Competition and Regulation:
The Development of Oligopoly
in the Meat Packing Industry

**INDUSTRIAL DEVELOPMENT AND
THE SOCIAL FABRIC, VOLUME 2**

Editor: Glen Porter, Director, *Regional Economic History Research Center,*
Eleutherian Mills—Hagley Foundation, Greenville, Delaware

INDUSTRIAL DEVELOPMENT AND THE SOCIAL FABRIC

An International Series of Historical Monographs

Series Editor: Glenn Porter
Director, Regional Economic History Research Center,
Eleutherian Mills—Hagley Foundation, Greenville, Delaware

To the employees and boss of Ray Ranch,
Conrad, Montana

Competition and Regulation:

The Development of Oligopoly
in the Meat Packing Industry

by MARY YEAGER
Department of History
University of California,
Los Angeles

 JAI PRESS INC.
Greenwich, Connecticut

823393

Library of Congress Cataloging in Publication Data

Yeager, Mary.
　Competition and regulation.

　(Industrial development and the social fabric; v. 2)
　Bibliography: p.
　Includes index.
　1. Meat industry and trade—United States—History.
2. Competition—United States—History.　3. Oligopolies—
United States—History.　I. Title.　II. Series.
HD9415.Y4　　　338.8′26649′00973　　　76-52011
ISBN 0-89232-058-3

Copyright © 1981 JAI PRESS INC.
165 West Putnam Avenue
Greenwich, Connecticut 06830

ISBN: 0-89232-058-3

Library of Congress Catalog Card Number: 76-52011

Manufactured in the United States of America

CONTENTS

Tables

Figures

Maps

Preface

This book confirms what my populist father anticipated when I left the family farm in Montana and boarded the train for college in the East. "Get out there," he warned, "and you'll become a bookworm, just like the rest of those ivory-towered intellectuals." If blame is to be allocated, the railroads deserve most of it. Three days and four sleepless nights in coach accommodations effectively transformed my image of railroads from "triumphant" to "monster" machines. I spent my college years trying to discover how the railroads lost their soul.

Had it not been for Alfred D. Chandler, Jr., who directed this study as a dissertation at Johns Hopkins, I still might be trying to give them one. Chandler's pioneering framework for the study of big business directed my attention away from black-hatted railroad robber barons and soulless corporations to railroad managers and to the large, integrated modern corporation. Chandler analyzed the evolution of big business in terms of the dynamic and interrelated forces of markets and technology. In *Strategy and Structure* he suggested that strategies adopted by firms in response to new market opportunities and technological innovations largely shaped the structure of organization through which resources were administered. Chandler's framework encouraged more systematic comparisons of the patterns of corporate development and more precise testing of his strategy-structure hypothesis for different industries in different countries.

This history of meat packing began as a test of the strategy-structure hypothesis. I chose meat packing in part because it was expedient to focus on an industry with origins in the rural-agrarian economy. I knew that unless I quieted family fears about my transmogrification into a city slicker, my return trips to the Big Sky country would be blazed with

xvii

controversy. Since the industry did not remain rural-agrarian but evolved into a modern, integrated industry, I also could study meat packing without severing my links to the East.

Meat packing was the logical choice. My family already had its own history of the industry. Stories of unscrupulous middlemen and extortionist railroad rates had colored many a table conversation. Whenever cattle prices did not yield the expected return, which seemed to be more often the case than not, the "beef trust" reared its ugly head. Moreover, as a voyeur at branding festivals and a sickly spectator of home-slaughter, I had been steeled for the worst of meat packing details. *The Jungle* did not trigger a wince. Nor did Norman Mailer's "collective diarrhetics of an hysterical army of beasts"* invoke more than a feeling that his description of the Chicago stockyards was too "eastern," too "urbane." A farmer simply did not see cattle or slaughterhouses in that way.

Meat packing also fed my continuing interest in the railroads. I held out hope that competitive rate struggles between railroads and shippers of livestock and dressed beef might provide clues to the disappearance of the "corporate soul." As the nation's first modern oligopolies, the railroads pioneered competitive patterns that came to characterize the meat packing industry. By examining how meat packers and railroad executives solved similar problems, I hoped to generate some useful hypotheses about the behavior of oligopolists in general.

My interest in the relationship between railroads and packers took me beyond Chandler's strategy-structure framework to an analysis of intra- and inter-industry competitive patterns. Competition itself became an important determinant of managerial strategies, a force that not only affected industry structure but also helped shape the political responses to industry growth. The government attacked the "beef trust" not long after oligopoly had emerged. Before the turn of the century, however, government did not have as significant an impact upon managerial decision making as did the forces of markets and technology. Nevertheless, public policy did affect the distribution of power between and among groups, and thereby indirectly affected industry development. By devising laws and developing institutional capabilities to protect "free" competition and to balance the demands of contending interest groups, the government fine-tuned the market in subtle ways and often with unintended consequences.

This focus on political factors was sharpened considerably by Professor Alfred S. Eichner, whose fine study of oligopoly in sugar refining provided a challenging model for my own study. Although our approaches to oligopoly remain substantially different, I profited greatly from Professor Eichner's suggestions. His encouragement throughout every stage of the writing process was invaluable.

Among the many others who have assisted me are Tom Weiss, James Patterson, and Louis Galambos. My friend, Margaret Walsh, offered her considerable expertise on the early history of pork packing and unhesitatingly shared much of her data. Her "small is beautiful" perspective served as a reminder that big is not necessarily better. I am especially indebted to William Bruce Catton and to Travis Jacobs for starting me on this journey into history. The Johns Hopkins seminar fueled my take-off. The staff at Baker Library, Harvard University Graduate School of Business, particularly Kay Beaver, Shirley Wayne, and Arthur Cornelius, eased the transition into sustained growth by helping to search for materials in the corporate records division.

Mr. Arthur R. Curtis, legal counsel, Swift and Company, provided access to invaluable court records and to Minutes of the Board of Directors' meetings. Friends in the Manson community of Montana generously donated their schoolhouse as a research and writing center. Grazina Kulawas of Providence, Rhode Island, prepared the typescript.

My friends, Gilbert and Jody Kujovich, Joan Zimmerman, Ann Jones, and Ed Perkins performed the drudgery of proofreading and editing as stoically as the underpaid Slavic workers of *The Jungle*. This book is hardly payment for the surplus labor power I exploited, but it could not have been done as quickly without them. Michael White and Jonathan McLoud of UCLA helped to compile data; Victor Jew, Barbara Cohen, and Christopher Cocoltchos assisted with bibliography; K. L. Freedman and N. L. Dias prepared graphic illustrations. The Faculty Senate of the University of California, Los Angeles, provided financial assistance.

Finally, I must thank Dad for helping me to keep one foot *out* of the ivory tower. His sobering assessment of the dissertation was not unexpected. "Shucks, I could have told you all that in two hours."

I only hope that the book warrants at least three hours of your time.

Mary A. Yeager
Los Angeles

Miami and the Siege of Chicago (New York, 1968), p. 88.

Introduction

In the latter part of the nineteenth and the early part of the twentieth centuries, the American economy developed from its traditional mercantile, rural-agrarian orientation to its present status as a modern industrial giant. In the 1870s most major industries, including iron, leather, lumber, and implements, still serviced an agrarian economy. Many small firms handled only a single activity—either manufacturing, distributing, or engaging in wholesale or retail sales. Owned and managed by one or a few men, with relatively small amounts of labor and capital, they competed independently in local or regional markets. More distant markets were reached through distribution networks of wholesalers, jobbers, or commission merchants. These middlemen were among the most critically placed economic agents in the agrarian economy, distributing the nation's goods and often financing their production as well.

By the early twentieth century a number of the nation's industries, such as oil, meat, tobacco, and steel, were oriented to the economic needs of rapidly growing cities. These industries were often concentrated and oligopolistic, dominated by a few large corporations that not only manufactured but also frequently integrated purchasing, transporting, and marketing functions. Requiring huge amounts of capital, these new giants seldom engaged in traditional patterns of price competition. With shares of the market sufficient to influence the pricing and output strategies of rivals, no single firm could increase its proportion of the market without diminishing that portion of a competitor's share. Price competition consistently threatened to become "cutthroat."[1] Saddled with high fixed costs which did not vary with the volume of traffic, each firm was under severe pressures to keep resources fully utilized in order to keep down unit costs. Competitive pressures to reduce prices continued even if prices fell below acceptable profit levels. The danger, of course, was negative feedback; if price competition was carried to its logical conclusion these firms could, figuratively, cut each other's throats, forcing financial ruin.

Determined that their large investments should be fully utilized but afraid or reluctant to let competition be the sole determinant of prices, corporate executives began to cooperate to maintain market shares. Instead of competing on prices they chose to compete with brands, product quality, and service. This new kind of competition was often supplemented by cooperation. Prices came to be set or "administrered,"[2] as a function of costs rather than merely of market forces, so that whether cooperation was achieved through explicit agreement, tacit understanding, or simply custom, the results were similar: the achievement of relatively stable market shares and prices, at least in the short run.

Long accustomed to a business world of independent decision making in unconcentrated markets, the contemporary public found the concentrated, administered world of oligopolies to be a threat to openness and mobility as well as to the integrity of the political process. To protect the revered tradition of independent competition and individual enterprise and to assure that these newer, larger, integrated businesses operated according to traditional standards of "fair" competition, many Americans demanded new regulatory laws.

In the creation and implementation of those laws, there was very little awareness that the industrial sector was fast dividing into two realms, and that the free and independent competition so characteristic of small firms was not viable for industries dominated by large, integrated, and interdependent firms. The antitrust laws institutionalized the older, more familiar view of price competition and forbade monopoly. The hatred of monopoly focused on giant firms, especially those in manufacturing, and on explicit conspiracies in prices and markets. Oligopoly conformed neither to traditional competition nor to monopoly, so that efforts to discipline the behavior of oligopolists by applying sanctions against monopoly frequently failed. As government prosecutors in the meat packing cases came to learn, proof of conspiracy to fix prices or market shares was extremely difficult to obtain. When prices and markets were stabilized without overt collusion, or when oligopolists competed on nonprice considerations, the difficulties were exacerbated. By the time the law was refined and reinterpreted to apply to oligopolies, the structure as well as patterns of cooperation had become institutionalized.

The inability or unwillingness of Americans to discriminate between forms of competition made communication between the public and corporate executives difficult. Attempts by either side to educate the other about competition or regulation often proved counterproductive, making businessmen's professions of fair competition seem hypocritical. With laws reinforcing and expressing traditional beliefs in a competitive ideal, most Americans saw the economy as a corrupted version of an ideal, where evil monopolists gobbled up small businessmen, and every large firm looked the same.

As some modern economic historians and economists have pointed out, however, oligopoly and concentration did not occur in all industries, but primarily in those such as oil, steel, electricity, meat, and chemicals, which were able to reap the benefits of large-scale production and distribution by capitalizing on new technological processes and exploiting the opportunities of growing urban markets. In cases where monopoly preceded oligopoly, such as sugar refining and tobacco, government action appears to have played a more critical role. Industries such as woodworking, papermaking, textiles, and furniture, on the other hand, remained relatively unconcentrated until the late twentieth century because they derived fewer advantages from large-scale production and distribution processes and found customary methods more adequate.[3]

This growth pattern produced what Robert T. Averitt has described as the dual economy, characterized, on the one hand, by a new *center economy* of firms large in size and influence and, on the other, by the more traditional *peripheral economy* populated by relatively small firms.[4] Yet, despite the importance of oligopoly to the emergence of the dual economy, relatively few attempts have been made to analyze why oligopoly and concentration developed when they did, and in some industries and not in others.

To understand the modern economy, questions about the evolution of oligopoly and its role in the dual economy need to be examined carefully. Why did oligopoly come to characterize the nation's central industrial structure? Why did it precede monopoly in certain cases, and follow it in others? What were its consequences for the structure of industry and the larger American economy? If markets and technology were crucial to its development, then how and in what ways did these interrelated forces operate to stimulate change and competition within various industries? And if government's role was important, how, why, and in what ways did it exert its influence, and what were the consequences of government action?

These and related problems are the focus of this study, which I hope will be of value to economists and economic historians as well as to public policy makers interested in the problems of oligopoly. Though my subject is a single industry, meat packing, I will use an analytical framework that is relevant to many of the industries in Averitt's center economy, and which derives largely from the work of Alfred D. Chandler, Jr.[5] This analysis of oligopoly focuses on the histories of the strategies and structures of individual firms. It examines the reasons why the strategies and structures changed, identifies the forces that promoted or impeded the effective implementation of those changes, and assesses their impact on the larger industry structure.

The meat packing industry is an especially significant case for analysis. It was intimately involved in the transition of the American economy at the end of the nineteenth and beginning of the twentieth centuries. Traditionally a seasonal, local, and atomistic industry, by the late 1880s it was dominated by a small number of large firms operating in national and international markets. As one of the first major manufacturing industries to become oligopolistic, it pioneered new administrative techniques and competitive patterns that later came to characterize other technologically based industries oriented to urban markets. Its status as an oligopoly, in turn, made it an early target of governmental and public pressure against big business.

To be sure, developments in meat packing were in some ways peculiar to the industry. The rapid perishability of fresh meat, and thus the need for a relatively speedy refrigerated transportation and distribution system, made marketing the packers' primary and major problem. Entrepreneurs in other industries, such as oil or sugar, had to deal with other problems, such as overproduction, that resulted from technological innovations in refining. Not surprisingly, because they faced different technological and marketing problems and because their products differed, these entrepreneurs adopted different strategies of growth, which in turn, affected their markets differently. Meat packing grew large by a strategy of vertical integration because Gustavus Swift and those who followed him recognized that before they could market their perishable fresh meat effectively in a national market, they needed a fleet of refrigerator cars and a more efficient distribution system. Oil magnates like John D. Rockefeller, on the other hand, first tried to solve the problem of overproduction by combining with other producers and refiners.

Nevertheless, despite these important differences, nearly all firms that grew large also eventually became vertically integrated and administratively consolidated enterprises. An analysis of how and why the leading packing firms achieved their position of dominance, a study of the factors that enabled them to maintain their lead, and an examination of changing government-business relations, should tell us much, not only about one of the nation's most important industries, but also about the underlying processes of change in other oligopolistic industries.

The history of the meat packing industry has not yet been studied in detail. The only wide-ranging history is a 600-page monograph published in 1923 by Rudolf Clemen.[6] Clemen, however, did not probe what now seem to be some of the most important developments in the industry. The few studies that were made prior to Clemen's work were hampered by contemporaneity with their subjects; they were either aggressive antipacker tracts or defensive, propacker testimonials. Titles such as *The Dark Side of the Beef Trust, The Greatest Trust in the World,* or *Packers, the Private Car Lines and the People* indicate their biases.[7]

The public antagonism and corporate defensiveness that produced these studies also effectively sealed the archives of the major meat packing firms. While the packers' reluctance to open their sources to scholarly inquiry is understandable for relatively recent information, their lack of cooperation concerning nineteenth- or early twentieth-century materials is regrettable. Of all the firms and families contacted, only Swift & Company provided assistance, and that was limited primarily to access to public records, government documents, and briefs and transcripts of antitrust cases. Nevertheless, thorough use of these and other sources enabled me to address the basic questions of this study.

What follows then, is in one sense, the first thorough economic history of this industry in a critical period of its past. We shall analyze the growth and development of the packing industry from the prerailroad era to roughly 1912, by which time oligopoly was firmly established; review the entrepreneurial activities of Gustavus Swift, Philip Armour, and other notable packer pioneers; and examine antitrust and related legal actions that their aggressive entrepreneurship evoked. However, we shall not forget that these strains were interwoven in a complex, interrelated process of economic change. By considering the interaction of those elements, it is possible to understand the larger reference of our study—the development of oligopoly in the industry.

NOTES

1. The best discussion of the concept is still Lloyd G. Reynolds, "Cutthroat Competition," *American Economic Review*, 30 (Dec. 1940):737–747. "Competition becomes cutthroat when prices and profits fall below a specified level.... [It] can arise only where there is excess capacity of the fixed factors engaged in the industry.... [Excess capacity is] the amount which, if withdrawn from production, would bring a rise in prices sufficient to restore normal profits" (p. 737).

2. Gardiner Means first introduced the term "administered" in the 1930s in conjunction with the notion of "price inflexibility," which he considered an important factor in explaining the severity and duration of the Depression. Administered prices were defined as prices that were "set by administrative action and held constant for a period of time." He distinguished them from "market prices," which he said were "made in the market as the result of the interaction of buyers and sellers." (*Industrial Prices and Their Relative Inflexibility,* a report prepared for the Secretary of Agriculture and published as Senate Document

No. 13, 74th Cong., 1st Sess., Jan. 1935. The major portion of the report is reproduced in Means, *The Corporate Revolution in America* [New York, 1962], pp. 77–96, to which this and subsequent citations refer.)

Although the line between administered and market prices is admittedly difficult to establish, this study accepts Means's definition and concentrates on the problem of explaining why, and under what circumstances and conditions administered pricing first occurred in the meat packing industry. See F. M. Scherer, *Industrial Market Structure and Economic Performance* (Chicago, 1970), pp. 284–286.

3. Alfred D. Chandler, Jr., set the pace for historical studies of oligopoly and concentration in his pathbreaking *Strategy and Structure* (New York, 1962). See also his more comprehensive, *The Visible Hand* (Cambridge, Mass., 1977), and "The Structure of American Industry in the Twentieth Century: A Historical Overview," *Business History Review*, 43 (Autumn, 1970):255–281. For a particular industry study, see Alfred S. Eichner, *The Emergence of Oligopoly: Sugar Refining as a Case Study* (Baltimore, 1969), and Eichner, "Business Concentration and Its Significance," in *The Business of America*, Ivar Berg, ed. (New York, 1968), pp. 169–200.

Most economic studies of oligopoly focus on developing indices of concentration and describing the behavior of firms and the nature of market structures in concentrated industries. Among the best studies are Morris Adelman, *A & P* (Cambridge, Mass., 1959); Adolph Berle, *Power Without Property* (1st ed., New York, 1959), and *The Twentieth Century Capitalist Revolution* (New York, 1960); William J. Baumol, *Business Behavior, Value and Growth* (rev. ed., New York, 1967); John M. Blair, *Economic Concentration* (New York, 1972); Betty Bock, *Dialogue on Concentration, Oligopoly and Profit* (New York, Conference Board, 1972); William J. Fellner, *Competition Among the Few* (1st ed., New York, 1949); John Kenneth Galbraith, *Economics and the Public Purpose* (Boston, 1973); Michael Gort, *Diversification and Integration in American Industry* (Princeton, N.J., 1962); A. D. H. Kaplan, *Big Enterprise in a Competitive System* (Washington, D.C., 1954); Ralph L. Nelson, *Merger Movements in American Industry, 1895–1956* (Princeton, N.J., 1959); Warren G. Nutter and Henry A. Einhorn, *The Extent of Enterprise Monopoly in the United States, 1899–1939* (New York, 1959); Willard Thorp, *The Integration of Industrial Operation* (Washington, D.C., 1920).

4. Robert T. Averitt, *The Dual Economy* (New York, 1968). Although the terms *center* and *periphery* convey important functional distinctions, they also establish a hierarchy of structures that tends to slight the important interrelatedness of the two economies.

5. *Strategy and Structure* and *The Visible Hand.*

6. Rudolf A. Clemen, *The American Livestock and Meat Industry* (New York, 1923).

7. Herman Hirschauer, *The Dark Side of the Beef Trust* (Jamestown, N.Y., 1905); Charles Edward Russel, *The Greatest Trust in the World* (New York, 1905); J. O. Armour, *Packers, the Private Car Lines and the People* (Philadelphia, 1906).

Chapter I

Development of the Meat Packing Industry, 1800-1870: Many Sellers and the Power of Market Forces

Before the introduction of the refrigerator car in the 1870s, the meat packing industry[1] was ruled by Mother Nature with a mighty invisible hand. Because fresh meat was perishable it had to be consumed quickly or preserved by salting, smoking, or pickling during the cold winter months. Constrained by the weather, the industry remained diffuse and unconcentrated. Packing required no huge investments or sophisticated technology, only a supply of meat, salt, and a good curing recipe. Entry and exit were easy and frequent, with numerous buyers and sellers competing independently on the basis of price. The industry's seasonality made packing a part-time activity and limited specialization. Neither the packer's role nor functions were clearly defined. Slaughtering, butchering, and packing activities were disintegrated. Relationships between those in the industry were fluid and unsystematic, depending largely upon local conditions, the weather, availability of supplies, and distances to market.[2]

Because meat was a bulky, low-value good that could not bear high transportation costs, transportation heavily influenced the industry's location. Indeed, from the beginning of the nineteenth century transportation played a key role in influencing the development of meat packing.

TRANSPORTATION'S ROLE IN WESTERN MEAT PACKING PRIOR TO THE COMING OF THE REFRIGERATOR CAR

The progressive improvement of transportation facilities resulting from the innovation of the steamboat, canal,[3] and railroad was highly important to the expanding agrarian economy and to the industries that processed agricultural products. By making transportation faster, cheaper, safer, and more certain than before, these innovations stimulated western settlement, increased the production of agricultural foodstuffs, and hastened the growth and geographical concentration of processing industries that laid the foundation for the industrialization of the West.[4]

Since processing involved the conversion or refining of a natural resource, such as lumber, agricultural produce, or livestock, into usable and marketable form, it has always developed alongside major areas of agricultural production.[5] In colonial times, when the frontier hugged the western seaboard, the farmer was often his own processor. With the growth of the eastern cities of New York, Boston, Baltimore, and Philadelphia, however, processing became more than an on-the-farm activity. The growing demand for food in these cities created a market for the farmer's output and led to the rise of specialized processors and slaughterers.

As the distance between markets and agricultural producers widened with the westward push of the frontier,[6] it sometimes became uneconomical to transport unprocessed, bulky items like corn and wheat from the frontier to distant cities. People began to process farm output nearer the source of supply in response to the transport differential between processed and nonprocessed agricultural commodities. Thus, some farm products could be marketed beyond their immediate environs, in regional markets in the South and East, even before significant improvements in transportation.

Nevertheless, not until the steamboat hastened the growth of trade and population in cities strategically located on major western waterways did western processing become a major industry. Agricultural processing industries not only utilized new forms of transportation to widen the market for western goods, but their spread led to the diffusion of the manufacturing technologies they embodied.[7] Following closely the lines of trade drawn by successive innovations in transportation, the industry centered first in Cincinnati and the Ohio Valley, and then moved with the railroad in the 1850s to producing regions nearer Chicago and the Great Lakes.[8] By 1860 the western processing industries contributed 53 percent of the total value added by the nation's processing industries, and processing had emerged as the West's leading industry. The importance of agricultural processing in western manufacturing is clearly reflected in Table I.1.

The linkages between the growth of processing industries, the development of new modes of transportation, and the resulting expansion of agriculture are clearly revealed in the history of the meat packing industry, which quickly emerged as one of the West's most important

Table I.1. Manufacturers in the Western States in 1860,
Selected Industries[a]

Industry	United States	Western states[b]	Western states as percentage of United States
Agricultural implements	$11,961,791	$6,279,616	52.59%
Blacksmiths	8,224,176	2,051,679	24.94
Cooperage	7,238,018	3,016,947	36.68
Flour and meal	40,083,056	18,018,704	44.95
Liquors (malt)	11,313,610	4,395,878	38.85
Leather	22,785,715	3,141,605	13.78
Lumber, planed and sawed	53,569,942	19,957,259	37.25
Provisions	7,091,809	3,802,003	53.61

Source: Eighth Census, 1860. Manufacturers. Vol. III.
[a] By value added, in current dollars.
[b] "Western states" include Ohio, Indiana, Michigan, Illinois, Wisconsin, Iowa, Minnesota, Nebraska, Missouri, Kansas, and Kentucky.

processing industries. By the 1880s meat packing was also one of the largest industries in the nation.[9] The fact that live hogs, cattle, and sheep lost valuable weight when moved to market and fresh meat was highly perishable made the relationship of transport innovations to the industry a complicated one. On the one hand, livestock could always walk to market if the distances were not too great or weight losses too high, or meat could be cured before shipment. On the other hand, fresh meat could never be distributed beyond local markets without speedy, efficient, refrigerated transportation. Thus the available transportation influenced both the form of the product to be marketed and the trade patterns.

In the early 1800s the growing settlements west of the Allegheny-Appalachian mountain barriers relied upon flatboats or keelboats on the Ohio-Mississippi river systems to send surplus agricultural goods to distant markets. Shipping low-cost, bulk goods such as flour eastward by wagon was more time consuming and far more costly than using the water transport system of riverboats to New Orleans and oceangoing vessels from there to the eastern seaboard.

Most meat that moved to market also followed the river transport system, but it was shipped in equal quantities on the hoof, in the form of bulk meat, or in barrels, for there was no cost advantage in marketing cured meats. A cheap and dependable supply of salt, which was the main ingredient for packing, was unavailable.[10] Sea salt could be imported from the Gulf but only at prohibitive cost, while the salt obtained from the nearby Kanawah works in western Virginia contained large amounts of impurities that were said to "putrefy" rather than preserve the meat.[11]

In addition to the west-south river trade there was a small west-east trade in livestock. After Alexander Hamilton's excise tax made it unprofitable to market corn as whiskey, farmers in northern and western Ohio began to feed corn to livestock, thereby increasing livestock production. Lacking easy access to rivers, some of the most enterprising farmers drove small herds, seldom exceeding 100 cattle and hogs, across the mountains to markets in Philadelphia, New York, or Baltimore, where the animals were slaughtered to provide fresh meat or to be cured for export. Others sold stockers or "thin" cattle to farmers along the way, who fattened them on grass and marketed them a few months later. Despite the time and risks involved, high initial profits made the drives worthwhile, encouraging more farmers to drive herds to market.[12] The overland trails did not provide an outlet for cured meats however. Wagon transport of such a bulky, low-value, semiperishable good was uneconomical.

The innovation of the upriver steamboat in 1816 widened the markets for meats generally, but had a greater impact on pork packing and the trade in cured meats than it did on beef packing and the overland trade in livestock. By reducing upriver freight rates and providing more reliable, speedier, and more flexible means of river transport, the steamboat reduced the cost of importing salt and encouraged a greater volume of processed meats. Growing trade in turn promoted rapid specialization and encouraged some concentration of slaughtering in packing towns strategically situated along the waterways (see Figure I.1). Hogs were easier and cheaper to raise than cattle, while pork was easier to cure and tasted better than processed beef; thus, more pork than beef was raised and packed. During the 1843–1844 season there were over 96 western towns packing over 1,245,000 hogs. Of these towns, most packed under 8,000 hogs annually. The top five cities accounted for 35 percent of the packing; the first ten, 47 percent; the first twenty, 60 percent. Cincinnati, Ohio, and Madison, Indiana together contributed 24 percent of the total pack, to capture the lead as packing centers. In the same season, Ohio alone packed 52 percent of the hogs; Indiana, 24 percent; Illinois, 13 percent; Kentucky, 9 percent; and Tennessee, Mississippi, and Iowa together accounted for the other 2 percent. Beef packing paled by comparison.[13]

The steamboat assured the predominance of cured pork and provisions in commercial trade flows, for it was ill equipped to haul livestock. Its belching noise and billowing smoke frightened animals, making loading and unloading difficult. Moreover, unless special facilities were

Figure I.1   Distribution of Hog-Packing in the West, 1850–51 Season.

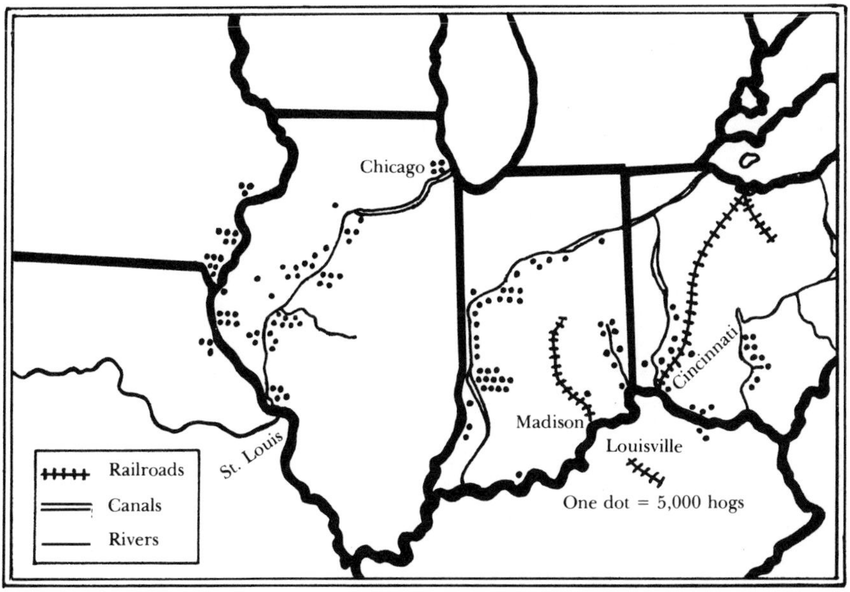

Based on figures in *Cincinnati Drovers' Gazette,* February 20, 1852, p. 3. Points with less than 3,500 hogs packed are combined or not shown.

constructed at considerable cost animals were often washed overboard or bruised.[14] Slaughtered meat, on the other hand, required faster transportation than the steamboat could provide and so remained confined to local markets. Most meat was therefore cured in the winter and shipped during the spring thaw.[15]

Although a large portion of the western pack was consumed locally in intraregional markets, interregional and international exports of provisions grew rapidly after the 1830s, providing the major impetus to the industry's growth and expansion.[16] Rough estimates of final demand markets indicate that the South consumed nearly one-third of the western pack in the 1840s. Despite higher per capita livestock figures than any other region, the South slaughtered fewer animals for commercial sale, forcing the growing cities of the Deep South to rely increasingly on western foodstuffs. The East probably absorbed an even larger share than the South, especially after the 1840s, when serious meat deficits began to appear in some of the major coastal cities. Then, with the reduction of the English tariff on American livestock and meats in the 1840s, a new and rapidly expanding foreign market for western meats was opened up as England joined Canada and the West Indies to become leading importers of American meats. By 1860 eastern and foreign markets absorbed nearly half of the western pack.[17]

Bacon and bulk meats comprised the largest portion of exports throughout the period. Most of the exports originated in a few of the fastest growing commercial and packing centers. In the 1840s Cincinnati, Cleveland, and Portsmouth, Ohio, contributed over 80 percent of Ohio's exports of provisions. Ohio accounted for over one-half of the West's total exports, and the West contributed well over three-fourths of the national total of meat exports.[18]

As cured pork and provisions became the mainstay of the western packing industry, more livestock tramped overland to meet the demand for fresh meat. Cattle were the favorites for the long distance drives, for they had more compliant driving dispositions, sturdier constitutions, and lost less weight than hogs. Since hogs often brought higher prices than cattle in western markets, most farmers found it more convenient and profitable to drive their hogs short distances to packing centers scattered along the rivers rather than risk the overland trails.[19]

Although data on the number of animals using the trails is unavailable, the volume increased significantly enough between 1820 and 1850 to support a group of specialized drovers and a new set of institutions to service the trade. Replacing farmers and stock raisers as the dominant marketing agents, drovers functioned as middlemen between producer and buyer, scouring the countryside for animals, selling them on the farmer's account for a commission in the marketplace, or purchasing them outright from farmers and marketing them on their own account. To accommodate and provide for the men and animals along the way, hotels, taverns, and livestock pens were built along the trails. These "drove stands," as they were called, sustained drovers and animals on a time consuming and arduous journey over some 400–1000 miles of rugged trails and streams.[20]

Like the trade in cured pork and provisions on the river systems, however, drives were seasonal. Animals had to be marketed during the most favorable weather conditions to avoid muddied and dangerous trails. Drives began any time from the middle of February until the first of June, and terminated at eastern stockyards sometime between April and August. Moreover, even when droving was at its height during the third and fourth decades of the nineteenth century, the west-east overland commerce in livestock was not as significant as the west-south trade in provisions.[21]

The rapid growth of a western trade in cured pork and provisions was both cause and consequence of several changes in the packing industry, perhaps the most spectacular of which was the rise of Cincinnati as the hog packing capital of the world. Situated on a bend in the Ohio River, near a major livestock producing region, Cincinnati grew more rapidly than did towns farther upriver, becoming the steamboat and commercial center of the West and gaining an early lead as a pork packing center. With a stronger commercial base than rival towns, Cincinnati not only attracted larger meat flows but also was better equipped to meet the seasonal needs of the growing industry.

Cincinnati's hog pack jumped from just over 15,000 hogs in 1822–1823 to 86,000 by 1833–1834. By the 1830s Cincinnati was the most populous western city and the largest pork packing center in the nation. The construction and completion of a system of canals in the 1830s and 1840s opened interior parts of the state and further secured Cincinnati's lead. By the 1840s Cincinnati produced nearly 30 percent of the western pack, which averaged about 481,000 hogs annually during 1832-1841.[22] In 1840 packing was Cincinnati's major industry. Packers produced some $3 million worth of provisions, or 58 percent of the value produced by food processing industries, and 17 percent of the value produced by all manufacturers in the city.[23] Pork products dominated the city's export trade as well, accounting for roughly 30 percent of the total value of the city's export products in 1825 and 44 percent in 1839.[24] Pork continued to hold the lead through 1860, with flour, grain, and whiskey next in value. By 1851 processors of provisions contributed over $5.9 million of the city's $17 million total, or 35 percent of the total value added by manufactures.[25]

With steadier and larger supplies resulting from improved transportation and the concentration of slaughtering and packing operations, Cincinnati also forged ahead of other river towns in the utilization of by-products. Their manufacture, though tied to the packing industry, developed independently of it, and was carried on not by packers but by independent manufacturers who traditionally had served local markets only. Unlike earlier producers of candles, soap, lard, and tallow, however, Cincinnati manufacturers produced for regional, national, and even international markets.[26] In the 1840s Cincinnati lard, used in the United States for cooking purposes, was marketed in Cuba as a substitute for butter. Lard oil adulterated with sperm oil was used in Atlantic port cities as a home lighting fuel. In England and France the same product was used to dilute and thereby reduce the cost of olive oil. Other products included "Star" candles made of stearine extracted from lard in the manufacture of lard oil; grease produced from the offal and used to make soap; fertilizer, the end-product of bones that had been compressed by steam; glue taken from the hoofs of hogs; prussiate of potash made from hair, hoofs, and offal and used extensively in the print factories of New England for dying; and prussian blue manufactured from the blood of hogs.[27]

The increasing value of by-products enabled Cincinnati packers to pay higher prices for hogs. In the 1840s hogs brought from 5–25 cents more in Cincinnati than in rival towns along the rivers.[28] Higher prices, in turn, attracted even larger meat flows to the city.

Packing's linkages to by-product industries, and its demand for complementary and subsidiary activities, such as drayage and cooperage, made it an important factor in the growth and development of Cincinnati and the western economy, even though actual slaughtering operations were seasonal. By-product manufactures contributed significantly to the city's manufacturing output. In 1841 candles, lard, and oil added $354,000 to the city's $17,432,670 total manufacturing output, as compared with $817,000 accounted for by flour and feed together. By 1851, when the value added by all manufacturing had jumped to $55,017,000, by-products accounted for $4,491,000 and feed and flour, $1,690,000.[29] That same year meat packing and satellite industries were the city's largest employers, providing jobs for an estimated 10,000 individuals who, "but for its existence," reminded one packing house admirer, "would be earning little or nothing one-third of the year."[30] Along with slaughterers, packers, and pork and beef house workers, the industry supported a host of auxiliary workers. There were coopers who made lard kegs, pork barrels, and hogsheads; drayers, who hauled the meats from the slaughtering houses on the outskirts of town to packing houses in the center; hoop pole cutters, box makers, soap makers, bristle dressers, steam renderers, candle makers, and mattress makers.

As significant as were the industry's growth and expansion during this period, however, the process of change did not involve fundamental alterations in the packing industry's organizational structure, competitive patterns, or methods of production and distribution. One of the most fundamental characteristics of the industry—its seasonality—remained. The arrival of cold weather led packers to speed up operations and accelerated the flow of goods to market, while a warm spell slowed down the market and often forced packers to cease operations. As long as the business was seasonal there were probably few advantages to integration. Although packers would from time to time expand operations forward and backward from the single function of boxing cured meats for shipment, the separation of slaughtering, packing, and marketing activities that had characterized the industry since colonial days was still evident in Cincinnati in the 1830s and 1840s.[31] The institutional array of supporting activities, such as drayage and cooperage, which had evolved with the industry in the early 1820s, continued to service the industry's needs adequately throughout the period.

Without major innovations in transportation and refrigeration technologies, the industry could not circumvent the constraints of seasonal markets. It adjusted to seasonal demands. To handle larger volume meat flows and variable production schedules, slaughterers and packers found new ways to rationalize and speed up the product flows. The killing, cutting, and processing activities that had previously been carried out unsystematically became part of a larger "disassembly process." New mechanical devices and steam driven machinery were installed to assist the product flows. Tasks were subdivided and arranged to produce the largest output in the least possible time. By the 1840s slaughtering houses in Cincinnati used a system of overhead rails to move the carcasses at a carefully predetermined rate, while workmen at fixed stations performed a single specialized task: one split the animal, the next removed its entrails, another removed specific organs, and the last man washed down the carcass.[32]

Packers kept up with slaughterers by standardizing and regularizing their operations wherever possible. From wagons hogs were taken directly to the pork houses where they were piled in rows as high as possible. Another group of laborers carried them from piles to scales where they were weighed before being taken by another group to the "blocks" where the hogs' parts were "struck off." Another group proceeded to subdivide the animal, distributing every piece "with the exactness and regularity of machinery, to its appropriate pile." Trimmers then took over, to prepare the meats for different markets. Bulk and smoked meats were handled by another set of workers who piled the meat, covered it with salt, and placed it in a barrel for pickling. In the early 1850s Cincinnati packers were cutting and disposing of the hogs at the rate of one every minute.[33] By increasing the rate at which products flowed through the plants,[34] Cincinnati slaughterers and packers gained economies of speed that lowered costs and permitted more efficient handling of larger volume flows.

Such economies played an important role in securing Cincinnati's lead as a packing center, but their impact upon the western packing industry remained limited. The disassembly process, like all packing and packing-related activities, followed the rhythm of the weather and seasons, discontinuing with the end of the packing season and the arrival of cold weather. Because slaughterers and packers could implement the disassembly process without undertaking major structural changes or making huge capital investments, entry into the industry remained relatively easy. The costs of building a packing plant ranged from $6,000 to $10,000.[35] In Cincinnati substantial growth in the number of firms took place concurrently with a rapid increase in the volume of production. Whereas 26 firms packed approximately 240,000 hogs in 1844, by 1855–1856 the number of firms had jumped to about 42 and the output had increased to an average annual pack of 424,000 a year.[36] The seasonality of the business meant that there were few economies to be gained by building capacity large enough to meet peak periods of demand. Rather, plants remained relatively small, and packers were numerous. There were only a few firms whose hog output exceeded 15,000 during the six-month season.[37]

A more serious impediment to entry was the requirement on short notice of substantial amounts of working capital, ranging anywhere from $50,000 to $100,000, to purchase the growing volume of animals and other raw materials needed to meet the increased demands of the trade during peak seasons in the early spring and late fall.[38] Often it was months between the purchasing and marketing of meats, a fact which created additional problems for those in the industry. But even this barrier proved inconsequential in Cincinnati. New entrants and smaller operators could compete effectively with larger operators, who occasionally financed their purchases out of profits, simply by tapping the city's growing financial institutions, or more commonly, by working on commission, selling packed meats on the accounts of farmers, drovers, or eastern meat distributors. The latter had by the late 1840s become relatively prominent in the Cincinnati industry.[39]

Although Cincinnati packers had more opportunities to lessen the risks and financial uncertainties of the business than those not as strategically situated on waterways and farther from a growing commercial center, packing remained a precarious enterprise. Speculation and "guesstimation" prevailed. In good years, with good weather and reliable supplies, packers could reap large profits, but the bad years more often outnumbered the good, giving the industry a rapid turnover and high mortality rate.[40] Price competition between numerous buyers and sellers quickly weeded out the inefficient and unlucky.

The weather and seasonal nature of the business tied packing to the growth and expansion of the rural-agrarian economy. Because a packer's profits depended on such varied factors as the weather, the availability of capital, the anticipated demand, the actual supply of animals and labor, and the cost and capacities of satellite operations related to packing, most packers could not afford to specialize. They continued to function primarily as middlemen, acting as general commission merchants, distributing meat products along with other provisions and grocery items, and packing on commission for others. Sometimes a packer bought directly from the farmer or drover, did his own slaughtering and curing, or marketed the meat on commission for others or on the farmer's account. But whatever the case, neither his function nor his relationship to other functional agents was firmly defined.

The most successful packers and the firms with histories were those with the connections, through credit ties to more established meat and provision dealers in the East or in foreign markets, or through relatives who engaged in some aspect of the meat or general commission business. A few carved a more permanent niche in the market by capitalizing on new opportunities to expand their general line of goods or later, by building fine reputations as quality producers of particular products, which they carried in addition to other goods. S. Davis, Jr. & Co. of Cincinnati, for example, advertised as beef and pork packers, commission merchants, and curers of extra-family hams of the "Diamond Brand." By the 1850s Schooley & Hough had earned a reputation as the "Queen City ham establishment" on the basis of their "special skill and care" involved in curing hams.[41]

Product specialization, however, was never very extensive before the 1850s. The city's reputation as a pork packing center was built more on its quantitative contributions to the western trade in provisions than on the qualitative differentiation of its products. Only after the railroad began to carve new commercial trade routes and to stimulate interregional competition with the Northwest did Cincinnati packers begin to devote serious attention to the improvement of breeds or the quality of their products.[42] Until then, geographical concentration of packing operations in a relatively small number of cities left the industry's structure atomistic and unconcentrated. As has been indicated, small river towns remained competitive with Cincinnati and continued to market meat in export markets. The existence of over 96 packing points, most of which packed under 8,000 hogs annually, and the seasonal nature of both the packing business and the west-east overland trade in livestock, were visible reminders that the steamboat, for all of its contributions to the growth of the western economy, had nevertheless not revolutionized the packing industry.

Before the coming of the Civil War, the full impact of the railroad was to bring change to the industry, not only in terms of business organization and behavior but also in terms of the locus of the industry's geographical center. Cincinnati could not compete with Chicago as a rail center. Its slaughterers and packers had few alternatives but to adjust. Although they attempted to broaden and improve their product lines, their efforts ultimately failed. Cincinnati's share of the total western hog pack slowly declined from 28 percent in the 1840s to 19 percent in the 1850s. In the latter decade nearly one-fifth of the hogs exported from Cincinnati were shipped live by rail. In 1862 Chicago pushed ahead of Cincinnati to become the world's largest hog packing center.[43]

THE RAILROADS: PACESETTERS OF CHANGE IN THE MEAT PACKING INDUSTRY

The coming of the railroad in the 1840s and its accompanying technology, the telegraph, had a more significant long-run impact upon the livestock and packing industry than had the steamboat and canal.[44] These new innovations not only made transportation and communication faster, cheaper, and more reliable, they also helped to create a national market, providing year-round transportation for a wide variety of goods across the nation. Because livestock could be shipped on the hoof in simple railroad cars, the railroad converted what had previously been a minor and seasonal enterprise—the west-east overland drives—into a major year-round shipping business. In so doing, the railroad stimulated the growth of the eastern packing industry as well as that in the West, and sparked new interregional competition. By lowering the costs of transportation and thereby lowering the final prices of meat, the railroad broadened the demand for both fresh and cured meats and altered patterns of production and distribution.[45]

Whereas in the prerailroad era more pork was packed than beef and trade in provisions to New Orleans exceeded that in livestock driven to southern or eastern markets, the extension of the railroad network into the West in the 1850s, and the completion of the major east-west trunklines to Chicago in the 1860s,[46] encouraged a year-round commerce in provisions and livestock that soon surpassed the west-south river trade. Lower freight rates and shorter total distances made west-east rail routes preferable, and pushed livestock and corn production into the upper Mississippi River Valley and farther into the interior along the rail routes. Because rails went where steamboats and canals did not, new areas of beef production were opened in the West and as far south as Texas.

Perhaps the major change in the industry's locational pattern, the rise of Chicago as a major livestock and packing center, was directly related to the spread of the railroad network. Before rails penetrated the interior of Illinois in the 1850s, Chicago was little more than a way station for livestock en route to other states. In the 1830s the city's six packers produced a pack of about 10,000 hogs annually, and most of it was consumed locally. River towns like Alton and Beardstown, Quincy and Peoria, which were more strategically located to participate in the river trade than Chicago, were the state's leading hog packing centers. Then, beginning in the late 1840s, a network of lines spread throughout the interior of Illinois, linking Chicago to the interior cattle raising districts.[47]

The most immediate impact of these intrastate rail lines was to stimulate the livestock trade and beef packing business. With the demand for pork and provisions being met largely by the steamboat and river trade, there was ample opportunity to expand the domestic market for beef. An additional stimulus to beef packing came from abroad in 1844–1845, when England reduced tariffs on American livestock and foodstuffs.

The English did not share the American antipathy to cured beef and proved to be some of Chicago's best customers in this early period. Utilizing new rail links to interior cattle raising districts and the lower cost lake and canal routes to eastern port cities, Chicago quickly forged ahead of rival towns, becoming the largest beef packing center in the West in 1849.[48]

Yet even in beef packing, the greatest increase followed the coming of more direct through lines to the East in the 1850s and 1860s. Between 1851 and 1860 Chicago more than doubled its beef pack from 22,000 to over 56,000 cattle.[49]

Improved transportation ties enabled Chicago to draw its stock not only from the grassy prairies of the nearby states of Iowa and Indiana, but also from the entire beef growing territory of the Northwest. Even large droves of Texas cattle made their way to Chicago, where handsome prices more than covered the cost of the long drives. During the two years 1857-1858, Chicago's trade in Texas cattle tripled.[50] Although most of the Texas cattle were slaughtered and packed in Chicago, cattle from Ohio, Iowa, and Indiana were often either driven short distances to rail heads or shipped live by rail to Chicago and then directly to terminal markets in the East. Eastward shipments of cattle by rail quadrupled between 1852 and 1858, increasing from 11,200 to 42,600. New York cattle receipts jumped 112 percent during the 1850s, with most of the increase coming from the western states.[51]

In the late 1850s Chicago's superior facilities gave that city the first "daily cattle market" in the country. As the Chicago Board of Trade boasted in 1858:

> In no other city on this continent is there a daily cattle market which has been as regularly represented throughout the year as our grain and provision markets, with the publication of our daily receipts; and this enables the drover to sell out almost as soon as he arrives, without the delays or hindrances which annoy and harass the drovers in the East, if circumstances should delay them beyond the special market day. In Chicago, there is generally a good shipping demand; there is a demand by beef packers, and there is also the constantly increasing requirements of our city butchers, so that cattle traders have generally little difficulty in disposing of their stock.[52]

With better transportation and livestock facilities it did not take Chicago long to catch and surpass rival hog packing centers along the rivers. Whereas the city ranked thirteenth among pork centers in 1850-1851, by the 1856-1857 season Chicago stood fourth. By 1862 it had moved into first place. Between 1856 and 1862 its hog output had doubled.[53]

The Civil War further accelerated Chicago's lead in both beef and hog packing. With the Mississippi River blocked as an avenue of interregional commerce, rail links became the preeminent method of transporting raw materials and finished products. With improved wartime prices, animals flooded the Chicago market. Hog receipts increased 258 percent, from 392,000 in 1860 to 1,410,000 in 1864–1865, while cattle receipts jumped 189 percent, from 117,000 to 339,000.[54] Government war contracts and speculation on the provisions market also lured more businessmen to Chicago and away from other packing points along the rivers. A few netted windfall profits that provided the basis for postwar expansion.[55]

Chicago was made even more attractive as a marketplace with the construction of the gigantic Union Stockyards in 1865. Until then Chicago's livestock business had been handled at several stockyards scattered throughout the city. These yards had been built and supported by different railroads in an attempt to compete for larger shares of the livestock business. The intensification of competition and the increase in volume during the war, however, convinced the railroads that it was in their interest to construct a central livestock facility. Of the $1 million amortized capital invested in the yards, the railroads contributed $925,000; city packers supplied the rest.[56] Business commenced on Christmas day 1865. "No other city in the country could boast of near perfect arrangements for the loading and unloading of stock," claimed one enthusiastic Chicago booster.[57] Stock pens stretched over 130 acres. There were, in addition, a large and handsome brick hotel, a commodious Bank and Exchange Building, and conveniently constructed scale houses. By bringing together buyers, shippers, and sellers, the Union Stockyards reduced the time and expense of marketing, intensified competition, and encouraged larger, steadier, and faster meat flows.

The higher volume and faster flows made possible by the railroads and their links to distant markets brought changes in the marketing of livestock and meats. In the early 1830s and 1840s, the relationship between farmers, drovers, packers, and commission merchants had been highly fluid. The drovers were the key figures in the early livestock and meat trade—they assembled, purchased, and sold the stock and often the meat as well. They seldom followed a single pattern when dealing with farmers or buyers, however. While some drovers bought animals directly from the farmer, had the beef slaughtered for a fee, and packed and sold the animals themselves, others sold the live animals on the farmer's account to a packer or commission merchant. The packer's role and his relationship to the drover were also not clearly defined. Some packers bought directly from the farmers and others packed on commission for the drover, farmer, or merchant. Indeed, many of the early packers got their start in the business as general commission merchants, packing meats as a sideline to supplement their income. As long as flows were small these part-time packers were ideally suited to the seasonal packing industry.[58]

With the coming of the railroads, marketing relations in the meat packing industry became more systematic and more specialized, the roles of marketing agents and packers, more clearly defined. Rather than functioning primarily as an intermediary between the farmer and the market, the drover pushed westward to collect herds for shipment on the railroads. Replacing the drovers in the market were specialized livestock commission merchants. Stock came to be consigned directly to these merchants by the drovers.

More familiar with the market because they spent more time in it and desiring to get the best prices in order to enhance their income—which was based on a percentage of sales—livestock commission merchants offered buyers and sellers an attractive service and lured more live-stock shipments to Chicago. By providing drovers with money from their own accounts to purchase animals direct from the farmers, these specialized commission merchants assisted in financing the larger meat flows and in expediting their disposal as well. Drovers could draw money from commission merchants as soon as the stock was delivered. This money could then be used to buy larger herds direct from western producers. The arrival of the first bona fide livestock commission firm in Chicago in 1857 marked a new phase in the marketing of meats, one that gave the city a new class of businessmen whose interests were closely tied to the railroads and the livestock trade.[59]

The railroads increased the interdependency among livestock commission merchants, packers, and meat wholesalers and retailers. Whereas most Cincinnati packers had ties to other lines in addition to meat, most Chicago packers were specialized meat commission merchants who sold to wholesalers more often than to retailers as earlier general merchants had done. Many Chicago packers moved into packing from the livestock commission business. Using profits derived from the growing trade, some established their own independent wholesale meat houses and bought and sold livestock on their own account, thus acting as meat jobbers rather than as commission merchants. By the mid-1860s some meat packers had even accumulated enough money to extend advances to eastern meat dealers who had once provided them with capital to conduct their operations. Others acted as livestock and meat commission agents for eastern wholesale firms, buying and shipping livestock and sending them quantities of cured provisions as well.[60]

The overlap between the meat commission and packing business was an important characteristic of the industry in the early railroad era. As long as the network of commission men and wholesalers provided an efficient and reliable outlet for packer products, there was little need or prospect for significant organizational change in the form of mergers or backward or forward integration.

Chicago packing firms were larger in size than their counterparts in Cincinnati, with larger capacities for handling both beef and pork, and they more often combined slaughtering and packing operations. Whereas only a handful of the largest Cincinnati packers produced an average annual pack of 20,000 hogs and cattle, in Chicago by the 1870s there were at least fifteen firms that packed over 20,000 cattle and hogs during the packing season, several that produced over 50,000 hogs, and at least four firms that had outputs exceeding 50,000 hogs and cattle per year.[61] With year-round businesses, Chicago firms reduced the risks of packing and tended to enjoy greater stability and longer life spans than had Cincinnati firms. The number of firms remained almost constant at 40 throughout the 1860s and 1870s. Nevertheless, these larger meat flows were handled by a work force not much larger than that employed by large Cincinnati firms. Firms continued to function effectively with only one or two partners to manage the business and perhaps no more than 100 or so employees to slaughter, cure, and pack the meats at peak periods.[62]

Internal economies were achieved by systematizing and rationalizing work processes, but Chicago firms also reaped the benefits of improvements in steam-driven machinery. Moreover, since most plants were located alongside railroad tracks, meat could be loaded for shipment direct from the plant, increasing the rate at which products flowed through the enterprise and allowing greater volumes to be handled.[63]

Afforded larger, steadier meat flows, Chicago by-product manufacturers produced a greater variety and number of by-products than had Cincinnati manufacturers. Although most by-products continued to be produced in independent establishments, a few packers also began to manufacture lard, tallow, and even barrels in their own plants.[64]

Some packers even attempted to capitalize on opportunities provided by the year-round movement of livestock by using ice to extend the slaughtering and packing season. Storage houses cooled by blocks of ice that had been cut and stored during the winter began to appear in Chicago in the 1860s. The summer pack remained relatively insignificant, however. In 1872 Chicago's summer hog pack accounted for only 10,350 of the yearly total of over 1,225,000 hogs. Of the nearly 6 million hogs packed during 1872 at principal slaughtering and packing establishments across the country, only 505,500 were put up during the summer.[65]

Until refrigeration technology permitted the marketing of a new product, the most fundamental limitation on the packing business remained. It continued to be a seasonal industry dependent upon cold weather to prevent spoilage between the processes of slaughtering and packing the cured meat. Most packers, like their predecessors in the eighteenth and early nineteenth centuries, continued to rely upon Nature for necessary refrigeration facilities. Packers remained essentially preparers of cured pork products and merchandisers of meat. In Chicago their functions were more specialized than previously, with many more acting as jobbers as well as commission merchants, but their business was still largely a seasonal affair confined to the early spring and late fall months. Thus, even after the coming of the railroad, the packing industry remained unconcentrated, disintegrated, and non-oligopolistic.

The railroads did not revolutionize the packing industry. Nevertheless, the changes they introduced were qualitatively different from those effected by the steamboat. The railroads not only improved upon existing methods of transportation and brought about quantitative changes in meat flows, as had the steamboat, they also created entirely new patterns of commerce and competition and extended the packing season as well. Whereas the steamboat simply enlarged the seasonal market for pork and pork products and increased the seasonal volume of meat flows, the railroads created a year-round west-east commerce in provisions and livestock that encouraged the rise of specialized livestock and provision merchants, who soon replaced drovers as the key figures in the marketing of meats.

These qualitative changes, in turn, significantly influenced the course of change in the meat packing industry. Already by the mid-1860s the rate of growth of Chicago's hog and beef packing industry had begun to decrease, while shipments of livestock east from Chicago had continued to increase dramatically. The most perceptible decline came in beef packing. Not until 1876–1877 did the cattle pack reach its wartime peak established in 1864–1865 of 92,500 cattle. The hog pack recovered earlier, surpassing its wartime high in 1870. These developments did not pass by unnoticed. The Chicago Board of Trade commented in 1870 that "Beef Packing has so largely fallen off at Chicago, that it has ceased to command any large degree of attention."[66]

By making it economical to slaughter and pack nearer the source of supplies in Kansas, Iowa, Minnesota, Missouri, and Nebraska, the railroads tended to push the packing business west from Chicago. On the other hand, by speeding year-round shipments of livestock to the East, they also broadened the demand for fresh meats and stimulated competition between the eastern and western packing industries. In both cases, they nurtured a symbiotic relationship with livestock shippers that suggested to a few eastern and western meat dealers that a still more efficient alternative would be to consolidate national packing and shipping in a single center and to ship the fresh meat rather than live animals.[67]

To understand how and why this alternative was successful in the late 1870s, it is first necessary to examine the evolving relationship between the railroads and the livestock shippers. The full implication of the growing coincidence of interests for the history of meat packing became clear only in the 1870s and 1880s, when the railroads faced new and severe competitive pressures of their own.

NOTES

1. The wide variety of nonintegrated and nonspecialized activities involved in meat packing and the scattered and diffuse nature of rural markets make precise definitions of the industry difficult. In the early 1800s the term *packer* referred specifically to those who literally "packed" meat into containers. However, during the mid-nineteenth century, packers also frequently performed related activities of slaughtering, curing, and marketing the meats as well, depending upon local conditions. Until refrigeration technology allowed year-round operations in the 1870s, the industry is most accurately described as consisting of a number of interrelated but independent activities associated with the production, distribution, transportation, and sale of meat and meat-related products.

2. Few studies have carefully analyzed the changing nature of the packer's functions or his relationship to other functional agents. The information that does exist must be gleaned from more general sources. See Clarence H. Danhof, *Change in Agriculture* (Cambridge, Mass., 1969), pp. 27–48; Isaac Lippincott, *A History of Manufacturing in the Ohio Valley* (Chicago, 1914), pp. 112–116; Thomas S. Berry, *Western Prices Before 1861* (Cambridge, Mass., 1943), pp. 215–246; Charles Leavitt, "Some Economic Aspects of the Western Meat Packing Industry, 1830–1860," *Journal of Business of the University of Chicago*, 4 (1931):68–69; Victor S. Clark, *History of Manufactures in the United States*, Vol. I (1929; rpt. New York, 1949), pp. 481–484; Charles Kuhlmann, "Processing Agricultural Products in the Pre-Railway Age," *The Growth of the American Economy*, Harold Williamson, ed. (New York, 1944), pp. 386–391; Charles Cist, *Cincinnati in 1841* (Cincinnati, 1841), especially the advertisements, and Cist, *Sketches and Statistics of Cincinnati in 1851* (Cincinnati, 1851), pp. 228–231; Clemen, *American Livestock and Meat Industry* (New York, 1923), pp. 92–105, 123–124; Harper Leech and John C. Carroll, *Armour and His Times* (New York, 1938), pp. 2–8; *Hunt's Commercial Chronicle and Review*, 19 (July–Dec. 1848):171.

3. Canals played a relatively negligible role in shaping the structure and trade patterns of the livestock and meat packing industry and are not dealt with in detail in this chapter. Only the Erie Canal carried significant numbers of livestock or quantities of meat products, and compared to the quantities sent down the Mississippi River aboard flatboats or steamboats, those sent by canal were relatively insignificant. Canal traffic continued to depend upon relatively crude modes of transportation, most commonly the flatboat, and later the steamboat, and upon weather conditions. While some farmers sent livestock aboard flatboats, such journeys were often hazardous and costly. Most meat shipped on canals was cured to avoid spoilage and consisted primarily of pork and bacon.

Canals stimulated livestock production in inland regions remote from major water arteries, but in Ohio, at least, canals were constructed in the northeastern part of the state, away from swine raising districts in the southeast. Since most pork packing plants were also concentrated along the Ohio river and its tributaries, the canals served primarily as trade gatherers rather than traffic makers. While canals in Indiana and Illinois were more strategically located with respect to livestock production—in the northern part of the state—by the time population reached significant levels there, the railroads had already eclipsed the canals as the major livestock and meat carriers. See Charles Leavitt, "Transportation and the Livestock Industry of the Middle West to 1860," *Agricultural History*, 8 (Jan. 1934):21–23; Albert Fishlow, *American Railroads and the Transformation of the Ante-Bellum Economy* (Cambridge, Mass., 1965), p. 266; Berry, *Western Prices*, Table 17, p. 222; John G. Clark, *The Grain Trade in the Old Northwest* (Urbana, Ill., 1966), pp. 18–21.

4. The close ties between agriculture, the processing industries, and improvements in transportation are most clearly described in Alfred D. Chandler, Jr., ed., *The Railroads* (New York, 1965), pp. 3–12; Fishlow, *American Railroads*, pp. 225–230; Berry, *Western Prices*, pp. 215–246; Elmer A. Riley, *The Development of Chicago and Vicinity as a Manufacturing Center Prior to 1880* (Chicago, 1911).

Few studies deal specifically with the processing industries. Victor Clark, *The History of Manufactures*, Vol. II (1929; reprinted New York, 1949), pp. 481–485, devotes only a few pages to them and generally dismisses their importance. More helpful are regional studies that focus on western manufacturing and thus necessarily deal with processing. One of the best is Margaret Walsh, *The Manufacturing Frontier* (Madison, Wis., 1972). See also Lippincott, *A History of Manufacturing in the Ohio Valley* (Chicago, 1914).

5. Walsh, *The Manufacturing Frontier*, p. ix.

6. See cartography, Robert James McFall, *The World's Meat* (New York, 1927), pp. 127–141. An early effort to measure the growing imbalance between supply of and demand for cattle is Silas L. Loomis, "Distribution and Movement of Neat Cattle in the United States," U.S. Dept. of Agriculture, *Report of the Commissioner, 1863*, pp. 254–259. "The Provision Trade of the United States," in U.S. Bureau of Statistics (Dept. of Commerce and Labor), *Monthly Summary of Commerce and Finance of the United States for the Fiscal Year 1900*, Vol. III, p. 2280, shows the South leading the nation, with 46 percent of national swine production in 1840, 52 percent in 1850, and 46 percent in 1860 (see the accompanying tabulation).

Swine Per One Hundred People by Region, 1850–1860

	Regions				
Year	Northeast	Midwest	West	South	Pacific
1850	13	41	181	215	23
1860	10	31	149	175	101

Source: U.S. Dept. of Commerce and Labor, U.S. Bureau of Statistics, *Monthly Summary of Commerce and Finance of the United States for the Fiscal Year 1900*, Vol. III, p. 2280.

7. The processing industries, including milling, meat packing, and tanning, were among the largest employers of steam power and of steam-driven machinery in the United States in 1870. Processing entailed higher productivity per worker than most western industries and utilized some of the most advanced labor techniques and organizational methods in the West, laying the foundation for modern assembly-line methods of production (Fishlow, *American Railroads*, pp. 225–230).

8. Riley, *The Development of Chicago*, pp. 124–125. Receipts of cattle increased 624 percent between 1840 and 1880, while hog receipts showed a spectacular 3,234 percent increase.

9. Measured by means of the construct "value added by manufacture," which represents the value created in the process of manufacturing by deducting from the gross product the

cost of materials consumed, the fuels used, and other costs incurred in manufacturing the finished product (Walsh, *The Manufacturing Frontier,* p. vi).

10. Berry, *Western Prices,* pp. 217–218.

11. *Ibid.*

12. George Renick drove the first herd of 68 cattle from Chillicothe, Ohio, to Baltimore, Maryland, in 1805, and netted a handsome profit of $31.77 per head [Clemen, *The American Livestock and Meat Industry,* pp. 72–73; Paul C. Henlein, *Cattle Kingdom in the Ohio Valley, 1783–1860* (Lexington, Ky., 1959), p. 8; Charles W. Towne and Edward M. Wentworth, *Pigs* (1st ed., Norman, Okla., 1950), p. 183].

13. Leavitt, "Western Meat Packing," pp. 76–79. By far the best account of early pork packing is Margaret Walsh, "Pork Packing as a Leading Edge of Midwestern Industry, 1835-1875," *Agricultural History,* 51 (Oct. 1977):702–717, especially 704–705.

The steamboat's major contribution was to shorten the length of the return trip. Rather than driving flatboats off the rivers, the steamboat actually stimulated the seasonal movement of meat and small quantities of livestock by flatboats, since it enabled flatboatmen, who were usually farmers, to make the return trip in a week rather than a few months as had previously been the case [James Mak and Gary M. Walton, "The Persistence of Old Technologies: The Case of Flatboats," *Journal of Economic History,* 33 (June 1973):444–452].

14. Clark, *The Grain Trade,* p. 37, and Henlein, *Cattle Kingdom,* Chap. V, describe the travails of a few who attempted the trip.

15. Clark, *The Grain Trade,* pp. 45-50, 138-140; Berry, *Western Prices,* pp. 219-221, provides scattered estimates of the volume and value of cured pork and provisions, and of livestock shipped on the west-south river system.

16. Attempts to compile figures on final demand markets for western foodstuffs are plagued with difficulties. During the era of river transportation, meat products were transported south for re-export to the East and to foreign countries. With the coming of the railroads some of the meat stocks shipped eastward by rail were also destined for export markets abroad. Efforts to derive estimates of the volume and value of internal trade on the west-south river system have focused on a determination of southern self-sufficiency in foodstuffs. Contemporary observers seem to have considered the southern market far more important than do historians of recent quantitative studies. The latter suggest that the South was relatively self-sufficient in foodstuffs (including meat) and that export and re-export markets in the Northeast and abroad were more important than the southern market (Robert E. Gallman, "Self Sufficiency in the Cotton Economy of the Antebellum South," in William N. Parker, ed., *The Structure of the Cotton Economy of the Antebellum South* [Washington, D.C., 1970], pp. 5–24; W. K. Hutchinson and S. H. Williamson, "The Self-Sufficiency of the Antebellum South," *Journal of Economic History,* 31 [Sept. 1971]:591-612; Sam B. Hillard, *Hog Meat and Hoecake* [Carbondale, Ill., 1972], pp. 186-212; Clark, *The Grain Trade,* pp. 137-140; Fishlow, *American Railroads,* pp. 281, 284).

The best critique of the literature is Lloyd J. Mercer, "The Antebellum Interregional Trade Hypothesis: A Re-Examination of Theory and Evidence," Mimeo. Margaret Walsh, "Pork Packing as a Leading Edge," pp. 715–716, discusses the relevancy of the trade hypothesis to the provision trade.

17. Leavitt, "Western Meat Packing," pp. 84–85, estimates that 18.5 percent of the total western pack was exported from New Orleans in 1844–1845, and that of this percentage, the South took somewhere between 15–25 percent. By 1850-1851, the South was absorbing from one-third to one-half the western pork and bacon.

18. Clark, *The Grain Trade,* p. 137.

19. Statistics are hard to come by and those available do not distinguish hogs and cattle,

but the logic seems compelling. Most of the available data are taken from incidental reports of travelers or observers living near the droving trails. See estimates of Paul C. Henlein, *Cattle Kingdom*, pp. 103–129; Edmund Cody Burnett, "Hog Raising and Hog Driving in the Region of the French Broad River," *Agricultural History*, 2 (April 1946):86–103; L. N. Bonham, "American Live Stock," in Chauncey M. Depew, ed., *One Hundred Years of American Commerce, 1795–1895*, Vol. I, (New York, 1895), pp. 225–226; Leavitt, "Transportation and the Livestock Industry," p. 29; Lippincott, *History of Manufacturing*, p. 13; Clemen, *The American Livestock and Meat Industry*, pp. 58–60, 72–75, 81–82, 84, 174–181; James W. Whitaker, *Feedlot Empire* (Ames, Iowa, 1975), pp. 18–34; Charles W. Towne and Edward N. Wentworth, *Cattle and Men* (Norman, Okla., 1955), pp. 218–223, and *Pigs*, pp. 98, 102, 114–115, 118, 121–125.

20. The hazards of droving are colorfully discussed by drover Joseph McCoy in *Historic Sketches of the Cattle Trade of the West and Southwest* (Kansas City, Mo., 1874; rpt. Columbus, O.: Long's College Book Co., 1951), and analyzed in Henlein, *Cattle Kingdom*.

21. Based on rough estimates in Clark, *The Grain Trade*, pp. 39–40, 138–140; Henlein, *Cattle Kingdom*, pp. 103–129; Leavitt, "Transportation and the Livestock Industry," pp. 22, 26, 29; Berry, *Western Prices*, p. 222.

22. Berry, *Western Prices*, pp. 218–226; Walsh, "Pork Packing as a Leading Edge," p. 704; Leavitt, "Western Meat Packing," pp. 69–90; Clark, *The Grain Trade*, p. 138.

23. Compiled from Cist, *Cincinnati in 1841*, p. 56; Berry, *Western Prices*, pp. 219–226.

24. Berry, *Western Prices*, p. 220; Clark, *The Grain Trade*, pp. 17, 49, 137–140.

25. Clark, *The Grain Trade*, p. 138; Berry, *Western Prices*, p. 220.

26. Berry, *Western Prices*, pp. 226–229; Leavitt, "Western Meat Packing," pp. 70–77; Clemen, *American Livestock and Meat Industry*, pp. 135–145, and *By-Products in the Packing Industry* (Chicago, 1927). *National Provisioner*, September 8, 1906, p. 15, includes a helpful list of by-products and their origins.

27. Cist, *Cincinnati in 1851*, pp. 283–286; Philip Armour, "The Packing Industry," in *One Hundred Years of American Commerce*, Vol. I, p. 388.

28. Berry, *Western Prices*, p. 232; Lippincott, *A History of Manufacturing*, p. 179; Armour, "The Packing Industry," p. 384; Cist, *Cincinnati in 1851*, p. 286.

29. Berry, *Western Prices*, p. 220. Total value added by manufacturing computed from Cist, *Cincinnati in 1851*, pp. 258–261.

30. Cist, *Cincinnati in 1851*, p. 288.

31. Local ordinances in Cincinnati prohibited slaughtering within city limits. Although some historians have suggested that this regulation may have retarded integration, it does not appear to have blocked the move toward integration in the 1850s. Had there been more advantages to integration at an earlier date, entrepreneurs probably would have at least attempted to circumvent the regulation in some way.

Another reason why integration came more slowly to the Cincinnati industry is that in the early 1830s Cincinnati slaughterer and real estate investor John C. Coleman obtained a virtual monopoly of slaughterhouses. Because he had control over the slaughtering business, he was able to effect contracts with local packers, whereby the latter turned over all of their animals to him. Such a development may have increased the costs of entry and of integration. For information on Coleman and his activities, see Berry, *Western Prices*, pp. 229–232; *R. G. Dun & Co. Mercantile Credit Rating Reports*, Manuscript Reading Room, Baker Library, Harvard Business School, Boston.

32. Cist, *Cincinnati in 1851*, pp. 278–288; Nathan Rosenberg, *Technology and American Economic Growth* (New York, 1972), pp. 109–110; Siegfried Giedion, *Mechanization Takes Command* (New York, 1969), pp. 86–101.

33. Charles Cist, "The Hog and Its Products," U.S. Dept. of Agriculture, *Report of the Commissioner, 1866*, pp. 390–391.

34. Chandler, *The Visible Hand*, p. 242, describes the process as increasing the speed of "throughput."

35. Estimates of capital invested in plants are necessarily crude because of the difficulty of distinguishing packing from related activities. The U.S. Census follows no consistent patterns in enumerating packing plants, frequently including pork and beef packers, slaughterers, butchers, and sausage makers under the general description of meat packers or provision dealers, sometimes omitting one or several activities. U.S. Bureau of the Census, *Twelfth Census of the United States: Manufactures*, Vol. 9, Pt. III, Special Reports on Selected Industries, Harry C. McCarty, "Slaughtering and Meat Packing," p. 387, lists 185 slaughtering and meat packing plants, with a total capital of $3,482,500. Capital invested per establishment averages $18,824.32. Leavitt, "Western Meat Packing," p. 70, n. 6, states that eleven packers of Chicago had from $3,000 to $45,000 invested in their plants, for an average of $14,700.

36. Berry, *Western Prices*, p. 228; Cist, *Cincinnati in 1851*, pp. 228–229.

37. Estimated from data in Cist, *Cincinnati in 1849*, pp. 278–281, and Cist, *Cincinnati in 1851*, pp. 228–233; Berry, *Western Prices*, pp. 218–231.

38. Berry, *Western Prices*, pp. 229–230, and n. 43, p. 236; Leavitt, "Western Meat Packing," p. 73, cites an outlay of $50,000 to $80,000 for medium-sized packers during the 1854–1855 packing season. More generally, see Forrest M. Larmer, *Financing the Livestock Industry* (New York, 1926); Clemen, *The American Livestock and Meat Industry*, pp. 135–145.

39. Berry, *Western Prices*, p. 228; Walsh, "Pork Packing as a Leading Edge," pp. 709–712.

40. Walsh, "Pork Packing as a Leading Edge," p. 712.

41. Cist, *Cincinnati in 1851*, pp. 228–231.

42. *Ibid.*, pp. 228–229, 278–281.

43. Henlein, *Cattle Kingdom*, p. 163; Margaret Walsh, "The Spatial Evolution of the Mid-Western Pork Industry, 1835–1875," *Journal of Historical Geography*, 4, No. 1 (1978):1–22, gives an excellent overview and illustrates with invaluable maps.

44. The telegraph is often neglected in studies of transportation. Its simultaneous spread with the railroads played a significant role in the rapid growth of Chicago's packing industry. See *Hunt's Commercial Chronicle and Review*, 19 (July–Dec., 1848):165, for a contemporary view of the importance of the telegraph and its spread with the railroad.

45. Fishlow, *American Railroads*, pp. 205–236, 266–298, discusses the railroad's impact upon western agriculture and on patterns of commerce. Fishlow gives special emphasis to the provision and livestock trade, pp. 266, 281, 284, Table 39. See also, Philip D. Armour, "The Packing Industry," in Chauncey M. Depew, ed., *One Hundred Years of American Commerce, 1795–1895*, Vol. II(New York, 1895), p. 385.

Among the earliest advocates of a system of refrigerated transport were animal lovers who considered the shipment of livestock on the hoof cruel and inhumane ("The Market Systems of the Country: Their Usages and Abuses," U.S. Dept. of Agriculture, *Report of the Commissioner, 1870*, pp. 250–253).

46. The building of east-west through rail connections was rapid. By 1851 rail connections between New York City and the Great Lakes had been established. Philadelphia and Baltimore secured contact with the Ohio in 1852 and 1853, respectively. Chicago and points in Indiana and Ohio had through connections to the East by 1853. Most of Ohio's network was built between 1853 and 1857. By 1860 Ohio and Illinois led the nation in railroad mileage, and Chicago, with eleven major railroads, was the greatest railroad center in the world. Riley, *The Development of Chicago*, pp. 109–111, 123–128; Leavitt, "Transportation and the Livestock Industry," pp. 26–27; George Rogers Taylor, *The Transportation Revolution, 1815–1860* (New York, 1951), pp. 84–86.

The New York Central and Pennsylvania railroads had reached Chicago by 1869; the Baltimore & Ohio did not obtain a connection of its own until 1874. The Grand Trunk Railway of Canada constructed its own line to Chicago in 1880. William Z. Ripley, *Railroads, Rates and Regulation* (New York, 1924), pp. 1–42, includes a concise historical survey of the development and spread of the transportation network. See also, Chandler, ed., *The Railroads*.

47. For a general history of Chicago, see A. J. Andreas, *History of Chicago*, 3 vols. (Chicago, 1884); *City of Chicago: A Half Century of Progress, 1837–1887* (Chicago, 1887); Charles Cleaver, *History of Chicago, 1833–1892* (Chicago, 1892); Riley, *The Development of Chicago*; Bessie Louise Pierce, *A History of Chicago*, 3 vols. (New York, 1957). For more detailed information on the livestock and packing industries of Chicago, see Clemen, *The American Livestock and Meat Industry*, pp. 102–106; *Griffith's Annual Review of the Livestock Trade and Produce Trade of Chicago, Fifth Annual Report, 1869*, pp. 19–20; *Annual Review of the Commerce, Manufacturers and the Public and Private Improvements of Chicago, 1856–1857* (Chicago, 1857), especially pp. 20, 26.

Illinois laid its rail network quickly. The Galena & Chicago Union Railroad paved the way. Two years later came the Illinois Central, linking Chicago with Cairo, Illinois. In 1852, the Michigan Central, which ten years earlier had been constructed between Detroit and Ypsilanti, chugged through Illinois to Chicago. That same year witnessed the arrival of the Aurora Branch Railroad, the first of a series of lines, which by consolidation four years later, produced the Chicago, Burlington & Quincy Railroad. Another competitor, the Chicago, Rock Island & Quincy line, began operations in 1852, the same year that the Pittsburgh, Fort Wayne & Chicago was incorporated and the Chicago & Alton received its charter. By 1857, these local lines secured through connections to the East. In 1855 the Michigan Southern and Northern Indiana gave those states access to Chicago's rapidly growing market. By the end of the decade, there were lines "formed in almost every possible direction" (*Griffith's . . . Eighth Annual Report, 1872*, pp. 16–17; *Fourth Annual Review of the Commerce, Manufactures, Railroads and General Progress of Chicago for the Year 1855* (Chicago, 1856), pp. 66–76).

48. Chicago killed 20,000 cattle in the fall of 1849. The firm of Wadsworth & Dyer entered the business in 1844–1845 and immediately began to send its beef to the English market. Within a year, the firm controlled over two-fifths of the beef packing in the city, putting up about 100 beeves daily during the packing season. At that time Chicago boasted of six packers. One of the earliest to enter the business was Archibald Clybourne, a butcher under government contract for the Potawotomie Indians. Clybourne pioneered in sending the first shipment of beef to eastern markets in 1843, packing over 3,000 head of cattle for William Felt & Company, farmers and commission merchants of Rochester, New York (Clemen, *The American Livestock and Meat Industry*, pp. 83–84, 104–105; Towne and Wentworth, *Cattle and Men*, p. 310; Henlein, *Cattle Kingdom*, p. 167). The increasing shipments of beef to eastern markets brought high prices for cattle, ranging from $1.50 to $2.00 per pound.

49. Edward W. Perry, "Live Stock and Meat Traffic of Chicago," U.S. Dept. of Agriculture, *Report of the Bureau of Animal Industry, 1884*, pp. 245–246; Chicago Board of Trade, *First Annual Report, 1858*, p. 24, and *Fourth Annual Report, 1861*, p. 37.

50. This figure represented a 200 percent increase. Total cattle receipts in the city numbered 48,500 in 1857; 140,500 in 1858; 111,700 in 1859; 177,100 in 1860 ("The Texas Cattle Trade," U.S. Dept. of Agriculture, *Report of the Commissioner, 1870*, pp. 346–352; "Provision Trade of the United States," p. 2286).

51. New York Produce Exchange, *Annual Report, 1874*, pp. 380–381; Perry, "Live Stock and Meat Traffic of Chicago," p. 247; Leavitt, "Transportation and the Livestock Indus-

try," pp. 29–31. Fishlow, *American Railroads,* pp. 266, 284, 289, and Berry, *Western Prices,* pp. 91, 226, provide statistics on the differential impact of railroads on eastern shipments of livestock and salted meats.

52. Chicago Board of Trade, *First Annual Report, 1858,* pp. 24–25.

53. Perry, "Live Stock and Meat Traffic of Chicago," p. 246; Chicago Board of Trade, *First Annual Report, 1858,* p. 24, and *Fourth Annual Report, 1861,* p. 37.

54. Chicago Board of Trade, *Third Annual Report, 1860,* pp. 32–33; *Fourth Annual Report, 1861,* pp. 32–33, 36–38; *Fifth Annual Report, 1862,* pp. 32–34, 38; *Seventh Annual Report, 1864,* pp. 46–51; *Eighth Annual Report, 1865,* pp. 36–42; *Ninth Annual Report, 1866,* pp. 46–52; Riley, *The Development of Chicago,* pp. 127–137.

55. Nelson Morris walked to Chicago from Michigan City, Indiana, in 1850 to become a livestock dealer and packer. Philip D. Armour, a grain and provision merchant and successful speculator, came to Chicago from Milwaukee, Wisconsin, in 1865. Both men capitalized on wartime opportunities. By the 1870s they were among Chicago's leading livestock dealers and pork packers. Armour had established his own distribution outlet in New York for the firm's cured pork and provisions (Clemen, *The American Livestock and Meat Industry,* pp. 149–159).

56. Nine railroads participated in the agreement. Many of the roads were connecting lines of the major east-west trunklines: the Pittsburgh, Fort Wayne & Chicago Railway Co.; the Michigan Central Railroad Co.; the Chicago & Great Eastern Railroad; the Chicago, Burlington & Quincy Railroad; the Chicago, Rock Island & Pacific Railroad; the Chicago & Alton Railroad; and the Illinois Central Railroad. The city packers provided $50,000; the public put up $25,000 (Pierce, *A History of Chicago,* Vol. II, p. 93; Federal Trade Commission, *Report on the Meat-Packing Industry, 1919,* 5 vols. [Washington, D.C., 1920], Pt. III, "Methods of the Five Packers in Controlling the Meat-Packing Industry," p. 194; Jack Wing, *The Great Union Stockyards of Chicago* [Chicago, 1865], pp. 8–11).

57. *Griffith's . . . Eighth Annual Report, 1872,* pp. 6–7.

58. Because packers sometimes acted as commission merchants for wholesalers, it is important to distinguish the various types of marketing agents. I have used the typology adopted by Glenn Porter and Harold Livesay in *Merchants and Manufacturers* (Baltimore, 1971), p. 5. They define the agents as follows:

a. *Generalized merchant* The all-purpose, nonspecialized merchant of the colonial and early national periods. Synonyms include merchant capitalist, colonial merchant, and sedentary merchant.

b. *Broker or factor* A mercantile creature who is entirely a middleman. He never sells on his own account, but acts for others in his task of bringing buyer and seller together. He is more specialized than the colonial merchant, for he deals in a single line of goods, such as groceries, dry goods, drugs, iron, hardware, etc. Like the commission merchant described below, he takes a commission on his sales.

c. *Commission merchant* Differs from the broker or factor in that he sells partly for his own account as well as for others. He, too, is a specialized man of business, and this differentiates him from the generalized or colonial merchant.

d. *Jobber* A wholesaler who buys and sells entirely on his own account, distributing his purchases either to other jobbers or to retailers.

e. *Manufacturer's agent* Acts solely as middleman, never selling on his own account. He differs from the broker or factor only in that he is even more highly specialized; he usually acts for a relatively small number of larger producers and sells to a smaller circle of customers than does the broker. If a particular firm authorizes him to be its sole representative in a specified geographic area, he is an exclusive manufacturer's agent; otherwise he is a nonexclusive manufacturer's agent. An exclusive manufacturer's agent acts for more than one producer; however, he is exclusive in the sense that he is a particular manufacturer's only sales agent in the area.

Other terms, including *wholesaler, merchant, middleman, commercial agent,* and *mercantile agent,* are general terms that cover any and all of the above types.

59. *Griffith's ... Fifth Annual Report, 1869,* pp. 19–28, and *Eighth Annual Report, 1872,* pp. 5–14; McCoy, *Historic Sketches of the Cattle Trade,* pp. 78–115.

60. Clemen, *The American Livestock and Meat Industry,* pp. 87–89, 136–138; *Griffith's ... Fifth Annual Report, 1869,* p. 26; McCoy, *Historic Sketches of the Cattle Trade,* pp. 280–300. The increasing importance of both specialized packers and specialized commission merchants in Chicago's trade is reflected in the following figures extracted from occupational and membership lists of successive *Annual Reports* of the Chicago Board of Trade. Whereas Chicago had at most thirty "general commission stores [nonspecialized]" and six packing houses in 1848, by 1863, there were nearly 447 specialized commission merchants and 45 packers. Of the 45 packers, nearly all were also specialized meat commission merchants and slaughterers who more often sold to wholesalers than to retailers as earlier general merchants had done.

61. Compiled from Chicago Board of Trade, *Annual Reports, 1858–1875.*

62. The internal activities and organizational structure of selected Chicago packers are described in Chicago Board of Trade, *Third Annual Report, 1861,* pp. 36–37, and H. D. Emery, "Hogs and Pork Packing," U.S. Dept. of Agriculture, *Report of the Commissioner of Agriculture, 1863,* pp. 211–215.

63. Chicago meat packers also benefitted from improvements in mechanization of slaughtering and processing. Giedion, *Mechanization Takes Command,* pp. 232–233, claims that the basic mechanizing principles were developed during the period 1867–1877. Among some of the most important were devices to catch and suspend the hog, machines for spine-cleaving and hog scraping.

It was less a failure of entrepreneurship than a fact that new technologies and market opportunities constrained Cincinnati packers and narrowed their range of alternatives. Put another way, the railroad gave Chicago a comparative advantage in livestock production and meat processing. Wyatt Belcher, *The Economic Rivalry Between St. Louis and Chicago, 1850–1880* (New York, 1947), details the intercity competition for trade that resulted.

64. Emery, "Hogs and Pork Packing," p. 211. See also, Chicago Board of Trade, *Third Annual Report, 1861,* pp. 36–37.

65. "The Provision Trade of the United States," III, p. 2290; Chicago Board of Trade, *Twenty-Third Annual Report, 1881,* p. 34; *Thirty-Third Annual Report,* pp. 52–53; New York Produce Exchange, *Annual Report, 1883,* pp. 344–347.

66. Chicago Board of Trade, *Thirteenth Annual Report, 1870,* p. 146; *Fourteenth Annual Report, 1871,* pp. 143–147; *Fifteenth Annual Report, 1872,* pp. 164–168; *Sixteenth Annual Report, 1873,* pp. 13, 47–49; *Seventeenth Annual Report, 1874,* pp. 12, 42, 46–47; *Eighteenth Annual Report, 1875,* pp. 15–17, 42, 46–47.

67. "The Market Systems of the Country: Their Usages and Abuses," U.S. Dept. of Agriculture, *Report of the Commissioner, 1870,* pp. 250–253.

Chapter II

The Livestock Industry and Railroad Instability: The 1870s and 1880s

In addition to encouraging growth, specialization, and geographical shifts in the packing industry, the railroads also influenced this business very significantly as a result of the chaotic freight rate structure that came to characterize American railways in the nineteenth century. This chaotic rate pattern grew out of the underlying economics of the railroad industry, which was the first to face new and severe competitive pressures.

As the nation's first capital intensive, oligopolistic industry, the railroads confronted problems far different from those that beset the smaller firms that dominated the economic landscape of the prerailroad era. Trunkline railroads of the 1850s were far larger than any enterprises of the day, with a vast network of through and local lines stretching from the East as far west as Chicago and beyond, and they required much larger amounts of capital to build and operate. Whereas the very largest and best steamboat could be secured for a price between $40,000 and $60,000 in the mid-1850s, the construction of railroad companies and lines often involved a fixed capital investment of more than $5 million; the capitalization of the longer, intersectional trunk lines that connected the West and East ranged from $17 to $35 million. Working capital for the east-west trunklines ran between $2 and $3 million annually, while that of a steamboat seldom exceeded $30,000. Heavy capitalization limited entry so that markets quickly came to be dominated by a few large firms, each with market shares large enough to influence the price and output behavior of rivals.[1]

The capital needs and cost structure of the industry led to new and distinctive competitive patterns. The railroads were saddled with high fixed costs for machinery, buildings, and land that had to be borne whether they carried traffic or not. In addition, they were faced with high operating costs that varied with the volume of goods carried. Because fixed costs usually comprised at least 60 percent of total costs, and often more, railroads were under severe pressures, especially during times of depressions and low prices, to attract traffic. Unless resources were fully utilized, unit costs would soar. Yet the concentrated, oligopolistic structure of the market made competition necessarily interdependent. Price cuts by one firm to draw traffic away from another invariably provoked a competitor to respond in self-defense in order to avoid losing too much revenue. Such competition quickly became "cutthroat," since each firm had the resources and was under similar pressures to continue to compete even if it became unprofitable to do so. Unlike the independent price competition between small firms in unconcentrated markets, which simply drove inefficient firms out of the market, interdependent oligopolistic competition between giants could threaten the survival of an entire industry.[2]

The particular combination of high fixed costs and the need for the maximum utilization of capacity made the railroad industry inherently chaotic and unstable, with rates that fluctuated wildly and dissimilarly over time and in different regions. Rate wars were commonplace, and bankruptcies, the rule more than the exception. Given the uncertainties of interdependent behavior and the complex nature of costing and pricing problems—which involved a determination of hundreds of kinds of costs and prices for thousands of different commodities in different regions across the country for connecting roads as well as trunklines—it was usually impossible to confine rate wars to a specific product or to a specific group of roads. Whether rates were cut on livestock or grain, each road often felt the impact and was forced to inaugurate similar cuts in order to maintain its total share of the traffic for any one product or business in general. A rate war that began with cuts on livestock, for example, easily spread to rates on grain, for if one road was unable to secure livestock even at reduced prices, it would frequently reduce rates on another product in an attempt to compensate for losses on livestock.

The interdependent nature of oligopolistic competition, which made it impossible to treat the problems of any particular road or traffic in isolation of the general state of railroad affairs, also made efforts to cooperate a common occurrence in the railroad business. Cooperation took various forms, as knowledge permitted and experience demanded, but the purposes and results were usually the same. First, informal verbal agreements, then loose associations and pools, and finally, stronger regional federations or cartels of railroads were devised in an attempt to maintain rates and provide steady profits to the industry. Each method involved agreement on uniform rates and a determination of allotments of traffic or profits between competing roads.[3] Although each device was theoretically more advanced than the previous, providing more effective means of control and more severe penalties for noncompliance, the agreements were not enforceable in courts of law, so that compliance continued to rest on the good faith of participating roads. Good faith, however, was always easier to profess than to practice in a concentrated and oligopolistic market where it was often more profitable, in the short run at least, for a firm in the agreement to cut rates in order to secure a larger share of the market for itself.[4] Moreover, by wooing customers away from a competitor with lower prices, there was at least the possibility of securing their loyalty in the long run.

The impact of these new patterns of railroad competition on the livestock and packing industry was considerable. No sooner had the four great east-west trunklines reached the western interior in the late 1850s than their search for freight and their consequent rate wars began to tie them to western livestock shippers in a financial arrangement that neither interest wished to abrogate. Competition for livestock was especially severe, for it was one of the heaviest and most lucrative trades.[5] Since the major western roads and east-west trunklines intersected at Chicago, fierce competition centered there. The first roads to build their Chicago extensions, the New York Central and Pennsylvania, gained early leads as major livestock carriers. Although the Erie did not reach Chicago with a line of its own until the early 1880s, it nevertheless received a good portion of the trade via its western connections.[6]

To secure a larger share of the trade individual roads began to offer inducements to shippers. Secret rate cuts were the earliest and most common device, but railroads also began very early to invest in stock cars, stockyards, and terminal facilities in order to encourage larger shipments and lure traffic away from competitors. When railroads first entered Chicago in the 1850s, each line secured its own stockyard facilities. In 1856 the Michigan Central, a subsidiary of the New York Central, leased the Myrick Yards and within the year had transformed them from "rough contrivances" into the most popular yard in the city. The railroad built 30 acres of pens capable of accommodating 5,000 head of cattle and 30,000 hogs, and hired John B. Sherman, a former manager of one of the city's earliest yards, to operate them. Three years later, in 1859, the Pittsburgh & Fort Wayne Railroad equipped its yards with attractive double-decker pens. Two or three more yards followed within the next four years, each more elaborate than the other, and designed to attract shippers and to handle larger meat flows.

None, however, proved very satisfactory for either railroads or shippers. Because the facilities were scattered throughout the city at considerable distances from each other, supplied from different sources, and serviced by different roads, no uniform prices could be obtained. A brisk day at one yard might be, and often was, a dull day at another. A difference of 25 to 50 cents per hundred pounds in the prices of the same class of animals was not unusual at different yards during the same hour of the day. A livestock dealer thus did not know whether the prices he received were more or less than those received at other yards, and the distance, costs, and time involved in transferring stock from one yard to another prevented a livestock dealer from traveling to receive the best daily price.[7]

Railroads found the system unsatisfactory for other reasons. The scattered locations of the yards necessitated considerable switching, which in turn involved a great deal of wear and tear on the rolling stock as well as investments in extensive switching facilities. Competitive improvements and competitive building also proved to be a costly and seemingly endless process. Recognizing that a larger, consolidated stockyards would be in their own interest, the stock carrying railroads in 1865 invested some $925,000 of the $1 million amortized capital for the gigantic Union Stockyards of Chicago. Tying the railroads even closer to the livestock business were their investments in livestock cars, terminal facilities, and stockyards throughout the country.[8]

Competition for the livestock trade was also fierce among the specialized livestock commission merchants who handled the growing meat trade. These shippers, who provided railroads with high volume meat flows, pressed for and received rebates from the railroads, often playing one road off against another. The depression of the early 1870s further intensified competition for traffic, making tighter control over the trade seem imperative. In attempting to control rate cutting on livestock, however, the railroad managers created some new problems for themselves.[9]

COMPETITION AND COOPERATION AMONG THE RAILROADS

In 1875 the three major livestock carrying roads, the New York Central, Erie, and Pennsylvania, devised an *evener system* to divide the cattle and hog traffic at fixed percentages from Chicago to New York and thereby stop the scramble for livestock and the resultant rate cutting.[10] Drawing on the principles laid down by Pennsylvania Railroad President Thomas Scott, who had first proposed an evening scheme to oil refiners in 1872 as part of his South Improvement Company project,[11] these three roads each selected two of the country's major cattle and hog shippers as *eveners* to guarantee each road its agreed-upon portion of shipments and to see that no road got more than its share. The Erie and Pennsylvania chose Chicagoans Nelson Morris and O. H. Tobey, Samuel Allerton and D. H. Sherman, respectively, while the New York Central selected William Tilden of Chicago and New Yorker Tom Eastman.[12] If a road was unable to secure its quota of shipments through the normal distribution of traffic, these eveners were to make up the quotas with their own stock or purchase it in the market. For effecting the distribution, the eveners received a rebate of $15 per carload, or 7½ cents per 100 pounds (which amounted to about 15 percent of the total carload rate, or about $100) on every shipment they made.[13]

Although the evening system for hogs quickly broke down,[14] that for cattle worked well, returning profits to both participating roads and shippers, at least for a while. The system "had good results to us in every way," Erie General Freight Agent Simon Sterne admitted several years later.[15] In 1873–1874, before the evener system was inaugurated, the Erie hauled 5,025 cars of cattle. In 1875, the same year the system began operating, the Erie carried 14,459 cars, or almost three times the previous number. The Erie's livestock traffic and revenues more than doubled. Whereas it earned over $96,000 on 40 million pounds of cattle in 1875, in 1876 it carried 140 million pounds that brought revenues of nearly $255,000. Sterne claimed that the three cattle eveners had shipped over one-third of the Erie's business, for which they received $69,000 in 1875–1876, and more than $1,050,000 between 1875–1877. During 1875–1876, when rate wars plagued grain and other traffic and revenues dropped, rates on livestock held firm and profits remained steady.[16]

The relatively smooth operation of the evener system during these years contrasted significantly with the chaos that characterized the railroad business generally. The depression-ridden decade that brought severe rate cutting and decreasing profits to nearly all other types of traffic except livestock, also undermined the railroaders' sanguine belief of the early 1870s that informal alliances and the "good faith" of those involved could bring stability to the business. In February 1877 A. J. Cassatt of the Pennsylvania lamented to Vice-President John King of the Baltimore & Ohio that "this matter of meeting and agreeing on rates, and patching up these treaties is of no avail, and matters gradually are getting worse and worse, until there is almost universal ruin."[17] Groping for a solution, many executives believed "that a pool for all of the through traffic . . . would be advantageous and practicable."[18]

The need for tighter control over the business was evident. This time the railroads organized a more formal regional federation of roads—the Eastern Trunkline Association—and patterned it after the already successful Southern Railway and Steamship Association, formed in 1875 and headed by German-born engineer Albert Fink. The Eastern Trunkline Association was designed to maintain reasonable and uniform rates to all shippers and to stabilize rates by pooling profits or traffic, thereby removing the incentive for secret rate cutting.[19] In an attempt to mimic the success of the southern group, trunkline executives invited Fink to come north to manage their new organization. Under his guidance, administrative structures were established to carry out the Association's provisions. By December 1878 the Association had established a Trunkline Executive Committee, a Western Executive Committee, and a Joint Executive Committee to maintain rates.[20] As commissioner of the Association and chairman of the committees, Fink saw to it that the railroads carried out their contracts (i.e., rate and traffic agreements). He also adjusted the contracts after an examination of railroad tonnage and referred any disputed contracts on other matters to arbitrators, if necessary. Any complaints were to be sent to Fink, who referred them to the proper committee for a hearing. Under the provisions of the Joint Executive Committee (to which livestock problems were referred), if a resolution failed to receive unanimous approval, Fink's decision was binding. Although the Association was "empowered to specify and enforce against all companies such rules and regulations . . . as it may from time to time adopt," it lacked legal authority to do so. That is, "contracts" reached under the Association's aegis were not enforceable in courts of law because, under the common law, such organizations had no legal standing. Consequently, stabilization depended upon the voluntary cooperation of all roads.[21]

After the Trunkline Association was organized it became the mechanism for dealing with livestock shipments. At the first trunkline meeting in 1877, railroad executives extended their pooling efforts to general westbound traffic. Livestock, as eastbound traffic, continued to be pooled separately, through the evener arrangement.[22]

The two methods of pooling soon proved incompatible. Although both the Association and the evener system pooled traffic, the Association method was more formal and lay under the railroads' own control; the latter was more informal and lay as much in the hands of the eveners as the railroads. By allowing livestock to be pooled separately by a few roads who had informal understandings with a few select shippers, the railroads created the potential for trouble within and outside their own Trunkline Association. In contrast to the secrecy of the evener system, the Association operated openly, providing a forum where disgruntled shippers and roads could voice objections. Using the umbrella of the larger, more formal Association, they attacked the evener system, widening the cracks in its operation until participating roads decided to use the

Association to extricate themselves from their predicament with excluded roads and shippers.

Trouble began in September 1877, not long after the Trunkline Association was organized. Western connections of the American trunk-lines charged that the Grand Trunk Railroad of Canada was giving rebates on livestock from Chicago to New York. The Grand Trunk had been a source of annoyance to American trunk lines since the early 1870s. Handicapped as a carrier by its long and circuitous route, which wound through Canada from Chicago over connections with the Michigan Central to Montreal and over the Vermont Central into Boston, the Grand Trunk had practiced the art of rate cutting with a skillful aggressiveness that made even the most mischievous of American lines look amateurish. With no Canadian rivals to restrain its action, with debts piling up, and only foreigners to subdue, it cut rates on both grain and livestock unabashedly throughout the 1870s. Although agreeing to join the Association, Grand Trunk executives greeted the organization coolly, with an annoying indifference that troubled American railway managers.

Unruffled and undaunted by the charges of rate cutting on livestock, Grand Trunk General Manager Joseph Hickson calmly explained that "the 'eveners' charge paid by the Trunk Lines on all livestock to New York" meant that the American trunklines "control nearly all the stock to that market." Only by giving its shippers "equal facilities by paying rebates on stock from Chicago," he pointed out, "could the Grand Trunk secure stock [shipped] to New England."[23] The Baltimore & Ohio, and western connecting lines, such as the Illinois & St. Louis and the Ohio & Mississippi Railways, which had been unable to compete with the trunklines for the livestock trade, agreed with their Canadian ally. To eliminate what they considered to be unjust discrimination, they joined with the Grand Trunk to support the following motion:

> That this meeting regards the existing system of "evening" on live stock, not only as an unnecessary expense to the roads, but as an obstacle to the general maintenance of rates on live stock and they recommend to the Trunk Lines the abolishment of that system.[24]

By a slim two-vote margin that pitted roads in the evener system against those excluded, the motion carried.[25] But under Committee rules requiring unanimity, it could not be implemented.[26]

Although the roads in the evener system had not supported the motion, that fact was hardly reassuring to eveners when news of the attempted action reached the press and public. Nourished on a system of rebates that secured their dominance of the trade, eveners branded the resolution an attempt "to legislate them out of existence" and retaliated by threatening to withold their stock.[27]

The eveners' retaliatory action, together with growing complaints from excluded shippers and the public and losses from deteriorating livestock rates, soon reminded all railroads of the system's dangers. A resentful William Vanderbilt, who was away in Europe when difficulties flared up, refused to be bullied by the eveners: "They said the evening system should not be broken up; they would force the New York Central road to continue it; I told them to make an issue on that and fight it . . . the only question is, whether I would have had pluck enough to stand out if I had been there."[28] Western roads proclaimed their determination "to put eveners down to a level with other people."[29] The *New York Times* charged the "cattle ring" with depriving other cities of trade and gaining "control of the business by entering into a conspiracy with the great railroad companies."[30] The *Railroad Gazette* believed the railroads had "made 2 or 3 times as much profit as they were able to do without it."[31] St. Louis livestock shippers, angered that they were not included, asserted that it had enabled Chicago to forge ahead of St. Louis as the leading commercial center.[32]

Railroad executives participating in the evener system naturally saw things differently. To them the system was not a device for dominating the livestock trade or discriminating against any particular group of shippers, but, as Livestock Agent J. B. Dutcher of the New York Central tried to explain, "simply a way to get rid of this fearful competition . . . a method to enable the railroad companies to get some compensation for doing this business that would be remunerative to them."[33] The railroads had "not the slightest" interest "to see who controlled the traffic," another railroad employee insisted, "so long as they got the traffic."[34]

Just as the evener system and its livestock pool came under attack, so did the larger, more inclusive pools organized by the Trunkline Association. Eastern packers like Jacob Dold of Buffalo, who paid the railroads higher local rates to New York than other shippers paid on through traffic from Chicago to New York, blamed railroad pools for his troubles, charging that "since they got the pool, railroads have been able to maintain western rates." "We [eastern packers] have been unable to compete with the western shippers," he complained. "The Chicago folks, the western folks, are bound to have the best of us."[35] Shippers were often annoyed when freight billed over one route reached its destination by another as a consequence of trunkline reallocation of traffic. Demanding the right to choose their own routes, they argued that the railroads should not have the prerogative of diverting freight to other routes, since that frequently caused delays in shipments.[36] The public distrusted the pools, feeling that railroads were combining against consumers to promote their own self-interest.

The pool was, of course, designed to maintain rates at profitable levels, but the railroads nevertheless insisted that the public would benefit from this interference with competition. A suitable division of traffic, they argued, would eliminate the wild fluctuations in rates that always accompanied a railroad war.[37] The rail managers' declared confidence in pools, however, could not guarantee their effective operation. The lack of legally effective enforcement procedures and mutual distrust by participating members made any pool at best a temporary solution to the railroads' competitive problems.[38]

From September 1877 to August 1878, railroad affairs deteriorated as they continued to rely on the evener system. Not only did rates on livestock drop; this period also saw increases in the protests from an angry public and shippers unhappy with the pools.[39] The evener system was particularly susceptible to breakdown in the atmosphere of distrust that prevailed during this period. The lack of a formal agreement and of a structure to administer an informal agreement, coupled with the difficulty of reconciling the interests of railroads and the eveners, were the most important inherent defects of the arrangement. The declining rates on livestock and the consequent increase in relative costs to railroads of the $15 evener rebate further strained these already tenuous relationships.

Moreover, the appearance of a working refrigerator car late in 1878 presented the roads with an external and unanticipated problem. Although the innovation was still in its infancy, concerned livestock shippers, recognizing its cost cutting advantages, had already begun to pressure the railroads to slow the still small but increasing traffic in refrigerated dressed beef.

In an attempt to solve these problems, Fink and the Joint Executive Committee conferred in Saratoga, New York, in August 1878. Foremost in the minds of the Joint Executive Committee was the need to procure remunerative rates and to diminish the influence wielded by the eveners. To accomplish both goals, they reduced the amount of rebate to eveners from $15 to $10 a carload.[40]

The railroad managers' response to the problems presented by the infant dressed beef traffic on refrigerated cars was made without much deliberation. Embroiled in difficulties with livestock shippers, they paid little attention to the full implications of the new innovation for traffic or rates and simply resolved that "the net rates on dressed meat shall be 50 percent above the net rate for cattle."[41]

The policies implemented at Saratoga in 1878 were hardly designed to win new friends for the railroads. Eveners were angry that their rebates had been reduced, livestock shippers wanted still higher rates on dressed beef, and dressed beef shippers could hardly applaud rates that were arbitrarily pegged a certain percentage above those for a competing product. The railroads' action, however, did have an added significance: at Saratoga, both livestock and dressed beef shippers saw the railroads move to gain greater control over transportation rates. That development obviously was an ominous one for shippers.

Relations between livestock shippers and the railroads in the Trunk-line Association continued to worsen after 1878. While roads and shippers outside the evener system were using their own methods to undermine the evener arrangement, roads in the system were at war, with chaotic results for shipping rates. Each road suspected the others of "cheating" on the evener agreement formally recorded at the Saratoga Conference in 1878. Obviously, the charge of cheating was comprehensive enough to encompass nearly every railroad malpractice and ambiguous enough to hide what may have been the real motive for moving toward abandonment of a system which was not as profitable as the railroads had anticipated. According to the New York Central and Erie version of the feud, the Pennsylvania withdrew from the system and began carrying livestock at lower rates. The New York Central and Erie then discharged their eveners, Morris and Allerton, who resented the dismissal and began to ship exclusively on the Pennsylvania. A rate war on livestock resulted.[42]

The rate war apparently began when shippers outside the system pressured competitors of the participating New York Central, Pennsylvania, and Erie to lower rates. A combination of outside shippers could provide quantities of stock substantial enough to induce rate reductions. Testifying in New York before the Hepburn Committee, which in 1879 began its investigation of alleged railroad abuses, G. H. Blanchard, general freight agent of the Erie, seemed to verify the Grand Trunk's earlier prediction that roads outside the system would be forced to give rebates to their own shippers in order to compete with roads in the evener arrangement. According to Blanchard, such collusive action precipitated the breakup of the system:

> As this arrangement went on, from time to time these outside shippers did undertake a combination against the railroads; and the result was that the Canada Southern, for instance, about that time, would pay privately a drawback [rebate] to an outside shipper equal to the amount they believed these equalizers were getting for this service; the Canada Southern could not continue it for a great while without affecting the Grand Trunk, and the Grand Trunk would then begin the payment of something; a payment on their part would affect the Lake Shore, and the Lake Shore would begin to pay. . . . the result was that the action of the Lake Shore would

affect the Fort Wayne, and the Fort Wayne the Baltimore & Ohio, and Chicago would affect St. Louis, until, . . . the largest rebates were more than equal to the amount received during those times by the "eveners" themselves.[43]

The feud, whatever its origins, amply illustrates the complexity and instability of railroad affairs. No large road could change prices without affecting the pricing behavior of another; the industry was oligopolistic. Disagreement usually triggered rate wars that necessitated new rate policies. Pressures by large shippers further impeded the development of a clear-cut, rational policy toward ratemaking.

The war on livestock rates came to affect all eastbound traffic and soon brought the matter before the Eastern Trunkline Association again. What the railroads wanted most at this time was firmer control over the livestock business. In May 1879 the Trunkline Association produced a new policy that took control out of the hands of the eveners, who were shippers, and gave it to agents of the Association. Instead of there being a few eveners who received a $10 rebate per carload for their services, under the new arrangement, any shipper who shipped on the roads and routes designated by the joint agent of the associated roads received a rebate of $20 per car. As William Vanderbilt explained, now "every man could be his own evener." The principle and objective of the evener system remained the same: livestock shipments were pooled in order to equalize shipments between the different trunklines and to stabilize rates. In order to assure the effectiveness of the agreement the Trunkline Executive Committee adopted a double tariff rate on cattle. Under such an arrangement, if a shipper desired to give a particular trunkline more than its share of tonnage, he had to pay the higher tariff rate. The lower rate nearly always induced shippers to consign their shipments to the Trunkline Association agent and ship as he directed.[44]

Support from livestock shippers who had not been part of the old evener system came quickly. The livestock dealers of East Buffalo, for example, voiced gratitude for the railroads' equitable actions by adopting a resolution—a note of thanks—to "Vanderbilt, Scott [of the Pennsylvania], Jewett [of the Erie] and the Managers and Directors of the different railroad companies for the action they had taken in regard to this much-needed reform."[45]

Railroad executives did learn at least one important lesson from their difficulties with eveners and livestock shippers: the value of a neutral position. By putting shippers upon an equal footing, the railroads believed they had demonstrated their own neutrality and fairness toward all livestock shippers. No doubt the railroads also recognized the advantages of a policy that made them less vulnerable to exploitation by large shippers and to criticism by smaller shippers and the public.

The allocation system implemented by the Trunkline Association in the late 1870s marked the high point both of railroad attempts to achieve stability in the trade and of the close ties between railroads and livestock shippers. By including all major stock carrying roads and by providing incentives for cooperation to all shippers rather than favoring a few eveners, the Association diminished the threats to stability posed by combinations of smaller, excluded shippers and railroads outside the evener compact. More importantly, the scope of the new, more formal arrangement assured continued railroad involvement in the livestock trade. To secure the interest of stock carrying roads in the livestock business, the Trunkline Association had sought to establish an all-inclusive cooperation and to deal neutrally with each shipper. Whereas previously each stockman had to take his chances with individual roads, he now received a commitment from the railroads that if certain specified rules and procedures were followed, no one livestock shipper would receive preferential treatment, or that in case privileges were bestowed, the aggrieved shipper could take his complaints to the Association for a hearing. Thus, early informal agreements between a few roads and a small number of individual shippers had become, by 1880, a complex and relatively stable interrelationship between the businesses of livestock and railroad transportation.

THE IMPACT OF THE EVENER SYSTEM

Just what economic effect the evener system had upon the railroads' livestock business or the development of the livestock or packing industry is impossible to determine precisely. The available evidence suggests that it had little significant long-term impact. During its short four-year existence, the system hardly functioned efficiently; the same competitive forces that led to its organization also worked to undermine its operation and bring about its dissolution. It may have stimulated Chicago's livestock trade and helped to promote a more rapid expansion of the eastern and western packing industries. Yet these developments appear to be less a result of the evener system than a product of much more fundamental forces of changing technology and competition. Nearly a decade before the inauguration of the evener system, the railroads had begun to shift trade flows toward Chicago.[46] As early as 1865 the railroads had organized the Union Stockyards to expedite meat shipments to and from Chicago, and the stockyards were as much a result as a cause of changing and increasing meat flows. Nor did the evener system make Morris, Allerton, or other eveners "big" shippers. Nearly all of them were big shippers before they became eveners. In fact, it was precisely because they were large that the railroads chose them as eveners. While the system may have helped to make the railroads' livestock traffic more stable and therefore more remunerative for some roads some of the time, the New York Central's own eagerness to disband it suggests that it was not as profitable as had been hoped.[47]

The area in which the evener system probably had its major impact was in stimulating the export trade. Both Morris and Eastman began to export live cattle to England in large numbers in the mid-1870s, shortly after the inauguration of the system.[48] Eastman also began his experiments with refrigerated beef at that time. Morris' and Eastman's interest in the newer aspects of the trade could certainly have been related to their role in the evener system. In the first place, the eveners were bound, if unable to provide the railroads with agreed percentages, "to go into the Chicago market and buy this stock at any price, ship it by the different railroads at full rates and then sell it at the market prices, so as to keep up the various market arrangements."[49] While the system was designed to increase livestock shipments and equalize percentages on the railroads, there was little consideration given to actual market conditions at the place of destination. That the eveners might end up having to dump too many cattle on the market was of secondary importance to the railroads. The shippers, on the other hand, in order to realize the advantage of the $15 rebate, had to dispose of the cattle at the end of the line. Therefore, when supply in certain cities temporarily exceeded local demand, and the shippers had to continue sending cattle eastward in order to maintain proper percentages among the railroads, the export trade was a natural outlet.

This construction of events assumes that the eveners were forced or at least led into the export trade. A slightly different characterization of "the necessity for increasing the export trade" was suggested by a railroad employee, when testifying before the Hepburn Committee in 1879:

> My judgment is that in the beginning the eveners made a good deal of money out of this arrangement; that they had an interest in sending as many cars as possible over the trunk lines, so as to get the $15 on each and every car; that that stimulated them to find new outlets for the cattle business of the west over these railroads; that it [the export business] had been inaugurated in a small way at Montreal, and that Mr. Eastman himself, together with three other gentlemen, took up this question, not as a labor of love, but to increase the shipments at $15 per car; and that they entered into very much more prompt and effective cooperation and competition with Canadian shipments than they would otherwise have done; it was in an indirect way, therefore, that this matter [the evener system] helped.[50]

The employee's testimony that the eveners voluntarily sought to increase the flow of cattle to the East implies that the $15 rebate made the export trade profitable enough to act as an independent incentive for shipment.

That is, the stimulus for the export trade was not the imposed obligation to ship, but the profit that was realized from shipping.

The evener system also influenced developments in the packing industry in another, more indirect way. By involving the railroads even more deeply in the west-east livestock trade, it virtually assured their continued interest in protecting and preserving that trade. This, in turn, meant the protection of eastern packing and slaughtering houses in the form of more favorable rates on livestock vis-à-vis processed western packing products. The evener system thus helped assure that the railroads would become intimately involved in the competitive struggle that broke out between livestock and dressed beef shippers and western and eastern packing houses once the refrigerator car was perfected.

For the economic historian, the evener system is more important for what it shows about the nature of large-scale, oligopolistic competition than for either its short- or long-run economic impact on the industry. The demands that prompted railroad executives to inaugurate the system were a result of high fixed costs and unused capacity that created severe pressures to obtain traffic. The resultant competition, intensified during the depression of the 1870s, made some kind of cooperation imperative. Livestock, one of the most lucrative of western products and also among the most difficult to control, was one of the first commodities to be pooled.

CONCLUSION

The reasons that the railroad had such an impact upon the market for meats lay in large part in the capital intensive, large-scale nature of the modern railroad corporation and the oligopolistic, concentrated structure of the industry. The railroads were plagued by high fixed costs that in turn created severe pressures to compete for traffic. Unless resources were fully utilized, unit costs would soar. The competition that resulted was a new kind of competition—carried on between a few large-scale enterprises in the same markets. It was a type of interdependent rivalry far different from the independent competition described in Chapter I, between many small firms in diffuse and unconcentrated markets, and with a much greater impact upon the packing industry and the larger American economy.

The railroads attempted to mitigate the intense competitive pressures by engaging in various cooperative agreements. From particular commodity pools and informal arrangements like the evener system, they moved to establish a larger, more formal regional federation—the Eastern Trunkline Association. This larger cartel, however, ultimately proved no more effective in stabilizing rates than had the evener system.

Although different in scope and organization, both shared a common and fatal weakness—the lack of effective enforcement procedures. Neither shippers nor railroads could be legally forced to uphold their side of the agreements. As a result, whenever a road thought that more could be gained by cheating than by carrying out the agreement, secret rate cuts usually followed.

Despite the weaknesses of their organizations and associations, however, the railroads, by virtue of their size and ratemaking ability, did possess unprecedented power vis-à-vis other less well-organized groups. It was the power to discriminate, stemming from control over rates and the need for traffic, that understandably outraged many shippers and the public in general, and invited government regulation.[51] And it was such power over transportation services and costs that gave the railroads an important role in the history of the meat packing industry and other industries dependent upon rail transport to market their goods. Had railroads not become financially involved in the livestock trade, the subsequent history of the dressed beef industry might well have been different.

Already by the late 1870s both livestock and dressed beef shippers had begun to experience the effects of oligopolistic competition among the railroads. Unlike livestock shippers, however, dressed beef shippers were armed with a powerful technological innovation that was to enable them to counter railroad power.

NOTES

1. Alfred D. Chandler, Jr., ed., *The Railroads*, pp. 3–18, 21–24, 159–162; George Rogers Taylor, *The Transportation Revolution* (New York, 1951), pp. 74–103; William Z. Ripley, *Railroads, Rates and Regulation* (New York, 1924), and *Railroads, Finance, and Organization* (New York, 1923).

2. Lloyd G. Reynolds, "Cutthroat Competition," *American Economic Review*, 30 (Dec. 1940):737–747. The *Railroad Gazette*, April 24, 1885, p. 264, emphasized:

That the railroads, some of them being in desperate straights for money, have not been able to maintain rates during this period [1885] of extraordinary shipments is a further proof, of which there have been many, that growth of traffic cannot be depended upon to insure remunerative rates. Nothing but an unexpected growth of traffic can do this, for if the increase is foreseen, it will be provided for, and usually many times over, because it can be provided for at little cost, and comparatively little addition to existing appliances is required to enable the eight Chicago railroads to carry vastly more than they carried last March even. . . . The fact is not sufficiently appreciated that a reduction in the rate which is but a small proportion of the whole rate often destroys nearly all the profit. . . . It does not seem possible that this immense traffic, greater than any other of the kind in the world (the Chicago shipment being but part of the whole east-bound movement) should be incapable of yielding a profit to the carriers.

3. Chandler, ed., *The Railroads*, pp. 160–161.

4. The best discussion is Paul W. MacAvoy, *The Economic Effects of Regulation* (Cambridge, Mass., 1965).

5. *Proceedings and Circulars of Trunk Line Committees, 1881* (New York, 1881), p. 17, Statement No. 9, showing the eastbound dead freight forwarded from the western termini of the trunk lines.

6. The New York Central and Pennsylvania had reached Chicago by 1869. The Baltimore & Ohio did not obtain its own connection to Chicago until 1874. The Grand Trunk Railway of Canada constructed its line, the Chicago & Grand Trunk, in 1880. Both the Grand Trunk and Baltimore & Ohio, however, were handicapped as livestock carriers by their longer and less direct routes to the East; they initially concentrated more on procuring the grain and provision trade than in competing for the livestock trade.

7. *Griffith's Annual Review of the Livestock Trade and Produce Trade of Chicago, Fifth Annual Report, 1869*, pp. 19–25, *Eighth Annual Report, 1872*, pp. 4–7, 14–29, 24–27; Jack Wing, *The Great Union Stockyards of Chicago* (Chicago, 1865), pp. 1–11.

8. Insights into the growing interdependencies between railroads and stockyards can be found in New York, State Assembly, *Proceedings of the Special Committee Appointed to Investigate Alleged Abuses in the Management of Railroads Chartered by the State of New York*, including Report and Testimony, 8 vols. Assembly Doc. No. 38, 1879–1880, especially Vol. III, pp. 3299–3315, and Vol. IV, pp. 350–356, 261–269. Hereafter cited as the *Hepburn Report.*

9. G. R. Blanchard, general freight agent of the New York Central Railroad, in testimony before the Hepburn Committee (Vol. III, pp. 3315–3317), explained why control over the livestock trade was so difficult:

> The stock business was complicated by a great many matters; . . . The shipment of live stock was found to be different from any other class of freight in this, that when it was started from Chicago, the owner could sell at Pittsburgh to another man, and let it go through on the same rates at which it was contracted, or he could do the same things at the Bellair yards, on the Baltimore & Ohio Road, and he could do it at Buffalo; and in addition to that he could do it still further back at Toledo and Detroit; then as you proceed east, the market at Baltimore permitted another sale, the one at Philadelphia another one, the market at Albany another one, so that the ownership of this stock was continually changing, and the shippers of stock would mix their stock in all kinds of ways to evade the local rates of the railroads. . . . This live stock was a business that moved itself—went around on its own feet and legs, and could be driven here and there, and being so driven from one railroad to the other, it was liable to constant attempts at concentration. For example, all of the shippers of the Michigan Central and Lake Shore or Fort Wayne Roads being notified in Chicago today, that the rates had advanced, they would say, "we won't pay them;" therefore, it would be found that everybody called for cars on the Fort Wayne Road on one day, and the stock would all be driven over to their portion of the yards at Chicago, and delivered to that road; the effect intended to be produced by such shippers—that he had got a reduced price, or a drawback, was, at least believed, and the result would be that, in order to counteract that rate or belief, the Lake Shore would compromise; if the Lake Shore held out, the New York Central, finding they had lost their Chicago live stock business, would be instantly telegraphing to ask the reason of it; and Erie would similarly telegraph to know why the body of the stock was arriving at New York by the Pennsylvania Railroad; and the railway interest was constantly being prodded and spiked by the people who were in the habit of acting as commission merchants at the terminal yards. . . .

10. Testifying before the Hepburn Committee in 1879, John B. Dutcher, livestock agent of the New York Central, claimed that the livestock business had to be organized in 1875 because "rates . . . had run very low, so low that there could not possibly have been any money to the company in transporting cattle . . ." (*Hepburn Report*, Vol. II, p. 1742).

The *Railroad Gazette*, May 23, 1879, p. 479, attributed the difficulties to the entry of the Baltimore & Ohio Railroad into Chicago, November 15, 1874. Not part of the Saratoga Compact of 1873, which secured verbal agreement to maintain rates, the Baltimore & Ohio cut rates in order to secure their portion of traffic, and launched a full-scale rate war that dragged all roads into the fray and involved both east- and westbound traffic and even extended to passenger fares.

For additional information on the evener system see *Railroad Gazette*, Dec. 14, 1877, p. 552; *Railway Age*, Jan. 31, 1878, p. 67; U.S., Congress, Senate, *Select Committee on the Transportation and Sale of Meat Products*, Report and Testimony, No. 829, 51st Cong., 1st. Sess., 1889, pp. 56–57, 391 (hereafter cited as the *Vest Report*); Pierce, *A History of Chicago*, Vol. III, pp. 134–135, dates the evener agreement "somewhere" between 1873 and 1875.

11. For a description of the scheme and its outcome, see Harold F. Williamson and Arnold Daum, *The American Petroleum Industry*, 2 vols. (Evanston, Ill., 1959), I, pp. 346–352, 354–358, 360–362. Testimony of Simon Sterne, *Hepburn Report*, II, p. 3319, credits Tom Scott with the plan for evening cattle and hogs.

12. Eastman, Allerton, and Morris were cattle eveners; Tobey, Tilden, and Sherman were hog eveners. Biographical sketches of Eastman, Allerton, and Morris are given in *Dictionary of American Biography* (New York, 1936), pp. 217–218, 603–604. Timothy Corser Eastman was born in Croydon, New Hampshire, the son of Joseph Eastman, a carpenter, and Lucy Powers, a schoolteacher. Eastman moved to Cleveland, Ohio, in 1849. There he operated a dairy farm and began driving livestock from Ohio and Kentucky to the East. His livestock business grew so rapidly that in 1859 he moved his headquarters from Albany, New York, to New York City. It was in New York City that Eastman met Commodore Vanderbilt, and it was Vanderbilt who put him in charge of all the cattle business handled by the New York Central Railroads. When Eastman died in 1893, he was reputed to be one of the wealthiest men in New Hampshire.

Nelson Morris, a Bavarian Jew from Hechingen, Germany, walked to Chicago from Buffalo, New York, in the 1850s. In Chicago he worked at the stockyards as a head-hog renderer and cattle trader. Soon he secured contracts to supply the French and other European governments with beef and was instrumental in supplying the commissariat of the Union forces with livestock during the Civil War. By 1873 his company was earning more than $11 million a year. In 1874 he entered a partnership with Isaac Waixel (alleged by some to have been a hog evener). The firm of Morris & Waixel eventually became Nelson Morris & Company, and later Morris & Company. In addition to constructing one of the first packing plants at the Union Stockyards, Morris owned large cattle ranches in the Dakotas and in Texas, and was a cattle breeder and feeder as well.

Samuel Waters Allerton was a native New Yorker who began to purchase and sell livestock at Newark, New Jersey, in the early 1850s. About 1856 he moved to Illinois, began a stock farm, and started selling cattle in Chicago. In the early 1860s he cornered the market on pork and made windfall profits that he used to launch the First National Bank of Chicago, of which he was a director. He was instrumental in organizing the Union Stockyards of Chicago and founded the Allerton Packing Company. He invested heavily in the stockyards of Pittsburgh, Baltimore, and Jersey City, and, later, in the yards at St. Joseph and Omaha, and bought large tracts of farming land in Illinois, Ohio, Iowa, Nebraska, and Wyoming.

Information on hog shippers is scarce, but see the general discussion of the evener system in *Hepburn Report*, Vol. I, pp. 397–416; Vol. II, pp. 1625–1660; Vol. III, pp. 3315–3322. Also, *New York Times*, June 18, 1879, p. 8.

13. *Hepburn Report*, Vol. I, pp. 397–416; Vol. II, pp. 1625–1660; Vol. III, pp. 3315–3322; *New York Times*, June 18, 1879; U.S. Congress, Senate, *Report of the Senate Select Committee on Interstate Commerce*, 2 vols., S. Rpt. No. 46, 49th Cong., 1st Sess., 1886, I, p. 660 (hereafter cited as the *Cullom Report*); *Vest Report*, pp. 49–60.

14. Testifying before the Hepburn Committee, George Blanchard, general freight agent of the New York Central, explained that

weekly shipments were exchanged between the railroad companies of the arrivals of through cattle and hogs; but gradually the hog shipments were increased so much by way of the Pennsylvania Railroad, owing to the corn regions of Southern Ohio, where that company had access, and the New York Central and Erie had not, that the cattle dealers at a later date agreed that they would take the total hog and cattle shipments, and give us enough cattle shipments to equalize the hogs—that is, if we were short on hogs, they would increase the number of cattle to make good the correct and proper amount of tonnage, while we paid them, only on cattle. . . . so that a car load of hogs was equal to a car load of cattle; I think the agreement with the hog "eveners" lasted about eighteen months; when the payment to them [the hog eveners] was stopped because they did not equalize the stock in the manner in which they agreed to do, and the cattle men undertook to make good the total [*Hepburn Report*, Vol. III, p. 3319].

15. *Hepburn Report*, Vol. I, pp. 3328–3329. See also, testimony of John Dutcher, livestock agent of the New York Central, *Hepburn Report*, Vol. II, pp. 2427–2429, and R. C. Vilas of the Erie, *Hepburn Report*, Vol. I, pp. 413–418.

16. *Railroad Gazette*, May 23, 1879, p. 286, noted that "since the first contract with the eveners was made, which was in April 1875, the rates on live stock have been maintained at from 50¢ to 60¢ per 100 pounds, though for a great part of that time grain rates have been 20¢ or below. The great railroad war of 1876 did not disturb live stock rates, and generally when the railroads have carried their business without profit they have had the consolation that live stock was netting them something handsome."

17. Letter from John King, vice-president of the Baltimore & Ohio Railroad, to John W. Garrett, president, February 15, 1877 (Baltimore & Ohio Archives, Maryland State Historical Society, Baltimore, Maryland).

18. *Railroad Gazette*, May 18, 1877, p. 224.

19. In a traffic pool each road carried a prearranged allottment of traffic that had been decided upon by the Association's administrative office. A money pool, on the other hand, involved the forwarding of profits to the Association's office, where the money then would be divided up according to earlier arrangements. A money pool replaced the traffic pool. According to either method, rate cuts could increase neither traffic nor profits of a road, thus ideally removing the incentive for secret rate cutting (Chandler, ed., *The Railroads*, p. 161).

20. The Trunkline Executive Committee, composed of the four east-west American trunklines—the New York Central, Erie, Pennsylvania, and Baltimore & Ohio, and after 1880, a fifth trunkline, the Canadian Grand Trunk Railway—was in a sense the top-ranking committee, since its representatives indirectly controlled nearly all east-west traffic either directly or indirectly via connections. Usually other meetings were called at the request of the Trunkline Executive Committee. The Western Executive Committee, with headquarters at Chicago, was composed of the major western roads, while the Joint Executive Committee was composed of representatives of the trunklines and their connections. Increasingly, the Joint Executive Committee handled a large share of the problems. See *Hepburn Report*, Vol. III, pp. 3124–3132, for the articles of organization. A short but helpful article is D. T. Gilchrist, "Albert Fink and the Pooling System," *Business History Review*, 34 (Spring 1960):24–49.

21. Despite its weaknesses, the Association offered its members several advantages. The administrative structure that had been devised not only offered the railroads an opportunity to voice their complaints, but it also greatly facilitated their attempts to analyze and deal with their own competitive problems and to set rates and pool traffic on freight. Moreover, in some cases, the Association served as a counterweight to large and influential shippers. For general information concerning pools, see Chandler, ed., *The Railroads*, pp. 159–162. Albert Fink's opinion of pooling and his explanation of the Association's objectives are contained in *Hepburn Report*, Vol. I, pp. 483–490.

22. The decision to create a westbound pool was based on several considerations. Competition for westbound traffic was particularly severe and heavy. The Grand Trunk and all four American trunklines had terminal facilities in New York City. Westbound traffic theoretically would be more easy to control than that originating in the West and sent east,

for operation of an eastbound pool would depend upon the railroads' ability to make their western connections adhere to the pooling agreement. It was hoped that if the first pool were successful, they could effect similar arrangements on eastbound traffic. An eastbound pool was organized in 1879.

Since Grand Trunk cooperation was necessary if the Association were to succeed, the American trunklines persuaded the Canadian trunkline to join in 1880. Ironically, however, the Association's pools became a useful tool for the Grand Trunk. That road often forced American roads to comply with its demands by threatening to disrupt the pools.

For information concerning the organization of the westbound pool, see "Memorandum of Agreement made this 8th day of June, 1877, by and between the New York Central Railroad Company, the Erie Railway Company, by H. J. Jewett, Receiver, the Pennsylvania Railroad Company and the Baltimore & Ohio Railroad" (Baltimore & Ohio Archives, Maryland State Historical Society, Baltimore).

The formation of a pool often made it possible to lay off some workers, for the joint agent of the Association often accepted responsibilities of several workers. When railroad leaders met in 1877 to formulate plans for the westbound pool, they also agreed to reduce the labor force and to cut wages by 10 percent. Such action helped to precipitate the "Great Strike of 1877," which affected nearly every railroad corporation in the country and caused serious damage to the railroads' equipment and property.

23. *Proceedings of the Trunkline Executive Committee,* September 27, 1877, p. 9.

24. *Ibid.*

25. *Ibid.*

26. It was somewhat more complicated. Rules of the Joint Executive Committee indicated that "In case any question brought before this Committee fails to receive its unanimous action, such question shall be referred to the Chairman, who shall decide the case upon its merits, and whose decision shall have the same force and effect as the unanimous vote of the Committee." See "Articles of Organization," in *Hepburn Report,* Vol. II, pp. 3124–3132. Fink did not or could not enforce the resolution.

27. *Chicago Tribune,* September 28, 1877, October 3, 9, 1877, December 11, 12, 1877. Evidence concerning these counterthreats is most difficult to obtain, since eveners obviously did not broadcast or publish their activities. However, the proposals to deal with them discussed in various proceedings of the trunklines and joint executive committees, provide a good indication of the power wielded by eveners. References to such threats are also found in testimony before the Hepburn Committee, *Hepburn Report,* Vol. II, pp. 1625–1630, 1659–1660, 1742–1747, 3319–3322.

28. *Hepburn Report,* Vol. II, p. 1660.

29. Testimony of George Blanchard, *Hepburn Report,* Vol. II, p. 3335.

30. *New York Times,* May 21, 1888, p. 4.

31. *Railroad Gazette,* May 23, 1879, p. 286.

32. *New York Times,* May 21, 1888, p. 4. Testimony of J. M. Osborn, *Vest Report,* pp. 56–59, 70–72.

33. *Hepburn Report,* Vol. II, pp. 1745–1747.

34. *Ibid.,* Vol. III, pp. 3334–3335.

35. *Ibid.,* Vol. II, pp. 2151–2152. Speaking of the "Chicago folks," Dold claimed that "those big packing houses out West, they do not make any pork sausage; they do not take care of the little odds and ends; they put everything right into the tank, and it goes bumpety bump down; I try to make money out of everything that is possibly useful" (*Hepburn Report,* Vol. II, p. 2162).

36. Testimony of Gustavus Franklin Swift, *Cullom Report,* Vol. II, pp. 636–637.

37. Commenting on the pool, the editor of the *Railroad Gazette,* May 18, 1877, p. 224, asserted that "There will doubtless be a great deal of distrust to such a measure among the

community; but if it is carried out sensibly with the result of the maintenance of regular, impartial moderate rates, doing away with the enormous and violent fluctuations now so common, a year or two will suffice to reconcile all responsible men to it."

38. As early as October 1877, trunklines had become dissatisfied with percentages allotted only a few months before. Roads receiving more freight than their quota found it bothersome and aggravating to make repeated transfers to companies that were "short." Readjustments were demanded, and rumors circulated that the pool might be abandoned. (See *Railroad Gazette*, October 5, 1877, p. 457.) Further difficulties arose from the lack of a firm policy regarding the subdivision of pooled traffic among the western connections of the trunklines. It was one thing to divide the freight among four or five roads at a point of common origin in New York, but quite another to determine the percentages to be forwarded by the various connections—the Michigan Central, the Lake Shore, the Fort Wayne, and a host of others—that took freight to a multiplicity of destinations beyond the trunklines' western termini. These connections naturally fought for larger shares of this forwarded traffic, and stability in rate levels could not be achieved until further allocations were made.

39. *New York Times*, January 27, 1878, p. 1. In January a new threat to the westbound pool arose. Westbound traffic was allegedly being diverted from the trunklines at New York to the more roundabout "ocean-and-rail routes, chiefly by steamers to Portland and the Grand Trunk to the West" (*Railroad Gazette*, January 25, 1878, p. 44). Pressured by criticism and urged to act, the Trunkline Executive Committee descended upon the Grand Trunk and its ally the Vermont Central, threatening a "combined movement . . . to compel them to come to terms, or else to carry off their entire business by the establishment of rates with which they can never hope to compete without inviting ruin upon their own interests" (*New York Times*, January 28, 1878, p. 5). Apparently, the Grand Trunk was also disrupting westbound rates from Boston.

40. *Railroad Gazette*, August 30, 1878, p. 600, quoting proceedings of the Trunkline Executive Committee at Saratoga, New York. The agreement reached at Saratoga stipulated "that no return passes whatever should be given the shippers of livestock or men in charge of same," and "that the issue of free passes on account of livestock shall be confined to Chicago, and good only on trains on which their stock is being shipped." The strategy behind the reduction of rebates to the eveners is discussed by R. Vilas, general freight agent, New York, Long Island & Western Railroad, *Hepburn Report*, Vol. I, p. 405.

41. *Ibid.* Also, testimony of J. B. Dutcher, *Hepburn Report*, Vol. II, pp. 1740–1741.

42. *Hepburn Report*, Vol. I, pp. 397–410, 413, 418, 931; Vol. II, pp. 1625–1659, 1742–1745; Vol. III, pp. 3299–3322.

43. *Ibid.*, Vol. III, pp. 3321.

44. Testimony of Vanderbilt, *Hepburn Report*, Vol. II, pp. 1627–1630, Vol. III, pp. 3324–3328, records the new agreement in full. See also, *New York Times*, June 6, 1879, p. 5.

As to the public advantages of the agreement, Vanderbilt explained:

> if he [a shipper] had got ten car loads of cattle to ship, if he shipped them where the roads wanted him to ship them, so as to keep themselves even, his price would be 80 cents a hundred; and if he shipped them where he pleased, his price would be at 90 cents a hundred, and they do the evening, as we lose that 10 cents; before that they paid the 90 cents and the eveners got the 10; now every man is his own evener, and we got a great many more customers; instead of business being confined to half a dozen men, we have any quantity [*Hepburn Report*, Vol. II, pp. 1627–1630].

45. *Railroad Gazette*, May 30, 1879, p. 299.

46. See text, Chapter I, pp. 11–14.

47. Testimony of Vanderbilt, *Hepburn Report,* Vol. II, pp. 1627–1630.

48. This is reported in greater detail in Chapter III, pp. 55–58. Whereas approximately 68 cattle were exported between 1870 and 1874, a total of 31,407 were shipped to Great Britain between 1875 and 1879, the years during which the evener system was in operation (Richard Perren, "The American Beef and Cattle Trade of Great Britain, 1870–1914," *Economic History Review,* 20 [August 1971]: 430–432).

49. *Hepburn Report,* Vol. III, pp. 3332–3333.

50. *Ibid.*

51. Congress passed the Interstate Commerce Act in 1887. The congressional investigations behind passage of the Act are contained in U.S. Congress, Senate, *Report of the Select Committee on Transportation Routes to the Seaboard,* S. Rpt. No. 307, 43rd Cong., 1st Sess., 1874 [known as *Windom Report*]; U.S. Congress, Senate, *Report of the Senate Select Committee on Interstate Commerce,* S. Rpt. No. 46, 49th Cong., 1st Sess., 1886.

Chapter III

Growth Strategies in the Early Dressed Beef Industry

Before the 1880s no fresh meats carried the "Armour Star," "Swift Premium," or "Morris Supreme" labels. The refrigerator car was little more than an "ice-box on wheels," ridiculed by cynics as a "sweatbox." "You might as well have shipped the meat in a clothes basket," Philip D. Armour quipped from hindsight.[1] Western refrigerated beef was a novelty item of questionable quality in the food budgets of eastern consumers. Shipments of refrigerated meat were sporadic, small-scale, and seasonal, and distributed through the traditional network of jobbers and commission merchants.

By 1886 the Chicago packing firms of Armour, Morris, Swift, and Hammond were transporting large-scale shipments of dressed beef from west to east on a regular and year-round basis, in fleets of company-owned and insulated commercial refrigerator cars, and distributing meat through company-owned distribution outlets. The emergence of the "Big Four" marked the beginning of a new method of supplying beef to the consumer. The business was becoming more systematized, more structured, and more complex. Central distribution points were becoming larger and under more centralized control, while the area of product distribution widened.

The key to the industry's transformation was the progressive improvement of the refrigerator car and its application to the long distance transportation of meats. The refrigerator car enabled dressed beef to be slaughtered in Chicago and shipped to the East at a lower cost than livestock, which had to be transported to the East and then slaughtered. The latter method was relatively costly and inefficient, since nearly 60 percent of the animal was inedible. Moreover, cattle lost weight or died on the trip, and they had to be fed and watered at terminal facilities along the way. Dressed beef, on the other hand, weighed less, was more compact, and took up much less space in the cars. As important, with the innovation of the refrigerator car, butchering could be concentrated at Chicago, rather than dispersed among the many consuming communities, thereby assuring higher volume operations and lower unit costs than the former methods of shipping stock in small lots to wholesale butchers throughout the East.[2]

The refrigerator car initially created almost as many problems for the packers as it later did for the railroads and livestock shippers. The long distance distribution of a perishable product was a novel undertaking. There were no master plans to follow to develop the trade, and the few interested packers wrestled with many difficulties during the late 1860s and the 1870s.

Initially, rules of thumb and a strategy of experimentation characterized the business. Knowledge of refrigeration techniques was rudimentary, and losses occurred frequently in the early days. As Armour once explained, "our first experience with it was not very profitable, . . . we did not understand the methods of refrigeration and did not get our beef to the seaboard in proper condition. . . . We had to learn the methods and experiment."[3]

Even Gustavus Swift, who recognized better than most what was needed to make the business a commercial success, did not know at the outset what was the best strategy to develop the trade. Only after the railroads refused to build refrigerator cars did Swift decide to build his own, and only after early experiments had demonstrated the need for more efficient distribution networks did Swift decide to build his own. Then, once he implemented his strategy of vertical integration, his enterprise grew rapidly, even beyond his expectations. "Father had no idea at the outset that his business would or could become as large as it eventually did," Louis Swift explained later, "but he was heading it always in its given direction."[4] By 1884, only three years after he began sending summer shipments of dressed beef, Swift was the largest dressed beef shipper in the country. Those firms that adopted a similar strategy grew large in as short a time. By 1886 Swift and the three other firms that had successfully implemented his strategy controlled a major portion of the interstate dressed beef trade.

Yet the strategy of vertical integration did not assure the smooth operation or long-run profitability of the enterprises. In order to maintain their initial dominant position, these firms also had to solve complex administrative problems that arose as they grew large and undertook new functions. Without examining the problems facing those who entered the dressed beef trade, it is impossible to understand why some solutions were more effective than others and why the firms of Swift, Armour, Hammond, and Morris came to dominate the industry. By placing both the problems and solutions in historical perspective, this chapter illuminates both the origins and dynamics of oligopoly in this industry.

THE BEGINNINGS: INNOVATION IN THE DRESSED BEEF INDUSTRY

Unlike the farmer-packers of the early nineteenth century who slaughtered, pickled, smoked, and sold their meat directly to local consumers, western packers utilized a long distance transportation system to expand their markets. By the 1860s they were shipping cured meats by rail to eastern wholesalers and marketing centers during the winter months. Even as late as the end of the Civil War, nature remained the packers' ice-box, just as it had been in the early nineteenth century. Because cooling was necessary to prevent spoilage before the preservative mixture could penetrate all parts of the meat, meats were cured and shipped east only in the winter, while fresh meats were distributed locally.[5] Large blocks of ice had been utilized in packing houses to keep meats cold during the summer since the mid-1850s, but the output during the summer months was small because efficient refrigerated transportation had not yet been devised.

As railroads opened new commercial possibilities for western goods, interest in shipping perishable articles, such as fruit, fish, and fresh meats grew, stimulating efforts to apply the principles of refrigeration to transport systems. Most early efforts to ship refrigerated beef, however, were sporadic, small-scale, and almost always seasonal. Refrigerator car pioneers were commonly tinkerer-inventors who saw the technical problems but did not fully appreciate what it took to make the refrigerated beef business a commercial success or a year-round business. A few pioneers shipped beef for a time and made a profit. One such was Henry Peyton Howard of San Antonio, Texas, who made the first successful shipment of refrigerated slaughtered meat in his own steam freighter from Texas to the Gulf port of Indianola in 1868. Another was Thomas Rankin of Denison, Texas, who had organized in 1872 the "Refrigerating Cars Quick Transit Fresh Meat Company" to transport refrigerated beef from Denison to New York City. Before long, however, they ran into serious difficulties. Howard found that even though he had purchased his own steam freighter and acquired a 20- by 50-foot cold storage room in New Orleans to receive meat from San Antonio, he could not count on Mother Nature to provide suitable weather conditions. Often his shipments were destroyed en route by unpredictable storms in the Gulf of Mexico. Rankin's problem was different. He discovered that the business was not profitable unless a steady flow of supplies could be secured. Unable to enlist support to construct a packing plant in Denison, he closed down his company.[6]

The early experiments of Detroit meat dealer and packer George H. Hammond were more successful. Cautious, quiet, and a New Englander by birth, George Hammond became interested in refrigeration technology in the late 1860s, when his neighbor, William Davis, developed and patented a refrigerator car allegedly capable of conveying "meats, fruits and vegetables, in a perfectly fresh, unchanged condition, over any distance, and for any reasonable or required length of time."[7]

Described by William's son, D. W. Davis, as "extremely simple," the car was insulated by a wooden shell lined with hair felt. Wedgelike galvanized iron tanks located at the sides of the car held about 6,500 pounds of crushed ice and salt, which were loaded from the top of the car through funnels that were fitted with plugs to prevent air from entering the car after the refrigeration mixture was added. Drip pipes and pans underneath the ice tanks carried and collected the moisture that formed during the cooling process. There was no provision for mechanical circulation of air within the cooling chamber. Before loading the perishable items the car was allowed to stand for some 20 hours, until the temperature reached about 33 degrees, after which time another 1,000 pounds of ice was added and the meat was loaded for shipment. A 2,500-mile trip required yet another re-icing along the way.[8]

Although the car carried strawberries on its successful maiden voyage from Cobden, Illinois, to Buffalo, New York, in September 1868, Hammond was convinced of its adaptability to the meat trade. As a thriving wholesale and retail meat dealer with his own packing plant and solid connections in New England, Hammond was eager to use the innovation to expand his business. After plans were perfected in 1869, he engaged the Michigan Car Company of Detroit to build the car, persuaded the New York Central–Boston & Albany railroads to carry the shipments, and then made arrangements with the wholesale meat firm of Brown, Plumber & Co. in Boston to receive and distribute the meat.[9]

On April 2, 1869, the refrigerator car Davis had designed and the Michigan Car Company of Detroit had built, arrived in Boston over the tracks of the Boston & Albany Railroad. It carried 16,000 pounds of fresh beef and George H. Hammond. The *Boston Daily Advertiser* described the experiment and heralded the innovation's cost-cutting advantages:

> The improvement in the car consists in a new method of packing the ice, securing great economy. The amount of ice used in this car on the passage from Detroit was about 6,500 pounds, whereas the amount used on such a trip heretofore has frequently reached eleven tons. The ice is placed in narrow chambers at each side of

the car, opening at the top from the outside and does not, therefore, come in contact with the meat or with the air in the car which is kept dry and cold. . . . The invention is also applicable to stationary meat and fruit houses.[10]

Proud of his success and convinced that the business could be made profitable, Hammond immediately took steps to develop and protect his interests in it. His strategy was cautious, involving as few risks as possible. First, he secured financial backing from the private banking firm of C. A. Ives of Detroit as well as the two New England jobbers through whom he had distributed his first shipments. Then, with their help, he secured exclusive patent rights to the Davis car. He apparently remained content with the car, despite the difficulties it presented. Lacking a proper ventilation system, the car sometimes delivered green and smelly meat. Hammond solved the problem by confining shipments to the winter months. To secure supplies and ice, Hammond and his associates built a packing plant just across the Illinois state line in Indiana, a short distance from the Union Stockyards, on the banks of the Calumet River. The plant was also near the ice harvesting property and ice houses of P. J. Smith & Co. Hammond's investment amounted to $2,000; that of his associates totalled $4,000. Since his shipments were seasonal and still relatively small-scale, he continued to rely on the traditional network of wholesalers and commission merchants to distribute his meat, thus foregoing additional investment in marketing facilities.[11]

During the early 1870s the small-scale, seasonal nature of Hammond's shipments created little stir, either in the meat markets of the East, among railroad executives, or among wholesalers and commission merchants. Hammond as yet had no significant competition. Nor did he confront much opposition from the railroads. Having just begun to nurture the livestock trade, with the evener imbroglio still to come, the roads courted him and his trade. Some, like the Michigan Central, even built their own crude refrigerator cars, providing special rate contracts for his beef. In one instance, the New York Central donated land so that Hammond could build a warehouse "for the purpose of handling exclusively Chicago dressed beef" right alongside the tracks of the Boston & Albany Railroad in Worcester, Massachusetts.[12] Since Hammond distributed his meats through wholesalers or commission merchants, they welcomed his business, and like railroad executives, often went out of their way to cooperate with him. After learning of Hammond's shipments to Boston, the wholesale meat firm of H. A. Botsford & Co. of Hartford wrote to him, asking that he buy and dress cattle for them in Chicago.[13] Hammond agreed and continued to supply meat to the wholesale firm until about 1878. Having nothing to do with final sales and facing negligible competition or opposition, Hammond did not need, and so did not use, aggressive sales policies. As his biographer stated, "Hammond's methods were simple. There was no high pressure used, or threats."[14]

Another reason the new product seemed not to threaten the existing order was the fact that western dressed beef at first often cost the same or more than locally slaughtered meat. The *Boston Market and Produce Report* issue of March 26, 1874, listed Chicago dressed beef as selling for nearly 2 cents more per pound than Boston slaughtered beef.[15] Consumers were not yet the beneficiaries of the new shipping methods. Perhaps the cost of distributing and marketing the meat offset the cost-saving advantages of Hammond's refrigerator car. Moreover, in view of the substantial amounts of ice required to cool the meat, it is quite possible that the Davis car itself was simply not very efficient.[16]

What is important is that the new method of supplying meat to consumers was apparently economical enough and the demand brisk enough to give Hammond a profit and to lure others into the business. By 1873 the sales of the newly organized George H. Hammond Co., including products other than fresh meat jumped to more than $1 million a year. By 1875 the company's sales totalled almost $2 million annually.[17]

Wealthy Chicago packer and livestock shipper Nelson Morris watched with interest as Hammond carved out his monopoly of the New England trade, but he tended to see only the apparent profits, not the problems involved in developing the business on an extensive scale. To Morris the dressed beef trade provided an opportunity to extend his local fresh beef trade to eastern markets; he seldom considered it more than an extension of his larger pork packing and cattle shipping business. Clearly, he did not anticipate that dressed beef would provide the basis for a significant new industry. Always wanting it understood that "he was a cattleman to the core,"[18] Morris left the technical aspects of the dressed meat business to others and simply shipped his first carload of meat to Boston, frozen and in an ordinary box car, in the winter of 1874. After 1875 his growing involvement in the evener system may have discouraged a more active interest. Although he continued to send a few carloads every week during the winter season, his dressed meat business remained a small-scale, seasonal affair that required no new methods of distribution or production.[19]

Also displaying an interest in the trade were several western meat wholesale and commission firms, one of which was Nofsinger & Company of Kansas City. In the autumn of 1875 that company sent a carload of refrigerated beef to Philadelphia and Boston. Netting over $800 on those two carloads (containing meat from 103 cattle), the firm sought to build up its business. As it did so, however, it encountered serious difficulties with the railroads. By the mid-1870s, as we have seen, the railroads had inaugurated the evener system for livestock shipments. More concerned with the profitability of the livestock trade than with the much smaller dressed beef shipments, they arbitrarily set rates for dressed beef that eroded the profits in the new trade. Since the refrigerator car had not yet been perfected and old methods of distribution and marketing were still being used, a hike in the rates for dressed beef from 65 cents per 100 pounds to 75 cents per 100 pounds was prohibitive in the eyes of Nofsinger & Company. Moreover, that firm, like many early experimenters, relied upon the railroads and fast freight companies to furnish them with cars, and soon discovered that "the supply of refrigerator cars was too small to answer the demand of the traffic and [that] many of those furnished were defective." The company also complained that

> there was at times neglect on the part of the railroad employees in not supplying the cars with ice while in transit. For that reason beef would frequently reach its destination in bad condition. The delays in transit were often disastrous. The appliances in many of the markets where the beef was sold were crude and insufficient so that the meat got into bad order before it could be sold.[20]

The difficulties in building the domestic dressed beef market and growing opportunities in the export trade prompted packers and livestock shippers to turn their attention to the export trade.[21] The high demand for American meat in Great Britain in the mid- and late 1870s, and the high cost and high risk involved in transporting live cattle across the ocean, created strong incentives to find other methods of tapping overseas markets. Export cattle averaging about 1,200 pounds sometimes lost up to 100 pounds during the voyage and were often seriously bruised or injured. Moreover, special decks had to be built aboard freighters to insure the safety of cattle during storms.[22]

It was one of the participants in the evener system, T. C. Eastman, a wealthy livestock shipper and New York City packer, who inaugurated the export dressed beef trade. Unlike Morris, he recognized the technical and commercial problems as well as the opportunities associated with long distance transportation of a perishable product, and planned his strategy carefully. Sometime in 1875 Eastman secured patent rights to the Bates process of refrigeration. Meat was cooled in an airtight chamber by a cast iron fan or blower connected by a belt to a steam engine outside the chamber.[23] Installing such a system aboard a steam freighter, Eastman sent his first cargo of chilled meat from New York to England in October 1875. The beef arrived in good condition, and he set out to expand his business.

During the next two years he installed refrigeration systems on three of the major steamship lines, the White Star, Anchor, and the William & Gueton. Eastman paid premiums for refrigerator space and erected crude refrigerators at his killing yards in New York and New Jersey. In addition, he organized Eastman's Ltd. in England to make arrangements with retailers in markets all over England, Ireland, and Scotland. Within three months from the date of his first shipment, Eastman was shipping 100 carcasses weekly; by the close of 1876 and early 1877 his shipments averaged from 600 to 1,000 carcasses per week. The first week in February 1877 he shipped 1,022 cattle. By the end of the year he was shipping 4,000 carcasses a week.[24]

The savings as well as the profits were enormous. A live steer cost £8 10s. to send from New York City to London in 1878, as opposed to 30s. dressed.[25] It cost Eastman about $26 per head for preparation, freight, and cost of transit, including commissions to agents on the other side. The average price realized was about $90, netting him a profit of roughly $64 a head![26]

The enormous profits lured others into the export trade, among whom were fellow eveners Morris and Allerton, who shipped from Philadelphia, and George Hammond, who shipped chilled beef from Boston through the meat wholesale firm of Sawyer, Hollis & Company.[27] By January 1877 there were already eight firms exporting dressed beef to England as opposed to four carrying live cattle.[28] These other exporting firms followed the pattern laid down by Eastman, erected large chill rooms near the stockyards in the United States and installed their own special cooling systems aboard steamers. With the exception of Hammond, who sent his own sales representative to London, few, however, were as conscientious as Eastman about securing sales outlets.[29]

By 1877 competition was fierce in the London market, where distribution outlets were concentrated. When Englishman James MacDonald visited America in 1877, he reported that the dressed beef trade had expanded so rapidly under boom conditions that the exporting firms were soon engaging in severe competition. (See Table III.1 for an indication of how rapid the growth was.) As a result, most firms soon were operating at a loss and at least one, Lehman Samuel & Brother of New York, had been forced to declare bankruptcy.[30]

The losses had their origins on both sides of the Atlantic and reflected the need for more economical and efficient methods of distribution and marketing, and an improved system of refrigeration, as well as oversupply in the British market. Commenting on the nature of the business, the *London Mark Lane Express* of January 15, 1878, reported:

> The present supplies of American meat, if spread anything evenly over the country, would be absorbed without producing any noticeable effect upon the demand of home-produced meat. But the supplies are not, nor are they ever likely to be evenly spread over the country. Indeed, in hot weather, unless the cold-air process is kept

up after disembarkment and during transit by rail, the foreign meat cannot be sent far into the inland districts.[31]

Heavy cattle purchases for the export trade, which fed the railroads' livestock traffic, had forced up cattle prices in America to approximately 1d. (one British penny) per pound. Then, when the shipments reached England, they had to be dumped upon an overstocked London market and sold at prices that seldom covered costs.[32]

Developments in the export trade foreshadowed problems in the domestic dressed beef trade. Many of the difficulties lay in the unsystematic way the business was organized. As of 1877 only Eastman had made sure that interior sales outlets were secured, and he had established only one storage facility in all of England. If firms were unable to

Table III.1. Statement of the Quantity and Value of Refrigerated Beef Exported from the United States to Great Britain During the Eighteen Months Ended March 31, 1877, Furnished by Dr. Young, Chief of the Treasury Bureau of Statistics

		To England	
Year	*Month*	*Pounds*	*Dollars*
1875	October	36,000	2,800
1875	November	36,000	2,800
1875	December	134,000	10,700
1876	January	162,000	12,700
1876	February	292,000	24,000
1876	March	302,000	24,300
1876	April	1,256,000	106,409
1876	May	912,000	69,400
1876	June	940,000	72,000
1876	July	645,000	44,500
1876	August	1,037,000	101,811
1876	September	1,838,550	154,275
1876	October	2,202,685	185,088
1876	November	3,598,980	331,402
1876	December	3,364,480	286,055
1877	January	2,312,450	226,410
1877	February	4,410,610	543,000
1877	March	5,099,055	435,585
	Total	28,579,010	2,461,803

Source: "Fresh Meat Shipment to Europe," U.S. Dept. of Agriculture, *Report of the Commissioner, 1876,* p. 320. ("Fresh meat" refers to chilled, dressed beef.)

secure customers before shipments arrived in London, they risked losses. Even though meat could be left aboard the ships for a few days while customers were rounded up, such a delay cost money and also disrupted scheduled trips. Moreover, as was the case with early experiments in the domestic beef trade, refrigeration technology had not yet been perfected. As a result, summer shipments were frequently disasters.

When the English market became oversupplied, competition eliminated marginal firms and prompted those that remained in the business to continue the search for economies. Eastman clearly recognized what had to be done. He was confident that "in the course of time, at least ½¢ per pound will be saved by the substitution of condensed air for ice" and "that more refrigeration facilities would be installed in English meat shops." For the present, however, Eastman asserted that "the profits of the trade are too small to admit of this being done."[33]

Despite the crude state of refrigeration technology and the chaotic nature of the trade, exporters like Eastman and pioneers in the domestic dressed beef trade paved the way for Gustavus Swift and those who followed in the late 1870s and 1880s. Although domestic refrigerated meat shipments during the mid- and late 1870s remained small in comparison with those that would pour into markets when the refrigerator car was perfected and the business was more systematized, the volume was significant by the mid-1870s. In 1875 the Chicago Board of Trade noted that "the shipment of dressed beef from this city to the eastern markets has grown within the past few years to a very important traffic." A year later the Board of Trade reported that "the business of shipping dressed beef to England has assumed considerable magnitude."[34] The increasing volume of western dressed beef acquainted consumers with the product, but, more importantly, it exposed some of the problems in handling a perishable product on a large scale.

GUSTAVUS SWIFT'S WINNING STRATEGY

Gustavus Franklin Swift, a native of Cape Cod, Massachusetts, and cattle dealer and partner in the Boston wholesale meat firm of Hathaway & Swift, set out from Albany in 1875 en route to Chicago, determined to solve the problem of distributing fresh meat.

He quickly became the major innovator in the industry.[35] Arriving in Chicago the year Eastman made his first export shipments of dressed beef, when the domestic meat trade was still small-scale and seasonal, Swift made entrepreneurial contributions that extended beyond the utilization of a cost-saving refrigerator car to the organization and systematization of the business as well. Improving upon the earlier efforts of Hammond, he developed and then built his own cars to transport his meats all year-round, created his own distribution facilities to market the beef, and shipped it on a scale large enough to make the business profitable. By the early 1880s, Swift had become the largest dressed beef shipper in the domestic market.

When Swift arrived in Chicago in 1875, he was a relative newcomer to the city's packing business. He had limited capital and looked for ways of competing more effectively with his already well-established rivals. Always foremost in his mind was the problem of cutting costs of bringing meat to the eastern market. He wanted to avoid paying "freight on inedible portions of the cattle," commented his biographer, "and to avoid the loss of weight to cattle and the due hardships of travel." He was determined to end "the waste of buying cattle which had passed through the hands of too many middle men and against which too many charges had accumulated." As important, Swift recognized that "bringing about efficient distribution was the big problem with perishable food."[36]

In order to secure enough capital to purchase a slaughtering plant of his own and to finance experiments with refrigeration, Swift worked as a cattle buyer for several eastern wholesale meat firms during the first two years after his arrival in Chicago. At the same time he experimented with chilled meat shipments, paying the G. H. Hammond firm a slaughtering fee, then sending the carcasses to the wholesale meat firms of his brother Edwin, in Clinton, Massachusetts, and to Hathaway & Swift over the Grand Trunk's cold and northerly route. Like the early shipments of Hammond, those of Swift did not necessitate a radical change in existing railroad equipment, for Swift used ordinary box cars with temporary framings from which to suspend the carcasses. The cars were not iced and their doors were left open for ventilation. Although the meat arrived in good condition, Swift considered the shipments too costly. He then rented several refrigerator cars from fast freight companies engaged in similar experiments with the fruit trade, but the railroads' inability to supply enough cars soon made this method impractical. In 1877 he discontinued the winter shipments and set out to perfect the refrigerator car that could haul meets year-round.[37]

In 1878 Swift hired engineer Andrew Chase to help him perfect plans for an insulated and ventilated car. A year later blueprints were completed. Although modeled after the Zimmerman refrigerator car, patented in 1876, the Swift-Chase car featured a unique cold blast system that provided automatic circulation of pure dry air through the cooling compartment. Air was cooled by passing through ice bunkers in the upper corners of the car. As cooler, heavier air sank, it forced warmer, lighter air to escape through ventilators connected to the outside. The ice bunkers were filled from the exterior of the car through an opening in the roof.[38]

Lacking sufficient capital to build more cars, Swift sought ways to finance the project. When he approached the railroads to ask their aid in building the cars, he learned that they saw not the long-term advantages of the innovation, but its short-term expense and the serious and immediate problems it posed for them as livestock carriers and ratemakers. Because of the required large investments, railroads had generally been unwilling to provide specialized cars for individual shippers. They had concentrated on building fleets of general service cars (boxes, gondolas, flats, and so on), leaving construction and ownership of the more exotic types to private car lines. Their interest in building livestock cars and facilities, however, was different. Railroads built many of these cars not only because the traffic was very lucrative, but also because they were eager to develop eastbound traffic. Heavy investments in livestock cars and related activities, and the existence of a functioning evener system in the mid-1870s, increased the railroads' reluctance to build refrigerator cars. The Grand Trunk had only small investments in livestock facilities but it did not have the financial resources to undertake such a risky and expensive investment as the new refrigerated trade called for. All of the railroads flatly refused to build the necessary cars.[39]

Rebuffed by the railroads, Swift proceeded to Detroit, where he contacted his friends, the McMillens, owners of the Michigan Car Company and builders of Hammond's first cars, and persuaded them to construct ten cars by signing a mortgage on his business. Before the cars were out of the shop, Swift encountered new difficulties. Hammond, who kept a close watch on Swift, learned of his plans to build cars of his own. He immediately sued Swift for patent infringement and inaugurated injunction proceedings to prevent the cars from being released. The court eventually ruled in Swift's favor.[40]

Swift did not wait for the court decision. With an eye toward solving distribution as well as transportation problems, he returned to the Grand Trunk and this time persuaded the road's managers to carry the new cars and the prospective new trade. He had selected his road carefully. Swift's early career as a butcher and cattle dealer in New England, and that area's favorable weather conditions and growing meat deficit, made the New England market the most likely area for the country's first continuous shipments of dressed beef. The Grand Trunk was a natural ally in this region. The only other major connection to Boston, the New York Central–Boston & Albany combination, carried the dressed beef shipments of his rival, George H. Hammond, as well as a heavy livestock trade. By giving the Grand Trunk his business, Swift offered the road a product to compete with the largest carrier of livestock to New England, and secured a valuable ally in his attempt to compete with Hammond.

Realizing that to be effective the refrigerator car required an efficient distribution system, Swift moved quickly to buy ice harvesting rights in the Great Lakes in order to provide ice for cooling his beef and loading the ice-boxes of his cars in Chicago. Ice stations soon appeared along the route of his refrigerator cars all the way to the East Coast.[41] His brother's butchering business in Clinton, Massachusetts, and his several partnerships with leading wholesalers, such as Hathaway in Boston, and D. M. Anthony of Fall River, Massachusetts, provided ready-made sales outlets for his dressed beef.

Adopting a marketing strategy designed to allay the potential opposition of the wholesalers and secure additional sales outlets at the least possible cost, Swift chose to be cooperative rather than combative. Since the early nineteenth century, wholesalers, commission merchants, and jobbers had played a dominant role in the development of the meat industry and of the whole American economy. Not only were they the chief distributors of the nation's goods, but they were suppliers of capital and other services as well.[42] Just as their opposition might seriously hamper the expansion of the business, their assistance could be invaluable in developing the trade and eroding any prejudices against refrigerated meat. Moreover, their knowledge of the business would eliminate the necessity of hiring and training sales personnel, and if Swift could forge alliances with established wholesale outlets, it would lessen the initial investment costs in the creation of a distribution system.

Swift and his younger brother Edwin, who took charge of New England marketing, cautiously approached eastern wholesalers, offering to buy a minority interest in those businesses. Thus assured of retaining control over their businesses, many eastern wholesalers found alliance with Swift less threatening. Many of these wholesalers became the distribution agents of G. F. Swift & Co. of Chicago, and handled Swift's shipments on a commission or a consignment basis.[43] Where cooperation was not forthcoming, Swift hired a salaried manager to distribute meats directly from the railroad car. If necessary, he applied stronger pressure by lowering prices and forcing the wholesaler to capitulate. A good example of the latter strategy occurred in Fitchburg, Massachusetts. Unable to convince the leading wholesale firm of Lowe and Sons to distribute his meat, Swift decided to "feed Fitchburg" himself. To accomplish the task he built a branch warehouse in Fitchburg and enlisted the support of his brother William, instructing him to sell the meat any way he could. William Swift offered low prices and extended credit to his customers. The Lowes soon capitulated. Gustavus Swift then quickly capitalized on Lowe's managerial resources and hired the elder Lowe to manage Swift & Co.'s Fitchburg branch house and employed his sons in the slaughtering plant at Chicago.[44]

Swift's sales philosophy and keen business sense did much to make him a leader in the industry. Because he had only limited capital when he went into the business, he felt that "$1 had to be made to do the work of ten." Moreover, because dressed beef was perishable, rapid and high volume sales were crucial: "if you did not sell, then you stood no chance to make it." "As long as a manager sold plenty, G. F. Swift stood by him," explained his son Louis, "even if he made no money." Forced to economize and cut costs wherever he could, Swift was not content simply to keep goods moving just fast enough to avoid being spoiled. On the contrary, he worked to develop a technique "which kept his goods moving at a rate far faster than was needed." Part of that technique was more effective sales methods. Swift always told his salesmen to "cut [the meat] and scatter it out." He reasoned that wholesalers would be more willing to distribute his meat and customers more willing to buy if they were not forced to buy the whole carcass but were allowed to choose only those cuts they knew would sell. The policy was a sound one, for it lessened the dealer's financial risks and enabled Swift to expand his trade.[45]

At the core of his sales policy and general business philosophy was Swift's determination "not to let 'em nose you out." Because of the opposition that grew as more refrigerated meat poured into eastern markets and threatened the existing order, Swift knew that unless he stuck to his sales efforts, his beef might not be sold anywhere. Rather than allowing his sales agents to move to another area if the meat could not be sold where designated, Swift insisted that salesmen establish themselves and drop prices as low as was necessary to induce customers to buy.[46]

Because Swift shipped the carcass meat rather than the live animal, there was a fixed cost differential in his favor from the outset. By slaughtering in Chicago he was able to avoid the cost of shipping to New York the 45 percent of each animal that was waste and nonedible by-products. Consequently, he could sell his meat up to 75 cents per 100 pounds cheaper in New York or Philadelphia or Boston than could parties who shipped live cattle, despite the higher cost per pound of shipping dressed beef. Such advantages, however, did not bring high profits initially. The trade was new and required substantial investments in plants, cars, sales outlets, and cooling facilities.[47] "He made little money during the early years," wrote his son Louis, "for what he made on successful shipments he lost on failures. And he poured good money after bad on experiments which advanced his knowledge of refrigeration and so in the long run repaid their cost. But at the time, they looked like dead losses."[48]

Nevertheless, Swift's determination to expand the trade and his shrewd strategy of vertical integration soon paid off. By the early 1880s he was making money and his trade was expanding rapidly. Although statistics concerning the condition of his business and its rate of expansion are difficult to obtain, the credit reports of R. G. Dun & Co. provide some clues. When Swift began to ship dressed beef in the winter of 1877, he sent his products to his brother's shop in Clinton and to the wholesale house of Anthony, Swift & Co. in Fall River, Massachusetts. The latter had opened up branches in New Bedford and Taunton, Massachusetts and Newport, Rhode Island by 1880. In 1879 R. E. Holmes & Sons of Worcester, Massachusetts, was selling Swift's refrigerated meats on commission. The business was reported to be "progressing moderately." Around the same time Swift added two more distributors to his list: Francis Jewitt, meat dealer, banker, and former mayor of Lowell, Massachusetts, and his brother Abner of Providence, Rhode Island. In 1880 R. G. Dun & Co. reported that the partnerships of Francis Jewitt & Co., A. A. Jewitt & Co., and Jewitt & Co. were doing an "extensive business" as shippers of both live and dressed beef. A. A. Jewett was "shipping considerable to Europe." There was a branch at Nashua, New Hampshire as well. The influential and prosperous wholesale firm of Hyde, Wheeler & Co. began distributing Swift's meats in Boston in 1879. George Nye & Co. of Springfield, Massachusetts, and Edwin Tetlow & Co. of Providence were handling his products by 1881. That year, Swift Bros. & Co. of Chicago (the parent firm) was reportedly doing an "immense business." Swift was shipping some 3,000 carcasses per week worth $190,000, of which he exported about 1,000. He owned some 150–200 refrigerator cars, costing between $4,000 and $6,000 each; in addition, he had refrigerators on more than 20 steamships assessed at $3,000 each. By 1882 Swift's business was reportedly in "snugger condition." He was said to be "making money fast." Between 1881 and 1883 Swift moved into New York City, Washington, D.C., Baltimore, and also the Connecticut communities of Norwich and Waterbury. The company had over 43 branches.

Meanwhile, the ratio of liabilities to assets had been decreasing steadily. In 1884, when R. G. Dun & Co. described the business as having been "brought into permanent shape," net assets of Swift & Co., and the branches of Franklin Swift and D. H. Anthony, totalled more than $3 million. Liabilities were reported to be around $650,000.[49] Having recognized the problems of distributing perishable meat and having acted more quickly and effectively to solve them than had other packers, Swift drove his firm to the top of the industry only a few short years after he had perfected the refrigerator car. His rapid rise caught other packers by surprise.

THE RISE OF OTHER LEADING FIRMS

When Swift first began to ship dressed beef from Chicago in the winter of 1877, other packers at the yards dismissed him as a "mad man." "No one saw fit to give him much competition in the early days at Chicago," wrote his son Louis. "The general attitude around the yards was that if the Yankee newcomer was allowed enough rope he would hang himself."[50] Swift's status as a newcomer, however, proved to be an important factor in his early domination of the trade. By the early 1880s skepticism and apathy had been replaced by the sincerest form of flattery, as some of the leading Chicago packers—Philip Armour, Nelson Morris, and George Hammond—embarked upon similar strategies of growth in order to compete.

But entry was not easy even in the early 1880s. Unlike industries such as sugar refining, where new entrants were on a relatively equal footing almost as soon as they entered the business, those who entered the dressed beef business had to do so on a large scale almost from the outset.[51] Of the four firms that rose to the top, all except Swift began to ship dressed beef as an extension of an already established pork packing or cattle shipping business. Before Swift arrived in Chicago, Hammond had carved out a seasonal monopoly of the New England dressed beef business; he was an extensive hog packer, cattle shipper, and exporter as well, with sales totalling approximately $2 million a year by 1875.[52] Morris was one of the wealthiest livestock shippers in the country, an evener and seasonal shipper of domestic and export refrigerated meats. P. D. Armour had established a reputation for himself as the "Pork Baron" of the West. He and his four brothers had slaughtering plants at Chicago, Milwaukee, and Kansas City, and had begun distributing cured pork and provisions through Armour & Co.'s distribution house in New York City. Armour was also a speculator in provisions and a grain merchant, with extensive interests in elevators and warehouses in the Midwest. The firm's profits reportedly reached $2 million in 1880.[53] The firms of Cudahy & Co. and Schwarschild & Sulzberger (later Wilson & Co.), entrants into the trade in the early 1890s, were also already well established in the packing business, and therefore had considerable financial assets when they entered the dressed beef business.[54]

With the most extensive resources, P. D. Armour narrowed Swift's lead more quickly and effectively than did the others. A first rate salesman—actually more a merchant than a packer—and a shrewd businessman, P. D. was constantly looking for ways to expand his business.[55] He had watched the growing dressed beef trade with interest, and was especially impressed by Swift's persistence and rapid rise to success. More importantly, Armour admired and understood Swift's strategy of vertical integration. The more shipments Swift made, the more Armour became convinced that entry into the dressed beef trade could provide an excellent way to diversify and expand his own pork and provision business. "He needed the beef trade to fit in with his pork provision shipments," explained one trade journal, ". . . otherwise he would have to send only partly filled cars to points where beef could also be sold."[56] Diversification into dressed beef enabled Armour to employ existing resources more fully. Since he already had established distribution outlets for pork, he knew the value of company-owned branch houses, but he was also aware of the problems peculiar to the dressed beef industry and sought the advice of experts before entering the trade. He contacted the commission firm of Hyde, Wheeler & Co. of Boston, selling agents for Swift's meat, and offered Thomas H. Wheeler an opportunity to organize a beef department for Armour & Co. Wheeler took the offer.[57] Such expert distributing advice, coupled with Armour's capital, merchandising skills, determination, and drive soon made him one of Swift's closest rivals.

Armour shipped his first carload of meats to Boston in his own refrigerator cars over the tracks of the Michigan Central, New York Central, and Boston & Albany railroads in 1882, only four years after Swift's first warm weather shipments.[58] By 1883 he had established branches in New York for the storage and sale of dressed meat in Albany, Troy, Poughkeepsie, New York City, Utica, and Schenectady. He was already laying plans to expand into the North and Northwest. The Kansas City pork packing plant of Armour Co., established in 1869 and run by his brother Simeon, provided an excellent opportunity to expand into dressed beef in this region with no other investment than in cars. In 1883 after building his own cars, Armour began to ship dressed beef into Colorado and Minnesota, often selling the fresh beef directly from the door of his refrigerator cars. By 1884 the company was sending about two carloads of meat per day from Kansas City to St. Paul and Minneapolis, and had nearly 300 cars running over the lines of both eastern and western railroads.[59] In 1886 Armour controlled 24 percent of the total number of cattle slaughtered in Chicago, 7 percent less than Swift.[60]

Morris' efforts to compete were impressive but not as effective as those of Armour. In 1884, when Swift slaughtered more than 400,000 cattle for the dressed beef trade, Morris slaughtered only 36,000. Morris had begun constructing his own cars sometime around 1884. He built his first branch house in 1885, when he employed a man specifically to look after his refrigerator car business and to expand the firm's dressed beef trade. Within three years, Morris & Co. had nine branch houses in the East and a trade large enough to give the company the third largest share of the dressed beef trade in the country.[61]

Although Hammond never recaptured the lead he lost to Swift in the early 1880s, his quick and successful implementation of a strategy of vertical integration earned him a dominant position in the industry. He had invested more than $3 million in the business by 1886, including capital for 800 refrigerator cars and branch outlets in New York, Boston, and Connecticut, and a second slaughtering plant at Omaha, Nebraska.

The firm directed its major attention to the export market, erecting several sales outlets in Great Britain and one of the largest in Scotland.[62] Nevertheless, by 1886 Hammond lagged behind Swift, Armour, and Morris, with 14 percent of the Chicago cattle slaughter, compared to 24 percent for Armour, 31 percent for Swift, and 17 percent for Morris. Together, however, the Big Four accounted for an impressive 86 percent of all cattle slaughtered in Chicago.[63] (See Table III.2.)

The similarities between the patterns of development of Armour, Swift, Morris, and Hammond were not mere coincidences. One of the most notable exceptions proves the rule. In 1883 rancher, shipper, and cattleman Count Marquis de Mores began building what was described by the *Cincinnati Price Current* as a "colossal system." Naming his enterprise the Northern Pacific Refrigerator Co., the Count set out to put cheaper beef on eastern markets and to provide an outlet for dressed beef in the Northwest. De Mores and his wealthy father-in-law, Louis von Hoffman, a New York City banker, invested over $400,000 in the enterprise.[64] In 1884, a year after the project was undertaken, the *Cincinnati Price Current* reported that the system included packing houses at every beef market along the Northern Pacific, from Helena, Montana, to Duluth, Minnesota. There was a slaughterhouse at Medora, Dakota (Territory), reportedly the biggest west of Chicago, with a capacity of 700 cattle a day. Sales in 1884 were averaging over $6,000 a day. Shipments to Duluth, Minnesota, were three times larger than expected. To permit further expansion, a new company capitalized at $1,500,000 was being organized.[65]

Despite this encouraging beginning, five years later the *Breeder's Gazette* reported the fate of that "colossal scheme":

> To the outsider it looked at first a plausible scheme. The intention was to draw on the ranch herds of Montana, kill the animals close to their grazing grounds, thus saving shrinkage, bruising and railroad freights, and place the meat at a low figure in the East. The affair was badly managed and ended in disaster; but even if it had been run by the most experienced man in America the result would have eventually been the same. The supply of beef lasted only for four months in the year, the remainder of the season the plant was idle. The meat was all of one class, no regular customers could be held, and the business gathered up, say, in four months' time was scattered to the winds when the supplies stopped. Labor was high and uncertain, and lastly, the offal could not be used to advantage. The failure of this and similar schemes proves most conclusively that a dressed beef concern to be successful must be located at a central point, where it can draw a daily supply of all classes of cattle for its use, and where there is competition enough among the railroads to ensure moderate freights. Chicago and Kansas City of the western markets are the only points where it has been absolutely safe to build an extensive plant, although Omaha during the last two years has cured cattle enough to ensure a steady supply for the dressed beef men there.[66]

Table III.2. Percentage of Total Number of Cattle Slaughtered at Chicago for Dressed Beef, Packing, Canning, and City Trade by Armour & Co., Swift & Co., Nelson Morris (Fairbank Canning Co.), and Hammond & Co. During the Years 1884–1890

Firms	1884	1885 [a]	1886	1887	1888	1889	1890
Armour	22	22	24	25	26	28	27
Swift	34	32	31	28	30	24	26
Morris	13	13	17	21	22	23	24
Hammond [b]	15	11	14	11	11	11	12
Total	84	78	86	85	89	86	89

[a] From (and including) 1885 to 1890, the figures are for the year ending March 1.
[b] Slaughtered at Hammond, Indiana, and included in shipments of live cattle.
Sources: Chicago Board of Trade, *Annual Reports, 1884–1890*; Cincinnati Price Current, *Annual Provision and Grain Trade Statistics, Thirty-Ninth Annual Report, 1888*, p. 18.

The lesson was clear. Without a system and ties to retailers, a new concern could not hope to compete.[67]

The concentration of trade in the hands of a few large firms and the overall growth of the industry were inextricably linked to the building of cars and the spread and location of distribution networks. The competition triggered by the implementation of this strategy led to a rapid expansion of the trade that, in turn, created new problems of administration for the dominant packers.

COMPETITION IN THE NORTHEAST AND THE BUILDING OF ADMINISTRATIVE NETWORKS

From the late 1870s to the mid-1880s, Swift, Armour, Morris, and Hammond concentrated on acquiring cars and branch houses to expand the trade. Coupling their strategy of vertical integration with a strategy of competition, they rushed to fill the markets of the Northeast, where local supplies had been diminishing rapidly since the mid-1840s. Operating in yet unconcentrated markets that were rapidly growing, their major object was to sell as much meat as possible. Organization was not very crucial in the early years and little attention was paid to internal administration. Swift's instructions to his salesmen in New York City in 1882 were typical of the haphazard pricing and output policies the packers employed during this period of expansion: "Well, I'm going to ship you three cars next week. Sell it somehow."[68]

The result was a rapid invasion of the markets in the major northeastern cities. Between 1882 and 1883 shipments of dressed beef to the East showed a spectacular 127.5 percent increase. While percentage increases for earlier and later years were not as dramatic, an upward trend was unmistakable. (See Table III.3.) As important was the growth of the trade in specific marketing regions within the Northeast. Because packers had concentrated their initial marketing efforts in the New England region, beef poured in at a rapid rate. While the volume was not as large in New York, the percentage increases were enormous.[69] (See Tables III.4 and III.5.)

Concurrently with the development of the trade went the expansion of by-product manufacture. Although Armour & Co.'s pork packing business gave it a head start in manufacturing pork by-products, not until it entered the dressed beef trade did the sale of beef by-products become significant.[70] In 1882, the same year the company entered the dressed beef trade, it also began utilizing the blood, bones, and meat scraps of beef. These activities led in 1893 to the founding of the Armour Fertilizer Works. In 1884 Armour & Co. hired its first chemist. That same year, it took over the glue works of the Wahl Brothers in Albany, New York. In 1885 Armour organized his pharmaceutical laboratories to make pepsin from hog and cattle stomachs and pancreatin, a digestive aid. A new method of reclaiming materials from the water of rendering tanks, found that same year, reportedly netted the company more than $100 a day. By 1886 Armour and other packers were even selling pig and cattle hair to furniture makers at prices of 4 to 5 cents per pound. In 1896 came the Armour Soap Works, followed in 1897 by a glycerine plant. So extensive had by-product manufacture become by the 1890s that Chicago humorist Finley Peter Dunne (Mr. Dooley) observed that: "A cow goes lowin' softly into Armour's an' comes out glue, gelatine, fertylizer, celooloid, joolry, sofy cusions, hair restorer, washin' sody, littrachoor an' bed springs so quick that while aft she's still cow, for'ward she may be anything fr'm buttons to pannyma hats."[71]

Although Swift did not initially produce as many different by-products as Armour, the firm's sales were extensive. By the 1890s, when the first data are available, subsidiaries of Swift & Co. were producing more than 4 million pounds of glue, 30,600 tons of fertilizers, 2.5 million pounds of neatsfoot oil, 38.7 million pounds of butterline (butter oil made from beef skulls and jawbones and used as lubricants), and 53.36 million pounds of lard. In 1888 Swift & Co. obtained control of a majority of stock in the canning firm of Libby, McNeil & Libby, thus gaining an outlet for lower quality meats as well as canning facilities to compete

Table III.3. Comparative Statement of Shipments of Cattle and Dressed Beef from Chicago During the Years from 1880 to 1885[a]

Destination	Shipped Product	1880	1881	1882	1883	1884	1885
New York City	Cattle	222,262	265,367	257,281	238,828	191,736	182,199
	Beef		114	3,812	23,060	32,722	45,112
Boston	Cattle	81,914	96,222	56,391	75,689	54,845	39,931
	Beef	9,860	14,405	18,683	29,139	29,644	37,724
Philadelphia	Cattle	19,280	30,403	36,137	20,225	15,759	23,235
	Beef		10	475	9,033	14,299	22,825
Baltimore	Cattle	4,053	3,807	5,085	8,167	6,211	6,916
	Beef			1,393	4,160	4,208	7,676
New England States	Cattle	45,145	12,021	146	1,003	1,151	2,587
	Beef	20,845	29,227	38,627	52,936	53,066	60,252
New York State	Cattle	39,632	22,908	21,778	14,491	16,995	7,262
	Beef		18	907	16,605	24,552	25,506
New Jersey	Cattle	1,560	1,017	1,664	1,558	584	199
Delaware	Beef			630	6,237	10,619	14,041
Pennsylvania	Cattle	1,050	1,283	2,584	3,838	18,590	15,863
	Beef			370	5,893	8,746	9,438
Maryland & South	Cattle	1,308	572	2,594	8,415	4,539	2,830
	Beef			878	2,577	5,545	7,701
Eastern Canada	Beef					1,592	1,359
Total	Cattle	416,204	433,600	383,660	372,214	210,410	281,022
	Beef	30,705	43,774	65,775	149,640	184,993	231,634
Total Meats		446,909	476,374	449,435	521,854	395,403	512,656

[a] Tons of 2,000 pounds.
Source: "Dressed Meat Traffic," U.S. Dept. of Agriculture, Report of the Bureau of Animal Industry, 1886, p. 278.

Table III.4. Tons of Cattle and Dressed Beef Received at Boston and Other New England Points During the Years 1882–1889

Year		Cattle	Dressed beef
1882		76,410	89,150
1883		100,901	116,746
1884		74,505	121,017
1885		54,192	138,876
1886		52,431	153,544
1887		57,325	179,733
1888		70,186	187,732
1889		97,189	225,167
	Total Tons	583,139	1,211,965

Source: *New York Daily Tribune,* February 25, 1890, p. 7

with the large Armour & Co. canning works, established in the late 1870s.[72]

As significant as the rapid increase in volume of beef and beef by-products was the decrease in prices that occurred as the packers competed for larger market shares. Between 1883 and 1889 average retail prices for beef tenderloins dropped 10¾ cents—from an average price of 27½ cents per pound in 1883 to 16¾ cents per pound by 1889. While average prices for less expensive cuts of meat did not decrease as much, the decline of 3⅛ cents per pound was significant. The average value of cattle hides dropped from $6 in 1870 to about $4.50 by 1887. Tallow,

Table III.5. Tons of Cattle and Dressed Beef Received at New York City During the Years 1882–1889

Year		Cattle	Dressed beef
1882		366,487	2,633
1883		392,487	16,365
1884		328,220	34,365
1885		337,802	53,344
1886		280,184	69,769
1887		288,662	70,734
1888		327,406	96,224
1889		412,462	106,235
	Total Tons	2,733,818	450,260

Source: *New York Daily Tribune,* February 25, 1890, p. 7.

which sold for 8 cents per pound in 1883, was selling for 4 cents per pound in 1887.[73]

Such rapidly declining prices, coupled with the rapid growth of the trade and intensification of competition in the major marketing areas of the Northeast, turned attention to solving the administrative and managerial problems that had accompanied the growth of the firms and the assumption of new functions.[74] Only by setting prices more closely to costs and rationalizing their whole enterprises could they hope to compete effectively and continue to dominate the market. Because western packers sold one major line of products—meats—to hundreds of retailers and purchased supplies from thousands of livestock producers, the basic administrative problem was to coordinate the purchasing, distributing, and selling activities with the shifting demands of the mass market. This problem was further complicated because perishable dressed beef required efficient and rapid handling.

The geographical spread between the controlling company in Chicago and the selling agencies meant that records had to be kept at purchasing and receiving ends if supply and demand were to be coordinated. Information flows had to be established to assure rapid decision making and more efficient allocation of resources. Better communication and information depended upon standardized accounting and new methods of cost control and pricing.

Whereas during the early 1880s prices were set by impersonal forces of supply and demand in each geographic market, the expansion of the industry and the intensification of competition that accompanied growth made it imperative to set prices with some relation to costs. Unless costs or methods of costing were standardized or made uniform at the various plants, there was no way to compare the performance of the various branches and plants or to determine how well the enterprise as a whole was functioning. As important, without some knowledge of costs, there was no way to determine how one firm fared relative to its competitor. In short, if the various parts of the enterprise were to function as an integrated whole, the business had to be systematized.

Because Swift pioneered in large-scale, year-round shipments of dressed beef and was the first to create his own distribution network, he also was the first to confront these new problems of administration. Acting as quickly and effectively to meet these organizational imperatives as he had to meet the technological and marketing imperatives of the trade, he created a new form of administrative network that secured his dominant position in the trade. When completed by the turn of the century, this network consisted of a system of closely interrelated packing plants and sales offices. There were central and divisional headquarters, as well as territorial and branch offices, linked together by modern methods of communication and transportation and administered by new techniques designed specifically to coordinate high volume product flows with fluctuating market demands.

Until Swift had acquired a number of branch houses, however, administration played a relatively minor role in the growth of the business. From 1875 to 1885 Swift and his brother Edwin managed to run the business as a partnership. Swift handled most of the buying and financial activities from his small Chicago office, and Edwin managed the selling activities from his own meat shop in Clinton, Massachusetts. Together they issued orders for purchases and allocated supplies to a still relatively small number of branch houses with little assistance from branch house managers. But as the network was extended and competition intensified, they began to realize that rationalization of their resources was imperative. Branch house managers often complained that they could not sell all the beef sent to them and that frequently they had to sell at such low prices there was hardly any profit in handling the beef.

In 1885 they took the first major step toward building an efficient organization when they incorporated as Swift & Co. with an authorized, paid-in capital stock of $300,000 (99 percent of which was held by the Swift family).[75] Not only did the corporate form offer limited liability, but it provided the means of securing more capital for expansion through stock issues. At the same time they organized a centralized, functionally departmentalized administrative structure to achieve stronger internal control over the operation of their enterprise. Although increasingly centralized and enlarged to include additional departments and personnel as time went on, that structure remained basically the same for the next 50 years.[76]

Power in the corporation lay in the hands of family members and one or two stockholding executives who also sat on the Board of Directors (composed in 1885 of five members). Swift, as head of the family, was also head of the corporation. As chief executive, chairman of the board, and president, he had virtually complete control, his decisions being subject only to approval by the Board, (which rarely, if ever, vetoed his recommendations). In addition to the president there was a secretary and a treasurer and two vice-presidents. The latter supervised departments organized around basic functions, such as sales, purchasing, transportation, accounting, production, and finance, and around products—beef, veal, and pork. (Because by-products were manufactured by subsidiaries, no separate departments were organized to handle them.) As executive officers, stockholders, and members of the Board, these men made the day-to-day operating decisions, allocated supplies, controlled purchases, and also planned for the enterprise as a whole.

Directly subordinate to the vice-presidents who supervised the departments were the managers who operated them. These departmental managers worked with the vice-presidents to formulate policies for their respective departments, looked after the maintenance and repair of facilities in the departments, served on various ad hoc committees, and kept abreast of competitive activities.

To coordinate supply and demand more effectively, branch house managers were given substantial responsibilities. They sent in daily reports via telephone and telegraph regarding the supply of beef on hand in the branch houses. They requested shipments and ultimately determined the prices at which the meat was sold.[77] On the basis of the data sent from the sales outlets, executives at headquarters issued purchase orders and planned for the growth and operation of the whole enterprise.

Sometime during the mid- or late 1880s, the firm devised a system of "test costs" to achieve stronger internal control over pricing policies and to enable the enterprise to function more efficiently.[78] In determining the "test cost" of dressed beef, the accounting department at the central plant first calculated the average cost of a particular lot of cattle. To this cost was added an estimated killing cost (based on actual averages over time). From this sum they deducted an estimated value for by-products. The final figure, reduced to a dressed weight basis (and including an estimated profit), represented the cost per 100 pounds of dressed beef. Although simply a method of estimating average costs, this particular system proved to be an invaluable guide to pricing policies and day-to-day buying operations. By comparing the test cost at the plant with the actual prices received for the beef at the sales outlets, executives knew from day to day the results of the previous day's operations and also could compare the performance of various plants and selling outlets.[79] The rationale behind such a system was later explained by one of Swift's rivals, Ferdinand Sulzberger:

> We make the test uniform at our various plants as a line by which to measure results. . . . We have in one city perhaps five or six of our own branches to compare one with the other, and in this way we can compare results of branches. We can also compare results of one packing house with another . . . sometimes the beef may not be sold right, and sometimes we will trace it back to buying. This plan was the best that could be adopted after all kinds of experiments. I have been in the business since 1863 . . . and I found that that is the best plan when we went out west. In New York it was not necessary when we had the local business because we followed the sales up ourselves; but when we went out west, and had to distribute our beef from Maine to California, we found that this was the only plan where you could regulate your business for comparison's sake and also see your profit or loss in the results of cattle.[80]

The evolution of a centralized, departmentalized structure played an important role in the growth of the firm, but the full importance of this system of administration cannot be understood without recognizing the crucial relationships among competition, markets, and technology. Organization was not as crucial in the early years as it became later, once the market began to fill up and more competitors entered the field. It was the utilization of the insulated refrigerator car and the vigorous, speedy creation of a distribution network to market beef rather than the building of a well-defined administrative structure, that gave Swift an early edge over Hammond and other entrants. In 1884, even before Swift had begun seriously to fashion his administrative network, his company slaughtered nearly three times the amount of cattle for the dressed beef, canned meat, and city trade than any other Chicago firm, and was by far the largest dressed beef shipper in the country.[81] (See Table III.2.) The rapid growth of the business created a need for a structure to administer the business.

Because Armour, Hammond, and Morris encountered similar problems as they expanded their businesses, they solved them in similar ways. Until Armour began to ship dressed beef in the early 1880s, he had managed to meet most of the administrative problems that resulted from the growing size of his pork packing and provision business merely by enlisting the aid of his brothers. All five Armour brothers contributed in some way to the expansion of the business.[82] The family's entry into the packing industry had begun in 1863, when a wealthy merchant and packer, John Plankinton, invited P. D. Armour to become a partner in his Milwaukee firm. By 1869 Armour had become so disgruntled with the independent wholesalers through whom the firm was distributing its meats that he established Armour, Plankinton & Co. of New York to supervise the distribution of pork products and to take care of financial affairs in the East. P. D. persuaded his brother Herman, who had his own grain commission business in Chicago, to come to New York to take charge of the new firm; Joseph Armour took over Herman's Chicago commission business. In 1867 the hog packing firm of Armour & Co. of Chicago, a subsidiary of Armour, Plankinton & Co., began hog packing operations, and within five years the firm was slaughtering sheep and cattle as well. When Armour, Plankinton & Co. expanded operations and opened a packing plant in Kansas City in 1871, Simeon B. Armour served as manager. In 1871 Simeon was joined by another brother, Andrew Watson Armour, who became manager of the Armour Brothers' Bank of Kansas City. Joseph's failing health in 1875 brought P. D. to Chicago, where he remained to direct the business of Armour & Co. P. D.'s expert knowledge of merchandising and distributing meat products, as well as favorable economic circumstances and his strategic location in Chicago, made him the natural leader of the family business. Moreover, the profits he reaped from pork-speculating adventures in the 1860s and 1870s strengthened the Armour interests financially and assured Gustavus Swift a well-backed competitor when the firm began to ship dressed beef in the early 1880s.[83]

The centralized, functionally departmentalized administrative structure that existed at Armour & Co. of Chicago when P.D. entered the dressed beef trade was simply enlarged and increasingly centralized when new administrative problems arose. Although P.D.'s brother Simeon continued to operate the Kansas City packing firm as a business that was legally independent from Armour & Co. of Chicago until 1900, by the mid-1880s the central headquarters for the far-flung Armour empire were located in Chicago. It was in the Windy City that the Armour brothers and their top-ranking executives planned for the enterprise as a whole and coordinated supply with fluctuating market demands. From Chicago they gradually stretched an administrative network similar to that of Swift & Co. across the country.

In so doing, Armour drove his firm to the top of the industry. By quickly and effectively meeting the technological, marketing, and organizational challenges of the trade, the firm soon captured and maintained a share of the market second only to Swift's. Armour's rise to the top, however, was in many respects more rapid and less difficult than Swift's pioneering efforts. Whereas Swift had limited capital and was forced to build his company from the ground up, Armour had a flourishing and well-organized business even before he entered the trade. Similarly, Swift was the innovator who had to struggle and experiment; Armour was the follower who could profit from the innovator's example. The strategy of vertical integration pursued so successfully by Swift was easily followed and even improved upon on by his rival. Both moved forward into marketing and became distributors as well as manufacturers of dressed beef. They created similar distribution networks because they marketed a product that was highly perishable and required rapid and efficient service that the existing wholesaler network did not provide. Then, once they had created vast marketing organizations, they found they had to fashion administrative structures to rationalize and coordinate the high volume flows of goods within their respective firms. They then took on new product lines to make use of the integrated facilities.

Although the stories of the Morris and Hammond firms naturally differ in detail from those of Swift and Armour, they followed the same basic pattern. The results, however, were not uniformly successful. Competition among the Big Four in the Northeast caused market shares to fluctuate. Morris' firm increased its share of the Chicago cattle slaughter most significantly between 1884 and 1890, from 13 percent in 1884 to 17 percent in 1886, 22 percent in 1888, and 24 percent in 1890. Swift and Armour vied for first place. Swift's 34 percent share of the Chicago cattle slaughter in 1884 dipped to 31 percent in 1886, fell to 30 percent in 1888, and decreased again to 26 percent in 1890, while that of Armour climbed slowly from 22 percent in 1884 to 24 percent in 1886, 26 percent in 1888, and crept to 27 percent in 1890. Hammond's 15 percent share in 1884 fell to 14 percent in 1886 before leveling off around 11 or 12 percent. (See Table III.2.)

While it is difficult to account precisely for the ebb and flow of market shares without internal records, Hammond's relatively weak position in the oligopoly seems to reflect several factors. First, the firm's early monopoly of the New England trade may have dulled the incentive to compete so that when Swift effectively challenged Hammond's trade, the firm did not respond with the necessary speed and effectiveness. Secondly, Hammond's quiet, shy, and unaggressive character may have made him a less effective marketer than either Armour or Swift. Unlike his rivals, Hammond initially preferred to let his products sell themselves. While such a strategy may have been effective when the firm enjoyed a monopoly, it quickly proved inadequate when new competition appeared. And, finally, George Hammond's death in 1886 and the subsequent control of the firm by a group of English investors may have influenced the direction of growth. After 1886 the firm increasingly concentrated on building up the export rather than the domestic dressed beef trade. Hog packing became a more extensive activity than dressed beef. And while the firm engaged in by-product manufacture, it did not do so on a scale nearly as extensive as that of Swift or Armour. Foreign rather than domestic family control also meant that there was less resistance to sell the firm when an opportunity arose. In 1901 its owners accepted Armour's offer to buy.[84]

During the decade of the 1880s, however, the Big Four packers capitalized on the cost savings of the refrigerator car. In building the extensive distribution and administrative networks it required, they reaped economies of scale and acquired a measure of control that gave them distinct and significant advantages over their smaller rivals.

Although firms in 1886 were not as large, refrigerator cars were not as numerous, and administrative networks were not as clearly defined as they later came to be, the Bureau of Agriculture noted that:

> The dressed meat traffic in the United States is conducted almost exclusively, by firms employing large amounts of capital and many men in the work.... This trade is in the control of firms using their own capital, owning the slaughter-houses, and in some cases, the refrigerator-cars used in the business. These firms buy, kill,

transport, and in some places, even retail their meats to the consumers. At the termini they have built and own cold storage rooms for their own use, and are in almost every way independent of all outside dealers or agents so far as concerns the buying of the cattle in the markets of the East and all intermediate transactions necessary to the business, except the hauling of the refrigerator cars over the railways. . . . They do not carry on any part of the business as agents for others.[85]

The Big Four packers dominated the industry almost from the outset. By 1888, less than a decade after Swift perfected the all-weather refrigerator car, these four Chicago firms were producing almost three-fourths of the beef for Chicago's consumption, two-thirds of the nation's supply of dressed beef, and were slaughtering almost one-half of the nation's total meat supply.[86] The creation of administrative networks helped to secure their lead for the next several decades.

Once one packer had embarked upon the strategy of vertical integration, only those with financial resources and the foresight to adopt a similar strategy quickly, could hope to compete. It was important to get aboard fast. Not only were there barriers to entry due to high capital costs, but the early birds built long leads in terms of securing the most desirable locations in the market towns and establishing business ties to the local retailers and buyers. The market could only absorb so many integrated, "diversified" firms like these, and speed was critical.

The competition engendered by the utilization of the refrigerator car assured a rapid invasion of the market. It also made inevitable a struggle between the newcomers and those groups and interests threatened by the new order.

NOTES

1. *New York Times*, October 13, 1882, p. 4.

2. For a discussion of these and broader structural changes in the post–Civil War economy, see Alfred D. Chandler, Jr., "The Beginnings of 'Big Business' in American Industry," *Business History Review*, 33 (Spring 1959):1–31.

3. U.S. Congress, Senate, *Select Committee on the Transportation and Sale of Meat Products*, Report and Testimony, S. Rept. No. 829, 51st Cong., 1st Sess., 1889, p. 432. (Hereafter cited as the *Vest Report*.)

4. Louis B. Swift and Arthur Van Vlissingen, Jr., *The Yankee of the Yards* (New York, 1927), p. 130.

5. A useful general history of refrigeration is Oscar E. Anderson, Jr., *Refrigeration in America* (Princeton, N.J., 1953). For details of the early meat packing industry, see Rudolf A. Clemen, *The American Livestock and Meat Industry* (New York, 1923), and H. C. Hill, "The Development of Chicago as a Center of the Meat Packing Industry," *Mississippi Valley Historical Review*, 10 (1923):253–273.

6. W. R. Woolrich, *The Men Who Created Cold* (New York, 1967), pp. 104-105, 110-111; *Ice and Refrigeration*, September 1901, pp. 92-98.

7. *Ice and Refrigeration*, September 1894, p. 166. For details on Hammond's life, see

Rudolf A. Clemen, *George Hammond (1838–1886): Pioneer in Refrigerator Transportation* (New York, 1946); *Dictionary of American Biography*, p. 204.

8. *Ice and Refrigeration,* September 1894, p. 166, and November 1901, p. 207; Louis Unfer, "Swift and Company: The Development of the Packing Industry, 1875–1912" (Ph.D. dissertation, University of Illinois, 1951), pp. 24–25.

9. Clemen, *George H. Hammond,* p. 14.

10. Cited in Clemen, *George H. Hammond,* p. 14.

11. *Ibid.,* p. 16, and Bessie Louise Pierce, *A History of Chicago,* Vol. III, p. 115, mentions that when the George H. Hammond & Company was incorporated in 1881 it had a capital of $1.5 million; by 1888, capitalization had reached $2.5 million.

12. Clemen, *The American Livestock and Meat Industry,* pp. 232–236. The western railroads were more interested in refrigerator cars than were the eastern trunklines. The Chicago, Burlington & Quincy Railroad, for example, listed earnings of $7,209.22 on its refrigerator cars in operation from May 1 to October 22, 1879 (Chicago, Burlington & Quincy Archives, Newberry Library, Chicago, Record Group No. 33, File No. 7.2, "Statement Showing Average Tonnage, Trips and Earnings of East Bound CB&Q Refrigerators").

13. Clemen, *The American Livestock and Meat Industry,* pp. 232–236.

14. Clemen, *George H. Hammond,* p. 12.

15. The *Report* indicated that "All descriptions of fresh meat sell more readily, but trade is not very driving. Beef is higher, and the best Chicago in refrigerator cars is fully $1.00 per hundred dearer." The following table presents price data for selected months from the *Market Produce Report:*

Sale Prices* of Fresh Meat in Boston Market, Selected Months, Days, and Years, 1874–1877.

	3/26/74	4/19/77	7/26/77	9/13/77
Beef, Brighton, fore quarters/lb	6 @ 8	6 @ 6½	7½ @ 8	6½ @7
Beef, Brighton, hind quarters/lb	10 @ 14	10 @ 11	12 @ 14	12 @ 13½
Beef, Western choice/lb	9 @ 11	7 @ 8	10 @ 11	9½ @ 10

*Sale prices are within a low-high range of quotations, indicated by the symbol @.

16. Later refrigerator cars, such as that pioneered and made commercially successful by inventor Andrew Chase and Gustavus Swift, not only economized space and ice but also were insulated and provided for automatic circulation of air. For details on the Hammond car and later improvements, see *Ice and Refrigeration,* September 1894, pp. 166–167; September 1901, pp. 92–98; November 1901, pp. 207–208; December 1901, pp. 223–224; U.S. Patent No. 78,932, "Refrigerator," D. W. Davis, Boston, June 10 and September 15, 1868; U.S. Patent No. 219,256, "Refrigerators," George H. Hammond, Detroit, September 2, 1879; U.S. Patent No. 199,343, "Refrigerator Car," A. W. Zimmerman, New York, January 15, 1878; U.S. Patent No. 193,357, "Improvement in Refrigerator Cars," Joel Tiffany, Chicago, July 24, 1877; U.S. Patent No. 210,995, "Improvement in Refrigerators," Andrew J. Chase, Boston, December 17, 1878; U.S. Patent No. 215,572, "Purifying, Circulating, and Rarifying Air," Andrew J. Chase, Boston, May 20, 1879; U.S. Patent No. 220,422, "Refrigerator Cars," Thomas L. Rankin, Lyndon, Kansas, October 7, 1879; U.S. Patent No. 229,956, "Refrigerator," Andrew J. Chase, Boston, July 13, 1880. See Appendix A.

17. *R. G. Dun & Co.* (Manuscript Room, Baker Library, Harvard Business School, Boston), Mass., Vol. 87, Boston, Vol. 18, p. 50, November 4, 1879, lists Hammond engaged in the beef business in Detroit, Michigan, and worth about $300,000 to $400,000. He had apparently formed a partnership with George W. and N. E. Hollis. George Hollis was the largest mutton butcher in Brighton, Massachusetts, worth between $150,000 and $200,000. N. E. Hollis was of the firm of Sawyer, Hollis & Company. The latter had engaged several refrigerated steamers to export beef to Europe, and was represented in London by William Murray. "Cash capital" was reportedly $100,000. R. G. Dun & Co. characterized the group as "first class businessmen." By 1880 Geo. H. Hammond & Co. was reported to be "shipping cattle and making money." In 1881, the Hollis' bought out Hammond.

18. *National Provisioner,* August 31, 1907, p. 114.

19. Clemen, *American Livestock and Meat Industry,* pp. 156–158.

20. Edward W. Perry, "Livestock and Meat Traffic of Chicago," U.S. Dept. of Agriculture, Bureau of Animal Industry, *First Annual Report, 1884,* p. 266, citing Nofsinger & Company's complaints to the bureau.

21. Another factor that may account for the interest in the export trade is that exporters faced fewer obstacles or conflicts of interests than did domestic dressed beef shippers. In the domestic market vested interests had grown up to cater to the livestock trade. Railroads had invested huge sums of capital in stock cars and stockyards as well as in feeding and watering facilities along their tracks. Commission merchants and wholesalers carried out the functions of distribution and marketing. The export live cattle business, on the other hand, was not nearly as profitable or as highly developed. Until the mid-1870s the demand for American meat in Great Britain was too low to warrant the investment in the trade. Moreover, a dressed beef exporter could continue shipping livestock from west to east and benefit from economies introduced by refrigeration.

22. Clemen, *The American Livestock and Meat Industry,* pp. 269–275; Richard Perren, "The North American Beef and Cattle Trade of Great Britain, 1870–1914," *Economic History Review,* 20 (August 1971):431; "Statement from William Colwell, Boston, Mass., to Joseph Nimmo, Chief of Bureau of Statistics," in U.S. Congress, House, *The Range and Ranch Cattle Business,* Exec. Doc. No. 267, 48th Cong., 2nd Sess., 1886, p. 197, discusses early shipments of cattle and dressed beef to Europe. Hereafter cited as the *Nimmo Report.*

23. Perry, "Livestock and Meat Traffic of Chicago," pp. 314–315, explained that the Bate's patent "preserved meat fresh by inclosing it in an air-tight chamber and forcing among it a current of cold dry air." To use the patent, an elaborate system was required:

Refrigerators, or air-tight chambers, are . . . between decks. . . . These immense air-tight chambers are surrounded on all sides by three air-tight walls made of matched lumber covered with air-tight paper, which is made so by being saturated with resin. Between these surrounding walls there is an open space of an inch and a half, making the walls as perfect non-conducters as possible.

An ice-house is constructed on one side or end of the refrigerator, as is most convenient, and is filled with ice. The ice-compartment is in proportion to the size of the refrigerator, and is linked with galvanized sheet-iron. Fifty tons of ice are required by the Bate process for saving 60 tons of meat. A cast-iron fan or blower is placed inside of the meat chamber, connected by a belt to a small steam-engine on the deck above. The fans vary in size, according to the work required. The belt is enclosed in an air-tight box. Flues, or air passages, ten inches high and sixteen inches wide, made of matched boards, extend from the fan along the bottom of the floor to the sides of the refrigerator, where they connect with upright tubes or pipes, of half the size, which stand against the outer wall, into which the air of the refrigerator is drawn by the suction of the fan, and driven into the middle of the ice-chamber through a large flue made of matched boards, where it circulates through the ice and is drawn down and passed back into the refrigerator through an open space about three inches wide left at the bottom of the ice. The fan makes about eight hundred revolutions per minute, and is kept going constantly. These fans are large or small, according to the capacity of the meat-chambers. In this way a constant circulation of cold air is kept up during the entire voyage. A thermometer, suspended in a tin pipe which reaches from the upper deck down into the refrigerator, indicates the temperature, which is kept as near 38 degrees as possible. A cap is kept over the top of the pipe to prevent the escape of the cold air from the meat chamber. A more rapid circulation of air, which can be made by increasing the speed of the fan, will lower the temperature. The steam to run the fan-engine is supplied by the steamer's boiler.

24. Clemen, *The American Livestock and Meat Industry*, pp. 276–281; James McDonald, *Food From the Far West* (London, 1878), pp. 253–254; "Fresh Meat Shipment to Europe," U.S. Dept. of Agriculture, *Report of the Commissioner, 1876*, pp. 314–319; Perren, "The North American Beef and Cattle Trade of Great Britain," pp. 432–433; Testimony of T. C. Eastman, *Vest Report*, pp. 513–534; Statement from T. C. Eastman to Joseph Nimmo, *Nimmo Report*, 1886, pp. 172–173.

25. Perren, "The North American Beef and Cattle Trade," p. 433.

26. "Fresh Meat Shipment to Europe," p. 316.

27. R. G. Dun & Co., Geo. H. Hammond & Co., Mass., Vol. 87, Boston, Vol. 18, p. 50; Geo. W. Hollis, Mass., Vol. 86, Boston, Vol. 17, p. 261; Sawyer, Hollis & Co., Mass., Vol. 86, Boston, Vol. 72, p. 421.

28. Perren, "The North American Beef and Cattle Trade," p. 432; "Fresh Meat Shipment to Europe," pp. 316–319.

29. See Note 24 above.

30. MacDonald, *Food From the Far West*, pp. 294–296; Perren, "The North American Beef and Cattle Trade," p. 423.

31. Quoted in "Fresh Meat Shipment to Europe," p. 319.

32. Perren, "The North American Beef and Cattle Trade," p. 433.

33. MacDonald, *Food From the Far West*, pp. 255–256, paraphrasing Eastman.

34. Chicago Board of Trade, *Seventeenth Annual Report, 1874*, p. 14, and *Eighteenth Annual Report, 1875*, p. 17.

35. For an excellent analysis of the entrepreneurial function, see Joseph A. Schumpeter, *The Theory of Economic Development* (Cambridge, Mass., 1934), especially Chap. II.

36. Louis B. Swift and Arthur Van Vlissingen, Jr., *The Yankee of the Yards* (New York, 1927), pp. 8–9, 26, 183; Louis A. Neyhart, *Giant of the Yards* (Boston, 1952), p. 38.

37. Failure to distinguish Swift's early experiments from his first successful year-round shipments has produced a confusing chronology. The Chase patent was obtained in December 1878. I have dated the first successful year-round shipments 1879, but December 1878 probably marks their inauguration. Pierce, *A History of Chicago*, Vol. III, p. 119, gives 1877 as the date; "Report of the Half-Yearly Meeting, April 30, 1886: President's Speech," in *Annual Report of the Grand Trunk Railway of Canada, 1886*, includes a brief history of the dressed beef trade and mentions 1878 as the year for Swift's first shipments; Federal Trade Commission, *Report of the Meat-Packing Industry, 1919*, Summary and Pt. I, p. 238, lists 1878; Swift and Van Vlissingen, *Yankee of the Yards*, p. 190, declare it a "success" by 1880.

38. The Swift-Chase car seems to have been modeled after the Zimmerman refrigerator car, patented in 1878 (U.S. Patent No. 199,343). Chase patented a refrigerator (U.S. Patent No. 210,995, Dec. 17, 1878, and U.S. Patent No. 229,956, July 13, 1880), but his real contribution seems to have been the method by which the car was ventilated (U.S. Patent No. 215,572, "Purifying, Circulating, and Rarifying Air," Boston, May 20, 1879 [filed April 1878]). For a discussion see Louis Unfer, "Swift & Company: The Development of the Packing Industry, 1875–1912," (Ph.D. dissertation, University of Illinois, 1951), pp. 24–28; Siegfried Giedion, *Mechanization Takes Command*, pp. 218–222; Anderson, *Refrigeration in America*, pp. 51–52; Clemen, *The American Livestock and Meat Industry*, p. 222.

39. Swift and Van Vlissingen, pp. 186–189; Federal Trade Commission, *Report on Private Car Lines* (Washington, D.C., 1919), p. 28. The best history of the Canadian road is A. W. Currie, *The Grand Trunk Railway of Canada* (Toronto, 1957).

40. Swift and Van Vlissingen, *Yankee of the Yards*, pp. 189–190; Neyhart, *Giant of the Yards*, p. 93.

41. Swift and Van Vlissingen, *Yankee of the Yards*, p. 191; Neyhart, *Giant of the Yards*, p. 95. See also Swift's statement concerning his icing stations, in "Report Upon the Relative Cost of Shipping Dressed Beef and Livestock," *Proceedings and Circulars of the Joint Executive Committee* (New York, 1883), p. 73.

42. For an excellent analysis of the merchant's role in the American economy see Glenn Porter and Harold C. Livesay, *Merchants and Manufacturers* (Baltimore, 1971).

43. The distinction as well as the respective advantages of the "consignment" or the "commission" system is explained in detail, *National Provisioner*, June 5, 1909, p. 21. Consignees referred to independent wholesalers who distributed refrigerated meats for the packers on their own account. Goods to be distributed were sold to consignees before leaving the plant. When the packers owned their sales outlets, goods were shipped on commission, and the branch house manager received a certain commission or percentage of the sales.
For details on Swift's financial strategy see U.S. Bureau of Corporations, *Report of the Commissioner of Corporations on the Beef Industry, 1905* (Washington, D.C., 1905), pp. 286–287.

44. Swift and Van Vlissingen, pp. 70–71.

45. *Ibid.*, p. 73, 65, 76–77.

46. *Ibid.*, p. 67. By these methods, Swift increased the rate or velocity at which goods moved through his enterprise, thereby reducing risks and also the costs of distribution. On the general meaning and significance of the concept, see Alfred D. Chandler's treatment of "through-put," in *The Visible Hand*, p. 241.

47. The precise amount of capital tied up in plants and equipment is difficult to determine, since in the early years at least, many of the distributing outlets were not yet company owned. *R. G. Dun & Co.*, 1880–1884, lists assets and liabilities of Swift & Co. and some of its major partners, but neither the assets nor liabilities are divided into meaningful categories. Between 1880–1881, net assets approximated $700,000 but the worth of assets climbed to over $1 million by 1884. (See Note 46 below)
The cost of doing business is described in detail in two reports by Albert Fink, "Report of the Commissioner Upon the Testimony Furnished at the Conference held at New York, April 11 and 12, 1883, between the Trunk Line Executive Committee, the Chicago Committee and Dressed Beef and Livestock Shippers, regarding the Relative Cost of Shipping Dressed Beef and Livestock from the West to the Seaboard," pp. 1–132 ("hereafter cited as "Report Upon the Relative Cost of Shipping Dressed Beef and Livestock"), and "Final Report Upon the Relative Cost of Transporting Livestock and Dressed Beef, containing Abstract of Proceedings of April 11 & 12, 1883, and Proceedings of the Trunk Line Executive Committee of May 31 and June 1, 1883," pp. 1–92 (hereafter cited as "Final Report Upon the Relative Cost of Transporting Live Stock and Dressed Beef"), in *Proceedings and Circulars of the Joint Executive Committee* (New York, 1883).

48. Swift and Van Vlissingen, p. 200.

49. *R. G. Dun & Co.*, G. F. Swift & Co., Ill., Vol. 1, Cook County, Vol. 59, pp. 166, 280; F. Jewett & Co. (Francis Jewett, E. C. Swift, David Anthony, L. F. Swift, "Beef Packers and Exporters"), Mass., Vol. 87, Boston, Vol. 18, p. 175; A. A. Jewett & Co. of Providence, Rhode Island, Vol. 12, Providence, Vol. 4, p. 192; A. A. Jewett & Co. of Lowell, Mass., Vol. 52, Middlesex County, Vol. 3, pp. 105, 320.

50. Swift and Van Vlissingen, p. 26.

51. Alfred S. Eichner, *The Emergence of Oligopoly: Sugar Refining as a Case Study* (Baltimore, 1969), pp. 44–45, estimates the cost of entry into sugar-refining in the 1870s to be

between $500,000 and $700,000. Although the cost of building a packing plant seldom exceeded this sum, interstate meat packers also had to build their own distribution network. Sugar refiners, by contrast, continued to use the old distribution network to market their product. To assure safe and speedy delivery of fresh meats, branch houses were built or acquired. Interstate dressed beef packers purchased fleets of refrigerator cars, the cost of each car approximating about $1,200 in the 1880s. Cooling houses and icing stations were also built alongside railroad tracks. In addition to employing a large workforce at central slaughtering plants, there was also a large sales force and administrative staff. Judging from estimates submitted by some of the large packers to the trunkline association ("Relative Cost of Transporting Live Stock and Dressed Beef," pp. 106–131), and the mercantile reports of R. G. Dun & Co. (see Note 47 above), the costs of entry in the 1880s approximated between $1 and $2 million. By the turn of the century, entry required between $15 and $65 million (*Report of the Commissioner of Corporations on the Beef Industry, 1905,* pp. 39–51).

52. Clemen, *George H. Hammond,* pp. 15–16.

53. Federal Trade Commission, *Report on the Meat-Packing Industry, 1919,* Pt. V, "Profits of the Packers," pp. 21–22.

54. *Ibid.,* pp. 32–33.

55. Leech and Carroll, *Armour and His Times,* pp. 1–3.

56. *National Provisioner,* February 6, 1904, p. 39.

57. After several years as head cattle buyer and beef department manager for Armour, Wheeler returned to his firm in New England to supervise the sales efforts in that area and to establish more distribution outlets throughout the East. See his obituary in *National Provisioner,* November 7, 1908, p. 19. By the time of his death he had served all of the packers, except Morris. In the early 1890s Wheeler was also establishing branch houses for the G. H. Hammond Company.

58. *National Provisioner,* February 6, 1904, p. 39; Clemen, *The American Livestock and Meat Industry,* p. 236; Pierce, *A History of Chicago,* III, p. 120, reports that Armour started shipping refrigerated dressed beef to consumers in East Saginaw, Michigan in May 1882.

59. Letter from W. H. McDowell, general south-western freight agent, CB&Q railroad, Kansas City, Mo., to E. P. Ripley, general freight agent, Chicago, June 13, 1884 (Chicago, Burlington & Quincy Archives, Newberry Library, Chicago, Ill., File No. 33-2.1).

Armour also innovated the so-called "peddler car service," which distributed dressed beef to points where the population was too small to warrant the establishment of branch houses. The term originated in the 1880s when Armour & Co. sent out a salesman from Chicago with a carload of hams and lard, with orders to "peddle" the products to small towns where meat market men were to meet the train. Initially, peddler car service was sporadic, but by 1887 Armour had established two regular car routes, one in southern Wisconsin and Minnesota, and a second in northern Indiana. This came to be adopted by all the packers when it proved a valuable way to expand markets (Clemen, *The American Livestock and Meat Industry,* p. 401).

60. See Table III.2, above.

61. *Ibid.,* and Clemen, *The American Livestock and Meat Industry,* pp. 156–167; Pierce, *A History of Chicago,* Vol. III, p. 119; FTC, *Report on the Meat-Packing Industry, 1919,* Summary and Pt. I, p. 153; *Report of the Commissioner of Corporations on the Beef Industry, 1905,* p. 270.

62. R. G. Dun & Co., Mass., Vol. 87, Boston, Vol. 18, p. 50; Mass., Vol. 86, Boston, Vol. 17, p. 261. For additional details of the Hammond firm and its history, see Clemen, *George H. Hammond; State of Missouri* v. *Hammond Packing Company and St. Louis Dressed Beef and Provision Company,* No. 16090. Joint Abstract of Record and Transcript of Evidence, 6 vols., 1913 (Swift & Company Archives, Chicago, Ill.), Record Vol. I, 802–817.

63. See Table III.2 above. The Hammond Company was purchased by Armour in 1901,

in anticipation of a gigantic merger of the Big Three. Pierce, *A History of Chicago,* Vol. III, p. 116, claims that "The firm was at times hard pressed financially."

64. *Cincinnati Price Current,* October 2, 1884, p. 3.

65. *Ibid.*

66. *Breeder's Gazette,* July 3, 1889, p. 5.

67. Small packers who attempted to integrate forward into marketing, like de Mores, found problems of flow maintenance particularly difficult. See letter from T. A. Carroll, July 13, 1904, to Commissioner of Corporations (U.S. Bureau of Corporations, Record File No. 666, National Archives, Washington, D.C.).

Livestock shippers Joseph Stern of New York and Isaac Waixel of Chicago (an old evener for the New York Central), tried to compete with the Big Four by contracting with the Omaha Union Stock Yards Company to build a slaughterhouse for them, under lease agreement, and to operate a refrigerator car line. This attempt also failed (*Cincinnati Price Current,* February 7, 1884, p. 1).

A group of St. Louis livestock shippers organized in 1885 and began to sell dressed beef in Boston directly from their own refrigerator cars, auctioning it off to consumers. These direct sales to the public, however, did not continue (*Cincinnati Price Current,* April 2, 1885, p. 1).

68. Swift and Van Vlissingen, p. 66.

69. "Dressed Meat Traffic," U.S. Dept. of Agriculture, *Report of the Bureau of Animal Industry, 1886,* p. 278; Perry, "Live Stock and Meat Traffic of Chicago," U.S. Dept. of Agriculture, *Report of the Bureau of Animal Industry, 1884,* pp. 266–267; *Railroad Gazette,* February 20, 1890, p. 152; *Railway World,* December 6, 1884, p. 1161.

70. By-product activities and the economics of by-product manufacture of the various packers are described in Pierce, *A History of Chicago,* Vol. III, pp. 123–125; Clemen, *The American Livestock and Meat Industry,* pp. 347–378; Leech and Carroll, *Armour and His Times,* pp. 44–45; FTC, *Report on the Meat-Packing Industry, 1919,* Summary and Pt. I, pp. 369–389; *Report of the Commissioner of Corporations on the Beef Industry, 1905,* pp. 211–248; E. L. Rhoades, *Merchandising Packinghouse Products* (Chicago, 1929); *National Provisioner,* September 8, 1906, pp. 15–17.

71. Pierce, *A History of Chicago,* Vol. III, p. 124, quoting Dunne.

72. Minutes of the Board of Directors Meeting, March 25, 1893, Swift & Company Archives, Chicago, Ill.

73. Less expensive cuts dropped from about 11½ cents per pound in 1883 to about 8 cents per pound in 1889. For data and an analysis of the relationship between prices for by-products and dressed beef and the cost of cattle, see *Report of the Commissioner of Corporations on the Beef Industry, 1905,* pp. 85–196; *Vest Report,* pp. 418–423; Fred C. Croxton, "Beef Prices," *Journal of Political Economy,* 8 (March 1905):200–215.

74. Porter and Livesay, *Merchants and Manufacturers,* pp. 166–179, discuss some of the administrative problems.

75. The previous partnership was called Swift Brothers & Company. Incorporation on March 31, 1885, brought 103 stockholders into the business, many of whom were friends or independent wholesalers who had agreed to distribute Swift's meats. The Minutes of the Board of Directors Meetings list officers as G. F. Swift, president, Edwin C. Swift, 1st vice-president, Louis Swift, 2nd vice-president, L. A. Carton, treasurer, and Louis Hartwell, secretary. See also, Unfer, "Swift & Company," p. 55.

76. Unfortunately, without internal records only a brief history of organizational developments is possible. The timing of the developments is particularly difficult to pinpoint. The information that follows has been pieced together from various sources. Minutes of the Board of Directors Meetings list real estate transactions that provide clues as to the size, value, and geographical distribution of investments and sales. *Moody's Manual of Industrial*

Securities for consecutive years provides information on company executives, the numbers and titles of which indicate the growth of administrative structures. Annual reports of the various companies are also of some help. Harold P. Alspaugh, "Marketing of Meat and Meat Products" (Ph.D. dissertation, Ohio State University, Columbus, Ohio, 1936), is concerned primarily with the packers' organization as it existed in the 1920s and 1930s, but he provides a good analysis of the administrative structure with helpful organizational charts.

Perhaps the best source for tracing the evolution of administrative structures are court records, particularly *U.S.* v. *National Packing Company*, Cr. 4384 (N.D. Ill., 1910), and *State of Missouri* v. *Hammond Packing Company and St. Louis Packing and Provision Company*, No. 16090, Joint Abstract of Record and Transcript of Evidence, 6 vols., 1913. Swift & Company Archives, Chicago, hold the record and evidence of *U.S.* v. *National Packing Company* in "Old Veeder Files," in black loose-leaf notebooks, and *St. of Mo.* v. *Hammond Packing Company . . .*, 6 vols (titled "Briefs"), Joint Abstract of the Record and Testimony. Lawyers of Swift & Company also prepared an elaborate report when interviewing possible witnesses for the National Packing Company case. Copies of that report are also in the company's archives, in black loose-leaf notebooks.

77. This is true only in a limited sense. Branch managers set the prices insofar as they were the ones who had to sell the meat, but they followed general instructions concerning profit margins.

78. There are few good histories of the evolution of new accounting methods. Histories of accounting societies are more numerous. William D. Miles, a former employee of Armour & Company, testified in *St. of Mo.* v. *Hammond Packing Company*, Joint Abstract of the Record, pp. 352–353:

> that in the early days of the dressed beef business prior to 1887 there was no such thing as what it termed a margin, neither were there any regular shipments of beef. The custom was to ship beef and demand that a certain price be obtained for each lot of beef. But they learned this was impracticable and a margin system was thought of in order to prevent the necessity of asking the branch house managers to obtain an arbitrary price and also prevent the danger of selling unsound beef held too long for such a price. A system was devised asking the branch house managers to obtain a certain margin over what the beef cost. . . .

For more sophisticated explanations of the test cost system, see Howard C. Greer and Dudley Smith, *Accounting for a Meat Packing Business* (Chicago, 1943), pp. 27–46; George E. Putnam, "Joint Cost in the Packing Industry," *Journal of Political Economy*, 29 (December–January, 1921):293–303.

79. Putnam, "Joint Cost in the Packing Industry," p. 297, claims that the test cost "is the guiding factor" in the packer's buying operations. In a footnote he adds:

> It is true that unit costs are also a factor in the packer's selling operations, but they are not a guiding factor. Beef is a perishable product and must be sold in the market for what it will bring. A change in the weather or industrial conditions may so reduce the demand for beef, and therefore the price, as to compel the packer to sell below cost, in which case he will bid less for cattle. On the other hand, if he can sell at a profitable margin over cost, he will increase his purchases and develop more volume.

80. *St. of Mo.* v. *Hammond Packing Company*, Joint Abstract of the Record, pp. 417–418.

81. Chicago Board of Trade, *Twenty-Seventh Annual Report, 1884,* p. 44. "City trade" refers to the products consumed locally, within city limits.

82. Speaking of the Armour brothers, the family's biographers emphasized: "These brothers understood each other, from the days they had played together. They knew the

value of teamwork, one for all and all for each" (Leech and Carroll, *Armour and His Times,* p. 37).

83. Philip Armour's pork speculating ventures in 1879 reportedly brought the Armours more than $1 million profit. (Leech and Carroll, *Armour and His Times,* p. 34; Pierce, *A History of Chicago,* Vol. III, pp. 114–115, claims the Armour Company "profited to the tune of from six to seven millions" from pork speculation.)

84. *St. of Mo.* v. *Hammond Packing Co.,* Record Vol. I, 802–817. When the Hammond firm was purchased in 1901 by Armour in preparation for a gigantic merger, it owned 1,195 refrigerator cars, representing an investment of more than $620,136. Investments in branch houses totalled over $1,553,964. The firm had three major slaughtering plants at Hammond, Indiana, South Omaha, Nebraska, and South St. Joseph, Missouri, worth more than $2,528,152 (*St. of Mo.* v. *Hammond Packing Co.,* Record Vol. I, 802–817).

85. "Dressed-Meat Traffic," U.S. Dept. of Agriculture, *Report of the Bureau of Animal Industry, 1886,* pp. 277–278.

86. Figures compiled from reports of the Chicago Board of Trade, the Bureau of Animal Industry, and annual trade statistics of the *Cincinnati Price Current.*

Chapter IV

Challenge of a New Order: The Three-Cornered Struggle

Although cost-savings made possible by the refrigerator car and the distribution networks it required eventually brought victory to western packers who utilized the new innovation, this outcome was not at all clear in the late 1870s and early 1880s. Eastern wholesale butchers and packers, livestock dealers without a packing business, railroads, and the beef-eating public all had some interest in the livestock business. Wedded to a tradition that set the live steer on a pedestal, the public initially viewed cattle coming on the hoof to New York or Boston as freer from disease and healthier than the alleged "foul-smelling and impure" dressed beef. Eastern packers and wholesalers, exploiting this view, waged a fierce campaign against the western packers who, they claimed, were threatening their livelihood. Across the country wholesalers boycotted retail butchers who patronized western packers.[1] To these groups technological progress was a painful reality. In the words of one cattle dealer, "it was useless to try to compete with men who buy cattle in Chicago, slaughter them here and then ship to the East direct."[2] The facts supported their worst fears. It cost nearly twice as much to ship one animal live as it did to send one carcass of beef.[3]

Without some form of assistance in the form of favorable discriminatory railroad rates, these groups could not hope to compete in the long run with the new breed of western packers. They therefore demanded that railroads lower the rates for livestock, relative to those of dressed beef, in order to offset the cost advantages of their opponents' product and put them on an "equal footing" in the market. The old established production and distribution system could only survive through special protection from the railroads.

As we have already seen, the American railroads could be expected to provide this protection. To attract and serve the lucrative livestock trade, the railroads had made substantial fixed investments in stockyards and terminal facilities along their routes. Dressed beef not only threatened to eliminate the livestock business to which railroads had been catering, but it also was a new product that required expensive transportation equipment—fleets of refrigerator cars—which the railroads were reluctant to provide. Moreover, even if the railroads had had no vested interests in the livestock trade, the uncertainty of a new business made the prospect of investing in refrigerator cars and new storage facilities unappealing. Overshadowing these problems peculiar to the meat industry was the familiar and all-pervasive need for railroads to maximize their carrying trade. To the railroads, the ideal solution seemed to be to protect the livestock trade while simultaneously carrying the products of the dressed beef industry (but avoiding investing in refrigeration equipment and employing a rate structure that seemed neutral but in fact favored the livestock trade).

In an attempt to implement this "solution," the railroads adopted what they called a "principle of neutrality." According to a statement issued in 1883 by the Eastern Trunkline Association, railroad neutrality would be achieved by placing "dressed beef and livestock shippers upon an equal footing, so that a man who buys in the Eastern market dressed beef that is shipped from Chicago as such, and dressed beef that is derived from livestock which is shipped from the West and slaughtered here, will have to pay the same money per pound."[4] The railroads thus promulgated a rate differential that clearly penalized dressed beef shippers and discriminated in favor of the established livestock trade.

"Neutrality"—even as the railroads defined it—eventually proved unworkable, but there were several reasons why the railroads found it an expedient policy in 1883. It had been used in the past to try to resolve difficulties with large and small livestock shippers and packers of cured pork in the West and East.[5] Furthermore, the force of public opinion influenced the railroads' position. The "principle of neutrality" carried with it the rhetorical advantage of seeming to reassure the public that the railroads were operating "fairly" toward both groups of shippers.

Attempts by trunkline railroads to maintain this "neutral" stance were seriously eroded by the same forces that made their Association unable to enforce other rate stabilization policies. A maverick road, finding the Association's pools harmful to its own interests, could easily disrupt rate agreements. Because the railroad industry was oligopolistic, rate cuts by one road drew traffic away from the other roads, thereby prompting them to follow the rate cutter's lead.

The Canadian Grand Trunk Railroad was well-suited to play the role of maverick in this struggle. The long, circuitous, and cold northern route that made it a relatively unattractive livestock carrier and a troublesome participant in the American Trunkline Association, also made it an enthusiastic patron of dressed beef traffic. By agreeing to haul the new refrigerator cars, it obtained an early lead in the dressed beef trade to New England. Not as concerned as American livestock carriers to place livestock and dressed beef shippers on an "equal footing," it favored a rate structure that allowed dressed beef shippers the cost advantages of their product. Thus, the Grand Trunk could be expected to veto resolutions of the Association designed to thwart an increasing dressed beef trade. Allowing dressed beef shippers to realize their cost advantages, however, inevitably affected the livestock traffic on the American roads. Moreover, when the Canadian and American roads competed for traffic in the same product and region, the Grand Trunk frequently demanded differentials[6] to offset the disadvantages of its longer route. If the American roads denied the request, rate cutting by the Grand Trunk usually followed.

The railroads' competitive vulnerability contributed to the western packers' success. On the one hand, competition enabled individual packers to exploit the always precarious equilibrium between livestock shippers and railroads and among American trunklines, and maverick roads like the Grand Trunk, to enhance their own position in the market. On the other hand, it undermined stable rate structures. With no assurance of uniform rates and the nagging possibility that a livestock shipper or rival packer had obtained secret rebates, the drive to reduce costs was a critical factor in a firm's ability to survive.

The story of the opposition to the new order in meat packing, then, describes still another way in which a new cost-cutting technology and marketing strategy revolutionized the industry and effectively challenged the old order in transportation and distribution.

RAILROADS SEARCH FOR A SOLUTION

Technological innovation in the form of Swift's refrigerator car disturbed the always precarious equilibrium among railroads and livestock shippers. Seemingly unaware of the direction of change, the Trunkline Association attempted to meet the challenge of western packers and the growing dressed meat trade by brandishing their "principle of neutrality." It was inevitable, however, that the roads would have increasing difficulty in maintaining the differential that protected an older form of distribution against the newer, less costly means. When applied to a new situation in which products were competitive—indeed were almost perfectly substitutable—"neutrality" or the "equal footing" concept became practically useless, retaining only a public relations advantage.

The Grand Trunk, of course, was unconcerned with the "equal footing" principle. Primarily interested in promoting its own traffic by encouraging the new industry, it used its connection to Boston over the Vermont Central as a means of diverting traffic from the New York Central–Boston & Albany combination. The cost-savings made possible by the refrigerator car were so great that the Grand Trunk was able to charge dressed beef shippers a rate high enough to compensate for the longer route yet still permit dressed beef to compete effectively with the products of livestock shippers.

To counteract potential Grand Trunk threats in New England, William Vanderbilt of the New York Central secured control of the Canadian Southern in 1877 and the Michigan Central in 1878—the routes that carried the Grand Trunk's shipments from Chicago. Naturally, the Grand Trunk interpreted Vanderbilt's move as a serious threat to its interest, for Vanderbilt could at any time block the Grand Trunk's connection with Chicago. To counter Vanderbilt's strategy, the Grand Trunk built its own line to Chicago in 1880.[7]

Christened the Chicago & Grand Trunk, the new extension gave the Grand Trunk control of a complete line from Chicago to the New England market. In a stronger position than previously, the Grand Trunk joined the Trunkline Association's eastbound pool and quickly angered the American roads by demanding higher percentage allotments on all traffic than its rivals were willing to give.[8] Moreover, complaints of rate cutting on livestock and dressed beef to Boston and New England poured into the Trunkline Committee. The Grand Trunk, representing the dressed beef interests, and the New York Central, representing livestock interests, each claimed that the other had inaugurated the cuts.

Meanwhile, Swift's dressed beef shipments continued to increase, and alarmed livestock shippers and eastern wholesalers became convinced (or at least argued) that it was the rate cuts that enabled him to sell more cheaply. "If full tariff were charged him," they claimed, "he would be unable to sell at such low prices." Consequently, New York Central shippers pressured their carrier to lower cattle rates in order to protect their trade. They claimed that Swift was underselling them in the market by offering New England consumers his meat at 7 cents per pound while "no one could ship live cattle there and sell them at less than 8¢." Thus pressured, railroad agents with an interest in the livestock trade defended their shippers' arguments before the Trunkline Executive Committee and urged lower cattle rates relative to dressed beef.[9]

Railroad traffic managers with an interest in the dressed beef trade naturally interpreted matters differently. For example, Lansing Millis of the Vermont Central (a Grand Trunk ally), asserted that he had no doubt that Swift was selling at cost. He argued, however, that the trouble stemmed not from problems in the railroad rate area, but from Swift's

Trunk Lines and Major Subsidiaries

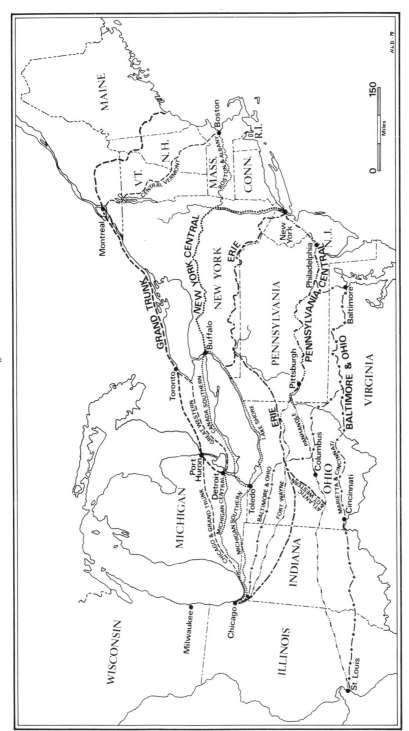

rivalry with his competitor, Anthony Comstock (an eastern wholesale butcher). Comstock apparently "was provided with funds and backers to carry on the [price] war as long as necessary." Millis believed the increased shipments stemmed from the changes brought about by the refrigerator car, and informed representatives that "an increase in the yearly amount of dressed beef must be expected, as large amounts of capital had been invested for the purpose of developing the business." The shipments were "entirely legitimate," he claimed, "and should not occasion any surprise."[10]

Albert Fink of the Trunkline Association agreed with Millis' interpretations, but he also recognized the railroads' delicate position. "There was a bitter competition between the dressed beef and livestock dealers," he emphasized, "[and] they would no doubt draw the railroads into the struggle, unless the agreements as to tariffs, etc., were strictly maintained, and perfect confidence established between the Trunk Lines."[11] As Fink himself knew, however, "perfect confidence" among the trunklines was an impossibility: "even with the most sincere intentions," he later admitted, "it is impracticable."[12]

But perfect confidence is just what the railroads tried to achieve when the Trunkline Association met on April 1, 1881 to determine the relative rates between the two products and to put a stop to alleged lower rates on dressed beef.[13] They attempted to fix the rate for dressed beef at a certain percentage above that of livestock, basing the percentage on the cost advantages of dressed beef. Representatives haggled over specifics, disagreeing on shrinkage allowances (the amount dressed beef shrank in transit). When these efforts to agree on a rate adjustment failed, the trunkline committee decided that *all* dressed beef shippers were temporarily to receive the lowest existing rate. That low rate had, of course, been offered by roads violating the Trunkline Association's guidelines. The Association hoped to discipline the roads that had cut the rates, and they hoped to do so by establishing such low rates as to make the traffic unremunerative. Hoping that this object lesson would halt the "past practice of carrying from 5 percent to 25 percent of weight without compensation [or below the Association's rates] will now cease," the Committee took no further action. Not surprisingly, the Association's new rate proved no more enforceable than the old one, and a rate war resulted.[14]

These difficulties concerning the rate structure persisted, and the Joint Executive Committee drew up a new livestock and dressed beef contract in April 1882, trying to halt the warfare. The contract was simply another pool, differing from earlier ones only in that it was a revenue rather than a traffic pool and applied to dressed beef as well as to livestock. Cattle rates were set at 40 cents per 100 pounds, those for dressed beef at 64 cents per 100 pounds. This money pool sought to divide the livestock and dressed beef traffic over all lines between the western cattle markets and the East.[15]

The new contract was evidence of changes occurring within and outside the railroad industry. Not until the railroads had experienced the damaging rate war of 1881 and the difficulties stemming from the livestock and new dressed beef traffic did they recognize the need to create another commodity pool to handle the new product. The new contract was more complex and more detailed, but proved to be no real solution to the problem.

The difficulty, of course, was that somebody was going to get hurt and cry discrimination no matter what the railroads did about rates. The question of what was a "fair" rate was almost impossible to answer.

By March 1883 conditions were explosive. Whereas in 1880 livestock tonnage to New York was 14 times greater than that of dressed beef, by 1883 it was only three times greater.[16] (See Tables III.4 and III.5.) The potential annihilation of livestock shippers by the lower cost dressed beef shippers spurred livestock carriers to take new action. The president of the Pennsylvania Railroad Company insisted that "it would be absolutely necessary to make a greater relative difference in rates on the two kinds of traffic."[17] The railroads were not the only ones to define the neutrality principle in terms of their own interest. Just as railroads refused to allow dressed beef shippers to realize their cost advantages, livestock shippers wanted the railroads to absorb the cost disadvantages of shipping live animals. As a compromise, Philip Armour suggested that, on the one hand, the railroads should pay charges for yardage, bedding, and feed that put livestock at a cost disadvantage relative to dressed beef; on the other hand, he argued that since the price of dressed beef in Chicago was substantially lower than that in New York (implying of course that the transportation rate was excessively high), the railroads should lower rates on dressed beef. The Grand Trunk supported Armour's proposal, and at a trunkline meeting its officials argued that "some concessions should be made in freight rates to dressed beef shippers" since market quotations in New York "showed dressed beef worth 50 cents per 100 pounds less than New York slaughtered beef."[18] Such arguments illustrate the complexity and difficulties of ratemaking: each group had its own particular conception of a rational rate structure, and their differences became apparent in their various interpretations of "equality" and "neutrality." At the request of both dressed beef and livestock shippers, Albert Fink brought all groups together in New York City at the Windsor Hotel on April 11, 1883, to seek a solution once more.

Quite correctly, Vermont Central representative Millis reprimanded all interests for believing that equality was possible: "It is simply nonsense for these gentlemen to come here and ask for a decision placing them on an equal basis," he complained, "because there is not equality about it." Although all interests undoubtedly wanted their own version of equality implemented, the Trunkline Association had to make the ultimate decision, and not surprisingly, based it upon the railroads' version of "neutrality."

When the meeting opened, Fink expressed his view that in arriving at a decision they could "leave entirely out of view the railroad side of the question—whether it is more or less profitable for the railroad companies to carry one of these commodities." Relative rates on dressed beef and livestock were to be determined after an examination of the cost accounts of the two shippers. In order to place both shippers on an "equal footing" in terms of prices in eastern markets, the railroads would charge a lower transportation rate to the group claiming the highest shipping costs. This meant, of course, that each side, in the complex discussion that followed, would want to claim the highest shipping costs for its own product in order to persuade the railroads to increase the rate on an opponent's product. Naturally, both dressed beef and livestock shippers threw in every possible detail that might affect costs, even including the bruises that the steers and dressed beef suffered in transit! Dressed beef shippers were at a disadvantage, for regardless of how many costs they calculated, their aggregate figures remained significantly lower than those of the livestock shippers. Obviously, under the railroad principle of neutrality, the cost advantages of western dressed beef became liabilities when the Trunkline Association used them to devise a rate structure. (See Tables IV.1 and IV.2.)

At the Windsor meeting, Fink and the railroads struggled to devise a rate structure that assisted livestock shippers without negating the cost advantages of dressed beef shippers. They decided to charge a 77-cent per 100 pound rate on dressed beef and a 40-cent per 100 pound cattle rate. Predictably, dressed beef shippers viewed the differential as discriminatory. After the meeting, Swift described the differential as "a lingering matter of annoyance."[19] Armour castigated Fink for being the expounder of an "odious doctrine" to prevent competition through railroad rate adjustments.[20] Both naturally agreed that the cost of transportation should be the sole determinant of transportation charges. Nor were the livestock interests satisfied. The rate differential between the two products was still not great enough, they thought, to enable them to compete effectively with the new packers.

The only area of agreement between the two groups of shippers concerned the need to eliminate the instability of such admittedly discriminatory rates. Regardless of their position on the question of relative

Table IV.1. Statement of Comparative Earnings on Live Stock and Dressed Beef[a]

Comparative earnings on live cattle and dressed beef:	
35,000 cattle @ 42,870,000 lb @ 40¢ to New York	$171,480
55% dressed 23,578,000 @ 64¢ to New York	150,900
12.02% hides, etc., 5,152,000 @ 30¢ @ 35¢ to N.Y.	17,600
42,870,000 cattle @ 20,400 lb per car − 2,101 cars @ 35 cars to train	60 trains
2,101 stock cars @ 19,000 lb each	39,919,000 lb
Add cattle	42,870,000
Total to haul	32,789,000
Weight of train of 35 cars	1,379,817 lb
The dressed beef @ 22,500 lb per car would require	1,048 ref. cars
The hides, etc., @ 26,000 lb per car would require	198 comm. cars
1,048 ref. cars @ 35,000 lb	36,860,000 lb
Ice for same @ 4,000 lb	4,192,000 lb
198 comm. cars @ 20,000 lb	3,960,000 lb
Dressed beef, hides, etc.	28,730,000 lb
Divided by weight of train of livestock 1,379,817 lb	53 trains

[a] Presented by Mr. John Newell (furnished by Mr. G. F. Swift).
Source: "Relative Cost of Shipping Dressed Beef and Livestock," *Abstract of Proceedings of Conference Between Trunk Line Executive Committee, Chicago Committee and Livestock and Dressed Beef Shippers* (New York, April 11–12, 1883), p. 106.

rates, both livestock and dressed beef shippers preferred stable rates. "Every man shipping a lot of beef should have the same rate, and should know what it is," Swift protested in 1886. "It would suit me better."[21] As long as a shipper had to compete for rebates and could not depend upon all railroads to give the same or equal rates, he was unable to determine whether he or his competitor had the cost advantage, or for that matter, what his true costs were. Stable rates meant greater stability for shippers as well as railroads.

The railroads endorsed their shippers' views on this point but proved incapable of stabilizing rates for either livestock or dressed beef. In the months that followed the Windsor meeting, rate cutting on dressed beef and livestock continued. Although a new settlement was drawn up in October 1884 by an Association arbitrator, a significant rate differential remained; cattle rates stayed at 40 cents per 100 pounds, and dressed beef rates were lowered 5 cents per 100 pounds, to 70 cents per 100 pounds.[22]

The discriminatory rate structure was not so discriminatory, however, as to erase the cost-cutting advantages of the refrigerator car. Western packers continued to expand and to use the Chicago & Grand Trunk

Table IV.2. Statement of Messrs. P. D. Armour & Co., of 21,913 Shipping Cattle, Killed at New Slaughter House, from February 8th to May 8th, Inclusive

Cost of cattle on foot		$1,384,693.57
Slaughter house expenses		5,720.63
Reclamation allowances		1,204.86
Icing and salting expenses (cooling house and cars at starting and salting hides)		5,163.32
Labor, salaries, office expenses and rent		43,375.41
OR		
Dressed beef sales	$ 791,702.46	
Dressed beef consignments *en route*	386,034.77	
Sales of hides	11,674.91	
Stock on hand:		
beef	47,455.67	
hides	131,913.90	
sundry offals	50,963.07	
Balance loss	20,413.01	
Total	$1,440,157.79	$1,440,157.79

Source: "Relative Cost of Shipping Dressed Beef and Livestock," *Abstract of Proceedings of Conference Between Trunk Line Executive Committee, Chicago Committee and Livestock and Dressed Beef Shippers* (New York, April 11-12, 1883), p. 131.

Railway as their preferred shipper. In 1885 some 59 percent of all the dressed beef shipped eastward from Chicago was carried on that line.[23]

As they expanded their hold on the market, the Big Four packers began to cooperate as much as compete—working together to put pressure on both their suppliers and the railroads. Testifying before the Senate Select Committee on the Transportation and Sale of Meat Products in 1889, Philip Armour's brother Samuel, a Kansas City packer, revealed one aspect of the packers' business strategy in the area of purchasing. As Samuel explained, "here is a man who has got a string of cattle and will not divide them. I want part of those cattle and perhaps my neighboring packer wants part of them. I may go to that man and say, 'Here, there is no use of our bidding against each other; I will take half of them and you half.'"[24]

The packers also used their competitive strategy and influence as large shippers to play one road off against another for lower rates. Complaining of Armour's pressure tactics in 1885, Henry Ledyard, president of the Michigan Central, wrote to A. Mackay, his general freight agent, "While I appreciate fully the value of Mr. Armour's business, we cannot take a position with him different from that which we take with other, and equally important shippers."[25] Hammond, an old customer of the New York Central, tried to persuade that road to aid him in building his branch plants in Armour's territory in New York.[26]

Capitalizing on the ownership of their refrigerator cars, the packers exacted rebates for the privilege of hauling their voluminous freight. As early as 1883 Armour, who was described by some observers as "just as good a railroad man as he was a butcher," was receiving a rebate of ¾ cent for each mile that an Armour refrigerator car traveled east of Chicago and 1 cent for each mile it traveled west of the Windy City. Although he was not the first to use that particular kind of rebate system, (it had been used previously by his friend George Pullman), he was the first to apply it to refrigerated meats. Mileage payments to other specialized car owners soon became the rule rather than the exception.[27]

For the livestock shippers and packers in cities and towns unable to compete with Chicago and its growing livestock trade, such methods confirmed suspicions of a monopoly among Chicago packers. "You can readily see that these dressed beef people hold a dangerous power," claimed one critic. "Buying cattle thus as they do at their own price they are enabled to put retail meat on the market at prices which run the butchers out of the business in the East, and for that matter in the West as well." Interpreting such tactics as a drive to monopolize the whole earth, he prophesied that "these people will find that they have run counter to the interests of too many classes. They antagonize the railroads, the butchers, the stock yards, the cattle raisers, and the beef consumers."[28]

In a letter to the *Chicago Tribune,* February 20, 1886, wealthy livestock shipper and packer Samuel Allerton warned that unless rates were adjusted to permit livestock shippers to compete with the packers, Swift, Armour, and Hammond would soon have a monopoly greater than Standard Oil. Allerton charged that Swift had received nearly $1,000,000 in rebates from the Grand Trunk and that rebates, not economic efficiency, were the key to Swift's rapid growth.[29]

Swift and his fellow packers naturally denied the charges, insisting that it was the livestock shippers who had received rebates.[30] In an unusual display of charity toward the big packers, the *New York Times* reminded its readers that several years previously, "the Chicago cattle ring deprived other cities of trade and gained control of the business by entering into a conspiracy with great railroad companies." Expropriating a common symbol, the *Times* compared the ring's methods to those of the Standard Oil Trust, and claimed that "it had established its power by means of iniquitous bargains with common carriers. . . . [just as had] the Association of Eveners in Chicago."[31]

In testimony before the Vest Committee in 1889 Armour denied

> that rebates unduly favoring the business were paid to dressed beef shippers by the railroads carrying dressed beef. This is not true in any respect, and, on the contrary, the dressed beef business has from its inception been treated in an unfriendly manner by all the trunk lines with the exception of the Grand Trunk and Baltimore and Ohio systems. . . . Owing to the fact that these cattle rates were continually cut the dressed beef men were put to the necessity of ascertaining the exact amount of such cuts—a task of great difficulty—and were then obliged to make claims upon the roads carrying their dressed beef for an equalization of the dressed beef rates which they had paid.[32]

In an era when secret rebates were more the rule than the exception, both interests undoubtedly received their share.[33]

As participants in the rebate game, the traffic hungry railroads recognized the dangers of the system, but were powerless to change the rules. Complaining that "most of the ground for irritation [over rate wars] was created by shippers who desired to fracture the existing agreements,"[34] the railroads resorted to their usual ineffective defensive policy. In 1886 the Trunkline Executive Committee passed a resolution declaring that such attempts should be reported to the commissioner "so that members of the committee could guard against the usual methods resorted to by shippers, in misrepresenting the action of one road for the purpose of influencing other roads in making reductions in rates."[35]

In 1886 further unsatisfactory attempts to agree on and enforce a rate differential for dressed beef and livestock inevitably led to more rate cutting and the breakdown of railroad pools. Earnings reports from all trunkline business indicated that the traffic carried during the previous two years had generally been unremunerative.[36] During that period, rates had dropped and remained at an unusually low level. Taking advantage of the low rates, dressed beef shippers increased the shipments of their product sent eastward from Chicago. In 1885, 51.5 percent of such beef shipments (dressed and live) had been dressed beef; by the end of 1886 the share of dressed beef had risen to 57.1 percent.[37]

To rectify the roads' increasingly unprofitable position and perhaps to thwart the increasing dressed beef shipments, Fink inaugurated a rate advance on March 1, 1886, which increased cattle rates 10 cents (from 25 to 35 cents) per 100 pounds and those for dressed beef 22 cents (from 43 to 65 cents) per 100 pounds. Fink explained that according to his "new" principle, "the cost of transportation on a pound of beef from Chicago to New York shall be the same whether the cattle are slaughtered in Chicago or slaughtered in New York." Rates were to be adjusted for each class of traffic separately rather than pegging the rates for dressed beef at a fixed percentage above the cattle rates.[38] In effect, however, Fink raised the rates, using the old principle but increasing the differential from 75 percent in 1885 to 86 percent in 1886.[39] The railroads' new policy was no less vulnerable and no more workable than their previous ones. Secret rebates and railroad rate wars, always disruptive, became a regular feature of the struggle to place dressed beef on the market. Despite the increased rate differential, dressed beef continued to pour into eastern markets, prompting the *Railroad Gazette* to conclude:

> This increase in the relative rates on the two classes of traffic does not appear to have interfered much with the growth of the dressed beef business; but as it is generally acknowledged that the rates have been maintained, it is possible that the differences in the tariff rates as agreed upon to take effect March 1, last have not been observed in making private arrangements with shippers as to what the actual rates should be.[40]

The new railroad policy excited fierce opposition from both groups of shippers. Dressed beef shippers joined Armour in branding Fink as the "executioner" of their industry. The *New York Times* reported rumors of a combination of dressed meat men preparing to resist the rate advance.[41] Livestock shippers also found Fink's increase objectionable, despite their improvement relative to the dressed beef firms, and interpreted it as an "extortion which should not longer be endured."[42]

As competition intensified, antagonism toward the big packers began to crystallize into collective opposition. In 1886 the National Butcher's Protective Association was formed, ostensibly to protect the butchers but actually to drive out the dressed beef trade.[43] Retail butchers' associations formed in cities where the innovators had penetrated. These groups not only waged aggressive propaganda campaigns against western dressed beef but also organized mass boycotts against butchers who patronized western packers.[44] Periodicals like the *Butcher's Advocate* of New York, the *Butcher's National Journal,* and the *Breeder's Gazette* sprang up to rally sympathy for the little butchers and packers.[45] The Chicago Livestock Exchange endorsed resolutions adopted at the National Cattle Growers' Convention urging the railroads to "make rates that will not so unjustly discriminate against the cattle interests." Attached to the resolution was a plea addressed to state legislators requesting that "suitable legislation be adopted" to limit the opportunities for discrimination.[46]

Legislatures in 19 states responded with bills to prevent the importation of dressed meats. Of the bills introduced in Arkansas, Colorado, Connecticut, Delaware, Florida, Illinois, Indiana, Kansas, Michigan, Minnesota, Mississippi, New York, New Jersey, Nebraska, New Mexico, Ohio, Pennsylvania, Tennessee, Vermont, and Wisconsin, only those in the four states of Colorado, Indiana, Minnesota, and New Mexico became law. The Minnesota law, which prohibited "the sale of any fresh beef, veal, mutton, lamb or pork for human food" imported into the state, became the basis for a Supreme Court case, which in effect ruled such laws unconstitutional because they were state interference with interstate commerce.[47]

The opposition was costly to the interstate packers both monetarily and psychologically. "I want to tell you that we have all got ourselves into expenses by this opposition that has been brought against us," Simeon Armour told the Vest Committee investigating the industry in 1889, "and if it is not the legislature it is something else that is annoying us and taking our money away."[48]

ORGANIZED RESISTANCE AND GOVERNMENT INTERVENTION

By the mid-1870s, the situation in the livestock and dressed beef trade had deteriorated to the point that groups and organizations that had initially sprung up to counter packer power now joined with their foes to demand an end to the inequities and discrimination inherent in the railroad rate structure. Beleaguered, the railroads agreed with rival shippers on the need for some kind of federal regulation to help achieve some stability in the railroad industry. The railroads' difficulties with shippers had made clear the ineffectiveness of state solutions for problems that were national in scope. Having paved the way for the growth of big businesses in industries such as oil, meat, and sugar, the railroads were among the first to seek the federal government's aid in taming the competitive struggles they had unleashed.

On March 17, 1885, the Senate of the United States appointed a committee "to investigate and report upon the subject of the regulation of the transportation by railroad and water routes in connection or in competition with said railroads of freights and passengers between the several states."[49] Chaired by Senator Shelby Cullom of Illinois, the committee issued its report a year later, recommending the federal regulation of interstate commerce. The testimony of ranchers, butchers, and meat wholesalers figured prominently in the report.

Attention focused on rate discrimination and railroad pools. Recalling the struggle between livestock and dressed beef shippers, Greenleaf W. Simpson, president of the Refrigerator Car Line, insisted that "it would have worked itself out before this . . . had not [livestock shippers] been aided by the railroads. The live-cattle men could not possibly have competed with the dressed beef men. They did not have a purse long enough to do it."[50] Armour representative Edward J. Martyn blamed the struggle on railroad pools. Had they been ideal, he explained, "we should have been snuffed out of the business. We never could have lived under it."[51] Gustavus Swift considered the effects of pools "detrimental to both shippers and railroads. Their trying to do business under pool protection has hastened the demoralizing state of affairs in railroad circles," he said. Livestock shipper Lucien Prince of Worcester, Massachusetts blamed the pools for making his business unprofitable and lashed out at railroad executives who, he criticized, "are neither honest nor honorable; bound to rule or ruin any man that does not obey their behests."[52]

Railroad officers admitted that their rate structures were unstable and frequently discriminatory and that their pools seldom functioned as they had hoped, but they blamed these difficulties on the unenforceability of their agreements rather than on the nature of pools. Contrary to the views of most shippers and committee members, railroad executives advocated federal regulation that legalized pooling.[53]

The Interstate Commerce Act of 1887 incorporated the views of railroad shippers. To the dismay of railroad executives it abolished pooling and followed the state-level precedents of the Windom and Hepburn Committees in relying upon competition to regulate the railroads. It prohibited discriminatory rates, drawbacks, and rebates and made it illegal to charge more for a short haul than for a long haul over the same line. Although not authorizing rate-fixing, the Act mandated "reasonable" and "just rates." Tariff schedules were to be published and no changes could be made until a ten-day public notice. To enforce and administer the provisions of the Act, Congress created an interstate commerce commission and empowered it "to compel testimony and production of papers."[54]

The first federal regulatory commission of its kind, the ICC began its work during the formative stage of big business, in the midst of one of the more intensely competitive periods in American history. Some saw the significance of the Act extending beyond its impact on the railroad industry. "The Interstate Commerce bill . . . will serve the people by undermining the power of the beef trade combination," rhapsodized the editor of the *New York Times*.[55] The more pragmatic *Railroad Gazette,* on the other hand, predicted a rocky road ahead for the railroads and the Commission.

> Where the shippers in a given line of trade are comparatively few in number and have it in their power to dictate terms to the railroads, the law becomes especially hard to enforce. There is a danger . . . that the prohibition of pools will have the effect of enabling those industries which are most nearly monopolized or most

closely organized to dictate terms to the railroads and receive the lowest rates for shipments.[56]

The eruption of a new war between livestock and dressed beef shippers made it evident that adjustment to the new law would be easier for shippers than it would be for the railroads.

COMPETITION AND THE ICC

Although the Interstate Commerce Act ostensibly outlawed pooling, it did not directly threaten railroad associations. Nor did it tamper with the system of differentials that enabled roads to receive allowances from the original rate to offset natural disadvantages of distance or routes. What it did was to establish a commission to see that railroads voluntarily enforced prescribed rules and regulations. Whereas previously railroads struggled to maintain agreements of their own devising, they now competed to maintain rates subject to the Commission's approval. With pooling outlawed, requests for differentials from the Trunkline Association became the only legal way for a railroad to secure a larger portion of the traffic.

The Grand Trunk's failure in 1887 to secure a greater differential on its dressed beef traffic put it in a rebellious mood.[57] Compounding the company's difficulties was a deterioration of its relations with Swift, the Grand Trunk's largest shipper of dressed beef. At the same time the road's relations with Armour, Swift's biggest competitor, improved. In mid-October 1887, Swift diverted his freight to the Michigan Central, Lake Shore, Canadian Southern, and New York Central roads. To Grand Trunk President Henry Tyler the reason for such action was obvious: the American roads had offered Swift lower rates.[58]

Whether or not that view was correct, a rate war exploded that accelerated the increase of dressed beef shipments to the East by lowering transport costs. The war also forced (or hastened) the conversion of the American roads to large-scale carriers of dressed beef. Angered by the loss of shipments, Grand Trunk General Manager Joseph Hickson notified the Joint Executive Committee on November 7, 1887, that the Grand Trunk intended to "make a differential rate by the main line of the Grand Trunk Railway, of 10 percent below that tariff on dressed beef traffic." Branding the action as arbitrary and unjustified, the Committee passed a resolution (in the Grand Trunk's absence), authorizing similar action by all roads.[59] Rates dropped on both dressed beef and livestock.

Still another rate war ensued. The month of November saw cattle rates drop almost 50 percent, and dressed beef rates plunged similarly. During the course of the rate war, Swift returned his shipments to the Grand Trunk. Relief came late in December 1887, when the trunklines finally agreed to give the Grand Trunk Railway a differential of 4 cents per 100 pounds to Boston and New England. Rates on dressed beef were restored to 65 cents, and the Grand Trunk was allowed a differential, being permitted to ship at 61 cents per 100 pounds.[60]

Before the agreement could be tested, however, Swift again diverted his shipments, this time to the independent and newly constructed Nickel Plate Railroad.[61] The packer indicated to the Trunkline Committee that "there are other than commercial reasons which prevent the continuance of those shipments."[62] Although the implication of his statement was unclear, the consequences of his action were immediate. Rates dropped. The Grand Trunk then demanded a greater differential, and the American roads reluctantly complied, giving their Canadian rival a 5-cent differential instead of the previous 4 cents, while at the same time advancing the rates on livestock and dressed beef. The differential brought Swift back to the Grand Trunk and intensified competition within the American trunkline network. A dissatisfied and restless Pennsylvania Railroad announced a lower rate for their own shippers. The Erie, angered by the Grand Trunk differential and desirous of having one of its own, lowered its dressed beef rates. The New York Central followed its rival by making an even lower cut. Completing the circle and starting things off again, the Grand Trunk then slashed dressed meat rates still further.[63]

No relief came as rates fell lower and lower. On July 7, 1888, the *New York Times* reported that railroad managers "Now . . . think there is no bottom."[64] After pointing out that the roads had ceased to make reductions on cattle rates after they had dropped to 5 cents to New York, 3 cents to Philadelphia, and 2 cents to Baltimore, a Chicago paper added that "the war on dressed beef rates . . . is continued with undiminished vigor."[65] Only the Grand Trunk refused to reduce its dressed beef rates below 26½ cents per 100 pounds. On July 17 the Erie slashed dressed beef rates to 6 cents.[66]

The depressed rates prompted the editor of the *Railroad Gazette* to express sympathy for the railroads' predicament. He blamed the war on shippers who had threatened the railroads with a loss of their "whole business" and had forced them "to a line of action that is neither good railroad economy nor good public policy." According to the editor, the Interstate Commerce Act was also partly responsible: "If the law prohibits railroad pools but cannot cope with rings of producers, it is simple madness to try weapons when there are other people whom you cannot control who are ready to take care of their weakness."[67]

The war ended as quickly as it had begun. The New York Central and

Pennsylvania refused to make further cuts. The Erie indicated its willingness to negotiate. All had realized that they were carrying the dressed beef business at unbearably low rates.[68] The Grand Trunk, on the other hand, found its proportion of the dressed beef traffic reduced by nearly 28 percent from the amount it had carried in 1887.[69]

The ICC had played a quiet but significant role in the three-cornered struggle between the railroads and shippers of livestock and dressed beef. By outlawing railroad pools and prescribing rules for the railroads without placing any constraints on shippers, it exacerbated competition among the railroads and made them even more vulnerable to demands of large shippers, especially those like Armour and Swift who also owned their own cars. Encouraged to play one road off against another, shippers received the government's tacit approval of their own attempts to cooperate and combine. With a public forum for adjudicating disputes, shippers intensified efforts to secure lower rates, flooding the Commission with petitions to correct past as well as present abuses. Shortly after the Act's passage in 1887, petitions flowed into the commissioners from dressed beef shippers protesting exhorbitant rates on dressed beef from Chicago to the East and demanding reclassification of their products and adjustment of rates.[70] By intensifying competition the ICC not only assured a more rapid invasion of the market by dressed beef shippers but also propped up the livestock trade.

When another dressed beef–livestock war erupted in 1890 after American railways again refused to grant the Grand Trunk a differential on dressed beef, the *Railroad Gazette* used the occasion to underscore the negative consequences of the ICC for railroads:

> The dressed beef rate war is almost a repetition of that which took place some two years ago. The Grand Trunk is fighting for a differential of three cents; the other roads are fighting against it; there seems to be no possible compromise. The serious thing is that the shippers, when as well organized as they are in the dressed beef industry, can precipitate such a war as often as they choose. They are organized; the railroads are not allowed by the ICC law to have any effective counter organization. If shippers threaten to withdraw their business from the Grand Trunk unless it receives a differential, the Grand Trunk must demand it. If other shippers threaten to withdraw theirs from the Lake Shore unless it meets the Grand Trunk's rate, the Lake Shore must enter the fight. A pool would enable them to protect themselves; without a pool they must fight, whether they want to or not.[71]

The disastrous effect of this competition on the railroad industry was manifest in the increasing tendency toward amalgamation and consolidation among the railroads during the 1890s.[72] Only by creating their own self-sustaining systems did railroads finally achieve the stability they had wanted for decades. By that time the battle to place dressed beef on eastern markets had already been won. Railroad resistance to the new trade had played an important role in assuring that victory.

CONCLUSION

By 1888 not even the rhetoric of neutrality persisted. Competition had hastened the spread of technological progress in the form of the new dressed beef industry—a development that forced American railroads to damage their own traditional interests in the livestock business. When the refrigerator car necessitated a change in railroad rate structures, old policies and attitudes, as well as existing investments, made adjustment painfully difficult. This experience clearly shows that the fragility of the pools—their constant disruption due to the lack of effective enforcement provisions—hastened the diffusion of technological innovation. Had pools been legal, it seems clear that their rigidity could have delayed the entry of the refrigerator car, perhaps for a much longer period.

In trying to implement their pools, the railroads also made use of the "principle of neutrality." The principle was defined loosely and according to particular circumstances. But, given the railroad investments in stockyards, cars, and other livestock facilities, "neutrality" was in fact, simply a means of promoting railroad self-interest. The Grand Trunk for its own reasons would not cooperate with the Trunkline Association. It gained an initial but transitory increase in freight for its efforts. More importantly, it opened up a major eastern market to the new dressed beef trade.

The ICC may have helped to break the Grand Trunk's monopoly of the dressed beef trade by exacerbating competition among the railroads, but in the long run it fostered railroad consolidation by driving out weaker roads and encouraging greater control through self-contained administrative systems.

Whatever the case, the dressed beef industry had already gained a secure foothold in eastern markets. The success of the refrigerator car and its effect on the industry were inextricably tied to the competitive forces of the day, especially to competition among railroads. Utilizing the new refrigeration technology, Swift, Armour, Morris, and Hammond intensified competition among rival groups of the old order and between the old and new orders in transportation and distribution. Guided by an entrepreneurial aggressiveness that thrived in a profit-oriented economy, competition and technology disrupted the railroads' "search for order" and thrust a few large, integrated, multifunctional meat packing enterprises into the center economy.

After the mid-1880s these same forces created new problems of adjustment for the new order as well. During the next two decades the big packers had to deal with the realities of oligopolistic competition in their own industry.

NOTES

1. *New York Times,* November 15, 1882, p. 5; October 10, 1882, p. 8; October 11, 1882, p. 5; *Vest Report,* pp. 131–136, 144, 260; *Cincinnati Price Current,* May 1, 1884, p. 1, details activities of the Eastern Butcher's Protective Society.

2. *New York Times,* October 11, 1882, p. 5. By November 1882 rumors were circulating that two of the largest livestock shippers, J. B. Dutcher and T. C. Eastman, were engaged in a scheme to drive out the dressed beef men. When the *New York Times* interviewed Dutcher, he denied the rumors and also the realities of competition between dressed beef and livestock shippers. He simply insisted that "beef shipped in refrigerator cars is an inferior article and cannot come into serious competition with the beef" slaughtered in New York. "The fact that dressed beef is brought here in refrigerator cars has very little, if any, influence on the market for prime beef killed and dressed here," he claimed (November 15, 1882, p. 5).

3. See Tables IV.1 and IV.2.

4. Crucial data for a thorough analysis of the struggle are contained in two reports by Albert Fink (discussed in text above, p. 80, n. 47): "Report Upon the Relative Cost of Shipping Dressed Beef and Livestock," pp. 1–132, and "Final Report Upon the Relative Cost of Transporting Livestock and Dressed Beef," pp. 1–97, *Proceedings and Circulars of the Joint Executive Committee, 1883.*

5. When Boston and New Hampshire pork packers asked railroads in 1879 to raise the transportation charge on the products of Chicago packers who, they protested, "can send to Boston for 35¢ meat for which the Boston packer cannot get the hogs carried for less than 81.8¢," railroads advocated "neutrality." The Trunkline Association implemented a policy similar to that which would be used in connection with the dressed beef trade: they allowed "that a rebate of 5¢ per 100 pounds be granted on all hogs that product of which is exported." This, they claimed, yielded "something to the Boston and New Hampshire packers" and at the same time placed "the packers on the Eastern seaboard upon an equality with the Western packers, so far as competing in foreign markets is concerned" (*Railroad Gazette,* September 26, 1879, p. 513, quoting a trunkline resolution adopted September 23, 1879).

6. Differentials—an allowance from the original rate—posed many problems for railroads. In some instances, railroads requested differentials to offset their natural disadvantages and to enable them to compete with more favorably situated roads. Differentials of this nature were designed to prevent excessive rate-cutting on these longer routes, where the need for traffic made them a threat to the more direct lines if they did not comply with such requests. Differentials were first allotted on April 5, 1877, according to the so-called Seaboard Differential Agreement. See *Report of Messrs. Thurman, Washburne and Cooley, Constituting an Advisory Commission on Differential Rates by Railroads Between the West and the Seaboard* (New York, 1882), and U.S. Congress, Senate, *Report of the Select Committee on Transportation Routes to the Seaboard,* S. Rpt. No. 307, 43rd Cong., 1st Sess., 1874.

The best analysis of Grand Trunk–New York Central difficulties concerning differentials is Edward Chase Kirkland, *Men, Cities and Transportation,* 2 vols. (Cambridge, Mass., 1948), I, pp. 495–528.

A "distance" differential, like that described above, is not to be confused with the rate differential between livestock and dressed beef discussed in the text. This latter differential refers simply to the difference between the rates for livestock and dressed beef.

7. Cleland B. Wyllie, "How the Grand Trunk Got to Chicago" (Master's Thesis, University of Michigan, 1953), p. 5; G. R. Stevens, *Sixty Years of Trial and Error* (Toronto, 1960), Vol. I of *Canadian National Railways*, p. 333; *The Commercial and Financial Chronicle and Hunt's Merchants' Magazine* (January–June, 1883), p. 663; Letter from John King to John W. Garrett, Baltimore, July 12, 1878 (Baltimore & Ohio Archives, Maryland Historical Society, Baltimore, Maryland).

8. *Proceedings of the Joint Executive Committee*, May 30, 1880, p. 136.

9. "Maintenance of Rates of Livestock and Dressed Beef to New England," *Proceedings of the Trunk Line Executive Committee*, October 8, 1880, pp. 23–32.

10. See Table III.3.

11. *Ibid.*

12. *Proceedings of the Joint Executive Committee*, August 10, 1881, pp. 85–88.

13. Problems plaguing the railroad business had intensified early in 1881, causing the *Railroad Gazette*, March 18, 1881, p. 156, to conclude that "The combination of the eastern and western roads represented by the Joint Executive Committee probably never was so near destruction as during the past few weeks."

14. *Railroad Gazette*, May 13, 1881, pp. 261–262; May 20, 1881, pp. 279–280; *Proceedings of the Joint Executive Committee*, April 27, 1881, p. 53; May 6, 1881, p. 61. The war was not as damaging to the Grand Trunk as it was to American roads (*Railway World*, January 14, 1882, p. 28).

15. *Railroad Gazette*, April 21, 1882, p. 240; *New York Times*, April 14, 1882, p. 8; April 15, 1882, p. 2; *Proceedings of the Joint Executive Committee*, March 3, 1882, p. 32; March 31, 1882, p. 46; April 13, 1882, p. 53; November 17, 1882, p. 241. The committee distinguished between "gross" and "net" rates for cattle. Gross rates for cattle were set at 50 cents per 100 pounds; net rates, at 40 cents per 100 pounds. The 10-cent difference was the amount rebated to a shipper after he had complied with the requirements of the joint stock agent who directed the shipments to certain roads in order to even the cattle traffic. The arrangement had been instituted to extricate the railroads from their difficulties with the first preferential evener arrangement, which had been instituted in the 1870s. No similar rebates were given to dressed beef shippers. However, an allowance for icing had been given by some roads to dressed beef shippers, but it was discontinued on April 13, 1882.

Unlike the old livestock pool, which physically divided the traffic and allotted percentages of livestock independently of dressed beef, the new contract transferred dressed beef, which had been handled separately, under the "dead freight" division, to the "livestock" division, and allotted percentages on the basis of aggregate livestock and dressed beef traffic (*Proceedings of the Trunk Line Executive Committee*, November 11, 1882, p. 84). This meant, in effect, "That, if said roads carrying dressed beef do not hereafter obtain the full amount of their percentages in dressed beef, they shall be evened in Live Stock as heretofore" (*Proceedings of the Joint Executive Committee*, November 17, 1882, p. 241). But percentages were adjusted not by moving traffic, but by compensating roads through transfers of revenue derived from the traffic.

16. "Dressed Meat Traffic," U.S. Dept. of Agriculture, *Report of the Bureau of Animal Industry, 1886*, p. 278; Perry, "Live Stock and Meat Traffic of Chicago," U.S. Dept. of Agriculture, *Report of the Bureau of Animal Industry, 1884*, pp. 266–267; *Railroad Gazette*, February 20, 1890, p. 152; *Railway World*, December 6, 1884, p. 1161.

17. *Proceedings of the Joint Executive Committee*, March 30, 1883, p. 34.

18. "Report Upon the Relative Cost of Shipping Live Stock and Dressed Beef," pp. 1–132, and "Final Report Upon the Relative Cost of Transporting Live Stock and Dressed Beef," pp. 32–39, in *Proceedings and Circulars of the Joint Executive Committee, 1883*.

In terms of the prices in eastern markets, if the buyer were to pay, say, one dollar per pound for dressed beef whether the steer had been slaughtered in New York or Chicago, and the livestock shippers could claim that his costs were seventy-five cents while those of the dressed beef shipper were only twenty-five cents, then the railroads, under Fink's equalization plan, would have to make the dressed beef shipper absorb this differential by adding a corresponding amount to his transportation charges.

19. Testimony of G. F. Swift, *Cullom Report*, Vol. II, p. 649.

20. "Dressed Beef Industry's Reply to Fink," *New York Times*, February 24, 1886, p. 3, quoting Armour, who provided a summary of conditions from 1883 to 1886.

21. *Cullom Report*, Vol. II, p. 651.

22. *Proceedings of the Trunk Line Executive Committee*, November 10, 1884, p. 10. The award was made October 2, 1884. For a detailed description, see *Railway World*, December 6, 1884, p. 1161. Briefly stated, it was based on the principle of charging each interest a rate proportionate to the value of service, a value arrived at by comparison of market values in New York on lots of live cattle identical in value at Chicago. The one shipment, however, was delivered as livestock and the other as dressed beef in New York, allowing to each shipper the cost of transportation exclusive of railroad charges and inclusive of any loss from shrinkage (Clemen, *The American Livestock and Meat Industry*, p. 241).

23. Grand Trunk President Henry Tyler was elated at his road's good fortune: "It is a matter of congratulation that we are not confined to the least profitable, but have a firm hold on one of the most expanding and lucrative classes of traffic" ("Report of the President's Speech at the Half-Yearly Meeting," in *Annual Report of the Grand Trunk Railway of Canada*, April 30, 1886, p. 32).

24. Testimony of Simeon Armour, *Vest Report*, p. 360.

25. The letter is contained in Thomas C. Cochran, *Railroad Leaders, 1845–1890* (Cambridge, Mass., 1965), p. 391. See also pp. 384–388, 401, 403, 433 and 497 for other letters relating specifically to the meat packing business.

26. *Ibid.*, p. 387, quoting letter from Henry Ledyard to H. J. Hayden, third vice-president, New York Central & Hudson Railroad, June 26, 1883.

27. Leech and Carroll, *Armour and His Times*, p. 162. Swift, Hammond, and Morris soon adopted the system in order to obtain similar advantages and to compete more effectively with Armour. Mileage fees created numerous problems for the railroads. For a discussion, see the "Special Committee on Car Service," *Trunkline Board of Presidents*, April 5, 1887, pp. 34–35.

The additional source of income from private cars often enabled owners to pay off their investments in a few years. Writing to his nephew Kirkland (April 23, 1897) of the advantages of private car ownership, P. D. Armour emphasized that "you cannot do anything that will make you money so fast as the car business. You don't need to be told this; all you have to do is look back on your records. . . . The refrigerator cars are the only cars that are good for anything" (Quoted in Leech and Carroll, *Armour and His Times*, pp. 163–164). See also, U.S. Congress, House, *Hearings Before the Subcommittee of the Committee on Interstate and Foreign Commerce . . . Relating to Private Car Lines*, 58th Cong., 3rd Sess., 1905, and Federal Trade Commission, *Report on Private Car Lines*, 3 pts (Washington, D.C., 1920).

28. *New York Times*, February 28, 1886, p. 2.

29. *Chicago Tribune*, February 20, 1886, p. 3.

30. *Ibid.*, March 4, 1886, p. 2; Testimony of P. D. Armour, *Vest Report*, p. 429.

31. *New York Times* (editorial), May 21, 1888, p. 4.

32. *Vest Report*, p. 429.

33. The role of railroad rebates in the rise of big business, however, remains a hotly debated issue. For a discussion of rebates in the oil industry, see Ralph W. Hidy and Muriel E. Hidy, *Pioneering in Big Business, 1882–1911* (New York, 1955), pp. 118–121; Harold Williamson and Arnold Daums, *The American Petroleum Industry* (Chicago, 1959), pp. 363–368, 401–402, 405, 412–429, 430–462.

34. *Railway World*, February 20, 1886, p. 174.

35. *Proceedings of the Trunkline Executive Committee*, March 3, 1886, p. 38.

36. *New York Times*, February 19, 1886, p. 1.

37. *Railroad Gazette*, February 4, 1887, p. 78, lists a 4.9 percent decrease in cattle shipments and a 20.3 percent increase in dressed beef shipments during 1886.

38. *New York Times*, December 7, 1886, p. 2; *Proceedings of the Trunkline Executive Committee*, February 17–18, 1886, p. 24. See Armour's statement, *New York Times*, February 21, 1886, p. 5, and February 24, 1886, p. 3; and Fink's explanation of the award, *New York Times*, February 27, 1886, p. 3.

39. *Railroad Gazette*, February 4, 1887, p. 78.

40. *Ibid.*

41. *New York Times*, February 24, 1886, p. 3; February 19, 1886, p. 1; December 7, 1886, p. 2.

42. *New York Times*, December 7, 1886, p. 2.

43. Clemen, *The American Livestock and Meat Industry*, p. 243; *Vest Report*, p. 150.

44. *Vest Report*, pp. 133–134, 144, 260, 326; Clemen, *The American Livestock and Meat Industry*, p. 244.

45. Clemen, *The American Livestock and Meat Industry*, p. 242.

46. *New York Times*, December 7, 1886, p. 2.

47. Miscellaneous Vol. No. 360, Swift & Company Archives, Chicago, Illinois, contains numerous pamphlets relating to legal prohibitions against the dressed beef trade. Among the more important are *An Address in Favor of Living and Letting Live: Dressed Beef Industry*, Argument of Hon. J. F. Merryman of the St. Louis Bar, before the House Committee on Benevolent and Scientific Institutions; *The War On Dressed Beef*, Argument of N. J. Hammond, Against House Bill No. 469, "To Prevent the Importation and Sale of Dressed Beef," before the General Judiciary Committee of the House of Representatives of Georgia, August, 1889 (Atlanta, Ga., 1889); *Opinion Upon the Constitutionality of State Legislature Prohibiting the Importation and Sale of Dressed Meats Without Previous Inspection of the Live Animal in the Locality Where the Meats Are Offered for Sale*, by George W. McCrary and Wallace Pratt (Kansas City, Mo., 1889).

48. *Vest Report*, p. 359.

49. *Cullom Report*, Vol. I, p. 1.

50. *Ibid.*, Vol. II, pp. 409, 665, 646–647, 662.

51. *Ibid.*, Vol. I, pp. 46–47.

52. *Ibid.*, Vol. II, pp. 642–647, 660–662.

53. *Ibid.*, Vol. I, p. 53.

54. The main features of the Act are described in Alfred D. Chandler, Jr., ed., *The Railroads*, pp. 199–210. See also, U.S. Interstate Commerce Commission, *Annual Report, 1887*, pp. 1–84. The first committee members included Thomas M. Cooley of Michigan, chairman; William R. Morrison of Illinois, Augustus Schoonmaker of New York, Aldace F. Walker of Vermont, and Walter L. Brag of Alabama.

55. *New York Times*, February 28, 1887, p. 4.

56. *Railroad Gazette*, December 2, 1887, p. 782.

57. The Grand Trunk wanted a "distance" differential—an allowance from the original rate—to offset the natural disadvantages of its longer, more circuitous route. For details, see *New York Times*, January 14, 1887, p. 2; January 20, 1887, p. 1; March 25, 1887, p. 5; *Railroad Gazette*, June 13, 1890, p. 418.

58. Apparently the Grand Trunk had been attempting to solicit Armour's business as well as that of their regular customer, Swift. Tyler explained the rationale behind such a policy to Grand Trunk shareholders: "Now, there are two powerful parties—Mr. Swift and Messrs. Armour—in this business. Mr. Swift is the gentleman whose traffic we previously mainly carried—the bulk of Messrs. Armour's went by other routes; but as they were trying

to set the companies by the ears in their favour, it was obviously not unjustifiable to deal with them separately" ("Report of the President's Speech," in *Annual Report of the Grand Trunk Railway of Canada,* June 7, 1888, p. 37).

59. "Minutes of the Standing Committee," *Proceedings of the Joint Executive Committee,* November 18, 1887, p. 104.

60. Paul MacAvoy, *The Economic Effects of Regulation* (Cambridge, Mass., 1965), p. 129.

61. The Nickel Plate (New York, Chicago & St. Louis Railroad) was one of several lines constructed in the early 1880s to compete with the trunklines. *Railway Age,* July 21, 1916, p. 91, observed that "It was built parallel to the Lake Shore not because there was any economic need for an additional road between Buffalo and Chicago, but to force the Vanderbilts to buy it through the practice of cut-throat competition."

62. The Swift-Armour feud was among the more important reasons. See *Proceedings of the Trunkline Executive Committee,* January 14, 1888, p. 4, quoting Circular No. 651, issued by the Trunkline Freight Dept.

63. *New York Times,* June 30, 1888, p. 2; "Report of the President's Speech at the Half-Yearly Meeting," in *Annual Report of the Grand Trunk Railway of Canada,* October 30, 1888, p. 29; MacAvoy, *Economic Effects of Regulation,* p. 129.

64. *New York Times,* July 4, 1888, p. 4.

65. *Railroad Gazette,* July 20, 1888, p. 483, quoting a Chicago paper.

66. MacAvoy, *Economic Effects of Regulation,* p. 130.

67. *Railroad Gazette,* December 2, 1887, p. 782, editorial opinion.

68. MacAvoy, *Economic Effects of Regulation,* p. 130.

69. Ripley, *Railroads, Rates and Regulation,* p. 434.

70. *Railroad Gazette,* January 9, 1891, p. 31; U.S. Interstate Commerce Commission, *Annual Report, 1887,* pp. 294, 303, 464, describes petitions of *Swift & Co.* v. *B&O Railroad; Nelson Morris & Co.* v. *Lake Shore Road; Annual Report, 1888,* p. 130, *Armour & Co.* v. *Chicago & Grand Trunk Railway, Swift & Co.* v. *Chicago & Grand Trunk Railway, Armour & Co.* v. *Lake Shore & Michigan Southern Railway Co.*

71. *Railroad Gazette,* June 13, 1890, p. 418.

72. *Ibid.,* January 31, 1890, p. 76. Chandler, ed., *The Railroads,* pp. 159–162, discusses the move toward consolidation.

Chapter V

Strains of Oligopoly: Competition and Combination in the Dressed Beef Industry from the Late 1880s to 1902

Just as the interrelated forces of technology and competition altered the packers' relationships with railroads, livestock shippers, and meat wholesalers, they also transformed the relations among the major packers themselves. Virtually a new industry in the 1870s, by 1886 dressed beef had become oligopolistic, with the four largest firms controlling a major share of the interstate dressed beef trade. With the coming of oligopoly, prices were no longer regulated entirely by the traditional, impersonal market forces of supply and demand. In order to assure a continuing return on their large investments in plant and equipment, the leading firms began to set prices with an eye to their costs. Unlike the old days of many small firms, the fact that there were only a few large firms in the industry made it relatively easy for the businesses to cooperate in setting prices and maintaining product flows. In 1886 the dominant packers organized a dressed meat pool in an attempt to eliminate price competition and stabilize the industry.[1] During the 1890s the Big Four made repeated but unsuccessful attempts to perfect these pooling arrangements. Finally, in 1902, the packers followed the path taken earlier by railroad executives and other large industrial firms and turned to increased consolidation.[2]

The transformation of the dressed beef industry's structure and competitive patterns took place in three distinct but overlapping stages that were defined principally by changing marketing and technological problems confronting the packers. During the first stage, covering roughly the years from 1870 to 1878, efforts were directed toward developing a

111

reliable all-year refrigerator car. That era was really the industry's gestation period, because the modern dressed beef industry was born only with the successful application of refrigeration in the beef trade.

The second stage, from about 1878 to 1886, saw packers build the market for dressed beef. Relatively low unit costs that resulted from the utilization of the insulated refrigerator car and the creation of company-owned or company-controlled branch houses enabled western dressed beef to compete effectively with that slaughtered on the east coast and distributed through wholesalers. The implementation of the new marketing strategy led to the rise of oligopoly, which in turn ushered in the third stage.

Between 1886 and 1902 the packers confronted the problems that followed the early growth of their enterprises and the extension of their distribution networks. This chapter examines the behavior of the industry in the era when the packers had largely "filled up" the market for their product, at least in certain areas of the country, and faced adjustment to a much slower industry growth rate in those areas.

OLIGOPOLISTIC COMPETITION

By 1887 Armour, Swift, Morris, and Hammond were supplying approximately 85 percent of the nation's supply of dressed beef. Of that percentage, Swift had captured 28 percent; Armour, 25 percent; Morris, 21 percent; and Hammond, 11 percent of the market.[3] (See Table III.2, p. 67.) As the initial period of rapid growth gradually drew to a close, the relationship among the innovating firms changed, necessitating new patterns of behavior. The rapid expansion of the early 1880s had by mid-decade brought the packers into direct and intense competition in markets where more than one competitor had established a branch house. In such a situation, further increases in one firm's business could only come at the expense of another firm. As the Big Four eventually realized, competition between a few large firms was far different from that between many small firms or between a few firms in a fast-expanding market.

As we have seen, the new dressed beef trade required substantial capital investments and the creation of a large distribution network with a large labor force. As in the railroad industry, the existence of high overhead charges and fixed costs, in turn, created an inexorable pressure to maintain high and steady volume. Unless the enterprises were kept running full time at near capacity level, unit costs would increase. Unlike their smaller, unintegrated rivals, the large dressed beef firms could not afford to shut down for long, even when conditions warranted it, for large expenses continued, regardless. As Edward Morris explained, "Your expenses goes on just the same; we can't stop doing business even if we wanted to."[4] Any decrease in volume meant that a firm's unit costs would increase while those of rivals who captured part of its market share would decrease.[5]

Naturally, the Big Four did not fully understand these new competitive conditions immediately; they went through a learning process. Sometimes they responded to competitive initiatives by pouring too much beef into the same cities, seeking to maintain their early growth. Glutted markets and falling prices resulted, driving profits downward.

As innovators, the major packers enjoyed in their early years the high profits that accrue to such successful new businesses in their initial growth periods, when the main problem is simply to try to meet the enormous demand. Figures for Armour & Company, for example, show that the rate of return on investment declined from 24 percent in 1884 to 12 percent by 1887, while net profits dropped from $1,618,000 to some $1,000,000[6]. Although figures showing the "net surplus" of Swift & Company are not strictly comparable to those of Armour & Company, nor available for the same years, they show a similar trend.[7]

The effects of growing competition in the dressed beef trade were further exacerbated by the fact that prices of by-products declined steadily in line with the general price decline of the period. "I do not care hardly what you name," complained Simeon Armour in 1889, "there has been a depreciation in the last two years in all kinds of business that is almost inexplicable."[8]

Like the railroad managers before them, the large packers came to realize that the growing competition for shares of a leveling-off market lowered profits, increased the instability and uncertainty of the business, and made the regulation of product flows and lowering of unit costs exceedingly difficult. These difficulties naturally made the packers less optimistic about the future than they had been in the early 1880s, when maneuvering room in the market seemed unlimited.

Such a situation nurtured a mood of cooperation in both the packing industry and the declining livestock trade. By the end of 1886, Swift, Morris, Armour, and Hammond reached an agreement among themselves and with rival livestock shipper and hog packer Samuel Allerton of Chicago. Under this agreement, a pool was organized to regulate meat shipments into the Northeast.[9] The formation of the first pool marked the beginning of an important stage in the industry. It was a clear sign that the industry had entered oligopoly and that the early days of rapid growth and extremely high profits had come to an end, at least in the Northeast.

From the adoption of the pooling strategy in 1886, until 1902, when they finally abandoned it, the packers tried repeatedly to perfect the pool. There were several major reorganizations and numerous minor ones; each attempted to provide stronger enforcement procedures and a more efficient administrative structure to increase the pool's effectiveness. Like the pooling agreements in other industries, however, those devised by the packers ultimately failed.[10]

COMBINATION IN THE DRESSED BEEF INDUSTRY: THE ALLERTON POOL, 1886–1893

Although the first pool was crude and unsophisticated, it was prototypical of the agreements that followed in the 1890s. Since the packers had not yet mastered the techniques of cooperation and were not yet completely convinced of the benefits of collusion, they were reluctant to sacrifice much of their independence. They confined their agreement to the Northeast where all major packers had marketing outlets and where the market "filled up" first. The pool theoretically would enable the packers to solve their competitive problems in that area without restricting their freedom of movement in other areas where they had just begun to build a market for dressed beef. In addition to an agreement on fixed market shares for each firm in the Northeast, the packers devised a crude system of uniform profit margins, arranged the same price lists for their dealers in certain areas, divided public contracts, made price agreements as to the buying of livestock, and frequently used their collective power to compel retailers to accept their meat.[11]

To the packers the need for some kind of cooperation had become quite obvious. "If we did not understand pretty nearly what everybody was shipping down into certain territory when we all have our houses in different places, and if we should dump a great lot of cars down there and the market would only command so much, we should just be slaughtered in no time," explained Simeon Armour.[12] That is, the problem of planning and matching supply and demand was now one that had to be faced jointly by the firms, whereas earlier it had been confined to each separate firm. P. D. Armour voiced a similar defense of collusion when he insisted that the uncertainties of the market and the constant threat of oversupply and declining prices in the Northeast had made it "absolutely necessary" to "arrange price lists for cut meats and canned meats from time to time with others producing the same commodities." Otherwise, argued Armour, there would be no way "to protect dealers in these articles from the sudden and violent decline in prices which would otherwise follow an oversupply."[13]

Sensitive to the need for cooperation, packers soon experienced the frustrations of trying to make their agreements work. Between 1886 and

1892, their firms expanded into new areas at a rapid rate. Armour stretched his distribution network into parts of the Northwest, near Minneapolis-St. Paul, and into the southern cities of Atlanta and Savannah, Georgia; Charlotte, North Carolina; Memphis, Tennessee; and Charleston, South Carolina. In all, he built 88 branch houses. Although the number and location of the Swift branch houses built during this same period cannot be determined, the New Englander undoubtedly maintained a strong position, for by the end of 1893, Swift had a total of 190 sales outlets, perhaps a dozen or so of which were in the Southeast and Northwest. To supply their rapidly expanding distribution networks, more slaughtering plants were built. In 1886 Hammond established a slaughtering plant at Omaha, Nebraska. In 1888 Swift established his second slaughtering plant at Kansas City and followed Hammond to Omaha in 1890; two years later, a Swift & Company plant was erected at the St. Louis Stockyards. Morris purchased the East St. Louis Packing and Provision Company in 1889.[14]

As the packers extended their distribution networks in the South and built more slaughtering plants to secure more meat, competitive marketing problems similar to those that first arose in the Northeast occurred in other areas. On May 30, 1891, Armour, Morris, Swift, and a representative of the Hammond Company organized another regional meat pool to allot meat shipments into Territory "B," including the states south of the Ohio and the Potomac rivers, and east of the Mississippi River and the states of Louisiana and Arkansas.[15] Precisely what the relationship of this pool was to the first regional agreement is difficult to determine. Whether it was a separate agreement or merely an extension of the earlier agreement in the Northeast, its objective was the same: the regulation of meat shipments and the stabilization of prices.

The entry of a new competitor, the Cudahy Packing Company, and the depression of the early 1890s, however, soon demonstrated just how unreliable such voluntary and piecemeal agreements were. Unlike those firms that attempted entry and failed, Cudahy moved at a propitious time,[16] breaking down barriers and expanding its business at a rapid rate. That company succeeded largely because it had the managerial and financial resources necessary to implement a strategy of vertical integration quickly and effectively. "Their credit, like their capacity is simply unlimited," commented one trade journal in 1892.[17] Even P. D. Armour had to admit, those "Cudahy boys are the . . . smartest irishmen [*sic*] in America."[18] The Cudahys, like the Armours and Swifts, were many in number—there being four brothers in all—and hardly newcomers to the business world. Edward and Michael, who were the packers of the family, learned the trade (and all its tricks) as top-ranking executives, first at Plankinton & Armour Company of Milwaukee and later at Armour &

Company of Chicago.[19] In 1875 Michael Cudahy accepted a partnership in Armour & Company of Chicago and assumed full control of plant operations. Edward, the younger of the two, joined Armour & Company two years later, serving first as a livestock buyer, then as a manager of an Armour branch house, and finally as assistant manager of plant operations. In 1887 the Cudahy boys enlisted Armour's help and moved to South Omaha to capitalize on the opportunities that were opening up as packing operations moved closer to the source of supply. That year they organized the Armour-Cudahy packing plant. Of the 7,500 shares originally issued, Armour purchased 2,350 and the remainder went to the Cudahys.[20] Three years later, complaining that the packers were "doing too large a business for the territory,"[21] Armour sold his share of the stock to Michael and Edward. The firm was then capitalized at $750,000 and its annual sales for 1890 totalled $13,471,000.[22]

Now in full charge, the Cudahys renamed the firm Cudahy Company, increased the capital stock, and set out to expand their business. Aware of the competition between the Big Four in the Northeast, the Cudahys wisely selected the South, Southwest, Northwest, and Pacific Coast as their major marketing targets. Following the strategy of vertical integration laid down by its predecessors, the company erected a packing plant in Los Angeles in 1892 and another in Sioux City, Iowa, two years later; built several branch houses in Chicago, one each in Omaha and Lincoln, Nebraska, and Minneapolis, Minnesota; and acquired a fleet of 90 refrigerator cars and several peddler car routes in the South by 1892.[23] Rapidly increasing profits accompanied and helped to finance geographical expansion into new areas. Between 1888 and 1891 the company's profits soared, jumping from $50,000 in 1888 to $825,000 by 1891.[24]

As Cudahy's business expanded into Kentucky, Tennessee, Utah, Oregon, and South Dakota, it undermined the pooling strategy of the Big Four. Clearly Cudahy could gain only at the expense of the packers' in many market areas. Fearing a loss of their individual market shares, the Big Four abandoned cooperation in an attempt to protect their interests. Before long the packers were at war. By May 1892, the pools were not functioning.

During the succeeding twelve months of competitive warfare, conditions became "intolerable."[25] The depression hit, intensifying competition and making it even more costly. Swift, in particular, felt the full impact of the squeeze. To finance the expansion of the late 1880s and early 1890s, Swift had borrowed heavily. With most of his capital tied up in plants, equipment, and real estate, he was hard pressed when the banks began to recall loans and demand payment. "We went into the Panic in May of 1893, owing about $10 million to the banks," recalled his son Louis; "for several months then, he [G. F. Swift] literally did not know two days in advance just where he was going to get the money with which to meet his obligations. Times were hard, hard as ever they had been in the memory of man."[26]

The depression affected all aspects of the meat business. Demand for meat products slumped and both beef and cattle prices dropped. Western banks refused to handle eastern paper, thereby limiting purchases. Across the country, loans were called in. Packers nevertheless had to continue to purchase livestock and supply their customers with meat if they hoped to have adequate working capital. Having taken the financial risks of allowing some of their dealers or customers to defer payment of goods until they were sold, they now found it difficult to collect payment. To protect themselves, Armour, Morris, Swift, and Hammond acted jointly to tighten credit measures, demanding settlement from their customers every Monday. Swift cut some of his losses simply by slashing wages 10 percent, while Armour bought gold in England to pay his workforce. Other meat wholesalers with fewer resources had fewer alternatives and simply cut credit to retailers. Retail butchers responded by combining against wholesalers in Cincinnati, Kansas City, and New York City. Some firms sold out to large concerns, while others simply disappeared.[27]

THE FIRST VEEDER POOL, 1893–1896

With future prospects of profitability jeopardized by the onset of a depression and the threat of unrestricted competition, it was soon obvious once more that much could be gained by cooperating. Having lost "considerable money,"[28] the old pool members undertook a major reorganization of their first pool. In recognition of Cudahy's successful entry into the industry, the membership was enlarged to include the new oligopolist. Also included was the Armour Packing Company of Kansas City and the Morris-controlled East St. Louis Dressed Beef & Provision Company. Although the pool was again confined primarily to the regulation of meat shipments into the Northeast, as was the case in 1886, shipments from Missouri River packing points as well as those from Chicago were included.[29] Allotments were made on the basis of each firm's percentage share of the total volume shipped into the territory by all members during the previous year (averaged on a weekly basis). Accordingly, the largest share went to Swift & Company. Armour & Company of Chicago earned the second largest; then came Morris, Hammond, and the Armour Packing Company of Kansas City. Cudahy, the newcomer, was given the smallest allotment.[30]

As the packers had learned from their previous pooling experience, the regulation of shipments by itself was not sufficient to assure the smooth operation and effectiveness of the pool. Close coordination between supply and demand and stronger enforcement provisions were also necessary if the agreement was to be effective. Moreover, unless there were some way to stabilize prices and achieve roughly equal profitability on each pound of beef sold, the packers realized that the agreement would be short-lived.

The packers therefore worked out a common method of figuring costs and margins, instituted fines and penalties for violations of the pooling agreement, and built a formal administrative structure to implement the various provisions of the agreement and handle the flow of information. The pact, implemented on May 13, 1893, was supposed to last for one year.

The use of margins and of what the packers termed "test cost" figures in administering prices, was not, of course, a new development. As we saw earlier, the test cost system arose simultaneously with oligopoly in the mid-1880s.[31] What was new was the systematic adoption by the five dominant firms of a uniform method of computing those test costs and margins. Again, the principles of systematization and rationalization originally worked out inside the separate firms were now being extended to include planning on an industrywide basis. To find the "test cost" of dressed beef, an agreed fixed killing charge was added to the cost of the live animal. From this sum, there was deducted a fixed allowance for by-products. An estimated selling price (or what the packers termed the "cost price") was obtained by adding to the "test cost" an agreed and uniform margin of profit.[32] By using the same method of costing and standardizing the profit included in the cost, the packers could arrive at a similar, desired selling price. Although prices for dressed beef would vary between individual firms because of differences in the cost of the live animal, in the long run they would tend to stabilize.[33]

Allocation of shipments and the provision and utilization of information on costs and margins required formal organization. Cartel headquarters were established on the sixth floor of the Counselman Building in downtown Chicago. Henry Veeder, lawyer and son of Albert Veeder of Swift & Company, was appointed official secretary of the pooling association and was put in charge of administration. He was assisted by 10 to 15 workers. Expenses for salaries, rental fees, supplies, etc., were to be shared by each of the members in proportion to their percentage allotments. To enforce the agreement a system of fines and penalties was instituted. So that prompt payment of shortages could be made, packers established a "clearing fund" of $7,500.[34]

Veeder's duties were carefully defined. His principal function was to compile the data sent to him every Monday by individual firms. That information consisted of the following "statements" or reports:

1. A "shipment" statement from each firm showing the quantity of beef shipped by it during the week ending the preceding Saturday into the northeastern territory.
2. A "margin" statement showing the difference between the test cost at the point of origin (packing plant) and the "closed selling price" (final average price at which the beef was actually sold) obtained by each party in the territory during the preceding week.
3. A small "summary" statement from each firm showing the "average margins" (average difference between the test cost and closed selling price) received for the territory.[35]

Veeder put the shipment statements from each party on a large sheet that showed the amount in pounds shipped by each firm into the territory and the total shipped by all the pool members into the territory. Margin statements from each firm were also transcribed onto one large sheet. The data showed how many cars of beef were sold, the closed (actual average) selling price and closed (actual average) margins received by each firm, and the total number of cars and the average margins received by all parties in the Northeast. Every Monday night Veeder mailed out to each member the statements showing the amounts shipped into the territory compared to the allotments of each party for the territory. If anyone had shipped less than his assigned percentage for that week, Veeder paid that firm (by a check drawn on his own account, established for him by the pool members) a sum equal to 40 cents for every 100 pounds "under." Similarly, if the statement showed that some company had shipped more than its allotment, that firm was to send Veeder a check covering overshipments, based upon the same payment per 100 pounds.

At pool meetings held every Tuesday, the chief executive officer and head of the beef department of each firm discussed the data. On the basis of margin and shipment reports, they appraised the general condition of the market, revised percentages whenever necessary, and formulated "working" margins for the following week.[36] Margin reports were used as a barometer of market conditions. Reports showing minus margins indicated that beef was theoretically selling below cost plus profit and that supply and demand were not coordinated to the packers' satisfaction. Frequently, margins were revised or shipments curtailed in order to correct the imbalance. Veeder explained in detail how the packers used the information:

The margin sheets prepared by me were used to determine the condition of the several markets. They showed the closed results [actual average sales] in each market during the past week. . . . [The margin] was a barometer. If the country as a whole showed there was too much meat on the market, that the markets were glutted, I would send out notices that shipments for the current week would be limited, to relieve the markets from the glut. . . . If prices were good in "A" [northeastern territory], that would be considered and the quantities would be increased. If the market was strong, the supply of beef shipped would be increased, and if weak, withheld to a figure. . . . I had the amounts shipped into the territory, but that would not determine whether the markets were glutted. Low prices did not necessarily mean less meat for the next week. The amount was determined upon the conditions of the market besides high or low prices.[37]

Decisions regarding allotments, the amount of profit, and the estimated fixed charges were made at pool headquarters by the presidents or representatives of participating firms. Instructions regarding the same were then wired or mailed to territorial supervisors in charge of branch houses in particular regions and sometimes to head buyers at Chicago and other packing plants. It was the responsibility of the territorial managers to communicate appropriate instructions to branch house managers.[38]

The provision of information concerning a competitor's business and the general condition of the market was perhaps the most important aspect of the pool—certainly the knowledge gained would be more than temporarily useful to the packers. But there were other ways in which they hoped to benefit. Market sharing, which also featured uniform methods of figuring costs and margins, was theoretically an ideal way to help solve the problems of coordination and competition. Under such an arrangement, the incentive to compete or cut prices could be expected to be reduced drastically, for each firm moved along a demand curve that was a fixed share of the industry demand curve and had the same elasticity as the industry curve at every price.[39] Uniformity in figuring costs and margins would prevent erratic reactions to changes in demand or supply. By standardizing the margin of profit included in costs and employing similar costing methods, the packers could gain some control over prices and equalize their profits per pound of beef, at least in the long run.[40]

Of course, the packers' view of the world was colored by considerations of self-interest. From a wider point of view, there was a danger of their manipulating the market and extracting very high profits from their control. Moreover, if they had tight control over themselves, the only check on their power would be the possibility of entry by new competitors.

As useful as the pooling agreement seemed to the packers in theory, in practice, harmony and complete cooperation were not so easily secured. A system of fines could deter but could not prevent those in the pool from acting in their own self-interest whenever it seemed necessary or more profitable to do so. Because it was legally unenforceable, the pool was potentially unstable; it soon became unstable in fact.

Before the year had elapsed, pool members were finding it difficult to cooperate. Although as late as 1893 only two regions—the Northeast and selective states in the Southeast—were subject to pooling, continued expansion in these areas triggered disagreement over percentage allotments. During 1893, Armour, Morris, and Cudahy built a total of 39 branch houses—the largest number established in any single year. Of that number, Armour built 17, Morris 8, and Cudahy 2, making their respective totals as of 1893—89, 52, and 18.[41] Tensions between the firms were inevitable.

Upon the expiration of the pool in 1894, each firm demanded an increased percentage as a condition for renewing the agreement. Arguments also arose concerning the accuracy of some of the shipment and margin reports submitted by the various companies. Only after a great deal of haggling did the pool members decide to extend the arrangement for another two years. At the same time, they extended their agreement in the Southeast to include more states.[42]

During the next two years competition coexisted alongside apparent cooperation. As the packers began to discover, the vast size of their enterprises and the geographical distance between controlling units of each firm and sales outlets in the field sometimes made complete cooperation difficult. Even if agreement could be secured at the top during pool meetings, there was a possibility that it would not always be achieved at the selling end. Not only were branch house managers tempted to engage in unauthorized price competition with their rivals in order to push sales, but the rapid perishability of meat often forced them to sell below the requested margins. Again, some members charged others with deliberately falsifying their reports, submitting inaccurate statements so that it would appear as if a firm were abiding by its allotments, when in fact, it was shipping more than its share and increasing its profits at the expense of other members in the pool.[43]

Meanwhile the packers continued to integrate backwards, building more plants and investing in stockyards. In 1893 the Swifts, Allertons, and Morrises became stockholders in the St. Louis National Stockyards Company. The capital of the company increased from $1.25 million in 1893 to $4 million by 1896. In the latter year, Swift organized the St. Joseph Stockyards Company with an authorized capital of $500,000. Together, the packers controlled over 500 branch houses in 1896; they had built a total of 17 slaughtering plants, and Swift owned one stockyard. Where beef comprised the only product at some plants, operations were expanded to include pork, lamb and veal.[44]

To utilize their marketing resources more fully and cut unit costs, packers began to diversify into new areas, such as poultry, cheese, and other dairy products, which could be distributed through the existing marketing organization at little additional cost. As the head of Swift & Company's Commercial Research Department, L. D. H. Weld explained years later, "These products could be placed in the same refrigerated cars, and sold through the same branches. . . . The handling of these additional products increased the volume of business with only a slight increase in overhead expense, with the result that the cost of selling per hundred weight of product was reduced on both the meat and the product handled."[45] Although the depression made such a cost-saving strategy especially attractive, the more immediate impact of diversification was to spread competition to new areas and make cooperation among pool participants all the more difficult.

A more serious threat to the pool's stability during 1894–1896, however, was the appearance of still another aggressive competitor outside the combine. This time the maverick firm was Schwarzschild & Sulzberger.[46] Until 1893, S & S had been a New York-based cattle exporting and shipping firm that also slaughtered meats locally for the city's kosher trade. With the westward movement of livestock production and the rise of the large western packing firms, however, S & S realized that if it was to continue to compete effectively it would have to secure slaughtering facilities in the West and extend a distribution network throughout the country, as had the Big Four and Cudahy. The purchase of the old Phoenix slaughtering plant in Kansas City in 1893 signaled its move into the new western regions. Not as careful as the Cudahys in locating their branch houses, S & S moved into areas already near saturation and where the others were already pooling. While expansion thereafter was rapid, there were problems inherent in the strategy which began to surface in the early 1900s.[47] Backed by eastern capital and the funds from an already flourishing business, S & S pushed their distribution networks into the Northeast and South, erecting their own sales outlets or making arrangements with commission merchants to handle their beef. By 1896 they had more than 50 branch houses, over three-fourths of which were in the Northeast. Somewhat amazed at the firm's rapid progress, the *National Provisioner* outlined part of the firm's expansion program:

> We are informed that they have in view a site in Chicago for the erection of a large distributing center. They are making direct sales by carload lots to Hazelton,

Figure V.1. Branch Houses of Major Meat-Packers in the U.S.: Regional Expansion 1886–1903

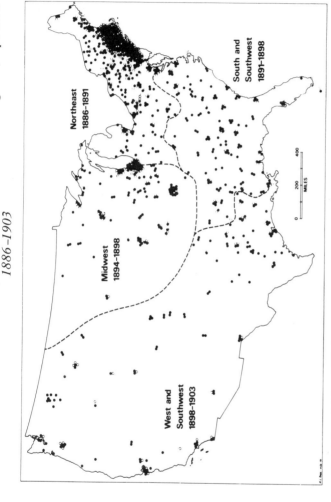

Source: Compiled from FTC, *Report on the Meat-Packing Industry, 1919,* Summary and Part I, p. 153, and Minutes of the Board of Directors, Swift & Company, Swift & Company Archives, Chicago, Illinois.

Pennsylvania; Joliet, Illinois; and St. Louis, Missouri; Worcester and Lowell, Massachusetts; and have made contracts with such houses as Nauss Bros. & Co., and Richard Webber, who are among the largest retailers in New York City. Their hotel and prime beef business in New York City is constantly on the increase. . . . To cap the climax, this concern, which has been running a line of refrigerator cars, has secured the improved Chase refrigerator car patent and has ordered an addition of 100 cars of the latest style. They have two establishments in Boston and many connections, like that with A. A. Taylor and John P. Squire and Company of Boston, as commission representatives.[48]

As was the case with Cudahy, S & S had both the financial and managerial resources necessary to implement the strategy of vertical integration swiftly and effectively.

S & S's rapidly expanding trade quickly became a source of concern to pool members. By 1895 the newcomer's share of the market had reached such proportions that it disrupted the pool. The members discovered that if they shipped their allotted volume into the areas where S & S competed, they flooded the market and were forced to sell beef at such a low price that there was little or no return on investment. On the other hand, if they attempted to cut back shipments, S & S might increase its shipments. Realizing that S & S's cooperation was necessary if the pool was to work, the pool members tried to persuade the newcomer to join. Negotiations proved unproductive.[49] On May 13, 1896, the packers suspended pool meetings, having been unable to control the industry satisfactorily.

By April 1897, although S & S still refused to join the pool, the old members were again convinced that they could not operate profitably without it. At the suggestion of Gustavus Swift and E. M. Martyn, head of the beef department of Armour & Co. and Armour's right-hand man, the pool was converted to a "statistical bureau" until more comprehensive arrangements could be made. The bureau was to serve solely as "a clearing house of information." There were to be no regular pool meetings, and no instructions concerning margins were to be sent out. Nor were there to be any agreements concerning market shares or any limitations on shipments. The members were simply to exchange information about margins and prices actually received and amounts actually shipped.[50]

Meanwhile the packers continued to exert pressure on S & S. This time, however, they strengthened their bargaining position with new and more convincing threats. Swift apparently spearheaded the drive against S & S. His plan was to enlist the help of other pool members in establishing a kosher beef house in New York City to compete with that of S & S. Only P. D. Armour remained aloof from the plan. Although he approved of it in principle, he preferred his own strategy. In a letter to the wife of his son Philip, Jr., dated March 5, 1898, Armour wrote: "Tell Phil that Swift has bought a piece of land in New York and is going to open a beef house for koshering as against S & S. I think it is a good move and I am very glad to see him do it. I think Morris is with him in the deal, and I don't know but [sic] Cudahy and Hammond. I know we are not, and he felt a little hard toward us because we would not join him. But Swift likes to fight so well, I thought I would let him have the game all to himself."[51] Armour did not intend to sit idle, however. Employing an old tactic, he tried to apply indirect pressure on S & S by wooing the Santa Fe Railroad, the main carrier of S & S's business out of Kansas City. In a letter to his nephew Kirkland in Kansas City, he explained the rationale of such a policy:

> The Santa Fe is a pretty big institution and it permeates an immense amount of territory that is tributary to Kansas City, and they can do a good deal of harm or a good deal of good, whichever way they are inclined. Now as a matter of policy you should try to court their favors a little bit, and make them passive friends, if not real friends. Simply do this as a matter of policy on general principles. They are great feeders to Kansas City, and your [opinion] that S & S would hold them . . . is simply boy talk. Perhaps they will hold them and perhaps they will not. The question, as far as we are concerned, is entirely for us to do our part in trying to hold them level.[52]

While such pressure tactics may have been effective, two years of uncontrolled competition probably proved more influential in persuading S & S to cooperate. Late in 1897 the newcomer made it known that it was ready to cooperate if an arrangement "could be made which would have the effect of terminating the war among the parties."[53]

THE SECOND VEEDER POOL, 1898–1901

On January 17, 1898, the old pool members reorganized the pooling association and began to work out an arrangement with S & S.[54] The most immediate problem was the readjustment of percentages. S & S's admission to the pool obviously meant that the market shares of some of the old members would have to be reduced. A related and even more serious problem was the pool's inability to enforce its allocations. The experience of the last six years made it obvious that unless new measures were implemented to strengthen the pool, it would suffer the same fate as earlier agreements.

The arrangement finally worked out was similar to the old Veeder pool, but included several new measures. Stiffer fines were to be levied against "cheaters." A task force of auditors was employed to verify reports and make periodic inspections of each firm's books. As before, shipments from Chicago and Missouri River points into the Northeast were to be regulated on the basis of each firm's share of the total volume shipped into that territory during a previous period, but in addition to this "general allotment," specific allotments were to be made for specific competitive points within the Northeast, where two or more packers competed. Similarly, margin statements were to be compiled not only for the general northeastern region but for every specific point where two or more packers competed. Under the new arrangement the packers were subject to two "fines."[55] If a firm exceeded its general allotment into the Northeast, it paid a 75-cent (rather than a 40-cent) fine for every 100 pounds "over"; if it also shipped in excess of its allotments to specific competitive points, it paid an additional $1.50 for every 100 pounds "over." Members had a right to withdraw after 30 days' notice. Meetings were to be held every Tuesday afternoon. The agreement, implemented on March 15, 1898, when S & S became a formal member, was supposed to cover three years, from 1898 to 1901.

Within four months the packers had extended the pool into three new territories. On July 9, 1898, agreements similar to that in the Northeast were concluded for Cook County, Illinois (designated Territory "C"); Territory "D," surrounding St. Louis and including all of Illinois (except Cook County) and Iowa (except Council Bluffs); and Colorado (Territory "E"). Since these areas were not considered as "competitive" nor as "important," there was simply one general allotment for each territory and a single, smaller fine of 50 cents per 100 pounds. These agreements were scheduled to last 131 weeks, or as long as the remaining period of agreement for Territory "A."[56]

As had been the case previously, the pool's extension signaled the continuing expansion of the industry and the need to cooperate to regulate the ever-increasing flows of meat into new territories such as Texas, California, Utah, and Colorado, where capacity had begun to outrun demand at profitable prices. During the three-year period from 1898 to 1901, the packers constructed more than 135 new branch houses and eight slaughtering plants, making the total cumulative number as of 1901, 618 branches and 28 plants. In 1898 a new Hammond Packing Co. (of Illinois) was organized with a capital of $1.7 million and a slaughtering plant at St. Joseph, Missouri. That same year, Swift & Co. and Morris & Co. also built slaughtering plants there. Upon receiving an attractive $1 million stock bonus from the St. Paul Stockyards Company of Minnesota in 1898, Swift constructed a plant in that city, prompting merchants of rival Minneapolis to offer Armour a similar contract.[57]

More supplies were needed to feed the growing distribution networks. In 1898 Armour & Co. contracted to build a plant at Omaha in return for land and a stock bonus from that city's stockyards company. A year later Armour acquired $300,000 worth of stock in the St. Louis National

Stock Yards Co. In return for locating a slaughtering plant in Sioux City, Iowa, Armour received another stock bonus of 4,000 shares and 12½ acres of land from the city's stockyards. The Cudahy Packing Co. made a similar contract with the Kansas City stockyards, agreeing to build a plant in Kansas City in return for $500,000 cash and land valued at $129,000. Meanwhile, S & S started their own slaughtering plant at Chicago without any bonuses.[58]

As we saw earlier, in order to use their growing capacity more fully, the packers turned to diversification. Along with poultry, they began to expand their line of by-products, entering the leather, soap, fertilizer, and glue businesses, usually setting up auxiliary plants or gaining control of stock in existing companies. By 1901 Swift had acquired nine produce houses, and Swift and Armour each built a fertilizer works in Atlanta, Georgia, in 1902. Swift built another fertilizer plant in Wilmington, North Carolina, acquired rendering companies in St. Paul, Minnesota, and Omaha, Nebraska, and organized the Ashland Leather Co. that same year. A more common means of diversifying was securing control of related companies through stock ownership.[59]

While the need to keep resources fully employed promoted extensive vertical integration and diversification, it also led the packers into new pooling arrangements. On July 2 and August 11, 1900, the packers began dividing allotments of mutton into the Northeast and Cook County, Illinois (Territory "C"), and allotments for veal to Cook County. A penalty of one percent per pound was to be levied against those who shipped in excess of their allotments. Before the end of the decade, the packers had also organized separate pools in the hide, canned meats, sausage and cut meat branches, as well as in fresh meats.[60]

Meanwhile, the packers undertook new measures in an effort to make their fresh meat pool work more effectively. In May 1900, percentages were again readjusted and a new resolution concerning overshipments was adopted. The problem was the familiar one. The expansion of the capacity of individual firms and the increase in the volume of meats shipped had brought substantial unused capacity in various markets. To alleviate the problem, the packers resolved that:

> Any member of this Association being shipped to any competing point, his over-shipment showing to be more than 19,000 lbs. above the maximum weekly ship-ment, shall reduce said average within the following two weeks, but failing to do so, shall pay a penalty of 1½¢ per lb. on average shown at end of said two weeks in excess of 19,000 lbs.; said penalty to be promptly collected by the Secretary and one-half by him applied towards the expenses of the Association and the other half promptly paid by him to the other parties who are shippers to such competing point, divided among them as their percentage interests shall appear.
>
> The payment of the penalty shall be continued at the end of each two weeks as long as an average of more than 19,000 lbs. is shown.[61]

An executive committee composed of representatives of the participating firms was also appointed to supervise the general operation of the agreement.

Yet as important as these measures may have been in the short run, they, like their predecessors, failed to provide the long-term stability the packers sought. As a result, their thoughts turned to the possibility of another, very different solution to their problems.

NOTES

1. Without internal records it is impossible to determine whether competition had become "cutthroat." However, the packers' pooling strategy suggests that prices and profits had dropped below a level that packers considered tolerable.

2. The National Packing Company was the product of their efforts. For details see Chapter VI, pp. 145–155.

3. See Table III.2.

4. "Exact Transcript of Shorthand Notes Taken at Interview with Edward Morris, February 2, 1905," U.S. Bureau of Corporations Record No. 122, File No. 738, National Archives, Washington, D.C.

5. *Breeder's Gazette*, June 6, 1888, p. 563, describes the nature and impact of this "new" competition:

> the cause of the difficulty, we believe, will be found to be not so much in the nature of combination as many good people suppose, but very largely in an unusual competition different in character from that which the market had previously known. Under the old condition of affairs the butchers enjoyed a large measure of profit which they appeared in nowise anxious to abridge by reducing the prices of meat to consumers, and any competition between them in this direction was purely local in its operations and temporary in its duration, while they were so numerous and their needs so imperative that the competition between them in the principal cattle markets had a tendency to steady and sustain values. All the tendencies and influences surrounding the market were then in favor of the producers. But with the growth of the dressed-beef interest all this has been changed. The large margin of profits of the local butchers presented an opportunity for this trade to gain a foothold, for those engaged in it doing business on a larger scale did not need such wide margins to render their business profitable.

Because oligopolistic competition often brought an end to the classic type of competition based on prices, economists have had difficulty analyzing the new competition. Many have associated the emergence of oligopoly with a decline of competition. (See Arthur R. Burns, *The Decline of Competition* (New York, 1936), pp. 165–166.) I argue that the nature of competition changed and that oligopoly meant the emergence of a new type of competition, based less on prices than on considerations such as product, quality, service, etc. The point is that competition did not disappear. Rather, it changed form.

6. FTC, *Report on the Meat-Packing Industry, 1919*, Pt. V, "Profits of the Packers," p. 21.

7. Minutes of the Board of Directors Meetings, 1885–1912, Swift & Co., Swift & Co. Archives, Chicago, Ill. See text, p. 156 for graphic illustration of packers' profits.

8. *Vest Report*, p. 369.

9. The *Vest Report* provides what little evidence there is of the Allerton pool. No doubt both the packers and Allerton recognized the advantages of such an agreement. The packers undoubtedly saw that part of their coordination and distribution problems stemmed from the movement of livestock, which continued, despite the increasing tonnage movement of dressed beef. Since Allerton was one of the city's leading livestock shippers

and also a former evener for the Pennsylvania Railroad, his cooperation in coordinating meat flows into eastern markets could prove invaluable. An agreement to divide market shares was probably even more attractive to Allerton, for it would enable him to maintain a share of the market for a longer time, despite significant cost disadvantages of shipping livestock. Just what Allerton's role in the pool was, however, is difficult to determine. Pool meetings were held in Allerton's Chicago office until the early 1890s.

10. There are few studies that attempt to integrate the strategy of pooling into a broader analysis of industrial developments. One good exception is Charles Wilson's study of the British soap industry, *The History of Unilever*, 2 vols. (New York, 1968), particularly, Vol. I, pp. 59–72. For general information on pooling in the United States see Wallace Belcher, "Industrial Pooling Agreements," in *Quarterly Journal of Economics*, 19 (November 1905): 111–123; William B. Stevens, "A Classification of Pools and Associations Based on American Experience," *American Economic Review*, 32 (September 1913):545–575; Eliot Jones, *The Trust Problem in the United States* (New York, 1921), pp. 6–18; Jeremiah Jenks, *The Trust Problem* (New York, 1903), pp. 108–109; William Ripley, *Trusts, Pools and Corporations* (Boston, 1905).

11. *Vest Report*, pp. 189, 208, 241, 328. The other major source of information on the packers' pools is the record of various court cases, in particular *U.S. v. Louis Swift, et al.*, 1910. Swift & Co. Archives, Chicago, holds transcripts and evidence in black, loose-leaf notebooks; reported *sub. nom.* 186 Fed. 1002 and 188 Fed. 92 (N.D. Ill., 1910); *St. of Mo. v. Hammond Packing Co. and St. Louis Dressed Beef and Provision Co.*, No. 16090, Joint Abstract of Record and Transcript of Evidence, 1913, Swift & Co. Archives, entitled "Briefs"; reported *sub. nom., State ex. rel. Barker v. Armour Packing Co.* 265 Mo. 121, 176 S.W. 382 (1915); *U.S. v. National Packing Co.*, Cr. 4384 (N.D. Ill., 1910). Most secondary sources rely on the *Vest Report* for information. See FTC, *Report on the Meat-Packing Industry, 1919*, Summary and Pt. I, pp. 46–47; Part II, "Evidence of Combination Among Packers," pp. 11–17; Richard J. Arnould, "Changing Patterns of Concentration in American Meat Packing, 1880–1963," *Business History Review*, 45 (Spring 1971), pp. 19, 23; Burns, *The Decline of Competition*, pp. 148, 154; Simon N. Whitney, *Antitrust Policies* (New York, 1958), Vol. I, pp. 27–94; William H. Nicholls, "Market-Sharing in the Packing Industry," *Journal of Farm Economics*, 22 (April 1940):225–241.

12. *Vest Report*, p. 455.

13. *Ibid.*, p. 446.

14. The building of branch houses and plants can be traced in the correspondence of railroad executives, Chicago, Burlington & Quincy Railroad Papers, Record No. 33-2.1, Newberry Library, Chicago, Ill.; R. G. Dun & Co. have information on Armour, Swift, and Hammond; *Vest Report*, pp. 366–367; FTC, *Report on the Meat-Packing Industry, 1919*, Summary and Pt. I, pp. 153, 239, provides a table showing the number of branch houses constructed by each of the packers (except Hammond) yearly, 1885–1917. See also Appendix C, pp. 261–266.

15. *U.S. v. Louis Swift*, p. 755, statement of Henry Veeder, Swift & Co. (Swift & Co. Archives).

16. The slackening demand that accompanied the depression made the pool particularly vulnerable to breakdown. Not only were pool members more likely to cheat in order to expand their shares of a dwindling market to keep their plants running full and steady, but a newcomer like Cudahy could take advantage of falling prices for livestock to undercut the pool's prices for dressed beef. Expansion during times of depression can also be less costly, since the cost of plant and equipment can be less than during periods of relative prosperity or growing demand.

17. *National Provisioner*, December 17, 1892, p. 15.

18. *Ibid.*, p. 15, quoting Armour.

19. The Cudahys need a historian. This account has been pieced together from the

following sources: John O'Rourke, "A History," Cudahy & Co. *Yearbook, 1890–1924,* Corporation Records, Baker Library, Harvard Graduate School of Business; Clemen, *The American Livestock and Meat Industry,* pp. 164–165; *National Provisioner,* December 17, 1892, p. 15; July 8, 1893, pp. 18, 23; July 15, 1893, p. 16; June 16, 1900, p. 15; January 31, 1903, p. 39. John Cudahy's adventures as a speculator are detailed in a series of articles on the so-called "hog-clique" in the provision market (*National Provisioner,* July 8, 1893, p. 14; July 29, 1893, p. 15; August 5, 1893, pp. 14, 16).

20. *Report of the Commissioner of Corporations on the Beef Industry, 1905,* p. 296.

21. *Vest Report,* p. 483.

22. FTC, *Report on the Meat-Packing Industry, 1919,* Pt. V, "Profits of the Packers," p. 32.

23. *National Provisioner,* July 15, 1893, p. 16. O'Rourke, "A History," states that the Cudahys arranged in 1892 with one of the western railroads to run a special train from Omaha at noon each day to transport their beef to Chicago. In return for special services the Cudahys guaranteed the railroad at least five or more cars of meat a day. To cut costs the firm built all its refrigerator cars in its own shops and erected its own repair shops. Before long the firm had installed private wires to connect the main plant at Omaha with branches at Kansas City and Sioux City, Iowa, and was communicating daily by phone to branch house managers in the East.

24. FTC, *Report on the Meat-Packing Industry, 1919,* Pt. V, "Profits of Packers," p. 32.

25. *U.S. v. Louis Swift,* pp. 754–755, statement of Henry Veeder of Swift & Co. (Swift & Co. Archives).

26. Swift and Van Vlissingen, *The Yankee of the Yards,* p. 30. Many of Swift's loans were with eastern banks. Thanks to the loyalty of many Swift employees and friends who poured money into the firm, however, his indebtedness to the banks had been reduced to $1 million by September 1893 (Pierce, *A History of Chicago,* Vol. III, p. 114).

27. Meats and provisions were in short supply in the East. Apparently, shipments from Chicago and western packing points were obtainable "only upon shipment of currency from New York or the receipt of drafts payable in Chicago." The National Live Stock Bank alerted shippers to eastern points that they would have to pay cash for their stock because the Bank would no longer honor Eastern drafts. The result "so handicapped shippers that they were obliged to remain idle, . . . Until eastern concerns forward sufficient funds to do business on a cash basis their agents here will enjoy a season of rest. This mean feature has given a bad odor to the cattle market, and has practically eliminated that element of competition which gives the most life and buoyancy to the trade." To ease financial stringency, the packers tightened their credit in the Northwest. In St. Paul, Minnesota, Armour, Swift, Cudahy, and several local packers agreed upon "A system . . . which binds the members of the combine not to give credit to any retailer longer than a week." Armour & Co. in August 1893 innovated in importing $500,000 worth of gold directly from Europe. A month later, in September, the *National Provisioner* noted that "Representatives in Albany, New York, of Armour & Company, Nelson Morris & Company, Swift & Company and Hammond & Company have combined for mutual protection. They will hereafter demand a settlement from their customers every Monday" (*National Provisioner,* August 12, 1893, pp. 16, 18; September 2, 1893, p. 19; June 9, 1894, p. 24; June 16, 1894, p. 25).

Actions such as these fueled rumors that the big packers were moving into the retail business. The packers consistently denied the charges but there is evidence to support the rumors (*National Provisioner,* February 10, 1894, pp. 18, 19; April 7, 1894, p. 21). However, independent wholesalers seem to have been more actively and directly involved in the move into retailing. The depression squeezed their profits severely. "So small have profits grown," explained the *National Provisioner* (November 3, 1894, p. 15), "that attempts have already been made on the part of wholesalers to run retail establishments in connection with their wholesale places, thereby eliminating the butcher's profit and eventually the butcher himself." In the case of both small and large packers, however, the move into retailing, if it was tried at all, proved unprofitable. The trade journal considered it an unwise strategy that would "only bring forth a greater competition among more powerful rivals and in the end the profits will not be larger while the risks are more unevenly distributed and will probably have increased."

28. *U.S.* v. *Louis Swift,* p. 755, statement of Henry Veeder of Swift & Co.

29. Much of what follows is from Henry Veeder's testimony, *St. of Mo.* v. *Hammond Packing Co.,* Record Vol. I, pp. 97–145; Vol. II, pp. 479–997; and from *U.S.* v. *Louis Swift,* pp. 1–775.

30. The court cases do not record the amount of the first allotments; they simply reveal who took the largest, smallest, etc., shares.

31. See text, Chapter III, p. 73.

32. Numerous descriptions of the early margin and cost system are found in the court cases mentioned above. For a more recent discussion, see George E. Putnam, "Joint Cost in the Packing Industry," *Journal of Political Economy,* 29 (December–January 1921):293–303, and "Unit Costs as a Guiding Factor in Buying Operations," *Journal of Political Economy,* 29 (October 1921):663–675.

33. The consequences of such market-sharing agreements are described in Burns, *The Decline of Competition,* pp. 146–194; William H. Nicholls, *Imperfect Competition in the Agricultural Industries* (Ames, Iowa, 1941), pp. 225–240.

34. Veeder drew money from the fund to pay packers who were "short" or did not receive the extent of their allotment, and deposited money into the fund from packers who were "long" or over their specific allotments. In one sense, the fund functioned as the pool's bank. The $7,500 was an arbitrary amount, contributed by the packers initially, to enable the pool to begin operations.

35. *U.S.* v. *Louis Swift,* pp. 758–759.

36. Margins generally refer to the difference between costs and prices, or the amount or percentage of profit derived from a sale. *Working margins* were the "targeted" profits, or what the packers hoped to get for their beef, as contrasted with what they actually received. The working margins, however, were based to some extent on past records of costs and prices. That is, packers devised working margins for each successive week, based on the past week's actual margins and supply and demand conditions in the market. Working margins were sent to territorial managers, who sent them to branch house managers as a guide to pricing policies. Because of different local conditions, branch house managers were often unable to meet the working margin; they had to sell below the requested price and therefore at a narrower margin than had been requested. The *closed margin* or *closed selling price* represented what the manager actually got for his meat. Although the working and closed margins might be the same, they often were not.

37. *U.S.* v. *Louis Swift,* p. 263, statement of Henry Veeder.

38. Although the following telegrams were relayed during a later period, 1910, they probably do not differ radically from the type of instructions sent out during the Veeder pool (*U.S.* v. *Louis Swift,* loose-leaf notebooks, Swift & Co. Archives):

> Send Swift & Co. . . . 6/30/10 to Number 1 New York, Number 1 Boston, Number 1 Philadelphia. We have taken some pretty low prices this week in beef, we think conditions will change; starting Tuesday beef each house for sale can be sold higher than sold last week, careful scrutiny of car sheets will show you some pretty cheap beef, some native so cheap that handsome plus margins should be shown as considerable native beef on the market next week will cost under 12 cents; we think shortage of cut beef will justify good plus margins which will materially help a higher selling price on other grades. Please carefully follow each house your jurisdiction accordingly. Have each house take full advantage, show improved results commencing Tuesday.

Chic. 7/19/10. To Number 1 New York, to Number 1 Philadelphia. Any house your jurisdiction not getting cost for beef get right after them. Get results asked.

Van Pelt, Boston. 8/23/10. You should make strongest kind effort to get 12½ cents on good cattle in Boston and every other house beginning Monday, there is just hell to pay around here this morn about our New England business and I have got to look to you to pull it out of the rut. T. G. Lee

39. George Stigler, *The Organization of Industry* (Homewood, Ill., 1968), p. 63.

40. Burns, *The Decline of Competition*, p. 165.

41. Compiled from data in FTC, *Report on the Meat-Packing Industry, 1919*, Summary and Pt. I, p. 153.

42. *U.S.* v. *Louis Swift*, p. 755.

43. Continued expansion and competition for resources also reintroduced the problem of adjusting percentage allotments. Between 1894 and 1896 Armour, Morris, and Cudahy built 89 additional branch houses. Armour again led the group with 44 houses; Morris built 11; and Cudahy, 16 (FTC, *Report on the Meat-Packing Industry, 1919*, Summary and Pt. I, p. 153).

44. *Ibid.*, pp. 240–241.

45. Swift & Co. *Yearbook, 1932* (Corporation Records, Baker Library, Harvard Graduate School of Business). The *National Provisioner*, January 12, 1895, p. 15, applauded the move to diversify, claiming that "it would help the packers and slaughterers during the dull times which generally set in during the so-called poultry season in the winter months . . . it would prove an advantage to the butcher if he could buy all his supplies from the slaughterer or packer instead of going all over to find them. Centralization means simplification and simplification means a saving of money."

46. *National Provisioner*, October 27, 1894, p. 26; January 12, 1895, p. 19; September 12, 1908, p. 15; *St. of Mo.* v. *Hammond*, Joint Abstract of Record, pp. 417–420; FTC, *Report on the Meat-Packing Industry, 1919*, Summary and Part I, p. 153.

47. For details, see FTC *Report on the Meat-Packing Industry, 1919* Pt. II, "Evidence of Combination Among Packers," pp. 159–210.

48. October 27, 1894, p. 26. The *National Provisioner*, April 25, 1903, p. 16, details the S & S expansion into Illinois and the southern states in the early 1900s.

49. *National Provisioner*, April 27, 1895, p. 28, describes the flurry that was caused when the Chicago packers visited the S & S firm in New York.

50. *St. of Mo.* v. *Hammond Packing Co.*, Joint Abstract of the Record, pp. 144–145; *U.S.* v. *Louis Swift*, p. 755.

51. Leech and Carroll, *Armour and His Times*, p. 110, quoting from Armour's letter.

52. *Ibid.*, pp. 152–153.

53. *U.S.* v. *Louis Swift*, p. 755.

54. There is some confusion regarding the dates of the pool's organization and the formal admittance of S & S into it. It appears that nearly three months elapsed before S & S was admitted. Whether or not pool members had decided to admit the newcomer when they reorganized the pool is uncertain.

55. It was, in reality, a compensatory payment that the pool channeled to packers who had shipped less than their allotment.

56. *U.S.* v. *Louis Swift*, pp. 762–763.

57. FTC, *Report on the Meat-Packing Industry, 1919*, Summary and Pt. I, pp. 243–244. Swift's move into St. Paul apparently strained cooperation between Armour and Swift and also angered merchants in the sister city of Minneapolis. No sooner had Swift signed the contract with the stockyards than Minneapolis merchants offered Armour a similar contract. The threat of another stockyards in a territory where one was considered suf-

ficient prompted Swift to undertake separate negotiations to persuade Armour to abandon the plan and become a joint stockholder in the St. Paul yards. Years later, when testifying before a Senate Agricultural Committee, Louis Swift explained why cooperation was so important. Armour's plan to move into Minneapolis "created a bad situation, as Swift was already at St. Paul . . . two stockyards in competition in the same town do not get along. It is ruinous for both of them." Undoubtedly a similar rationale had convinced Armour in 1898, for the stockyards at Minneapolis were not constructed. (See U.S. Congress, Senate, Committee on Ariculture and Forestry, *Hearings before a Subcommittee on S. Res. No. 221, in favor of Government Control and Operation of Meat Packing Industry,* 65th Cong., 2nd and 3rd Sess., 1919, p. 385.)

58. FTC, *Report on the Meat-Packing Industry, 1919,* Summary and Pt. I, p. 243.

59. *Ibid.,* pp. 260–283, 391.

60. *U.S.* v. *Louis Swift,* pp. 755–756, 771.

61. A penalty in addition to that on average shipments (*U.S.* v. *Louis Swift,* Government Exhibit No. 51).

Chapter VI

The Oligopolists Seek a New Strategy

Although the packers extended their pooling association in 1901 for another three years, they did so knowing that the days of the pool were numbered. For some 15 years the packers had put up with an unstable series of pools. That they did so for so long was probably due to several factors. Like most businessmen who had built up thriving enterprises, they were reluctant to abandon their identity and independence in a merger. Further, the fact that much of the country was still a relatively fertile growth area meant that they could continue to enjoy in some areas the kinds of good profits they had made in the early and mid-1880s. The process by which the whole national market came to be "filled up," as the Northeast had done first, was a protracted one. That fact helped preserve the unstable oligopolistic period for years. By the beginning of the twentieth century, however, there were few regions left for continued rapid growth.

In addition, the packers were beginning to react to growing public pressures. In 1899 the Supreme Court ruled in the Addyston Pipe and Steel case that cartel-type devices were illegal under the Sherman Act.[1] This point had been in dispute ever since the passage of the Sherman Anti-Trust Act in 1890, but the Addyston decision seemed to settle the matter. Clearly, if the packers were to continue their pooling association, they probably would be acting illegally. Meetings had to be shrouded in secrecy, and a system that had never worked very well would probably not work any better in such an environment.

The instability of such agreements had prompted industrialists in other key industries to abandon loose pooling associations for formal combination. John D. Rockefeller and his associates had devised the "trust" form of organization in the early 1880s after pools in that industry had proved to be nothing but "ropes of sand." By enabling the stock of different companies to be vested in a board of trustees, the trust permitted some real control over constituent companies and thus eliminated competition more effectively than had the pools. Such control, however, triggered public and legal attacks, and after the passage of the Sherman Anti-Trust Act in 1890, this often ineffective organizational form increasingly proved too risky to be of much use.[2]

The holding company superceded the trust. Sanctioned by the New Jersey corporation law of 1889, it permitted one corporation to hold stock in another and thus made merger—or the consolidation of like companies—much more feasible. Between 1897 and 1903, more mergers occurred than at any other time in the nation's history; most of these were accomplished by the holding company device. The period of the great merger movement saw combinations formed in steel, coal, copper, glass, biscuits, and sugar, to mention only a few.[3]

The pattern of combination in these industries was familiar to the packers. Swift in particular had watched the merger movement with interest. "The consolidation of all the packing companies into one huge unit was father's greatest business dream," wrote Louis Swift, "and the merger movement—especially the formation of U.S. Steel—suggested to him the possibility of fulfilling that dream."[4]

By the turn of the century some kind of merger was in the minds of all the dominant packers.[5] The idea received a powerful boost when some of the nation's railroads began to acquire significant numbers of refrigerator cars. Prior to 1900 only a few western and southwestern roads had invested in refrigerator cars. Beginning in that year, however, more and more roads began to build their own cars to avoid the mileage fees that had plagued them for more than a decade. In 1900 the Chicago, Burlington & Quincy organized a separate refrigerator car division within the traffic department and placed a man at the head of it to study conditions, provide for the proper carriage of perishable products originating along the lines of the roads, and stimulate the production of such goods. Within three years the tonnage of perishable freight on the CB&Q increased almost 100 percent. Other roads soon realized the profitability of such an investment and began making plans to organize their own refrigerator car divisions. Between 1900 and 1905 the number of refrigerator cars owned by the railroads increased almost 200 percent, from 10,760 in 1900 to 24,570 by 1905. The increase during previous years (with the exception of the period between 1885 and 1890) was not nearly as significant.[6]

The potential threat to the oligopoly was clear. Railroad ownership of refrigerator cars meant that the packers' control over product flows would be significantly reduced and that smaller packers might more easily enter the interstate beef trade, since entry costs would be lowered.

A further incentive to the concentration of packer power was the consolidation of several competing railroad lines into self-sustaining transportation systems.[7] These systems enabled the railroads to present a more unified bargaining position and reduced their traditional weakness vis-à-vis large shippers. Early in January 1902 the *Chicago Chronicle* reported that the Vanderbilt and Pennsylvania roads planned "to oust, so far as possible, the private refrigerator cars owned by the big meat packing companies and substitute their own cars." "This is another result," it claimed, "of the community of ownership and a further demonstration of the point that railroads of the country had reached in their combining process."[8] The propacker trade journal *National Provisioner* reviewed the situation in a March 22, 1902, article: "During the past two or three years the larger railroads of the country have been building thousands of refrigerator cars with the object of ultimately throwing out all private car companies and forcing the shippers to use the railway's equipment and save the mileage payments."[9]

Moreover, the individual packers were becoming increasingly concerned about what might happen to their enterprises and to interfirm relations after they themselves were gone. Only the Hammond firm, whose founder had died in 1886, escaped the possible succession crisis that threatened other firms at the turn of the century. The other pioneer packers were growing old. In 1900 Nelson Morris was 60 years of age, Gustavus Swift, 61, and Michael Cudahy, 59. Armour was the oldest of the lot, at 68 years, and was very troubled about his ailing health. Wistfully, he remarked to his nephew Kirkland of the Kansas City plant, "if I could clip a few years off the calendar, I would be all right."[10] The packers undoubtedly shared anxieties concerning the impact of a change in command upon interfirm relations. Representatives of the packers or their own heirs might fill the seats at pool meetings once occupied by the pioneers, but there was no assurance that relations would be as friendly or that even the usual fitful pattern of harmony could be maintained. The continuity in management built into large integrated bureaucracies was missing in firms making up the pooling association.[11] Death of one of the members could easily mean a decline of that firm's influence or the introduction of added uncertainty.

More than the others, Armour was particularly concerned about the future of his empire and the role that his family would take in managing it. By 1900 nearly all of his brothers had died. Joseph went in 1891; Andrew Watson Armour, the Kansas City banker, was the next to go, in 1897; Simeon Brooks Armour, of the Kansas City house, died in 1899. Then, on January 29, 1900, Philip Armour's younger son, Philip, Jr., died. That left only his eldest son, Ogden, and the sons of his brother Simeon, to look after the Armour empire.[12] P. D. had groomed his sons for the business from early childhood, but it had been Philip, Jr., not the older J. O., who had most emulated his father and had taken the greatest pride in the business. Ogden, on the contrary, showed little enthusiasm or interest. In a conversation with a friend at the yards one day, old P. D. described his oldest son: "Ogden was impressed with the fact that so many Englishmen had a leisurely life on a small income, with a lot of worthwhile things that he thought there would be something he would like to do instead of grubbing for money, when we already had more than enough. He thinks he should retire. I told him to be at the Yards in his working clothes at 7:00 in the morning."[13]

Unable to put much faith in his son's managerial abilities or interest, P. D. took steps to strengthen his empire before he died. Until 1900 the Armour Packing Company of Kansas City and the Armour Company of Chicago had remained legally separate corporations. P. D. pushed for a consolidation of the two interests. On October 26, 1900, he wrote to his nephew Kirkland that the consolidation was going through. In addition to that news, he slipped in several pieces of advice and expressed his opinion regarding the future of the consolidation:

> Ogden has forwarded to me your two telegrams of yesterday. I am glad the matter is so fixed that the consolidation can go through. No one can tell what the future of the consolidation will be, but I can say to you with all frankness that you have now got something that is worth something and is a piece of tangible, negotiable property. The future of the consolidation depends entirely upon management. I know it will not run itself. It wants somebody right at the head of it, but with its reputation and the soundness of the concern and the young men who have grown up about it, it ought to make its future very desirable.
>
> I know that if I had my health and strength that the concern in the next 20 years would make strides that we never dreamed of in the past, as we simply got the foundation well laid, but as I have said before, everything now depends on management.
>
> I suppose very soon some program of organization will be formulated, who should be in power, etc. It is everything in the organization in having the right men in the right places. We need more capital in the concern; in fact, I suppose we will do as we always have done, not divide very much, but try to strengthen the house in every way. I suppose the increase of the business and the development of the business will require more and more capital all the time.
>
> I feel this organization is an excellent thing for you boys; in fact, I think it is a good thing for everybody concerned. I told Combs to tell you every weak spot about Armour and Company, of your concern, so far as outside property, and all such things are concerned, and I hope they never will be allowed to get in any worse shape than they are.... As long as the old man lives, you can rely fully that the Armours will be taken care of, and I will always be loyal to anybody with the Armour name....[14]

It seems likely that Armour had been considering the possibility of some type of merger of the various packing companies, especially in view of developments that followed. On January 1, 1901, P. D. Armour died, leaving J. O. Armour in charge of the family empire. Only five months later, on June 1, 1901, Gustavus Swift presented to the pool members a proposal that was to lay the foundation for the formation of a consolidation—the National Packing Company. With the pooling association still operating, the packers began negotiations to implement a new strategy of merger.[15]

A further impetus came from the steadily growing governmental pressure. In January 1902, the Justice Department enjoined the packers from colluding in the buying or selling of their products. This made rapid agreement on a new strategy imperative. In April 1902 the packers disbanded their pooling association. On May 31, just ten days after the U.S. District Court in Chicago issued another injunction, J. O. Armour, Gustavus F. Swift, and Edward Morris signed a preliminary contract to merge their companies into a single enterprise.[16]

INITIAL MERGER CONTRACTS

The initial merger agreement of May 31, 1902, was clearly a prelude to a more detailed and comprehensive agreement. It included Swift, Armour, and Morris but not Cudahy or S & S. It provided that a "new corporation be formed" and that J. O. Armour, Gustavus Swift, and Edward Morris, as individuals,[17] would agree "to sell . . . to said corporation, when formed . . . [all] the shares of the capital stocks" of their respective companies.[18]

In return for the real property and shares of their respective companies, the packers were to receive 20-year gold bonds and preferred stock in the new company. The bonds and stocks were to be distributed according to the percentage each company contributed to the total tangible assets of the new corporation. As payment for intangible assets (including good will), and perhaps as capitalization of future earnings, the packers were to receive the same percentages of a block of preferred stock ($25 million par value) and an amount of common stock whose value equalled 25 times the actual earnings of the companies during a designated period in the recent past.

The relative division of stock among the three packers was significant. As certified on August 2, 1902, Swift, whose company's assets were appraised at $85 million, was to get about 46 percent of the stock of the new company. With assets of $73 million, Armour was entitled to approximately 40 percent of the stock. Morris, whose assets were valued at $24 million, was to receive the remaining 14 percent.[19] This percentage formula was also applied to a provision in which the three agreed "to purchase . . . for the use and benefit of the new corporation, when formed, the shares of stock . . . or the physical assets, *of other corporations* engaged in business now carried on by" Armour, Morris, and Swift.[20]

The companies marked for acquisition were some of the nation's largest integrated packing firms. These included: the G. H. Hammond and Hammond Packing Company with a capital stock of $1,750,000; the Fowler Packing Company, a Kansas corporation capitalized at $700,000, and its affiliates; the Anglo-American Provision Company, a Chicago hog packing firm capitalized at $200,000; the Omaha Packing Company of Illinois, with $500,000 capital and plants in Omaha and Chicago as well as its own refrigerator car line; the St. Louis Dressed Beef and Provision Company, capitalized at $1,250,000; and other smaller firms, such as the United Dressed Beef Company of New York with a capital stock of $300,000.[21] Payment for and stock ownership in these companies was to be based on the percentage formula. For example, Armour, who held 40 percent of the stock of the new company, would also hold 40 percent of the stock of each subsidiary of the new company and, in turn, would pay 40 percent of the cost of purchasing these companies. To assure that each of the participating members carried out the agreement, Swift, Morris, and Armour were each to deposit $1 million in securities or cash with the Illinois Trust and Savings Bank. Failure to meet the obligations of the contract would result in a forfeiture of funds to the other parties.[22]

Shortly after the signing of the merger contract on May 31, the packers began to implement its provisions, including the agreement to acquire other firms. The required securities were deposited, and a flurry of acquisitions began. On June 10, 1902, Morris contracted to buy the United Dressed Beef Company of New York. A day later, Swift purchased the Fowler properties, and Armour, the Hammond Company. On June 13, Armour bought the Omaha Packing Co., and Morris followed by acquiring the St. Louis Dressed Beef and Provision Co.[23] Meanwhile, negotiations were under way to arrange an $8 million loan to pay for the contracted companies, and tentative arrangements were made with the investment banking house of Kuhn, Loeb & Co. to provide $60 million to finance the overall merger.

Efforts were also under way in July 1902 to bring Cudahy and S & S into the agreement. It is unclear precisely why they were not part of the original merger.[24] Whatever the reason for their failure to sign the first merger contract, by the end of August 1902, both Cudahy and S&S had joined the merger.[25]

Cudahy was the first to join the Big Three. On July 18 a supplemental merger agreement was drawn up, the only difference between this and the previous one being the inclusion of Michael Cudahy. Like Armour, Swift, and Morris, he too deposited $1 million in securities with the Illinois Trust. Unlike them, however, he did not agree to acquire other competing companies.[26]

Soon thereafter, on August 26, S & S agreed to become a party to the combination. Another separate contract was drawn up, stipulating that at least 73 percent of the stock of the S & S Company would be exchanged for bonds and stock in the new company or for cash. Unlike the others, however, Sulzberger did not deposit $1 million in securities.[27] Thus, by the end of August 1902 there existed three separate, yet interrelated merger contracts: the initial merger agreement of May 31 between the Big Three, and the two subsequent contracts securing the participation of Cudahy and S & S.

Although the legal provisions dealing with the transfer of property and stock had been arranged, those dealing with the financing and promotion of the merger were not yet secure. As mentioned above, Kuhn, Loeb & Co. had tentatively agreed to underwrite the $60 million merger, but as of August 26, no firm contract had been signed. Instead, there was a detailed working agreement or tentative contract, the provisions of which were agreed to by the packers and submitted to the financiers for approval.

This tentative agreement combined the three related yet separate contracts described above (between the Big Three and Cudahy and S & S), and involved more than $264 million worth of assets. According to this main agreement, the "Big Company" (as the packers called it), was

> to acquire the properties and assets ... of Armour & Co., Swift & Co., the Fairbank Canning Company, and the Cudahy Packing Company, together with those of a large number of other corporations, and of certain firms and individuals, controlled or held by the principal stockholders of said four concerns respectively; also of a number of companies which have been purchased, in whole or in part, by some one of the vendors, including the Anglo-American Provision Company, the G. H. Hammond Company, Hammond Packing Company, United Dressed Beef Company, Omaha Packing Company, St. Louis Dressed Beef & Provision Company, and their several allied and subsidiary corporations.[28]

The Big Company was to be a holding company modeled after the United States Steel Corporation.[29]

The packers' selection of this organizational device was based on several advantages it had over other consolidation schemes.[30] Not only was the holding company considered to be a legally safe device, but it was also easier to organize, since only a majority of stocks or shares of subsidiaries was required to form a holding company, whereas fusion necessitated acquisition of all the stocks. The holding company form was flexible—it could provide whatever degree of centralized or decentralized control that seemed desirable. Subsidiaries could be tied together under the general control and supervision of a central management. At the same time, each subsidiary could retain its separate board of directors, staff, and system of accounts. More detailed operational problems could be left to officers of subsidiaries, while executives of the holding company were free to concentrate on broader questions of policy and coordination. Although under the centralized control of a parent holding company, subsidiaries could retain their own corporate identity and trade name.

Still another advantage of the holding company stemmed from the opportunity it afforded to standardize accounts. That would permit comparisons of similar businesses, supply the officers of the holding company with more precise information about the operating efficiency of each unit, and enable them to plan more effectively for the operation of the whole enterprise. Moreover, the mere fact of stock ownership did not impose upon the holding company a liability for the debts of its subsidiaries. The relative ease of dissolution gave the holding company still another advantage. Since the companies or properties held never had to lose their separate legal identities, they could easily be separated from the main or parent company.

Some of these advantages were of particular importance to the packers. Although years of informal cooperation and repeated but unsuccessful attempts to perfect their pooling arrangements had led them to search for a safer and more efficient way to cooperate, they nevertheless remained reluctant to undertake a full-scale merger that would force them to sacrifice their family firms entirely. Not only was the holding company legally less vulnerable than pools, but it enabled the packers to retain some elements of independence while at the same time reaping the advantages of consolidation. Moreover, by placing control of purchases and sales in the hands of a central, unified management, the packers could use the holding company to enforce the cartel arrangements worked out years before and rationalize competition as well. With properties and assets turned over to the holding company, the packers could, through their role as directors of the holding company, achieve a unity of policy impossible earlier.

The tentative contract, submitted to the financiers sometime in November 1902, embodied these objectives and spelled out the details of the proposed merger.[31] Undoubtedly aware of the difficulties in obtaining complete control of the stock of subsidiaries but alert to the fact that acquisition of a majority of stock was necessary to assure control, the packers agreed that at least 80 percent of the stock of companies to be included in the merger had to be acquired before the contract became binding. As mentioned previously, financial arrangements were made with various Wall Street powers—Jacob H. Schiff of Kuhn, Loeb & Co. (the principal underwriter), and with banker James Stillman and financier and railroader E. H. Harriman.

The proposed corporation was to have an authorized capitalization of $550 million: $75 million in 20-year, 5 percent bonds; $250 million in 6 percent preferred cumulative stock, and $225 million in common stock. In return for $60 million cash, the syndicate was to receive bonds totaling $35 million preferred stock with a par value of $36,875,000 and common stock worth $33 million. Ten million dollars of the bonds were to remain unissued, or, if so directed by Kuhn, Loeb & Co., were to be used in the conversion or retirement of existing underlying secured obligations of some of the companies recently purchased. In addition, the guarantors were to receive $10 million in common stock. For their property and assets and securities, Swift, Armour, and Morris were to receive, in proportion to their respective assets, $165 million worth of preferred stock and $182 million of common stock (based on the net earnings of each of the respective parties). Thus, the packers were to own a little less than four-fifths of the company and the syndicate's interests were to amount to a little over one-fifth.[32]

The syndicate was supposed to have some influence in the company. For at least three years it was to nominate three of the fifteen directors of the board, and three of the five members of a finance committee. The board of directors was to exercise "general control and direction" of the new company. An executive committee, composed of some of the directors, was to have charge of the "current business" of the company, and financial matters were to be the responsibility of the finance committee, whose office and headquarters was to be in New York City. J. O. Armour was to be the chairman of the board and of the executive committee; Gustavus Swift was to be president; Edward Morris, Michael Cudahy, and "others to be selected" were designated vice-presidents (and, as such, were also members of the executive committee).

A sudden, crippling blow was given the embryonic merger when, on November 18, 1902, at a meeting with Jacob Schiff of Kuhn, Loeb & Co., the packers were told that there would be no merger contract. Although the promoters left no evidence of the reasons for their withdrawal, both legal and financial factors appear to have been important. Legal uncertainty probably arose when government action threatened another of the same promoters' schemes, the gigantic Northern Securities Company. Albert Veeder, Swift's legal counsel, summarized the financial reasons for the financiers' withdrawal when he recalled the incident several years later:

> Mr. Schiff [of Kuhn, Loeb & Co.] told them [the packers] that they had been thinking this matter over very seriously, that it was a large transaction and that times did not look propitious, and that since the last interview he and his partners had had large discussions over the matter, and he did not say they were on the verge of a panic or anything of that kind, but he wanted to go out and sell everything of value

and go short on the market. Such being the case he thought perhaps they had better wait or postpone the matter and practically withdrew from it. . . . He [Schiff] suggested that they might get together on another basis but the other parties were disappointed and were not prepared to discuss any other basis, and no further negotiations resulted. So the purpose of the May 31st and July 18th contracts to form a large new company which should acquire all these properties they had been talking about, terminated. . . .[33]

The packers' unhappiness was understandable. "None of them were feeling very chipper when the question arose as to what should be done with those [newly purchased] companies," recalled Veeder. "There was an indebtedness of $8,000,000 [as a result of a loan to pay for acquisitions] coming due at the First National Bank of New York early in January."[34] They had all gone too far to turn back now. Numerous companies had been acquired that the packers claimed "never would have [been] purchased if they had known that the organization of the large company was to fall through."[35] They insisted, therefore, that the bankers should absorb at least some of the cost of financing them.

Nearly four weeks later, on December 19, Swift, Armour, and Morris signed another agreement with three guarantors and Kuhn, Loeb & Co., for a loan of $15 million to pay for the recently acquired companies.[36] As security for the loan, each packer deposited with the bankers a note for his proportionate share of the $15 million.

The December 19 agreement with the financiers was, however, more than a loan. Section 2 of the agreement suggests that the packers still contemplated the organization of another corporation: "This agreement shall not, however, prevent the consolidation of . . . said companies with one another, or with one or more other corporations, or the transfer of the property and business or the shares of stock of . . . said corporations to one or more other corporations, provided that the legality of such consolidation or transfer shall be approved by the counsel of the borrowers and the counsel of the lenders." This provision was an expression of intent on the part of the packers as well as a condition of the loan. The financiers undoubtedly did not wish to loan money without some guarantee that the purpose for which the loan was to be used was both legal and profitable.[37] The packers did not want to abandon previous objectives to eliminate competition and stabilize prices. On the contrary, they were more concerned than ever to achieve their previous goals. No sooner had the merger fallen through, therefore, than the packers and their lawyers, together with their financiers, began to consider other alternatives.

Apparently, three different propositions were advanced. The first was to divide the acquired properties among the major packers. The second was to operate the newly acquired companies under a partnership. The third involved the formation of a new corporation, more specifically a holding and operating company.[38] For what should by now be obvious reasons, the third alternative was considered the most feasible, and the packers chose it.

THE BUILDING OF THE NATIONAL PACKING CO.

Incorporated in New Jersey on March 18, 1903, the National Packing Co. was a smaller, less ambitious version of the earlier merger scheme. Whereas the proposed merger, with a capitalization of $550 million, had been designed to include all of the major packers, the National, with a capitalization of only $15 million, was organized and owned jointly by the Big Three packers only. Theoretically, it was to hold and operate only those companies acquired by them in preparation for the merger (see Figure VI.1). Just as the relative value of the tangible assets of each packer's firm had formed the basis for stock ownership in the Big Company, so too was it the cornerstone of stock ownership in the National Packing Co. Accordingly, Armour, Swift, and Morris held the same proportion of shares in the National Packing Co. that they would have held in the merger: 40, 46, and 14 percent respectively.[39]

Despite its apparently more restricted initial purpose, National soon became the vehicle through which the Big Three set out to control the entire interstate beef trade. Not surprisingly, the administrative structure fashioned at National was strikingly similar to the structures that had evolved in the Big Three corporations.

Legally a holding company, National was designed to be an operating firm as well. As defined by its articles of incorporation, the objectives of the company were

> To produce, manufacture . . . and . . . buy, sell, store, transport, distribute . . . and deal in . . . (1) animal and vegetable products and commodities (including meats and provisions), and (2) . . . articles and things in which, or in the production or preparation of which, any animal or vegetable product or commodity is an ingredient . . . and also (3) any materials, supplies or products which may be used in or in connection with the manufacture, production, preparation, use or sale of any of the products, commodities, articles and things aforesaid . . .
>
> To engage in any other manufacturing, warehousing, trading or selling business of any kind or character whatsoever.
>
> To . . . register, lease or otherwise acquire, and to . . . own, operate, sell [or] assign, . . . any trademarks, trade-names, patents, inventions, improvements and processes used in connection with or secured under letters patent in the United States.
>
> To carry on any other business whatsoever which the corporation may deem proper or convenient to be carried on in connection with any of the foregoing purposes, or calculated directly or indirectly to promote the interests of the corporation or to enhance the value of its property . . .[40]

Figure VI.1   Major Elements of the National Packing Co. System.

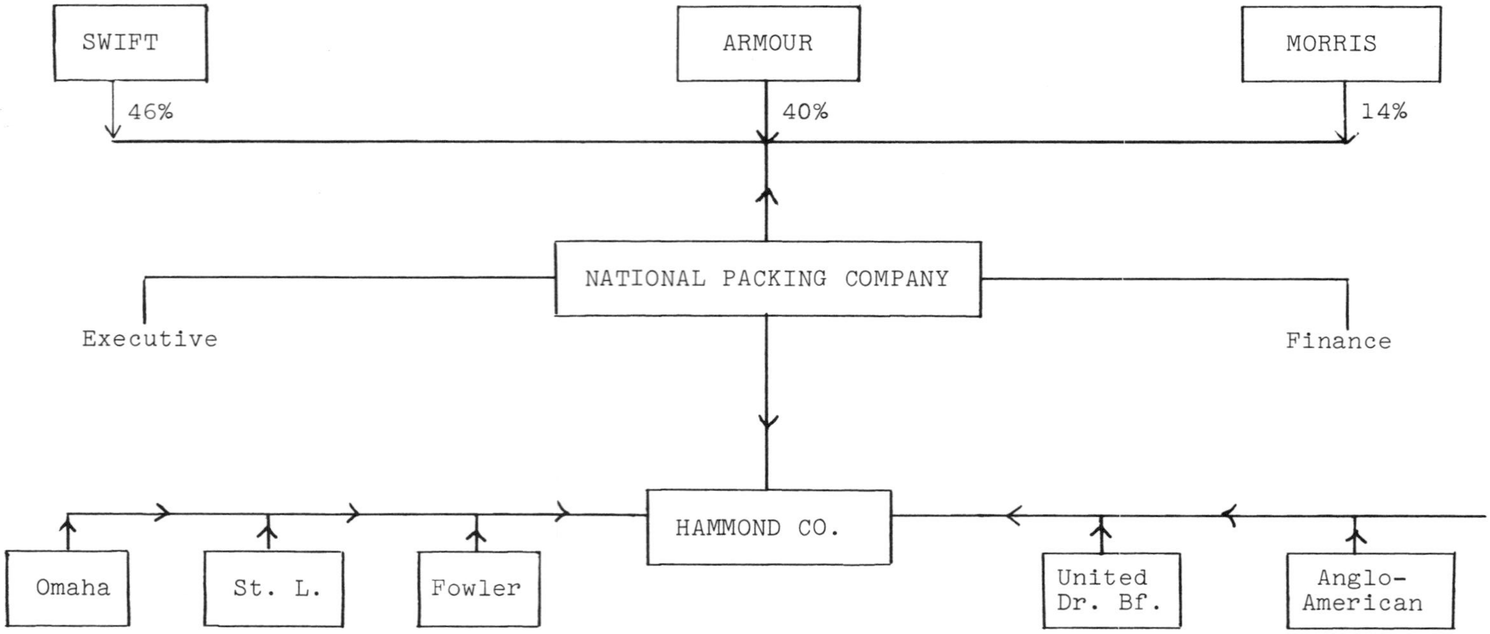

Since the most immediate problem facing the Big Three was the integration of the newly acquired companies into a unified corporate structure at National, they tackled organizational problems first. They combined managerial resources by placing control securely in the hands of a board of directors, which they and the immediate members of their respective families dominated. Other members of the 11-man board included some of the top-ranking executive officers and directors of the respective companies: P. A. Valentine, vice president and treasurer of Armour & Co.; Thomas J. Connors, director, Armour & Co.; Kenneth McLauren, officer, Armour Car Lines, the Corporation Trust Co., and the John P. Squire Co. (a Swift-controlled subsidiary); L. A. Carton, treasurer and director of Swift & Co.; Samuel McLean, general manager of the newly acquired Anglo-American Provision Co. and director of the Provision Dealer's Dispatch, a subsidiary of Swift & Co. Without exception, the directors had years of experience in the packing business; nearly all had decision-making experience and had been involved with the pooling association of the 1890s.[41]

The board made long-run strategic decisions as well as certain operational ones regarding prices and margins. It defined and delegated responsibility and authority, appointed and removed all executive officers, and planned for the whole enterprise. Not only did National's board determine the policies and affairs of its subsidiaries, but it also had the power "to fix and determine and to vary the amount of the working capital of the corporation, and to direct and determine the use and disposition of any surplus or net profits over and above the capital stock paid in." It could "sell, assign, transfer, convey, . . . the property and assets of the corporation, . . . and . . . issue the bonds, debentures, notes and other obligations or evidences of debt." To enable the executives to carry out their responsibilities and to assure smooth operation of the whole enterprise, meetings were to be held on the (by now) traditional day, Tuesday.[42]

The board created from among its own number, two top-ranking executive and finance committees. Consisting of five members, the executive committee was to exercise such powers as were conferred and authorized by the board. In the interim between board meetings, the committee was to "possess and exercise all the powers of the board of directors in the management and direction of the manufacturing, mercantile and transportation operations of the company and of all its other business and affairs. . . ." A five-man finance committee was placed in "special and general charge and control of all financial and legal affairs of the Company." As indicated earlier, however, it was the board and not the finance committee that determined dividends and issued stock. Any appropriation involving more than $20,000 required the approval of the board or the executive or finance committees.

Directly under the control of the finance committee were the treasurer, auditor, secretary, and general counsel of the company, all appointed by the board. The president of the company, appointed by the board and responsible to it, exercised a supervisory role, seeing to it that all orders and resolutions of the board were carried into effect.

All of these officers—the board, the two committees, president, treasurer, secretary, etc.—were housed in a general administrative office, located in the Rookery Building in downtown Chicago. All the officers were well-acquainted with the packing business and assured the managerial continuity so crucial to the smooth operation of the whole enterprise (see Figure VI.2).

The packers consolidated the lower-ranking managers of the various companies at the Hammond plant in the Union Stockyards.[43] The president was placed in supervisory control and two vice-presidents were put in charge of the product departments, initially beef and pork.[44] These vice-presidents, experienced managers who had usually transferred from the newly acquired companies, had control over both purchases and sales of a particular product by all subsidiaries, and, in addition, supervised other subdepartments, such as accounting, beef margins, etc. Working closely with them were the heads of these subdepartments, who saw to it that instructions from the vice-presidents were carried out at the individual plants. A vice-president exercised an important role in the company, for through his office flowed instructions concerning margins and prices from the board to district superintendents and information from the latter concerning the supply of beef on hand in coolers at branch houses, needs for the upcoming week, and daily margin and price reports.

Those lines of authority and communication required elaborate daily, weekly, and monthly reports from superintendents and managers in the field to the general auditor at National's administrative headquarters, as well as inspection visits to branch houses by district superintendents or their assistants. Information concerning prices and costs flowed down the administrative hierarchy from the board to the general manager to district superintendents and office managers at the various plants. Data concerning the supply of beef in the coolers, the volume needed for the upcoming week, and the closed (average actual daily) selling prices and margins flowed upward to the product vice-president for day-to-day operations and to the president and the general auditor of National, who with the board, used it as raw material for strategic planning decisions and day-to-day operating decisions.

Effective information flows, in turn, required a standardized accounting system. Without uniform accounting, it would have been impossible to operate the newly acquired companies and National as a unified

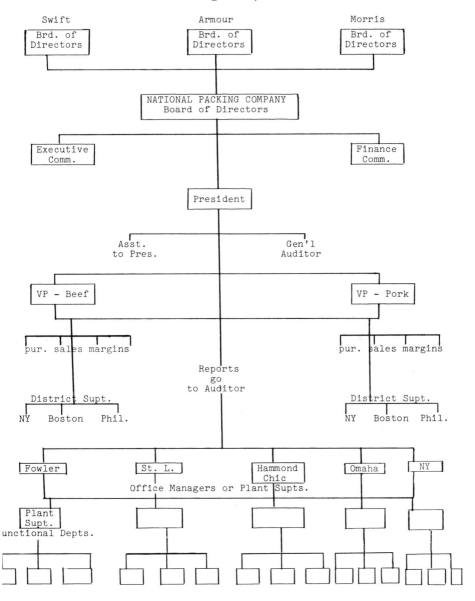

Figure VI.2 Internal Administrative Structure of the National Packing Co. System.

whole and to coordinate National's business with that of the packers' own companies. Shortly after National was incorporated, its three owners instituted standardized accounting forms for the calculation of costs at various plants. To assist them, they appointed a general auditor, who was to exercise supervision over the accounting of National and each of its subsidiaries. The auditor gave instructions to the head of the accounting departments at the various plants regarding the methods of computing costs and the procedures by which charges were made and products transferred. In addition to these activities, the auditor prepared departmental price lists on the basis of margin and price information received from the vice-presidents of the beef and pork departments. There was also a staff of auditors to inspect the books of subsidiaries. Although each subsidiary company kept its own set of books, it reported profit and loss statements to the auditor at National on a systematic basis.[45]

The subsidiaries of National were instructed to buy and sell through this general administrative structure. When they desired to purchase packing products, they communicated via telegraph or telephone to National, which then gave instructions concerning where to place the order. The system was explained in detail by A. N. Benn, assistant to the president of National, when he testified before the Supreme Court of Missouri in 1913:

> The National is a holding company for the subsidiary companies, does no special line of business aside from handling the affairs of the different companies, selling for them some of their products, and buying for them certain other products which they must buy. The subsidiary corporations when they desire to buy, shall buy through the medium of the National, but at times, and when they can buy to local advantage, they place the order directly themselves. If they can make a better deal themselves than the National can make for them, the National permits them to buy direct. They are advised each day as to the prices at which the National can buy for them. The National is connected with the principal office of most of the subsidiary concerns by a private wire. There is a private wire connecting all subsidiary concerns doing a slaughtering business with the National. . . . The National charges no commission on purchases made for the various corporations, but simply places the order for such concern. . . . Each of these subsidiary concerns makes daily reports to the National, which reports include the number of stock, cattle, etc., purchased by each on the market, during the day. They also report the prices which they have paid for such stock. Frequently the Chicago office tells its subsidiary concerns to buy at certain prices, but these orders cannot always, on account of market conditions, be strictly complied with. Each concern also reports each morning on the market that day, and the National then gives information to each concern, the general conditions, receipts and prices for the day.[46]

The policy of administrative consolidation was applied to the refrigerator car line services of the newly acquired companies as well. Unlike the sales and purchasing activities, however, car line services were not integrated formally into the administrative structure at National but instead, were operated by a corporation specifically created to take care of that end of the business—the National Car Line Company.[47]

The administrative structure at National, patterned as it was after that of the Armour, Morris, and Swift companies, assured cooperation and a uniformity of policy that worked to the advantage of these companies as well as to that of National. Utilizing this structure, the packers centralized information and data flows, then used this information to coordinate the product flows of National with those of their own companies, and to help stabilize and implement the old agreements on market shares that had evolved during the period of pooling in the 1890s.

All of the careful administrative reorganization just detailed would not have really made much difference in the industry if it had been simply the means of efficiently putting together the pieces from the abortive giant merger. National was, however, much more than that. It came to serve as a kind of forum in which the old goals of cartelization might be pursued legally. In a sense, National became a sort of corporate haven in which the packers could retain their independence yet collude, and perhaps collude more effectively than in the days of the pools. Because the National could be used as a clearing house of information, it became the nerve center or super-administrative network of the Big Three. A. N. Benn elaborated upon National's information-gathering role: "The National also reports to each concern the amount of stock that has been purchased on the market during that day by the Armours, Swifts, Morrises, and all other packing plants, and gives each subsidiary concern all the information it possibly can."[48]

Unlike earlier pooling agreements that covered allotments of dressed beef shipments and depended upon a system of fines for enforcement, now agreements among the packers could be implemented, they hoped, through the structure at National. Instructions to buy and sell given by the board of National to its subsidiaries were always based upon the data received from the beef departments of the respective parent companies, Armour, Morris, and Swift. Such data, reflected in price and margin reports, provided information on general market conditions as well as more specific information on the balance of supply and demand at various plants and branch houses of the various companies throughout the Northeast. Because they wore two sets of hats—one for National and the other for their respective members of the Big Three—the men who controlled National found their interaction there an easy way to exchange data on markets, prices, and costs. The National also improved upon the pooling arrangement by providing the Big Three with a common interest, namely the success of National as an operating company.

That was not decisive, but the day-to-day cooperation necessary to run this common enterprise did serve to reduce distrust among the packers.

While the Swift, Armour, and Morris companies continued to purchase their allotted market shares, National varied its purchases and sales, depending on what was required to "even" the packers. This it did in several ways. It varied its prices relative to those of Armour, Morris, or Swift. Frequently, when supply exceeded demand, it was National and not the Armour, Morris, and Swift companies that was instructed to get rid of the excess by lowering its prices. As one buyer observed, he was often able to obtain a cheaper price from Hammond (a National subsidiary) than from Armour or Swift on occasions when supplies seemed abundant.[49] The practice of National varying its purchases to suit the Big Three allegedly occurred on numerous occasions.[50] In a special report to the Bureau of Corporations in 1904, field investigator John Dickinson recorded what he had learned during an interview with Eugene Rust, general manager of the Kansas City Stockyards:

> Mr. Rust declares that Armour, Swift and Morris cooperate in this market through the plants of the National Packing Company located here. These are the plants of Fowler and Ruddy brothers. . . . A short time before the Fowler concern was taken over by the National Packing Company, through Swift, the Fowlers constructed stockyards near their packing houses. . . . Since the transfer of the Fowler concern to the National Packing Company there appears not to have been any change in the relations between the Fowler stockyards and the producers. . . . But Mr. Rust contends that Armour and Swift and Morris in combination are using this market. Solicitors for the Fowler yards are constantly in the field and the shipments to the yards are increasing. Of course there is no competition whatever at the Fowler yards, and *whenever the shipments there exceed the requirements of the Fowler plant, which are only about 800 a day, the surplus is turned over to any member of the combine who may need them or is prorated among the trio.*[51]

National functioned as an "evener" in the market, not only by "competing" for purchases but also, and probably more importantly, by permitting an interchange of product flows among the big packers and National and its subsidiaries. Because the Big Three jointly owned National and had fashioned information channels that permitted more effective communication, the packers could sell to and buy from National quickly and efficiently, whenever they found themselves "short" or "long" on the market. Or similarly, whenever National found itself without supplies, it could buy from the Big Three. With plants and branch houses scattered across the country, this meant that orders could be sent from the nearest plant of any of the Big Three or National, thus saving freight and distribution expenses.[52]

The packers also used National to allot supplies of provisions and to divide distribution responsibilities among those best able to supply a particular product. For example, meat dealers in West Virginia and Alabama found that "Swift & Company will supply him with fat backs; Morris & Company will supply him with beef ribs, and some branch of the National Packing Company will supply him with beef loins."[53]

Refrigerator cars also appear to have been exchanged on occasion. Having created a separate car line corporation—the National Car Line—to consolidate and operate the cars of National's various subsidiaries, the packers naturally turned to it whenever they needed cars. Although Swift and Armour "use their own refrigerator cars for the most part," reported John Dickinson from Fort Worth, Texas, "it is reported that a few weeks ago Swift & Company were liberally using the cars that bore the name of the German-American Packing Company of Chicago [a subsidiary of National]."[54]

Just as the packers cooperated to coordinate the product flows of National with those of their own companies, so too did they join together to coordinate their strategic decisions. The competitive race to build more productive capacity, which had proved so costly to the packers in the past, slowed down as National began to function. Whereas Armour had built 107 branch houses during the six-year period from 1891 to 1897, and 95 from 1898 to 1903, he built only 65 between 1904 and 1910, and, significantly, none of these were opened in a city in which he had a previous representative or in which there was already a house of Swift or Morris. Swift's rate of expansion also decreased. To the 193 branch houses built sometime between 1885 and 1897, Swift added 120 between 1898 and 1904. Between 1904 and 1910, however, he built only 75. Morris built 41 houses between 1891 and 1897, 38 between 1898 and 1903, but only 13 between 1904 and 1919. The rate of building slaughterhouses and the acquisition of stockyards also slowed perceptibly: whereas Armour had built or acquired stock in 4, Swift, 8, and Morris, 1, between 1898 and 1903, they built or acquired stock in only 2 yards during the next six years.[55]

Rather than engage in competitive building, the packers used National to acquire competing plants and more sales outlets. Between 1904 and 1910, National acquired some 23 slaughtering plants and stockyards, eight of which were not part of the original merger agreement.[56] The Ruddy Brothers' Packing Co. was purchased shortly after the formation of National in 1903. Incorporated in Illinois in 1882 with a capital of $100,000, it had confined its operations to the interstate dressed beef trade, using its own fleet of refrigerator cars. Serious financial difficulties, however, apparently convinced its owners to sell to the big packers, who probably saw its fleet of refrigerator cars as a useful asset and the elimination of a competitor as an obvious advantage.[57] That same year National paid over $1 million for the Continental

Packing Co. of Illinois, a Chicago firm incorporated in 1894 with $500,000 capital.[58] A year later, in 1904, National acquired the German-American Provision Co. and the Hutchinson Packing Co. of Kansas City, Missouri, as well as a majority of stock in the Provision Dealer's Dispatch. The latter firm was incorporated in Illinois in 1892 with $500,000 capital stock and operated primarily as a transportation company. The year 1905 saw the acquisition of the Milwaukee Stockyards Company, the Hamilton Stockyards Company, Ltd., of Canada, the Plankinton Packing Co. of Milwaukee, the Denver Union Stockyards, and 60 percent of the stock of the Colorado Packing & Provision Co. In 1906 National acquired 90 percent of the stock of the Smith Brothers Packing Co. of Denver, Colorado, the remaining 40 percent of the stock of the Colorado Packing & Provision Co., and 75 percent of the stock of the Union Rendering Co., also of Denver, along with the entire stock of the Northwestern Glue Co. National began to buy up the Butchers' Dressed Meat Co. in 1907, a cooperative meat packing firm organized in 1905 by the retail butchers of eastside New York to prepare kosher meats. The year 1908 saw National purchase the La Blanca Packing Plant in Buenos Aires, Argentina. The following year the remainder of the stock in the Western Packing Company of San Francisco was secured. In 1911 National acquired the Northern Reduction Company, a fat rendering concern in Bartel, Wisconsin.[59]

By 1911 National had branch houses in 153 cities in the United States and several in England and Scotland.[60] Its 2,600 refrigerator cars outnumbered those operated by the two biggest independent competitors, Cudahy and S & S.[61] The National's proportion of the total number of cattle slaughtered in the major markets of the U.S. averaged about 10 percent, and that increased the Big Three packers' share of the livestock slaughtered at the major markets from about 60 percent to 70 percent and their share of total beef sales from 29 percent to 36 percent.[62] As important, the National appeared to be making money for its owners. Even the first year of operation, which customarily is not a profitable one for a new company in the process of organization, brought $100,000 profit. Profits for the following year totalled $700,000.[63] Moreover, judging from the first payment of 1¾-percent dividends on April 1, 1908, and the 7 percent dividend rate maintained thereafter, the company's profits increased as time passed and operations became routinized.[64]

What gave the National such an important role in the industry was the fact that it permitted the centralization of some decision making and an efficient interchange of managerial resources, product flows, and equipment. The National is perhaps best described as a "half-way house" between pooling and complete merger, though it was really closer to pooling than to combination. Like a merger, it involved some institutionalization of decision-making processes. It differed significantly from a merger, however, in that cooperative planning was accomplished through the vehicle of an "outside" company. The internal structures of the Big Three companies remained intact, and, thus, like the pooling arrangement, the National did not eliminate the potential for conflict. If threats to individual interests surpassed damage to the common interests, the structures of the relationship permitted each packer to pursue an independent course, just as they had done ever since the 1880s.

THE IMPACT OF NATIONAL

While it is impossible to determine precisely what effect the National had on profits, prices, and margins of the packers, it is important to note that the oligopoly appeared to function more smoothly and profitably during the operation of National than before. Whereas the net profits of Armour and Swift averaged $1,850,000 and $1,460,000, respectively, between 1890 and 1900, they averaged $4,200,000 and $5,000,000 between 1900 and 1910.[65] Further, during the lifetime of National, market shares of the Big Three remained stable. Table VI.1 and VI.2 show no striking changes in the market shares of the four companies (Armour, Swift, Morris, and National) between 1907 and 1909, though of course the time period is too short to be decisive.[66]

Cudahy and S & S clearly managed to survive alongside National and the Big Three, maintaining their positions in the industry. Shortly after the merger agreement fell through, these two firms apparently disassociated themselves from further negotiations, but there is little evidence concerning any subsequent interfirm relations. Officers of Swift and National did attempt to acquire control of the stock of S & S throughout the decade.[67]

There is also some evidence to indicate that, while Cudahy and S & S

Table VI.1. Percentage of Total Cattle Inspected and Killed by Big Three Packers and National at Eight Major Livestock Centers in the United States, 1907–1909

Year	% Swift	% Armour	% Morris	% National
1907	33.9	27	17.5	21.6
1908	34.5	27.8	17.8	19.9
1909	34.8	28	17.8	19.4

Source: Compiled from data in *St. of Mo. v. Hammond Packing Co.*, Joint Abstract of Record, pp. 347–349.

Table VI.2. Distribution of Total Cattle Inspected and Killed by Big Three Packers (with National Figures Included) at Eight Major Livestock Centers in the United States, 1907–1909

Year	% Swift	% Armour	% Morris
1907	44.0%	35.7%	20.3%
1908	43.8	35.9	20.4
1909	43.9	35.7	20.3

Source: Compiled from data in *St. of Mo.* v. *Hammond Packing Co.,* Joint Abstract of Record, pp. 347–349.

may not have participated formally in the organization of National or in its directors' meetings, there nevertheless was some kind of cooperation, or at least a tacit understanding that these two smaller firms would not seek to disrupt the relative market shares established during the days of the pool, and that they would agree to follow where the Big Three led. In a letter to the Commissioner of Corporations, discussing the results of an interview with Chicago provision broker N. J. Weil of N. J. Weil & Co., field investigator T. M. Robertson suggested the possibility of price leadership: "Weil is of the opinion that the Cudahy and S & S are independent; but that in order to avoid open war with the National Packing Company and other large concerns have adopted the policy of following as closely as possible the prices fixed by the combination."[68] As was the case with the market shares of the Big Three and National, those of Cudahy and S & S seemed to have remained relatively stable throughout the period. Moreover, unlike smaller interstate firms, Cudahy and S & S generally shared in the profits of the industry. Whereas between 1895 and 1900 Cudahy's net profits had averaged only $440,500 a year, the next half decade saw that company averaging yearly net profits of $835,200. S & S also saw its net profits improve (although overexpansion would bring difficulties by the end of the decade). Average profits climbed from $624,200 a year during 1895–1900 to $815,200 during the next half decade.[69]

Collusion or some kind of formal cooperation is not necessary to explain the behavior of the "junior partners" in the oligopoly. It may well have been that these two independent and large, integrated, interstate firms benefited from the organization of National without actually participating in its operation. Stabilization of prices and elimination of competition between the Big Three meant a more secure position for

Figure VI.5. Net Profits in The Meat-Packing Industry, 1888–1912

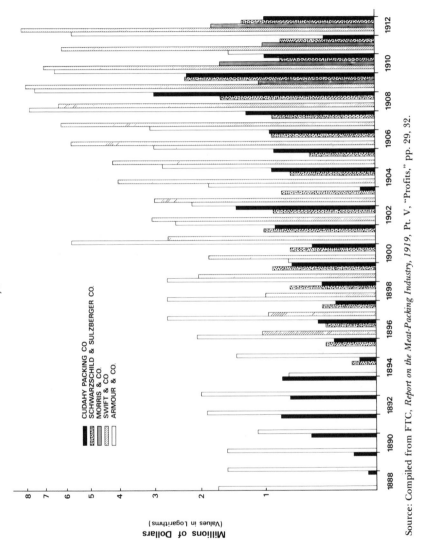

CUDAHY PACKING CO
SCHWARZSCHILD & SULZBERGER CO.
MORRIS & CO.
SWIFT & CO.
ARMOUR & CO.

Millions of Dollars
(Values in Logarithms)

Source: Compiled from FTC, *Report on the Meat-Packing Industry, 1919*, Pt. V, "Profits," pp. 29, 32.

157

Cudahy and S & S. Not only did they share these objectives, but they could profit from them as well if they followed the lead of the Big Three.

By the early twentieth century, the large packers had learned their lessons. They seldom engaged in price competition, practicing price leadership instead. By this time, all knew each other's costs, and all understood that only mutual trouble would flow from "rocking the boat."

NATIONAL PACKING COMPANY AND THE BIG THREE IN THE EXPORT TRADE

Not surprisingly, the National Packing Co. also played a role in diminishing competitive tendencies among the American oligopolists in overseas markets. Before 1908 interfirm relations in foreign markets were much the same as they had been since the late nineteenth century. The dominant American packers had initially directed their export efforts toward Great Britain and soon had come to control the American export trade. By the late 1890s, two-thirds of the cattle and three-fourths of the chilled beef exported to England had been bought in Chicago and exported by Armour, Morris, Swift, Hammond, and S & S.[70] Their extensive capital, organizational experience, and marketing abilities enabled them to move quickly into foreign markets, set up their own distributing agencies, and ship beef profitably, underselling their British competitors.

The same sorts of competitive conditions that led to domestic cartels during the late 1880s and 1890s created a need for regulation in the export trade. Agreements to regulate export shipments to England came soon after agreements upon percentage allotments in the domestic trade.[71]

Between 1900 and 1911, however, the American beef surplus diminished, and the United States lost its position as the major meat exporting country of the world. Demand in the U.S. market was so strong that less and less domestic meat was shipped abroad. The reversal came with almost startling rapidity in the dressed beef field, in which exports from the U.S. to England dropped dramatically, from about 370 million pounds in 1901, to less than 10 percent of that figure by 1911. Drastic declines occurred in shipments of pork, live cattle, sheep, and cured products as well. Pork exports fell from 31 million pounds in 1901, to less than 2 million pounds by 1911. Live cattle exports dropped from 459,000 head to 150,000 head, sheep exports plummeted from 297,000 pounds to 121,500 pounds, and exports of preserved beef and veal declined from 110 million pounds to 51 million pounds between 1900 and 1911.[72]

As prices rose and the demand for meat increased throughout the world, there were corresponding pressures for new sources of supply. The American packers had to keep a steady flow of products running through their overseas enterprises if they hoped to keep costs down. Because Argentina had become the beef producing center of the world, the packers quickly directed their attention there.

Swift & Co. moved first to capitalize on new Argentine opportunities. In 1907 Swift paid £350,000 for the La Plata slaughtering and cold storage plant in Buenos Aires.[73] As one historian of the Argentine meat trade put it,

> It was an auspicious purchase. The equipment of the plant was as good as any in the Plate and better than most. Its excellent situation on deep water was unrivaled and gave it a great advantage in the shipment of chilled meat; at La Plata the steamers could load and go directly to their destination, while most of the other plants were less accessible to ocean steamers and required double handling of goods. A further advantage was the exemption from taxes which the original concession provided. The company had by this time become the second largest shipper of beef. In 1906 its exports had amounted to 18.5% of the chilled beef exported, 15.5% of the frozen beef, and 15.1% of the mutton; the totals for 1907 were well on the way to exceeding these proportions. At one stroke Swift & Company became an important factor in the River Plate.[74]

Swift's unannounced move into the Argentine market alarmed Armour and Morris. Not wanting to be left behind, they, together with S & S, began to make their own plans to capture a slice of the Argentine export trade and to secure more supplies for their own organizations. Significantly, the next move into Argentina was made jointly by Armour, Morris, and Swift through the National Packing Co. Only a year after Swift's purchase of La Plata, National paid $1,700,000 for the La Blanca plant of Argentina. The third largest shipper of chilled (refrigerated) beef in Argentina, La Blanca had just opened its own sales outlets in England after finding the commission system inadequate. By 1910 beef exported from Argentina by the Big Three was being distributed to various of their sales outlets around the world by National's English subsidiary, the Hammond Beef Company, Ltd. In 1911 Americans shipped two-thirds of the chilled beef (the most profitable item in the trade), about one-fifth of the frozen beef, and about one-third of the mutton exported from Argentina.[75]

As usual however, the growing expansion into new markets led to a decline in packer profits in those markets. La Blanca, even without a depreciation write-off, showed a loss of $171,725 and paid no dividend in 1911. "La Plata, the aggressor in the price war, managed to maintain its twelve and one-half percent dividend rate," recorded Simon G. Hanson in *Argentine Meat and the British Market*, "but its earnings were cut in half. The earnings of the industry as a whole amounted to less than 4 percent on the share of capital, at a time when only Argentina could supply the quantity and quality of beef that England required!"[76]

Experience in the United States meat market foreshadowed the outcome. In November 1911 an export pool was organized to control product flows from Argentina to the English market. Consisting of all the major Argentine, British, and American exporting firms, the pool allotted each company a certain proportion of the total exports. Maximum quantities were to be established at meetings of representatives held every six weeks (probably on a Tuesday). Since the Big Three had made the largest gains between 1908 and 1911, they received the largest allotment. La Blanca and La Plata together shipped about 41 percent of the total output, while the other five Argentine and British firms shipped the rest.[77]

As the American domestic experience also foreshadowed, the peace was a fleeting one. The next years saw a repetition of the old pattern of the repeated creation and collapse of cartels. As had been the case in the domestic market during the period of expansion in new territories in the late 1890s, the packers oscillated between competition and cooperation, but National played an important role. Its entrance into the Argentine market shortly after Swift's independent purchase of La Plata suggests that Morris and Armour were reminding Swift that cooperation through National was in the long run more profitable than competition. On the other hand, even though Swift & Co. did not pass up the opportunity to cooperate in the centralization of the distribution of Argentine beef via National's English subsidiary, neither did it accept without complaint the constraints National imposed on its market behavior.[78]

National's days were numbered, however. It is impossible to judge how long it might have lasted if that determination had remained solely in the packers' hands. What is certain is that forces from outside the industry played a strong role in sealing its fate. They had been building for years.

NOTES

1. *U.S.* v. *Addyston Pipe & Steel Co.*, 1 F.A.D.641(1898); 175 U.S. 211(1899). In this case the government tried to enjoin the activities of six cast iron manufacturers who had organized the Associated Pipe Works for the purpose of rigging bids on municipal government contracts and pooling the receipts. When municipalities advertised for bids, the privilege of submitting the lowest bid was to go to the member that offered to pay the largest bonus into the common fund. The lowest court held that the arrangement was legal because like the American Sugar Trust in *U.S.* v. *E. C. Knight et al.*, 60 Fed.306 (1894), 60 Fed.934 (1894), 156 U.S.1(1895), the combination affected only manufacturing and therefore could not be reached by the Sherman Act, which applied to cases affecting interstate

commerce. It also claimed that the government had not proved the unlawfulness of the restraint. William Howard Taft of the Circuit Court of Appeals reversed the decision, arguing that the combination restrained competition and was therefore unlawful per se. Chief Justice Peckham, speaking for the Supreme Court, rejected Taft's interpretation that price fixing was illegal per se, but upheld the illegality of the combination. "Where the direct and immediate effect of a contract or combination among particular dealers in a commodity is to destroy competition between them and others, so that the parties to such a contract or combination may obtain increased prices for themselves, such a contract or combination amounts to a restraint of trade in the commodity, even though contracts to buy such commodity at the enhanced price are continually being made." See the discussion of the case in Donald Dewey, *Monopoly in Economics and Law* (Chicago, 1959), pp. 54–55, 161, 181, 218; Eliot Jones, *The Trust Problem in the United States* (New York, 1921), pp. 395–398; Alfred S. Eichner, *The Emergence of Oligopoly*, pp. 8–9, 17, 152, 187, 299.

2. Jones, *The Trust Problem in the United States*, p. 27.

3. The best recent analyses of the great merger movement are Alfred D. Chandler, Jr., *The Visible Hand*, pp. 319–344; Robert T. Averitt, *The Dual Economy*, pp. 4–22; Ralph L. Nelson, *Merger Movements in American Industry, 1895–1956* (Princeton, 1959); Alfred S. Eichner, *The Emergence of Oligopoly*, pp. 1–24. Contemporary accounts include Arthur S. Dewing, *Corporate Promotions and Reorganizations* (Cambridge, Mass., 1914), pp. 893–983; William Ripley, *Trusts, Pools and Corporations*, (Boston, Mass., 1905), pp. ix–xxx; John Moody, *The Truth About the Trusts* (Chicago, 1904). Shaw Livermore, "The Success of Industrial Mergers," *Quarterly Journal of Economics*, 50 (November 1935):68–96, explains why mergers were more successful in some industries than others.

4. Swift and Van Vlissingen, *The Yankee of the Yards*, p. 209. For Armour's view of mergers, see Leech and Carroll, *Armour and His Times*, pp. 205–206. *National Provisioner*, February 9, 1901, p. 12, claims that Armour was always opposed to the trust idea.

5. Leech and Carroll, *Armour and His Times*, p. 205. See also, later reports of the packers' attempt to merge in Bureau of Corporations, Beef Industry File No. 623, No. 738. Justice Dept. File No. 60-50-0(1) includes letter from Charles DeWoody, special examiner, Paris, Texas, February 2, 1910, to U.S. Attorney General Wickersham, which recounts the earlier testimony of Mr. Miles, general manager, Armour & Co., 1894–1903. Miles claimed that at a meeting held about June 1, 1901, G. F. Swift urged the packers to "form a 'rival' packing company . . . to destroy" one of the largest independent packing companies, the Omaha Packing Company. My interpretation generally supports the view that intensified competition may have been an important factor in the packers' decision to merge but also suggests that this factor alone is insufficient to explain packer actions at this particular time.

6. L. D. H. Weld, *Private Freight Cars and American Railways* (New York, 1908), pp. 28–30, provides the following statistics on railroad ownership of refrigerator cars (compiled from *Poor's Manual*):

Year	No. of refrigerator cars owned by railroads
1885	900
1890	3,398
1895	7,043
1900	10,760
1905	24,570

For additional details of the railroad's strategy toward the acquisition of refrigerator cars, see *National Provisioner*, January 25, 1902, pp. 11, 17.

7. See Alfred D. Chandler's discussion of their creation in *The Railroads*, pp. 159–163.

8. *National Provisioner*, March 22, 1902, p. 22, quoting the *Chicago Chronicle.*

9. *Ibid.*

10. Leech and Carroll, *Armour and His Times*, p. 97.

11. Edith Penrose examines the general problem of firm succession as part of *The Theory of the Growth of the Firm* (London, 1959), pp. 39–40, 186–190, and Chap. VIII. To see how other family firms coped with the problem of succession, see Alfred D. Chandler, Jr., and Stephen Salsbury, *Pierre S. Du Pont and The Making of the Modern Corporation* (New York, 1971), pp. 301–321. The relative advantages and disadvantages of pools and of formal administrative organizations are similar to those of informal, personal organization and to bureaucracy. See H. H. Gerth and C. Wright Mills, ed., *From Max Weber* (New York, 1958), pp. 197–244.

12. Leech and Carroll, *Armour and His Times*, p. 344.

13. *Ibid.*, p. 82.

14. *Ibid.*, p. 95.

15. Bureau of Corporations, Beef Industry File No. 623, No. 738, and Justice Dept. File No. 60-50-0(1), National Archives.

16. Simon N. Whitney, *Anti-Trust Policies*, Vol. I, p. 35; U.S. Congress, House, *Hearings Before the Committee on Agriculture on Meat Packer Legislation*, 66th Cong., 2nd Sess., 1920, p. 958, testimony of L. D. H. Weld, and pp. 959–965, testimony of Henry Veeder of Swift & Co.

17. In *U.S.* v. *Louis Swift*, 188 Fed. 1002 (1910), attorneys for the packers successfully argued that the distinction between the individuals and their corporations was important. They claimed that since the individuals had purchased the stock and properties in their own names, the charge of combination in restraint of trade against the Armour, Morris, and Swift corporations could not be supported. The FTC, *Report on the Meat-Packing Industry, 1919*, Pt. II, "Evidence of Combination Among Packers," p. 23, considered the distinction spurious.

18. The contract is submitted as evidence in *St. of Mo.* v. *Hammond Packing Co. et al.*, Record Vol. I, 571–590. The discussion that follows is based heavily on these records. The case first came to trial in 1913. State Attorney General John T. Barker charged the corporations with "unlawfully abusing their rights and franchise and unlawfully usurping authorities and privileges as corporations under the laws of Missouri, by entering into and becoming members of a pool, trust, combination, confederation, agreement and understanding. . . ." The final decision, rendered in April 1915 (reported sub. nom. *State ex. rel. Barker* v. *Armour Packing Co.*, 265 Mo. 121, 176 S.W. 382) found the corporations guilty. The packers were fined $25,000 each.

The initial merger contract—Articles 2, 3, and 4—show that the three packers were to turn over to the new company the stocks and properties of the following companies:

Armour
Illinois
    Armour & Co.
    Continental Fruit Express
    Rathbourne, Hair & Edgeway Co.
    Union Fruit Auction Co. of Chicago

New Jersey
    Armour Packing Co.
    Armour & Co.
    Armour Car Lines

Other states
    Earl Fruit Co. and California Manufacturing Co. (Iowa)
    Armour Packing Co., Ltd. (La.)
    Helmet Mining Co. (Mo.)
    Keystone Hotel Supply Co. (Pa.)
    Union Fruit Auction Co. (N.Y.)
    Hyde, Wheeler & Co. and T. H. Wheeler Co. (Mass.)

Swift
  Illinois
    Swift & Co.
    Swift Packing Co.
    Franklin Salt Co.
    Libby, McNeill & Libby, Inc.
    National Leather Co.
    Consumers Cotton Oil Co.

  New York
    Swift & Co.
    Butchers' Hide and Melting Assoc.

  Maine
    New England Dressed Meat and Wool Co.
    Swift Refrigerator Transportation Co.
    North Packing and Provision Co.
    National Manufacturing Co.
    Swift Live Stock Transportation Co.
    White, Peavey & Dexter Co.
    National Calf Skin Co.
    A. C. Lawrence Leather Co.
    Winchester Tannery Co.

  Other states
    Swift & Co. (N.J.)
    Swift & Co., Ltd. (La.)
    Libby, McNeill & Libby, Ltd., (La.)
    Springfield Provision Co. (N.H.)
    Merwin Provision Co. (Conn.)
    Union Rendering Co. of St. Paul (Minn.)

Foreign
    Swift Beef Co., Ltd. (Great Britain)
    National Oil and Hyde Co., Ltd. (Great Britain)
    Henry A. Lane & Co., Ltd. (Great Britain)

Morris
  Michigan
    Fairbank Canning Co.
    National Box Co.
    Morris Packing Co.
    Consumers Cotton Oil Co.
    Michigan Manufacturing Co. (Mich.)

Foreign

    Morris Beef Co. Ltd. (Great Britain)

    National Oil & Hide Co., Ltd. (Great Britain)

    American Live Stock Transportation Co. (including export cattle business)

Note: There were no slaughtering plants west of the 105th meridian (i.e., Colorado).

19. Until the properties were officially appraised, the packers agreed to accept temporary percentages. The ownership and liability of Armour, Swift, and Morris, respectively, equalled 40, 37½, and 22½ percent. Audit showed Armour having assets, profits, and liabilities totalling $73 million, $7.9 million, and $15 million, respectively. Swift's property was appraised at $85 million; profits amounted to $8.3 million; and liabilities equaled $35 million. Tangible assets of Morris totalled $24 million. No additional information on Morris was given (*St. of Mo.* v. *Hammond Packing Co.*, Record Vol. I, 590–591, 621, 697).

20. Emphasis added. *St. of Mo.* v. *Hammond Packing Co.*, Record Vol. I, 586.

21. *Commissioner of Corporations Report on the Beef Industry, 1905*, pp. 286–297, provides data regarding the various concerns composing or allied to Swift, Armour, Morris, Cudahy, Schwarzschild & Sulzberger, and the National Packing Company. *Moody's Manual of Industrial and Miscellaneous Securities* provides some information on the big packers but very little on smaller concerns. See *New York Times,* July 1, 1902, p. 2; August 1, 1902, p. 1; August 16, 1902, p. 1; August 19, 1902, p. 6; August 22, 1902, p. 2; February 24, 1903, p. 3; *National Provisioner,* May 19, 1900, p. 15; January 4, 1902, p. 13; January 3, 1903, pp. 13, 21, 31; April 11, 1903, p. 14; August 15, 1903, pp. 17, 23. Attorney Louis C. Krauthoff, representing J. O. Armour (Bureau of Corporations, Beef Industry File No. 5-738, National Archives), suggested this rationale for packer acquisitions: "It was possible that the large packing companies, after creating a market for their products in various parts of the country, or after establishing the ability to control prices in some measure upon the boards of trade, should find that the conditions which they had created were being taken advantage of by smaller companies which had no part in creating these conditions."

22. FTC, *Report on the Meat-Packing Industry, 1919,* Pt. II, "Evidence of Combination Among Packers," p. 23, states that "The capital stock in the so-called subsidiary companies of the National Packing Co. stood in the names of the stockholders of the National Packing Co. in the same proportion substantially as they were stockholders in the National Packing Company, so that on the books of the G. H. Hammond Co. there would be a certain proportion in the name of trustees who managed the Swift estate, a certain proportion of the stock standing in the name of Morris. Thus, for all legal purposes the National Packing Company might be wiped out of existence and the proportionate ownership in the acquired companies would go on undisturbed."

The Illinois Trust & Savings Bank of Chicago carried out the contract for the First National Bank of New York. There were many difficulties involved in drawing up the contract. Packers disagreed upon the specific properties to be included in the merger. Swift had to include D. M. Anthony & Co. of Fall River, Mass., and Bimbler, Van Wagener & Co., a hog and beef slaughtering firm of Newark, N.J., because "Armour and Morris insisted that those should be included in the sale, so that Mr. Swift would not have an opportunity afterwards, through a private partnership or corporation of which he was a member, of perhaps obstructing the business which he had recently sold through Swift & Co. It was because of his personal interest in these concerns that they insisted that they should be transferred to the large company when formed" (*St. of Mo.* v. *Hammond Packing Co.*, Record Vol. I, 599, 625).

23. The public had little knowledge of the packers' objectives. To most observers it appeared as though the Big Three were competing to acquire these additional companies

(*New York Times,* July 1, 1903, p. 2). The *New York Times* reported (July 3, 1902, p. 1) that Armour & Co. had made an offer to purchase the stock of Swift & Co. at $150 a share and that the offer had been refused.

Swift's purchase of the Fowler properties netted stockholders of that concern "a profit of between £4 and £5 a share." Preference and debenture holders received their capital. The ordinary shareholders of Fowler, Son & Co. received only £14 for each £7 paid up on £10 shares. The preference holders received their capital, plus seven years of unpaid dividends, making £14 for each £10 share. The holders of debenture bonds received their capital plus 2 percent (*New York Times,* July 3, 1902, p. 1).

St. of Mo. v. *Hammond Packing Co.*, Record Vol. I, 743-760, includes agreements between Swift and the Fowlers. Those between Armour and Morris and each of their newly acquired firms are nearly identical.

See the brief coverage of acquisitions and mergers in *New York Times,* August 1, 1902, p. 1; August 16, 1902, p. 1; August 19, 1902, p. 6; August 22, 1902, p. 2; August 25, 1902, p. 6; February 24, 1903, p. 3.

24. Several possible explanations can be advanced. First, merger simply may not have been as appealing to them. These two firms had traditionally been able to hold their own against the larger integrated corporations, and they may therefore have valued their independence more highly than they valued the proposed benefits of cooperation. Second, Cudahy and S & S may have been unwilling to negotiate on terms proposed by the Big Three. Third, the Big Three may not have wanted to include them in the agreement until after they had made the new acquisitions. The purchase of these additional concerns, in effect, would increase the bargaining position of the Big Three vis-à-vis Cudahy and S & S. Finally, Cudahy and S & S may have been unable to afford to purchase additional companies and, therefore, may simply have agreed with the Big Three not to enter merger negotiations until after those purchases were completed.

25. The Big Three may well have applied pressure to convince the two independents that it was in their best interests to join. John Dickinson, special investigator for the Bureau of Corporations, (Beef Industry File No. 623), learned from an interview with E. E. Matchette, general manager of the Kansas City House of S & S, May 19, 1904:

> that since the organization of the National Packing Co., the S&S house here had some trouble in getting refrigerator cars; that it was difficult to rent these cars from the National Car Line Co.; that the firm's own cars were not, in every case, handled by the railroads with the same dispatch as formerly, and that generally speaking, there was perceptible to him a disposition "all around" to hamper the operations of the S&S since the formation of the National Packing Co.

J. P. Cudahy related a similar story to Dickinson (Bureau of Corporations, Beef Industry File No. 623) in an interview, May 11, 1904, with regard to Cudahy's Kansas City plant.

26. The supplemental agreement including Cudahy is detailed in *St. of Mo.* v. *Hammond Packing Co.*, Record Vol. I, 778-787.

27. The contract between the Big Three and Ferdinand Sulzberger is in *St. of Mo.* v. *Hammond Packing Co.*, Record Vol. V, pp. 4158-4174. There were several major obstacles to acquisition of all the stock of S & S, the primary one being the fact that Sulzberger held only 22,090½ shares of the capital stock of S & S. There was included in the contract a provision stipulating that the Big Three would also purchase, on demand of Sulzberger, 7,312½ shares and 3,615 shares held respectively by Frederick Joseph and Samuel Weil (brother-in-law of F. Joseph). Outstanding shares numbered 43,734. Sulzberger and Weil and Joseph were to receive $190 per share for their stock. The total price of the stock purchase was $6 million. If the appraised value of stock was found to be less than $6 million, no diminution in the price of stock was to occur. In return for the stock Sulzberger was to receive common stock equal to "the proportion . . . applicable to those of the aforesaid

shares of said S&S Company which party of the first part [Sulzberger] shall deliver or tender to parties of the second part [Swift, Armour and Morris], upon the basis which the whole of the net earnings of said S&S Company for its fiscal year ending December 28, 1901, and before September 1, 1902" (p. 4162). The 43,734 outstanding shares, referred to as the "New England Stock," was to be purchased at a price not to exceed $110 per share.

28. The agreement is submitted as evidence, *St. of Mo. v. Hammond Packing Co.*, Record Vol. I, 649–670. The immensity of the merger is reflected in the value of the assets involved: $264 million, $90 million of which represented the plants and other fixed assets, including cars, of the vendor's companies and of the S & S Company; $130 million of which represented "the quick assets of all the . . . corporations and concerns"; $20 million of which represented the cost of the purchased companies and the amount to be set aside for working capital; and $24.5 million of which represented the aggregate net earnings of all the companies.

29. U.S. Congress, House, *Hearings Before the Committee on Agriculture on Meat Packer Legislation*, 66th Cong., 2nd Sess., 1920, p. 1293, testimony of Henry Veeder.

30. Holding companies are discussed in detail in James C. Bonbright and Gardiner Means, *The Holding Company* (New York, 1932); M. C. Wattersdorf, "Holding Companies," *Economic Journal*, 36 (December 1926):586–597.

31. *St. of Mo. v. Hammond Packing Co.*, Record Vol. I, 648–669. The discussion that follows in the text below, pp. 142–143 is based on details of the contract. See also, *Hearings Before the Committee on Agriculture on Meat Packer Legislation*, pp. 958–965, 1195, 1200, 1293–1295.

32. The syndicate was to withold its shares from sale for seven years, after which time the shares were to be offered to the packers.

33. *St. of Mo. v. Hammond Packing Co.*, Joint Abstract of Record, p. 89, testimony of Albert H. Veeder of Swift & Co.

34. *Ibid.* There were also a number of obligations outstanding as part payment of the purchase of additional companies.

35. *Hearings Before the Committee on Agriculture on Meat Packer Legislation*, p. 1293, testimony of Henry Veeder, son of Albert and also a member of Swift's legal counsel.

36. For details see *St. of Mo. v. Hammond Packing Co.*, Record Vol. I, 673–682. In the interim between November and December, Cudahy and S & S withdrew from the merger agreement.

37. Albert H. Veeder, lawyer and chief counsel, Swift & Company, considered approval by the bankers extremely important. "They did not give us free rope," he insisted when testifying before the Supreme Court of Missouri in 1913. "We planned the organization draft of charter and by-laws and general scheme, which were submitted to Mr. Cravath, as counsel for Kuhn, Loeb & Company, and taken by him under consideration, and when they finally met with his approval this supplemental agreement dated March 18, 1903 was made for the purpose of protecting Kuhn, Loeb & Co. and defining the rights of the parties" (*St. of Mo. v. Hammond Packing Co.*, Record Vol. I, 909). The packers believed that the bankers considered the merger perfectly legal.

The role of financiers in the promotion of consolidations is discussed more generally in Arthur S. Dewing, *Corporate Promotions and Reorganizations*.

38. *St. of Mo. v. Hammond Packing Co.*, Joint Abstract of Record, p. 93.

39. FTC, *Report on the Meat-Packing Industry, 1919*, Summary and Pt. I, p. 48; Pt. II, "Evidence of Combination Among Packers," pp. 22–23.

40. "Certificate of Incorporation of National Packing Company," *St. of Mo. v. Hammond Packing Co.*, Record Vol. III, pp. 1998–2005. The by-laws are found in Vol. III, pp. 2008–2011.

41. Information on officers is found in *Moody's Manual of Industrial and Miscellaneous Securities*, 1900, p. 814; 1905, p. 1862; 1907, p. 1919; *Commissioner of Corporations Report on the Beef Industry, 1905*, pp. 286–297; *National Provisioner*, February 21, 1903, p. 35; July 11, 1903, p. 13; August 15, 1903, p. 23.

42. "By-Laws of National Packing Company," Article No. 2, *St. of Mo. v. Hammond Packing Co.*, Record Vol. III, 2011–2013. The regularity of meetings shows that National was an operating as well as a parent-holding company. Such meetings were necessary if its directors were to make crucial decisions regarding routine matters of price and margins and those involving planning for the whole enterprise. The Federal Trade Commission interpreted the meetings as proof of conspiracy and claimed that because these meetings occurred the same day and hour as the pool meetings, they also indicated that National was simply a cover-up for another pooling association. As the text shows, the FTC was half right.

43. *St. of Mo. v. Hammond Packing Co.*, Joint Abstract of Record, p. 39, testimony of A. N. Benn, assistant to the president, National Packing Company.

44. It is difficult to determine precisely the number or the nature of departments. No official organization chart exists and information must be gleaned from the disjointed testimony of many employees. Edward Tilden, president of National, maintained two offices, one in the Rookery Building and another at the Hammond plant. *St. of Mo. v. Hammond Packing Co.*, Joint Abstract of Record, p. 218, testimony of W. E. Weber, general auditor, National Packing Co.

45. *St. of Mo. v. Hammond Packing Co.*, Joint Abstract of Record, pp. 146–216, testimony of W. E. Weber.

46. *Ibid.*, pp. 41–42.

47. *Commissioner of Corporations Report on the Beef Industry, 1905*, p. 295.

48. *St. of Mo. v. Hammond Packing Co.*, Joint Abstract of Record, p. 42.

49. Special Agent John Dickinson, Chicago, Ill., August 15, 1904, to the Commissioner of Corporations, regarding interview with Mr. Chapin of Chapin & Edwards, Provision Brokers, Chicago, Ill. (Beef Industry File No. 738).

50. Dickinson, Kansas City, Mo., April 16, 1904, to Commissioner of Corporations, regarding interview with U. S. Epperson, formerly general manager of Fowler Packing Co. (Beef Industry File No. 623). See also, FTC, *Report on the Meat-Packing Industry, 1919*, Pt. II, "Evidence of Combination Among Packers," pp. 26–92.

51. Dickinson, Kansas City, Mo., April 19, 1904, to Commissioner of Corporations, (Beef Industry File No. 623).

52. Without internal records it is difficult to "prove" the proposition. Yet in view of the fact that plant or branch managers at National never knew from where their shipments were sent, there is a good possibility that such was the case, Dickinson, Fort Worth, Texas, May 24, 1904 to Commissioner of Corporations, interview with J. B. Geogins, manager, Swift & Co. plant, Fort Worth, Texas (Beef Industry File No. 623). "Geogins explained that Armour and Swift were joint owners of a small packing house, the North Fort Worth Manufacturing Co. which "manufactures ice for the packing houses of both Armour & Swift and also boxes for both concerns. It also contains the rendering works for dead animals—diseased—for both houses. Judd [Geogins] explained that the disposition of all the plant's by-products, except stearine, is made from headquarters at Chicago, and all of its meats and meat products are sold or contracted for by the Armour house at Kansas City. All that he has to do is to prepare the manufactured article for market, and then to ship them to the points selected by the houses at Chicago and Kansas City.... Judd claimed not to know what prices are charged for dressed beef, declaring that all of these details are looked after by the Kansas City house under special arrangement, with the details of which he is not acquainted. He says all returns on meats are made to the Kansas

City house and returns on by-products are made to Chicago. For this reason he says he is unable to tell how the Fort Worth plant is getting along."

53. T. M. Robertson, special agent, to the Commissioner of Corporations, August 16, 1904 (Beef Industry File No. 738), regarding activities in West Virginia and Alabama meat territories. Robertson reported that "No transactions of the National Packing Company are made in its own name, the name of each branch being used in connection with transactions concerning it. When supplies are purchased the transaction is made with Mr. Ernest Brown, purchasing agent of the National Packing Company, and the seller is instructed to make bills to these branches. The National Packing Company sends out no price lists under its own name, but always uses the name of some branch."

54. Special Agent John Dickinson, Fort Worth, Texas, May 24, 1904, to Commissioner of Corporations (Beef Industry File No. 623); also his report on the Seattle trade, Seattle, Washington, September 8, 1904.

55. Figures compiled from data in FTC, *Report on the Meat-Packing Industry, 1919,* Summary and Pt. I, pp. 242–257.

56. *Ibid.*

57. For information on the Ruddy Brothers Co., see *National Provisioner,* August 11, 1900, pp. 29–30; *Commissioner of Corporations Report on the Beef Industry, 1905,* p. 295. Special Agent T. A. Carroll, Kansas City, Mo., November 18, 1904 (Beef Industry File No. 666), reported that "Mr. Ruddy did state, . . . that the National Packing Company had been after his old plant for a long time, but he refused to have anything to do with them; that after many unsuccessful attempts to purchase his plant and business openly and above board, trickery and deception of the most despicable kind was resorted to and that he never suspected what had happened until he found himself firmly within the clutches of the National Packing Co." See also, Special Agent John Dickinson, Kansas City, Missouri, April 26, 1904, to Commissioner of Corporations (Beef Industry File No. 623).

58. *Commissioner of Corporations Report on the Beef Industry, 1905,* p. 295. Bureau of Corporations, Beef Industry File No. 25-0-116, indicates that the Provision Dealers Dispatch was organized in 1892 "To carry on the business of constructing, manufacturing, purchasing, repairing, operating, managing, conducting, using, selling, leasing and otherwise disposing of freight cars for the carriage of live and dead freight; also to engage in and conduct a general trading and commission and storage business; also to engage in the business of forwarding agents, warehouse men, wharfingers, car and ship owners, charterers of cars and ships, shippers and freight contractors." Directors included John Cudahy (500 shares) and Henry Botsford (1000 shares), among others.

59. FTC, *Report on the Meat-Packing Industry, 1919,* Summary and Pt. I, pp. 47–48, 245–246; Pt. II, "Evidence of Combination Among Packers," pp. 22–25, 28–34. For additional information on the Colorado Packing & Provision Co., and Western Packing Co., see Dickinson, Denver, Colo., May 5, 1904, and September 27, 1904, to Commissioner of Corporations, (Beef Industry File No. 623). *National Provisioner,* September 9, 1905, p. 15, supplies information on the New York Dressed Meat Co. Simon G. Hanson, *Argentine Meat and the British Market* (Stanford, 1938), p. 149, details the move into South America. Information on the Northern Reduction Co. is from Swift & Co. *Yearbook, 1913,* p. 34.

60. *St. of Mo.* v. *Hammond Packing Co.,* Record Vol. V, 4962–4964.

61. The exact numbers are in dispute. M. Markham Flannery, special agent, Chicago, June 18, 1904, to Commissioner of Corporations (Beef Industry File No. 738), quotes 2600 from the books of Boyd & Lunham, Chicago pork and provision dealers. On June 24, 1904, Flannery submitted additional figures from Max Epstein, president and general manager of the German-American Car lines, indicating that National Car Lines owned 3,800, while S & S owned 1,600, and Cudahy, 959 cars. *Commissioner of Corporations Report on*

the Beef Industry, 1905, p. 270, lists Cudahy, S & S, and National as having 800, 1250, and 2197 cars, respectively, in 1905.

62. Market shares are necessarily approximate. *St. of Mo.* v. *Hammond Packing Co.,* Joint Abstract of Record, pp. 346–349, Record Vol. V, 4878–4879, states that 85 percent of fresh meats consumed in the eastern, southern, and middle-western states was slaughtered in eight central markets, and that Swift, Armour, Morris, and National supplied about 70 percent of that amount in 1910. See also, *Commissioner of Corporations Report on the Beef Industry, 1905,* pp. xix–xxiv; 52–84, FTC, *Report on the Meat-Packing Industry, 1919,* Pt. II, "Evidence of Combination Among Packers," pp. 31–41; Whitney, *Anti-Trust Policies,* II, p. 33.

63. FTC, *Report on the Meat-Packing Industry, 1919,* Part II, "Evidence of Combination Among Packers," p. 236, quoting from "Memoranda Relating to the Reorganization of Sulzberger & Sons Co., now Wilson & Co., Inc., by German F. Sulzberger, of Sulzberger & Sons, Co., December 1914."

64. Compiled from *Moody's Manual of Industrial and Miscellaneous Securities,* 1908–1911.

65. Compiled from FTC, *Report on the Meat-Packing Industry, 1919,* Pt. V, "Profits of the Packers," pp. 21, 24.

66. Compiled from *St. of Mo.* v. *Hammond Packing Co.,* Joint Abstract of Record, pp. 346–349. The impact of National on meat prices is less clear. During the first decade of the twentieth century, the prices of all commodities rose. Using the average prices for the years 1896–1900 as the base level (100), prices of all commodities reached their high point for the decade in 1906 (126.7). They then fell to 116.0 in 1908 and climbed again to 122.6 in 1909. Beef prices also rose considerably and at a higher rate than those of all commodities taken as a whole, but cattle prices, especially those for corn-fed steers, also increased faster than all commodities, which made a large increase in packers' profits unlikely. The accompanying chart, issued by the U.S. Department of Agriculture in 1909, compares wholesale beef and cattle prices.

	Prices index number	
Item	*1908*	*1909*
Best native steers, Chicago	136.4	139.9
Choice to extra steers, Chicago	126.3	——
All fresh beef sold in NY by leading packing house	119.8	——
Native carcasses, common to fair, NY	129.7	133.6
Native sides, NY (another authority)	120.1	——
Beef carcasses, Chicago	123.7	——
Export price, fresh beef	118.5	120.9
	Wholesale prices index number	
Extra mess beef, sale	151.9	——
Western sale hams (beef)	134.0	——
Tallow	139.9	——
Family beef, salt	165.0	154.8
Export price, salted or pickled beef	124.5	141.0
Export price, tallow	137.2	130.9

Source: "Prices of Meat," U.S. Dept. of Agriculture, *Yearbook, 1909,* p. 28.

The Department of Agriculture (*Yearbook, 1909*) found the explanation for increasing beef prices in conditions peculiar to the industry: (1) the decrease in cattle supply that resulted from the abandonment of ranges; (2) new demands for corn on farms for beef production; (3) the high price of corn; (4) high prices of all meat, partly because of high corn prices; (5) reduction of the stock of hogs due to the panic of 1907; (6) high farm land values; (7) increasing cost of meat production; (8) increasing imbalance between production and consumption, with production declining relative to consumption; (9) decreasing meat consumption per capita; (10) increasing consumption of meat substitutes; (11) sharp decline in the export meat trade.

As satisfactory as are the reasons for an explanation of high fresh beef and cattle prices, they do not adequately explain why prices for less perishable cured beef increased in greater degree than steer and fresh beef prices. The items for cured beef may be compared with steers and fresh beef in the tables above.

It seems likely that National's impact upon prices would have showed up more clearly in this area, since prices for goods such as cured beef and by-products could be more easily maintained than could those for perishable dressed beef. On the other hand, industry structure is a relevant consideration, too, as well as perishability. That is, if dressed beef is a more concentrated industry than, say, cured beef, those packers engaged in dressed beef operations would, theoretically, be in a better position to manipulate prices.

67. Changes in control of the S & S firm are traced in FTC, *Report on the Meat-Packing Industry, 1919*, Pt. II, "Evidence of Combination Among Packers," pp. 159–242; *St. of Mo. v. Hammond Packing Co.*, Record Vol. V, 4153–4232, testimony of Ferdinand Sulzberger; *National Provisioner*, January 4, 1902, p. 12; February 28, 1903, p. 17; April 25, 1903, p. 16; April 2, 1904, p. 13; June 11, 1904, p. 48; April 9, 1904, p. 13. In 1910, S & S became Sulzberger & Sons. In 1915 the Sulzbergers sold their entire capital stock to a group of bankers and shortly thereafter, Thomas Wilson, a former executive officer of Morris & Company, assumed the presidency. The company was renamed Wilson & Company.

68. T. M. Robertson, special agent, Chicago, Illinois, Aug. 2, 1904, to Commissioner of Corporations (Beef Industry File No. 738), "Memorandum of Interview with N. J. Weil of N. J. Weil & Co., Provision Brokers, Chicago."

69. FTC, *Report on the Meat-Packing Industry, 1919*, Pt. V, "Profits," pp. 29, 32.

70. Richard Perren, "The North American Beef and Cattle Trade of Great Britain, 1870-1914," *Economic History Review*, 20 (August 1971), p. 437.

71. *Ibid.*, pp. 437, 442. Perren's assumption that after 1903 "the combination became less close in respect to business both in the United States and in the United Kingdom" is more true for the export trade than for the domestic meat trade but is not supported by much concrete evidence in either case. See Simon Hanson, *Argentine Meat and British Market*, pp. 114-115, n. 2; Peter Smith, *Politics and Beef in Argentina* (New York, 1969), p. 34; FTC, *Report on the Meat-Packing Industry, 1919*, Summary and Pt. I, pp. 160-199.

72. Hanson, *Argentine Meat and the British Market*, pp. 152-154. See also, George K. Holmes, "Statistics of Live Stock, Meat Production and Consumption: Prices and International Trade for Many Countries," in U.S. Dept. of Agriculture, Office of the Secretary, *Meat Situation in the United States*, Dept. Repts. Nos. 109-113 (1916); *National Provisioner*, January 20, 1906, pp. 15, 44; February 17, 1906, p. 16.

73. Hanson, *Argentine Meat and the British Market*, p. 146.

74. *Ibid.*

75. *Ibid.*, pp. 149-150.

76. *Ibid.*, pp. 161-162.

77. *Ibid.*, p. 159.

78. *Ibid.*, p. 149, n. 13, interview with "an official of one of the Chicago firms."

Chapter VII

The Struggle Against
the "Beef Trust"

The coming of the large industrial corporation in the late nineteenth century soon convinced many Americans that their government should take steps to prevent private economic power from destroying competition. Along with the new oligopolistic competitive patterns that stressed cooperation alongside competition, came a concentration of power and influence that threatened old values and attitudes long associated with the sort of decentralized, atomistic decision making and individual opportunity that characterized the packing industry prior to the refrigerator car. Small, single-functional firms were no longer the rule in many sectors of the economy. Increasingly, decisions in such industries came to be made by a handful of men who operated the large, integrated enterprises that controlled a major share of their industry's market. Significantly higher capital investments and the market power of established oligopolists combined to make entry into many industries vastly more difficult than it had been earlier in the century.

Inevitably, these changes altered relationships between and among private and public interests. The result was widespread demands for government regulation. Such political pressures came first in the railroads, which had pioneered in the creation of oligopoly, then in industries such as oil, sugar refining, and meat packing, where the large corporation first appeared. Protests were spearheaded by the economic groups most adversely and immediately affected by these industries. The Interstate Commerce Commission was created in 1887 in an effort to prevent railroad rate discrimination and pooling. Three years later the Sherman Anti-Trust Act extended federal authority to prevent monopoly and combination in the entire economy, including manufacturing. In the 1890s dissident laborers joined disgruntled farmers to continue the earlier agrarian protest movements aimed at crush-

171

ing a "vast conspiracy against mankind," which they alleged was being conducted by Wall Street bankers, unscrupulous politicians, and businessmen. With the rise of progressivism at the turn of the century came more attempts to curb the power of the "soulless corporations." The creation of new governmental agencies, such as the Bureau of Corporations, the passage of new regulatory laws, such as the Pure Food and Drug Act, additional laws governing the railroads, and a stronger meat inspection law had substantially altered government-business relations by the end of the first decades of the twentieth century.[1]

The changing climate in the government's stance toward business affected the dressed beef industry almost from the first use of the refrigerator car. No sooner had Swift begun large-scale chilled meat shipments than hostility arose toward the packers. By 1888 the level of protests from the range country and from butchers and middlemen threatened by the packers had grown to the point where the Senate adopted in May of that year a resolution "to examine fully all questions touching on the meat product of the United States."[2]

The *Vest Report* that resulted from the subsequent inquiry reached Congress two years later, on May 1, 1890, the same day that the House was deliberating the Sherman Anti-Trust bill. Its critical analysis of the perilous state of competition in meat packing reinforced the belief of many congressmen that broad federal legislation was needed to prevent monopoly and assure competition.

THE VEST COMMITTEE AND THE PACKERS

The decline of the range cattle industry in the mid- and late 1880s provides the backdrop for the first congressional investigation of the meat packing industry.[3] That decline was linked to the changes triggered by the refrigerator car. The new innovation not only increased the demand for beef but also helped create a new demand for better grades of cattle and beef. Producers of range cattle were both the first to gain and the first to lose from the rapid changes in consumer preferences for beef. To meet the growing demand, they expanded production. During the boom period of the early 1880s they prospered, but by 1885 the boom had turned into a bust. High initial profits led to overproduction, glutted markets, and falling prices. Because cost-savings realized by the refrigerator car enabled consumers to buy the best grades of beef for what it had formerly cost them to buy the cheaper grades of range cattle beef, the prices of the usually lower quality range beef fell even lower. Consumers often preferred the better quality beef from corn-fed cattle rather than the beef from grass-fed range cattle.

With the end of the boom, rumors of a "beef trust" began to spread in the West. Cattlemen blamed Armour, Morris, Swift, and Hammond for their troubles. The Big Four, they contended, were colluding in the purchase of cattle to depress the price.[4] In response to the cattlemen's complaints, the Senate adopted a resolution on May 16, 1888:

> To examine fully all questions touching the meat product of the United States; and especially as to the transportation of beef and beef cattle, and the sale of the same in the cattle markets, stockyards, and cities, and whether there exists or has existed any combination of any kind either on the part of the Trunk Line Association, or the Central Traffic Association, or other agencies of transportation, or on the part of those engaged in buying and shipping meat products, by reasons of which the prices of beef and beef cattle have been so controlled or affected as to diminish the prices paid to the producer without lessening the cost of meat to the consumer.[5]

Chaired by Democratic Senator George Vest of Kansas City and manned by three other western Democratic senators and a Republican from Chicago,[6] the committee appointed to carry out the resolution sympathized with its stock-raising constituents from the outset. After interviewing a slate of witnesses heavily weighted to favor livestock interests, it concluded that "the principal cause of the depression in the prices paid the cattle raiser and of the remarkable fact that the cost of beef to the consumer is not decreased in proportion, comes from the artificial and abnormal centralization of markets, and the absolute control by a few operators thereby made possible." Suggesting that the railroads were to blame for the centralization of markets, and equating centralization with monopoly, the committee went on to charge that Armour, Morris, Swift, and Hammond had colluded (1) to fix the prices of beef; (2) to divide territory and business; (3) to divide the public contract business; and (4) to compel retailers to buy from them.[7]

Although testimony did reveal cooperative efforts (pooling) by the packers, the committee's report reflected the facts about the pools much less accurately than it reflected traditional attitudes about monopolistic competition and the value of individual enterprise in the marketplace. What most concerned the committee was the apparent failure of impersonal forces of supply and demand to regulate the market. Overlooking the consumer benefits resulting from the cost-savings of the refrigerator car and the resultant increased consumption of higher grades of beef, committee members focused on the overall stabilization of beef prices and saw it solely as the result of artificial restraints on the free market: "When a large supply of cattle is in the market, prices should decline, and with a decreased supply they should go up," the report opined. "Of course, no one can expect in any market a mathematical and procrustean rule to anything, but it should be as stated, supply being the controlling factor, prices should be governed accordingly, or the conclusion is irresistible that some other and more potent cause is controlling."[8]

Relying on the traditional model of the competitive market that equated small-unit production with independent and free competition, the committee could not believe that concentration could result from market and technological forces rather than collusion. Even when stockmen attributed lower prices to "natural" causes of overproduction and overmarketing, the committee insisted that concentration and pooling were the root of the problem.[9] After Texas rancher and cattleman A. P. Bush pointed to the oversupply of cattle, the committee pressed him about a combination:

"You do not think they would conspire to put up the price?" queried the committee.

"We do not see those sort of conspiracies very often," replied Bush.[10]

The committee pursued the conspiracy trail in questioning Armour as well, but heard merely a more sophisticated version of Bush's argument. "In my opinion," P. D. began:

> the leading cause of the decline in cattle values is the overproduction and overmarketing of cattle, especially of that grade of cattle known as range or southwestern cattle. The overmarketing of cattle has been brought about by the reckless investment and speculation in ranch properties, which placed a fictitious value upon cattle and resulted eventually in the withdrawal of money so invested, thus compelling many engaged in the business to prematurely market their cattle to realize on them.[11]

Pressed to act by a disgruntled constituency, the committee was in no mood to undertake the time-consuming analysis necessary to determine why cattle prices had fallen.[12] Since the causes were debatable, the committee focused on results. The creation of a national market for dressed beef and the resulting increase in firm size and industry concentration had widened opportunities for a few while narrowing those for the many. Cattle markets were more centralized and the business of buying and selling, more systematized than previously. There were fewer buyers and fewer markets but more sellers than before. To the committee, centralization and systematization were proof enough that the big packers had interfered with the market. "[While] we do not contradict Armour's statement," explained the committee:

> we are at the same time convinced that, even without agreement between the principals, their agents brought about all the possible effects of such an agreement. . . . No one acquainted with the motives and methods of business life can believe that under the circumstances existing in the Chicago market there could fail to be, as a rule, some concert of action on the part of the buyers against the sellers. . . . It is fair to assume that men found in combination from mutual self-

interest in one thing will combine as to another, if the motive and opportunity concur. That both motive and opportunity exist for combination among buyers in the Chicago and Kansas City markets as to the purchase of cattle cannot be questioned by anyone not determined to disregard all evidence.[13]

Several cattlemen, butchers, and independent wholesalers whose livelihoods had been threatened by competition from the interstate packers agreed. "There is not the same competition that there once was," complained one stockman. "Somebody up there seems to control the market," reported another. Chicago livestock commission merchant Samuel P. Cady found it to be a simple matter of "big fish eating up the little ones."[14]

Given the committee's predisposition against centralization and its attachment to the old model of price competition, the big packers' efforts to educate it and the public about a new kind of competition were doomed to fail. The Armours' testimony was self-incriminating. Although denying the existence of any "conspiracy" or "combination" to fix and depress stock prices, P. D. and his brother Simeon both admitted that they had found some form of cooperation to be necessary. "If we did not understand pretty nearly what everybody was shipping down into certain territory," Simeon asserted, "we should just be slaughtered in no time." "If we did not have some control over these [tenderloin] prices," echoed P. D., "there are so much more produced than we can use just at this time, that the price of cattle would absolutely decline just as much as these cuts decline."[15]

The American faith in the market as an automatic regulator of the economy saved the big packers any further explanation. Despite the committee's conviction that the packers had colluded to depress cattle prices, it saw no great need for government intervention in the marketplace. Their belief in the strength of free competition and a self-regulating market gave them a very limited view of the proper economic role of government.[16] That belief framed the committee's solution to the problem. It chose to rely heavily on "natural" economic forces and the continued expansion of the economy. "No combination," the report declared, "can keep the prices of beef cattle at the present quotations [and] the Chicago market [cannot] continue to control the cattle interests of the whole country as it does now, [nor can] a few large operators... retain their hold upon the market." As the committee explained:

This is a new country... not yet out of its first national manhood, and rapid development, with phenomenal transition from one commercial condition to another, must attend our future. The center of population is moving westward, and the centers of trade must change with changing population.

As lines of railroads penetrate the continent, and new territory is opened to commerce and production, the distributing centers must, of course, be affected, and it will continue to be until our country has reached the last stage of national development and danger—that in which the soil is sustaining human life to its fullest capacity.[17]

Optimistic that the passage of the Sherman Act, then pending before Congress, and the natural expansion of the country would cure the "evils" about which cattlemen complained, the committee offered this interim solution:

[Until] we escape from the abnormal and ruinous centralization of the cattle market and its domination by a few men and railroad corporations, every effort should be made by deep-water improvement of the Gulf of Mexico, diplomatic endeavor to remove quarantine regulations in Great Britain, national inspection, and the prohibition of monopoly in steam-ship transportation, to enlarge our foreign market.[18]

Of these remedies, the committee considered a national meat inspection law the most important. Meat inspection first became a national issue in the early 1880s. Until then, inspection had been left to cities and states. With the growth of the American interstate livestock and dressed beef trade, city and state regulations proliferated as competition with interstate traders intensified and periodic outbreaks of animal diseases, once confined to states or localities, threatened to become a national menace.[19] Compounding these problems for interstate traders were new foreign rules and regulations that increased with the growth of America's livestock and meat exports in the same decade.[20] In 1883 western pork packers appealed to the federal government for assistance in penetrating foreign markets closed by such regulations. The President appointed a commission of "impartial scientists," representatives of the Chicago Board of Trade and New York Chamber of Commerce, to investigate matters.[21] In 1884 the newly created Bureau of Animal Industry took over from the veterinary division, the inspection and research activities of the Department of Agriculture. Like most young government agencies, it soon found itself understaffed, underfunded, and overworked.[22]

The depression that hit the cattle industry in the 1880s made it difficult for the Vest Committee to ignore possible connections between inadequate inspection service, the decline in the export trade, and the glut in the domestic market. Livestock producers and large packers agreed that a national inspection system for export animals and meats was needed. Stockmen stood to benefit from higher livestock prices just as the big packers, who were the largest exporters, stood to gain from federally inspected exports.

There was general agreement that some inspection system was needed for livestock and meat that was exported. The central issue was whether inspection authority should be vested in the local, state or national governments, whether inspection should be mandatory or voluntary, whether inspection should be extended to interstate as well as to export livestock and meats. Stock farmer L. Leonard of Saline County, Missouri (which had no state inspection laws), contended that local inspection "would make numerous markets and competition." When asked whether he thought "the National Government would have the authority to provide for the inspection of animals produced in Missouri and killed in Missouri," he hesitated. "That would be a tolerably enlarged authority," he replied, but believed that "the state [not the national government] can do it." New York wholesale butcher Levi Samuels believed local inspection "would have the effect of opening the markets of the whole country to the producers of cattle. . . ." George Beck, a butcher and cattle dealer from Detroit, opposed national inspection of interstate meats "because if the inspector was appointed by the General Government there would be no move made to break-up the combination that we claim is by unholy methods concentrating this trade at one center." State inspection, on the other hand, "would increase the price of cattle by making competitive markets."[23]

The Vest Committee's support of a voluntary federal inspection law that applied only to the export trade met with widespread approval. Neither the major packers nor the stockmen nor American legislators were ready to support a more stringent law. The economic situation did not call for a stringent law and ideology was not yet finely tuned to support such an extension of federal control.

The committee's final report to Congress embodied a variety of recommendations that revealed hidden fissures in an ideology that, on the one hand, exalted free markets, but on the other, offered no guidelines for dealing with the capital intensive, concentrated national industries that such free competition had nourished. It confirmed popular suspicions of a beef trust, recommended a mild meat inspection law, and reiterated support for antitrust legislation then pending in Congress. "If the only result of the passage of the [Sherman] bill would be the elimination of that [beef] trust," proclaimed Democratic Senator Heard of Missouri after reading the report, "this would be sufficient to establish it as one of the wisest laws Congress ever passed with respect to commerce."[24] The Sherman bill became law on July 2, 1890, a month before Congress passed the first federal meat inspection law.

The packers considered these new departures in governmental policy relatively innocuous. The Vest Report did not lead to federal prosecution of the industry under the new antitrust statute. Further, the inspection law was voluntary, costless, and might well help to reopen foreign markets.[25] The Sherman Act would require judicial interpretation for years before its meaning or constitutionality could be determined.

Moreover, there was reason to believe, in view of the prevailing notion that government should have only a limited and negative regulatory role, that the Act might never be used against the packers. For many years, events were to justify the packers' optimism.

THE SHERMAN ANTI-TRUST ACT

The Sherman Act reflected the congressional conviction that government's role in the economy should be a negative one, designed primarily to free the market from artificial restraints on interstate trade.[26] Congress thought that once market forces could operate freely, competition would automatically be preserved by the market's self-regulating process. Section I of the Act prohibited contracts, combinations, and conspiracies in restraint of trade. Section II outlawed monopolies or attempts to monopolize. The Act, therefore, did not contemplate active and continuous governmental supervision; rather, it was designed to be triggered by occasional, specific deviations from the free market. Congress did not, however, explicitly articulate its conception of free competition. That state was assumed by all "to be too self-evident to be debated, too obvious to be asserted."[27]

This unarticulated, vague legislative certainty about the nature of free competition created enormous problems for the judiciary in interpreting and applying the new law. The ambiguous language of the Act, especially the keystone phrase, forbidding activities "in restraint of trade," provided little guidance for the courts. The judicial task was further complicated by the existence of an old, established, and limited common law doctrine against restrictive contracts.[28] The role of these precedents in enforcing the Act was not clarified by Congress. The resultant wide range of possibilities open to judges is described by William Letwin in *Law and Economic Policy in America:*

> For one thing, it could be read as condemning "every conspiracy, in restraint of . . . commerce among the several states," though many agreements that might be described—for instance, a malicious compact to derail a locomotive—would not have violated the common-law rules against monopoly. The word "every" also created doubts, for it could be taken to mean that the act went beyond the common law, which did not forbid "every" restraint but only "unreasonable" restraints. Uncertainty about the word "every" was contagious; judges who disagreed about its significance were apt to differ about the technical meaning of the succeeding words, "restraint of trade."[29]

As a result, the applicability of the Act remained unclear. Neither the lower courts, those affected by the Act, nor the attorneys general charged with enforcement knew exactly how to interpret it.

Nor was the government well-equipped to enforce or administer the Sherman Act. Compared to the large, integrated corporation, the executive branch of the federal government had not yet modernized or rationalized the administrative or decision-making processes within its relatively small bureaucracy. Decision making was highly decentralized and was carried out by a handful of officials performing the same functions in much the same way as they had during most of the nineteenth century, when commercial and agrarian problems dominated the government's attention on economic matters. As the case load in the Justice Department increased, neither funds nor personnel grew accordingly. In 1890 there was a total of 80 persons in the entire Justice Department, only 18 of whom were lawyers.[30]

Limited personnel and finances were only a few of the Attorney General's problems. As Letwin explained:

> If his Washington staff was overworked, at least it worked under his control. His subordinates in the field, including the district attorneys, were much more difficult to supervise. Troubles with them arose in part from the manner in which they were paid. Although district attorneys earned a fixed salary of $2000 a year, most of their income came from fees paid by the Government according to the number of cases they conducted. As might be expected, some of the district attorneys responded more enthusiastically to piecework pay than to the Attorney General's policies. . . .[31]

Nor could the Attorney General feel confident that his orders would be followed. With neither the power to appoint subordinates, nor much freedom to dismiss, he had to rely upon persuasion to implement his policies. Still another factor that complicated enforcement of the new antitrust law was the political nature of the Attorney General's job. As a political appointee he would be expected to adopt policies that reflected the attitudes of the party in office.

Such difficulties would have impeded even the most vigorous opponent of the trusts. They could be overcome only by a determined Attorney General who had the support of the President as well as the courts and who was willing to try new methods to enforce the Act.

Prior to 1903, the disinterest of the Attorney General combined with a conservative Supreme Court and two generally conservative, probusiness presidents, to make the Sherman Act ineffective.[32] William Miller, Attorney General during President Benjamin Harrison's administration in the early 1890s, left enforcement of the Act to his district attorneys. Richard Olney, Attorney General under Cleveland and a former lawyer for the Burlington, Quincy & Ohio Railroad, did little to invigorate the Act. Olney had little faith that the Sherman Act could affect monopolies to any great extent. The government's defeat in the E. C. Knight sugar trust case in 1895 convinced him that he was right. Drawing a distinction between "manufacturing" and "commerce," the Court ruled that American Sugar Refining's near monopoly of the manufacture of sugar in many states was not the same as a monopoly of interstate trade—commerce was not the same as manufacture and American Sugar was engaged in manufacture, not commerce. Therefore, according to that rather peculiar interpretation, the Sherman Act did not apply. The high court seemed to be saying that combinations or consolidations of manufacturing establishments were immune, but that collusive marketing arrangements might be vulnerable because marketing was "commerce." As a result, consolidations under a single management might well be safer than loose pooling associations.[33]

Despite the sugar trust case, Olney's successor, Judson Harmon, was convinced that the Act could still reach giant firms whose business involved interstate commerce. To test his theory, Harmon selected two circuit cases to argue on appeal: the Trans-Missouri Freight Association case, in which the circuit court had ruled that the Sherman Act did not apply to railroads; and the Joint Traffic Association case, in which the circuit court had declared that a railroad association whose object was "regulation" of competition, rather than "suppression," was legal. Harmon's theory proved correct. By early 1899 the Supreme Court had reversed both cases and thus provided new opportunities for enforcement.[34] In the process, it strengthened the view that pooling was less likely to be tolerated by the courts than were huge firms created by merger and run under a unified management.

More teeth were put into the Sherman Act when William Howard Taft, sitting on the Sixth Circuit Court of Appeals, ruled that the Addyston Pipe and Steel combination was illegal under the Sherman Act. That decision, upheld by the Supreme Court in 1898, made illegal all manufacturing cartels that "directly and immediately" restricted interstate commerce.[35]

The atmosphere of uncertainty that prevailed while the courts were searching for a meaning to the Sherman Act encouraged the packers to continue the pools they had first organized in the late 1880s.[36] They were greatly heartened by the circuit court rulings in the Trans-Missouri case in 1893 and the Joint Traffic Association case in 1896, which seemed to support the packers' view that their pools were legal. Even after the Supreme Court reversed those decisions and declared that Congress did not distinguish between "reasonable and unreasonable restraints," the packers could still base some hope on the language in the Addyston Pipe decision that suggested that combinations were illegal only if they "directly and immediately restricted competition and directly affected commerce among the states."[37] In view of the continuing expansion of the industry during the 1890s and the constant problems in enforcing the pools, the packers may well have believed that the Addyston Pipe ruling exempted their pools from the Sherman Act. This belief rested in part on hope and in part on a somewhat strained set of legal reasonings, but it was by no means an obviously wrong belief. As long as the pools provided real benefits to the packers, they apparently seemed to consider them worth the legal risks. Such was the case throughout the first decade following passage of the antitrust law.

By the turn of the century, however, the packers were reconsidering the costs and benefits of maintaining their pools. By 1902 the packers faced a more hostile environment than they had encountered during the depression decade of the 1890s. Not only had rising beef prices triggered a renewed public attack on the industry,[38] but eager middle class progressive reformers and an energetic new president, Theodore Roosevelt, appeared determined to tackle trusts in general, and the "beef trust" in particular.

In January 1902 the Justice Department initiated an investigation of packer activities. The *New York Herald Tribune* pressed the attack with a series of articles in late March and early April, exposing the possibility of a packer combination.[39] Already discontent with their pools, which had never been more than a partial success, the packers quickly concluded that they were not worth the legal risk. As we have seen, in April 1902, a month before the government filed suit under the Sherman Act, the packers abandoned their pooling strategy and embarked upon the eventually abortive negotiations to merge their respective companies into a gigantic holding company.

On May 31, only 10 days after the government presented its case, Armour, Morris, and Swift signed the agreement to purchase jointly those several independent companies that later became the National Packing Co. That agreement, if carried out, would have resulted in a near-monopoly of the interstate beef trade, but the packers did not seem particularly worried about the legal dangers of their would-be monopoly. Many industrialists had adopted a similar merger strategy earlier—especially in the merger wave between 1897 and 1902—and the courts had not yet ruled upon the legality of the holding company device. Indeed, the packers had interpreted the E. C. Knight case of 1895 as giving court approval to consolidations that were centrally administered. Speaking a decade later of the legal environment just after the turn of the century, Henry Veeder, attorney for Swift & Co., explained that "It was considered perfectly legal for one corporation, for one unit, to draw into itself other units and operate them; that is, the Steel Corporation had taken over the stock of other steel companies, and it was considered legal so long as there was one management and not two distinct managements who were operating together—was considered perfectly legal under the anti-trust law."[40]

It will be recalled that the promoters of the merger, Kuhn, Loeb & Co., voiced doubts about its legality when they backed out in November 1902. Another of their promotional schemes, the Northern Securities Company, was already threatened by court action.[41] The packers' joint acquisitions of other companies in preparation for the merger then became a problem. The solution, of course, was the incorporation of the acquired companies into the new, jointly owned, National Packing Co.

Concurrent with packer negotiations to form National was a court proceeding, begun on May 20, 1902, to enjoin alleged packer violations of the Sherman Act, including price fixing, collusion in livestock bidding, curtailment of fresh meat shipments, and imposition of uniform credit and cartage charges.[42] In response, the packers submitted a host of procedural arguments and two substantive defenses: they contended that, under the Sugar Trust case, their acts were not part of interstate commerce; and that even if they were, the purpose of the acts was not criminal; rather, they were done solely for the "public good." Making essentially the same argument that Armour had made before the Vest Committee nearly twelve years earlier, packer lawyers asserted that:

> Maintaining of prices . . . is synonymous merely with preventing a glut of perishable meats in the market. . . . If each acts without any knowledge of what the other is doing in that market, there will be an oversupply of fresh meat in their warehouses there. The meat has to be sold at that point. It could not be moved to another market without great loss; and it must be sold there quickly, or it will spoil and serious loss result. Even a cutting of the price would not dispose of such surplus before it would be injured and spoiled, because the demand there is substantially a fixed one, and increase in consumption and demand there in fresh meats is not quick enough to absorb the excess, and honest or prudent dealers would not at any price purchase—and unscrupulous or imprudent dealers should not be permitted to purchase—more meat than they could dispose of to their customers while it is still fresh and wholesome. If by reason of reduced price such oversupply should be disposed of by the defendants, either the dealers and public would be likely to suffer the loss of meats when spoiled and thrown away, or the consumers would have palmed off on them tainted and unwholesome meats.[43]

The circuit court, however, rejected the argument relating to the sugar case, and also ruled that each act had to be viewed as part of a whole, "for commerce is not restricted to specific acts of sale or exchange . . . [It] reaches backward to the purchase of cattle that come to defendants from States other than those in which defendants manufacture, and it reaches forward to the sale of meats, after conversion, to parties dealing with respect thereto from other States, followed by shipments into other States."[44] Nor did the court regard "good" motives or "reasonable" prices as sufficient to exempt the packers. Following the precedents laid down in the Trans-Missouri case, Circuit Judge Grosscup explained that a determination of the lawfulness of the packers' actions "is not dependent upon any consideration of reasonableness or unreasonableness in the combination averred; nor is it to be tested by the prices that result from the combination. Indeed, combination that leads directly to lower prices to the consumer may, within the doctrine of these cases, even as against the consumers, be restraint of trade; and combination that leads directly to higher prices may, as against the producer, be restraint of trade." The Sherman Act, emphasized Judge Grosscup, "has no concern with prices, but looks solely to competition and to the giving of competition full play by making illegal any effort at restriction upon competition. Whatever combination has the direction and necessary effect of restricting competition is, within the meaning of the Sherman Act as now interpreted, restraint of trade."

Finding the pooling agreements among the packers to be in restraint of trade, the Judge turned to the more difficult problem of injunctive relief. The court could not entirely dismiss packer arguments that an injunction "shows . . . to what extremes a paternal government might go in interfering and controlling the private affairs of its citizens." Nor could the Judge neglect the implications of the injunction, especially in the face of warnings from defense lawyers that "never before has a court been asked, upon a bill containing such general charges of violation and of intention in the future to violate the Sherman Act, to enjoin defendants from violating the law and assume the supervision of the future conduct of their private business. If that is authorized by the Act of July 2, 1890, it is suggested that it is an act designed to restrain and hamper, and not to promote, the freedom of trade." Judge Grosscup admitted that "it may be true that the way of enforcing any decree under this petition is beset with difficulties, and that a literal enforcement may result in vexatious interference with defendant's affairs," yet he also felt that he was "not at liberty" to stop before such considerations: "The Sherman Act, as interpreted by the Supreme Court, is the law of the land, and to the law as it stands both court and people must yield obedience."[45]

Therefore, on February 25, 1903, the Circuit Court for the Northern District of Illinois enjoined the packers from combining with respect to bidding in the purchase of livestock, fixing the prices at which meats are to be sold, establishing and maintaining rules for credit, imposing uniform cartage charges, and monopolizing or attempting to monopolize trade by means of railroad rebates or discriminations. Further, in an unusually broad prohibition, the court barred the packers from using "any other method or device, the purpose and effect of which is to restrain commerce."[46]

Standing alone, the prohibitory provisions of the injunction would have been a significant step forward in the development of the Sherman Act. In an ambiguous qualifying addendum, however, Judge Grosscup seriously undercut the force of the injunction, confused the entire matter, and provided the packers wtih a justification for future collusive activities:

> [Nothing] herein shall be construed to prohibit the said defendants . . . from curtailing the quantity of meats shipped to a given market where the purpose of such arrangement in good faith is to prevent the over-accumulation of meats as perishable articles in such markets.[47]

If the packers were at all concerned about the impact of the injunction before the Grosscup decision, they had even less reason to worry now. The qualifications allowed considerable room to maneuver and created loopholes that the packers did not hesitate to use.

The Supreme Court upheld the lower court's injunction on January 30, 1905, as well as the interpretation of the commerce clause on which it was based. Justice Oliver Wendell Holmes, writing for a unanimous Court, amplified Judge Grosscup's definition of interstate commerce into the now-famous *stream of commerce* doctrine. The Justice, however, was more sympathetic to packer arguments that the prohibition against "any other method or device," was too broad and vague: "we . . . are bound by the first principles of justice not to sanction a decree so vague as to put the whole conduct of the defendant's business at the peril of a summons for contempt. We cannot issue a general injunction against all possible breaches of the law." Agreeing with the packers that "the defendants ought to be informed as accurately as the case permits, what they are forbidden to do," Holmes modified the decree to cover only the specific acts prohibited by the injunction.[48]

So carefully had Holmes and Grosscup qualified the injunction that they made the government's victory a pyrrhic one. The many qualifications made the injunction weak and unclear, and it certainly provided no explicit threat to the continued operation of National. Packer lawyers realized the advantages of the jurists' modifications. Commenting upon the decision nearly a decade later, Henry Veeder of Swift & Co. pointed out that Grosscup "expressly permitted them to combine for the purpose of limiting the shipments to various consuming centers for the purpose of avoiding gluts upon the market" and that the Supreme Court, in affirming that decision, had extended the same privilege.[49] Another opinion of the decree, expressed by a stockman, was that the packers could violate "with impunity" the terms not expressly covered by the decree; that it was "merely a matter of good faith agreement between the Attorney General and the packers."[50]

President Theodore Roosevelt shared this stockman's skepticism of regulation by judicial decree. Indeed, while the packers were fighting injunction proceedings in the courts, TR was busily developing his own policy to deal with large corporations, a policy based more upon executive and administrative discretion than upon judicial interpretation of the Sherman Act.

PRESIDENT ROOSEVELT, THE BUREAU OF CORPORATIONS, AND THE PACKERS

TR's antitrust policy[51] was as much a reflection of his own presidential goals as it was an indication of his attitude toward industrial combinations. Roosevelt entered office in 1901 with three goals foremost in mind. He wanted to establish himself as a preeminent figure in the Republican party, to elevate the executive as the dominant force in the national government, and to make the government the most important single influence in national affairs.[52] To him, trusts were less an economic than a political, social, and moral problem. He viewed industrial combination as inevitable and generally desirable, but singled out for condemnation "bad" trusts—those which, in his own judgment, engaged in unfair competitive practices. He considered it the duty of government and the president to protect the public from corporate abuses and to assure proper business conduct.

In addition to the evils of bad business conduct, however, TR perceived another danger in industrial combination: the concentration of power and influence in the hands of a few men. He sensed that if he were to carry out his presidential goals, he needed to show the public that he, not the heads of giant corporations, controlled the government, and that government, not business, ruled the country.

Although court decisions gave ultimate sanction to antitrust enforcement, TR did not want to rely solely upon the Sherman Act and judicial interpretation to cure business evils. Not only were court decisions ad hoc, uncertain, and beyond the control of the chief executive, but they could not be relied upon to reinforce his own vision of antitrust as a weapon against certain types of business behavior without acting also against the prevailing form of industrial organization, which he did not want to alter. As he put it, "My desire is to strengthen the hand of the executive in dealing with these matters, and not to turn them over to what I regard as the chaos and inefficiency necessarily produced by an effort to use the courts as the prime instrument for administering such a law."[53]

For TR the best solution was increased executive and administrative discretion in antitrust enforcement, a solution he ultimately wished to implement through changes in the Sherman Act and the method of enforcing it. Prior to seeking such far-reaching changes in the antitrust law, however, TR's major weapon in his campaign against bad businesses was publicity. "Such publicity," he declared in 1903, "would by itself tend to cure the evils of which there is just complaint; it would show us if evils existed, and where the evils are imaginary, and it would show us what next ought to be done." To collect the needed information for a successful publicity campaign, TR proposed the creation of an "agency of publicity" under his own control and supervision that would have compulsory powers to obtain information and would report its findings to the president, who would use them for legislative recommendations to Congress.[54]

Despite some objections that such an agency would concentrate too much power in the hands of the President, Congress gave TR the agency of publicity he desired, as well as the power to control it. The legislators created in 1903, within the Department of Commerce and Labor, the Bureau of Corporations. The purpose of the bureau was to enable the President "to make recommendations for legislation" for the regulation of interstate commerce. TR was given authority to determine when and which results of the bureau's work were to be publicized, while the commissioner of corporations, who he appointed, was given the power to compel individuals to testify and to produce documents.[55]

The packers were among the first industrialists to learn that the bureau provided new opportunities to attack the large corporation. Having already singled out the "beef trust" as "evil" and having obtained an injunction against the packers, TR now successfully urged the bureau to respond affirmatively to a House resolution of March 7, 1904, requesting "the Secretary of Commerce and Labor . . . to investigate the causes of the low beef prices of cattle in the United States . . . and the unusually large margins between the prices of beef cattle and the selling prices of fresh beef."[56]

Concurrently with, though independent of the bureau's inquiry, the U.S. district attorney of the Northern District of Illinois undertook an investigation of possible violations of the 1903 injunction. In September 1904, the district attorney requested that the bureau turn over certain information that it had gathered concerning collusion in the meat packing industry. The request created a dilemma for TR, in whom the power to control information obtained by the bureau, had been vested. If he granted the request, he undercut the bureau's publicity function in favor of the judicial process that he had earlier eschewed. On the other hand, if he refused to transfer the information to the Justice Department, he "might have to forego a victory over the Beef Trust."[57]

Upcoming elections convinced TR to postpone his decision temporarily. In the meantime, Bureau Commissioner James Garfield made it clear to the President that he opposed using the bureau's power of investigation as an arm of the Justice Department. Such action "would be in contravention of the express provisions of the law," he wrote Roosevelt. Furthermore, since the bureau had obtained its information through what Garfield considered to be voluntary cooperation, he felt that it would be a violation of packer confidence.[58]

It soon became clear that TR did not interpret the bureau's functions so narrowly. On January 18, 1905, just twelve days before the Supreme Court affirmed the injunction handed down by Judge Grosscup in 1903, he directed Garfield to turn over to the district attorney any information that might aid in possible contempt proceedings then under consideration by the Justice Department.

The bureau's report on the industry was published on March 3, 1905. Stripped of the precise information on the combination, the report was a model of objectivity and restraint. Its approach—coldly analytical and cautious—was a significant contrast to that of the Vest Report just a decade earlier:

> All the statistics taken from the books of the companies were checked in the most thorough manner. Totals selected at random were verified by the items. Many typical bunches of cattle have been traced from the time of purchase to the time of sale as dressed beef, thus obtaining accurate information from the original records of costs, of actual selling prices, and of ultimate profits. In many cases the statements of cattle purchased by the companies were compared with accounts of the commission houses through whom the cattle were sold. The various checks thus employed insure the absolute accuracy of the figures. . . .
>
> In order to make certain of the accuracy of the results the Bureau adopted a double method of ascertaining profits. In the first place, it compiled from the detailed records of leading packers exact figures of the weights and costs of cattle, the quantity of beef, and all other products derived from them, the sales and transfer values of such products, and the expense of producing and selling them. The figures used were checked in selective cases by items on which they were based. From these elements the Bureau computed the profits of each of the packers under consideration and all together.[59]

The bureau was equally careful and cautious in drawing conclusions from the evidence. Refusing to accept popular beliefs, it evinced strong doubt that the packers exercised much control over prices or that they directly restrained commerce and competition. "Aside from the restraint imposed by potential competition of local butchers," explained the report, "an important check is placed upon the western packers by the possibility of the establishment of large concerns of the same general character and efficiency." Nor did it agree with the public and Congress that margins between cattle and beef prices were abnormally wide in 1903. On the contrary, it argued that "the margin of beef, instead of being unusually high during 1903, . . . was for each half of the year lower than the margin for any corresponding half year since 1898."[60]

Conclusions regarding prices and profits also contradicted popular opinion. "The high prices of beef which caused so much complaint among consumers at this time, were attributable wholly to . . . abnormal cattle prices," announced the bureau. High cattle prices, it argued, were due to the decreasing number and lower live weights of cattle slaughtered in "the face of . . . strong demand." It further concluded that profits—"which can not exceed at the outside 25 cents per head for all cattle slaughtered" or "2 per cent of sales"—were "reasonable."[61]

The public was shocked. Already exposed to muckraking serials like Charles E. Russell's "The Greatest Trust in the World," they expected the report to verify Russell's sensational charge that "here is something compared with which the Standard Oil Trust is puerile."[62] When it did not, they were convinced of a government whitewash. Describing the report as "very silly," "quite disgraceful," and "preposterous," the *New York Press* declared that "Commissioner Garfield, who has convicted himself of incapacity, should not wait for Beef Trust officials to go to jail before he gets out of office. He should get out now."[63] Russell, outraged and convinced that his story was more nearly correct, charged that the report "bears as much relation to the real operations of the real trust . . . as a treatise on Oriskany limestone would bear to the whole science of geology." He then queried rhetorically:

> Have we heard before of a Government department thus palpably and openly seeking to defend a lawless combination, and misstating, coloring and distorting the facts about it? Or have we ever before had advice from a Government bureau to consumers not to complain of the prices they pay, and to producers not to complain of the prices they get? How does it happen that this defence is issued just at the time when it is most needed for the packing interests? And how does it happen that the document had this peculiar aspect of the astute legal mind, making a difficult argument this airy skimming of dangerous facts, this agile turning of bad corners, doubling and twisting in and out among the air-holes.[64]

The report satisfied no one. Not only did the public criticize it because it protected the beef packers; but the cattlemen disliked it because it failed to understand their problems, and the packers claimed that it violated their confidences.[65]

TR's use of the bureau as an auxiliary arm of the Justice Department was even less effective than his use of it as an agency to turn the strong light of publicity on the packers. In March 1906, District Judge Otis T. Humphrey held that information obtained from the packers by Commissioner Garfield could not be used in the Justice Department case against them. Although the law establishing the Bureau of Corporations empowered the commissioner to take testimony and produce information, it remained unclear whether in obtaining that information the commissioner had given the packers immunity from prosecution. In conformity with immunity provisions of other congressional laws, immunity was granted specifically to individuals who testified under oath or in obedience to a subpoena. But in this case, the commissioner had issued no subpoena or asked the packers to testify under oath. The packers had rendered information—limited primarily to prices, costs, and profits—voluntarily and without coercion. The government claimed that since the packers furnished information without subpoena or oath and not in the formal manner of testimony, and without making any claim of immunity, they were not entitled to the privilege of immunity provided by the laws.[66] Upon hearing of the defense attorney's request for immunity, Attorney General W. H. Moody exploded:

> What would be the consequences? We might suppose that confessions and statements in obedience to the law might be made at Washington, possibly to the Interstate Commerce Commission, possibly to the Commissioner of Corporations, possibly to the Attorney-General. This is a great discovery of my learned friend, for which uncounted generations of captains of industry will thank him. Washington will become the Alsatia to which they can resort for immunity for their offences. It will be much easier, much better, instead of running away from a subpoena, to run toward the Governmental agent and serve a confession upon him.[67]

Dubbing this method of obtaining immunity, an "immunity bath," Moody provided verbal ammunition for TR's new attack on the packers. In a message to Congress on April 18, 1906, TR charged that Humphrey's interpretation of the immunity law "came near to making it a 'farce.' " TR was still seething in July when he wrote to the author of the bill that had established the bureau, Knute Nelson: "No one of us had the slightest reason for supposing that under it such a decision as that of Judge Humphrey was possible. Attorney General Knox has told me, as he has told you, that he did not regard Judge Humphrey's decision as good law."[68]

To prevent a recurrence of this "farce," TR immediately pushed for and received legislation extending immunity "only to a natural person who, in obedience to a *subpoena,* gives testimony under oath or produces evidence, documentary or otherwise."[69]

The public shared TR's outrage over the case. Educated by muckrakers to suspect the worst, and convinced that a beef trust existed, many Americans refused to accept the court verdict. Nor did the packers find much comfort in Judge Humphrey's decision. Although they termed it "gratifying,"[70] the decision did little to diminish the onslaughts against them. On the contrary, it seemed to make the President more determined than ever to press his attack and the public, even more interested in packer activities.

Thanks to muckraking journalists, the barrel of complaints against the packers had by no means been emptied. No sooner had they taken their "immunity bath," than the packers confronted new and even more ominous charges against them. These resulted from the uproar over the publication of Upton Sinclair's novel, *The Jungle*.

NOTES

1. Glenn Porter, *The Rise of Big Business, 1860–1910* (New York, 1973), pp. 85–101, provides a succinct analysis.

2. U.S. Congress, Senate, *Select Committee on the Transportation and Sale of Meat Products*, Report and Testimony, No. 829, 51st Cong., 1st Sess., 1889–1890, pp. i–xl. Hereafter cited as *Vest Report.*

3. See Ernest S. Osgood, *The Day of the Cattleman* (Minneapolis, 1929), especially Chapters IV and V. Samuel Hays, *The Conservation Movement and the Gospel of Efficiency* (Cambridge, Mass., 1959), p. 51, provides a brief but useful description of background conditions in the range industry.

4. U.S. Dept. of Agriculture, Bureau of Animal Industry, *Sixth and Seventh Annual Report, 1889–1890*, p. 415, includes the following letter from a Kansas City stockman, who complained:

> Many stockmen are of opinion that the profits of the business might be increased were it not for powerful combinations controlling the markets and contracting prices at their pleasure for cattle on foot, and at the same time maintaining such prices for the dressed meat that the poorer classes of people are prevented by the high price of beef from using it, and seek other meat or do without. This belief is so universal that I deem it worthy the careful consideration of the Department.

5. *Vest Report*, p. i.

6. Other members included P. B. Plumb of Kansas; S. M. Cullom of Illinois; C. F. Manderson of Nebraska; Richard Coke of Texas.

7. *Vest Report*, p. vi. The railroads' heavy financial investments in stockyards and livestock facilities, their participation in the evener system, and their discriminatory rate-making policies convinced the committee that railroads first concentrated the livestock trade at Chicago and then, in order to increase profits, conspired with the packers to concentrate the dressed beef trade there as well.

8. *Vest Report*, p. x.

9. The committee rejected the overproduction theory because it took "no account of the increased demand for beef caused not only by our enormous increase of population, but also by the establishment of dressed beef and canning industries." As for overmarketing, the committee disposed of it by showing that cattle prices rose with a rise in the supply of cattle. It also gave short shrift to the explanation offered by many of its witnesses, that the

great demand for the best parts of the carcass, such as the rib and loin beef, caused the price of these choice portions to remain unchanged despite the fall in the prices of cattle. Armour's data showed that average retail prices of top cuts increased slightly, about 1 cent between 1870 and 1889; those of medium cuts, such as round steak and shoulder, dropped most significantly, while the prices of lower cuts dropped about 1 cent. Nevertheless, the committee considered "preposterous" the view that a "revolution in tastes" had occurred to effect the price changes. In view of Armour's admission that the packers fixed the prices for finer cuts of meats, the committee's suspicion that "Some other more potent factor [was] at work" was based on fact. See *Vest Report,* pp. i–xvii.

10. *Vest Report,* p. 36. Some stockmen were not as concerned as the committee with the "evils" of combination. Georgetown, Texas cattleman and rancher Dudley Snyder told committee members that "It is as to whether we can better ourselves or increase our interest by having more or less of these combinations" (p. 14).

11. *Vest Report,* p. 414.

12. Even the Department of Agriculture, armed with staff and more data, found analysis roughgoing, and cautioned that "the actual beef supply which yearly goes upon the market is an unknown quantity. It becomes necessary, therefore, to judge of the supply by the total stock of cattle on hand in the country. Such deductions are subject at best to grave errors which are liable to arise from a larger proportion of cattle being marketed one year than another, in order to meet temporary financial emergencies, because of lack of feed, or because of a better price for cattle as compared with the price of corn and hay" (Bureau of Animal Industry, *Annual Report,* 1888–1889, pp. 64–73). "For this reason," it suggested, "the markets of the country have not felt the influence of the reduction of the stock of cattle in proportion to the population, which . . . has occurred and which must continue at an increasing rate from year to year . . . the price of steers for several years in the future will depend more on the price of hogs, upon the value of exports of cattle and beef products, and upon the proportion of steers marketed, than upon any changes likely to occur in the number of cattle per 1000 of population. . . ."

13. *Vest Report,* pp. v–vi.

14. *Vest Report,* pp. 387, 87, 212.

15. *Vest Report,* pp. 363, 454. Philip Armour's rationale for fixing the prices of tender-loins was "to protect our customer who is buying from us." "As an illustration," he explained, "80 per cent of these tenderloins are not produced except for two months in the year. There are but few hotels that take over one hundred pounds at a time except they may have some freezing facilities. . . . They are a luxury. . . . We take these cuts and distribute them through the year. We have refrigerators that we put them in. A tenderloin that I am putting down to-day I will perhaps sell in July or August. They would be utterly worthless if we should undertake to put them on the market. We freeze them. As I said before, very few ever buy over one hundred pounds at a time, and to show that our prices are moderate we make the statement of our prices."

16. Sidney Fine, *Laissez Faire and the General-Welfare State* (Ann Arbor, 1956), pp. 373–392, discusses the ideological underpinnings and practical application of laissez-faire attitudes in the late nineteenth and early twentieth centuries. The demise is traced in Harold U. Faulkner, *The Decline of Laissez-Faire, 1897–1917* (New York, 1968), especially pp. 366–382.

17. *Vest Report,* pp. 34–35.

18. *Ibid.,* p. 35.

19. D. E. Salmon, "Outlines of Work Pursued by the Bureau of Animal Industry," U.S. Dept. of Agriculture, Bureau of Animal Industry, *Fourteenth Annual Report, 1897,* pp. 26–36, and A. D. Melvin, "The Federal Meat Inspection Service," U.S. Dept. of Agriculture, Bureau of Animal Industry, *Twenty-Third Annual Report, 1906,* pp. 26–80. The *Vest Report* contains invaluable testimony regarding state and federal meat inspection.

In the early 1880s an outbreak of Texas fever prompted several western states situated along major south-north livestock trails to issue strict quarantine laws. To keep the trails open, range and cattle interests lobbied Congress for a national cattle trail. For details, see U.S. Congress, House, *The Range and Ranch Cattle Traffic*, by Joseph Nimmo, Jr., Ex. Doc. No. 267, 48th Cong., 2d Sess., 1885, pp. 1–199.

For the large packers' views on inspection, see Leech and Carroll, *Armour and His Times*, pp. 168–188; *The "Significant Sixty": A Historical Report on the Progress and Development of the Meat Packing Industry* (Chicago, 1952), pp. 70–98, 318. The legislative history of meat inspection is detailed in C. C. Regier, "The Struggle for Federal Food and Drug Legislation," *Law and Contemporary Problems*, 1 (December 1933):3–15. John Braeman, "The Square Deal in Action: A Case Study in the Growth of the National Police Power," in *Change and Continuity in Twentieth-Century America*, ed. by John Braeman, Robert H. Bremner, and Everett Walters (Columbus, Ohio, 1964), pp. 35–80, covers the 1906 Meat Inspection Act. Gabriel Kolko, *The Triumph of Conservatism* (Chicago, 1963), pp. 98–112, discusses meat inspection as part of a conservative drive on the part of the packers to secure regulation to protect their interests and profitability. Meat inspection is discussed as part of the increasing trend toward science in government by Hunter A. Dupree, *Science in The Federal Government* (Cambridge, Mass., 1957), pp. 152–182, and as indicative of the ideology of progressive reform, by Louis Filler, "Progress and Progressivism," *American Journal of Economics and Sociology*, 20 (April 1961):291–301.

20. Restrictions began with pork products. In 1879 Italy prohibited American pork because of the alleged presence of trichinae in several American shipments and the absence of a thorough microscopic examination to guarantee that meat was unaffected. Other countries quickly followed: Hungary in 1879, Spain and Germany in 1880, France, Turkey, and Rumania in 1881, Greece in 1883, and Denmark in 1888 (Melvin, "The Federal Meat Inspection Service," p. 69).

The rate of growth of America's exports of both beef and pork (fresh and cured) slowed considerably in the decade of the 1880s. The severest drop in tonnage (pounds) came in the years 1881–1883, when exports of fresh beef were cut almost in half. Total exports of fresh beef to England, Scotland, and France dropped from 106 million pounds to 70 million pounds, rising slightly to 81 million in 1883. Cattle exports to England were also cut in half (U.S. Dept. of Agriculture, *Report of the Commissioner of Agriculture*, 1883, pp. 286–287). See the accompanying table.

United States Exports of Fresh Beef and Beef Products and Fresh Pork and Pork Products in Pounds,[a] 1881–1889

Year	Bacon and hams	Fresh pork	Salted and pickled beef	Fresh beef
1881	747,000,000	—	41,000,000	106,000,000
1882	468,000,000	—	46,000,000	70,000,000
1883	340,000,000	—	42,000,000	81,000,000
1884	390,000,000	185,000	42,000,000	121,000,000
1885	400,000,000	424,000	48,000,000	116,000,000
1886	419,000,000	71,000	59,000,000	99,000,000
1887	420,000,000	24,000	36,000,000	84,000,000
1888	375,000,000	63,000	49,000,000	93,000,000
1889	400,000,000	23,000	55,000,000	138,000,000

[a] Rounded to nearest million.

Source: U.S., Congress, Senate, *Exports and Imports—Exports to Foreign Countries, 1789–1893*, Sen. Doc. No. 259, Pt. II, 53rd Cong., 2nd Sess. 1893–1894, Tables No. 2 and No. 7.

21. Headed by George B. Loring, the committee included Professor C. F. Chandler, F. D. Curtis, Professor D. E. Salmon of the Bureau of Animal Industry, and Eliphalet Wickes Blatchford of the Chicago Board of Trade. Under the guidance of Secretary of State Frelinghuysen, it sent a lengthy questionnaire to domestic packers and railroads, and received reports on inspection in the United States and Germany, Sweden and Austria. Reports on inspection of trichinae showed a rate of about 1.6 percent to 2.5 percent in American hogs, while the rate in hogs raised in Europe and inspected there, showed a somewhat higher percentage, between 2.9 percent and 9 percent, depending on locality. The Armours were convinced that "the epidemics of trichinosis in Germany were due to the eating of raw pork there" (Leech and Carroll, *Armour and His Times*, p. 180).

22. Salmon, "Outlines of Work Pursued by the Bureau of Animal Industry," pp. 26–36.

23. *Vest Report*, pp. 96, 109, 122, 136. Bill Roy, "Inter-Industry Vestings of Interests in National Policy Over Time" (Ph.D. dissertation, University of Michigan, 1977), quantifies packer–State Department exchanges.

23. Quoted in Hans Thorelli, *The Federal Anti-Trust Policy* (Baltimore, 1955), p. 205.

24. The first federal meat inspection law "provided for a careful inspection of salted pork and bacon intended for exportation, to determine whether it was wholesome and fit for food, when the laws, regulations, or orders of any foreign government required inspection, or when any buyer, seller, or exporter of such meats requested inspection; and also for the inspection of all cattle and sheep for export. Such inspection, it was provided, should be made at the place where the meats were packed or boxed, and the meats should be stamped or marked after inspection. The inspectors were authorized to issue certificates of inspection to the shipper of the meat and to the consignee and also for the Department of Agriculture." The new inspection system did not lead to a rapid increase in American meat and livestock exports. Although some countries relaxed their prohibitions, most quickly found other ways to keep out American meats. After microscopic examination was established in the United States, the German government then "claimed that the American certificates of inspection were not correct. France also imposed burdensome regulations on American pork even after it had been microscopically inspected. Belgium followed with a practical prohibition of American dressed beef in the requirement that the lungs of the animals accompany shipments" (Melvin, "The Federal Meat-Inspection Service," pp. 71, 76).

26. The origins and early application of the Sherman Anti-Trust Act are discussed in Thorelli, *The Federal Anti-Trust Policy,* and William Letwin, *Law and Economic Policy in America* (New York, 1965).

27. Thorelli, *Federal Anti-Trust Policy,* p. 226.

28. Philip Areeda, *Antitrust Analysis* (Boston, 1967), pp. 22–24.

29. Letwin, *Law and Economic Policy,* p. 144.

30. *Ibid.,* p. 103. Not until 1870 was the Attorney General made head of the Department of Justice. Prior to that time he had been a member of the president's cabinet.

31. Letwin, *Law and Economic Policy,* p. 103.

32. Thorelli, *Federal Anti-Trust Policy,* pp. 369–410; Letwin, *Law and Economic Policy,* pp. 143–181.

33. The case is discussed succinctly in Letwin, *Law and Economic Policy,* pp. 117–122; Thorelli, *Federal Anti-Trust Policy,* pp. 445–448; Alfred S. Eichner, *The Emergence of Oligopoly,* pp. 152–187.

34. The Trans-Missouri Freight Association case was reversed by the Supreme Court in 1897; the Joint Traffic Association case, in 1898. See Thorelli, *Federal Anti-Trust Policy,* pp. 452–462; Letwin, *Law and Economic Policy,* pp. 131–134, 152–154, 167–171, 178–180; Eichner, *The Emergence of Oligopoly,* pp. 8–9, 17, 152, 187, 299.

35. Letwin, *Law and Economic Policy,* pp. 130–137. Eichner, *The Emergence of Oligopoly,* p. 187, does not see this distinction and argues that "all cartel-type devices were illegal under the Sherman Act."

36. See Chapter V in text.

37. Letwin, *Law and Economic Policy*, pp. 169, 181.

38. Beef prices rose in 1898–1899, while cattle prices dropped, giving packers greater margins than previously. By 1900 beef and cattle prices and margins had leveled off. In January–June, beef and cattle prices rose sharply while margins increased only slightly, and after June 1902, beef and cattle prices declined. Margins increased slightly between March and July 1903. See *Commissioner of Corporations Report on the Beef Industry, 1905*, pp. 85–194, especially Diagram No. 14. The commissioner concluded: "It seems unquestionable that the high price of corn in 1901 and 1902 was one of the most important causes for the great advance in the price of cattle at that time, and the sudden drop in the price of cattle in the fall of 1902 was due in part, though by no means wholly, to a contemporaneous drop in the price of corn" (p. 141).

39. Quoted in Thorelli, *Federal Anti-Trust Policy*, p. 427.

40. U.S. Congress, House, *Hearings Before the Committee on Agriculture on Meat Packer Legislation*, 66th Cong., 2nd Sess., 1920, p. 1292.

41. A petition in equity was filed March 10, 1902, in the Circuit Court of Minnesota, against the Northern Securities Company, the Great Northern Railway Company, and the Northern Pacific Railway Company, and against James J. Hill, George F. Baker, and J. Pierpont Morgan, who were associated with the companies. The bill charged that the Northern Securities Company violated Sections I and II of the Sherman Act, prohibiting a combination or conspiracy in restraint of trade, in its purchase of the majority of capital stock of the two competing lines, the Great Northern and Northern Pacific Companies. The government sought to enjoin the Northern Securities Company from exercising any control whatsoever over the corporate acts of the railroad companies. (For details, see Thorelli, *Federal Anti-Trust Policy*, pp. 470–475, and Letwin, *Law and Economic Policy*, pp. 182–233.)

42. The motion was introduced by the government on May 10, 1902, in the Northern District of Illinois, for an injunction to restrain seven corporations, one co-partnership, and 23 other persons, for certain practices that the government charged, violated Sections I and II of the Sherman Act. The petition charged that these packers, controlling 60 percent of the total trade in fresh meats, combined and conspired:

1. to refrain from bidding against each other in the livestock markets in the different states, thereby inducing and compelling the owners to sell at lower prices than they would receive if such bidding were competitive;

2. to bid up "through their agent the prices of livestock for a few days" to induce cattlemen to send their stock to the yards and then to "refrain from bidding up such livestock, and thereby obtaining such livestock at prices much less than it would bring in the regular way of trade";

3. to fix prices at secret periodic meetings and to maintain these prices by a restriction of shipments, by establishing uniform rules for giving credit and by keeping a "black list" of delinquents and by refusing to sell to any such delinquents;

4. to impose uniform charges for cartage for delivery; and to secure less than lawful rates from railroads largely by means of discriminatory rebates;

5. to obtain a monopoly of the supply and distribution of fresh meat.

43. Brief for appellant at 70, *U.S.* v. *Swift & Co.*, 122 Fed. 529 (N.D. Ill., 1903).

44. The decision, handed down February 25, 1903, is reprinted in U.S. Congress, Senate, *Decision in Beef Trust Case*, by Peter S. Grosscup, S. Doc. No. 179, 57th Cong., 2nd Sess., 1903.

45. Grosscup, *Decision in Beef Trust Case*, pp. 6–7.

46. The injunction is reprinted in n. 1, pp. 393–394, *Swift and Co.* v. *United States*, 196 U.S. 375 (1905).

47. Quoted, pp. 394–395, *Swift and Co.* v. *United States,* 196 U.S. 375 (1905).

48. *Ibid.,* pp. 398–399.

49. U.S., Congress, House, *Hearings Before the Committee on Agriculture on Meat Packer Legislation,* 66th Cong., 2nd Sess., 1920, p. 1291.

50. *Ibid.,* p. 2156.

51. This section relies heavily on Arthur M. Johnson, "Theodore Roosevelt and the Bureau of Corporations," *Mississippi Valley Historical Review,* 45 (March 1959):571–590, and "Antitrust Policy in Transition, 1908," *Mississippi Valley Historical Review,* 48 (December 1961):415–433. See more generally, John Morton Blum, *The Republican Roosevelt* (New York, 1965 ed.); George Mowry, *Theodore Roosevelt and the Progressive Movement* (New York, 1946); Gabriel Kolko, *The Triumph of Conservatism* (Chicago, 1967), especially Chaps. III, IV, and V.

52. Robert H. Wiebe, *The Search for Order, 1877–1920* (New York, 1968), p. 190.

53. Quoted in Johnson, "Antitrust Policy in Transition," pp. 417–419.

54. Johnson, "Theodore Roosevelt and the Bureau of Corporations," pp. 573–574.

55. *Ibid.,* p. 575, and U.S. Bureau of Corporations, *Annual Report,* 1905, pp. 5–8.

56. *Commissioner of Corporations Report on the Beef Industry, 1905,* p. xvii.

57. Johnson, "Theodore Roosevelt and the Bureau of Corporations," p. 579.

58. *Ibid.,* p. 580.

59. *Commissioner of Corporations Report on the Beef Industry, 1905,* pp. xxvi, xxviii.

60. *Ibid.,* p. xxvi.

61. *Ibid.,* pp. xxxiv–xxxv.

62. Charles Edward Russell, *The Greatest Trust in the World* (New York, 1905), pp. 2, 5, 13, 145–147.

63. Quoted in Johnson, "Theodore Roosevelt and the Bureau of Corporations," p. 581.

64. Russell, *The Greatest Trust in the World,* pp. 142, 172.

65. Johnson, "Theodore Roosevelt and the Bureau of Corporations," p. 582.

66. *United States* v. *Armour and Company et al.,* 142 Fed. 808 (1906).

67. Quoted in Francis Walker, "The 'Beef Trust' and the United States Government," *Economic Journal,* 16 (December 1906):507.

68. Johnson, "Theodore Roosevelt and the Bureau of Corporations," pp. 582–583, quoting letter from Theodore Roosevelt to Knute Nelson, July 1906.

69. *United States Statutes at Large,* Vol. 38 (1906), Pt. I, p. 798.

70. *The "Significant Sixty,"* p. 91.

Chapter VIII

Beyond The Jungle

"That was their law, that was their justice! . . . Ten thousand curses upon
them and their law! Their justice—it was a lie, it was a lie, a hideous,
brutal lie, a thing too black and hateful for any world but a world of
nightmares. It was a sham and a loathsome mockery. There was no
justice, there was no right, anywhere . . . it was tyranny, the will and the
power, reckless and unrestrained!"[1] So raged Jurgis Rudkis, Lithuanian
immigrant, Chicago packinghouse worker, and one of the central figures
in Upton Sinclair's poignant novel about Packingtown. The justice of which
Jurgis spoke had little to do with the court's exoneration of the packers.
Rudkis spoke rather of the social injustice inherent in an economic system fueled by profits, where workers were treated as factors in the
production processes rather than as human beings whose skills, indi-
viduality, and effort entitled them to share in corporate decision making
and surplus profits.

Sinclair used Jurgis to deliver a fiery socialist message. Packingtown
was an ideal socialist target. "This was a place where modern commercial
forces held complete sway," Sinclair emphasized. Immigrants toiled in
plants run by bosses "who speeded up" a worker "till they had worn him
out, and then . . . threw him into the gutter."[2] Working and sanitary
conditions were deplorable. Elzbieta "had to stand motionless upon her
feet from seven o'clock in the morning till half past twelve, and again
from one till half-past five." She worked in "one of the dark holes, by
electric light, and the dampness, too, was deadly—there were always
puddles of water on the floor and a sickening odor of moist flesh in the
room. . . ." "Stern and ruthless economic laws" drove her "to work like a
prestidigitator— . . . so fast that the eye could literally not follow her,"
"hour after hour, day after day, year after year, twisting sausage links
and racing with death."[3]

Capitalism transformed humans into commodities, a process that
Sinclair described by relating the case of workers in "tank rooms full of

steam," who accidentally "fell into vats" and were sometimes "overlooked for days, till all but the bones of them had gone out to the world as Durham's Pure Leaf lard!"[4]

Capitalism also corrupted the state. Government was a tool of the packers, and the government inspection service, a farce. "The people of Chicago saw the government inspectors in Packingtown, and they all took that to mean that they were protected from diseased meat," wrote Sinclair. "They did not understand that these hundred and sixty-three inspectors had been appointed at the request of the packers and that they were paid by the United States government to certify that all the diseased meat was kept in the state. They had no authority beyond that; for the inspection of meat to be sold in the city and state the whole force in Packingtown consisted of three henchmen of the local political machine!"[5]

With the novelist's pen and the socialist's interest in revolution, Sinclair hoped to "open the eyes of the American people to the conditions under which the toilers get their bread. . . . [and to] blow the top off of the industrial-tea kettle."[6]

The kettle-top blew off—but hardly in the way Sinclair had hoped. As he lamented afterward, "I aimed at the public's heart, and by accident I hit it in the stomach."[7] First serialized in the socialist weekly *Appeal to Reason* in February 1905, *The Jungle* excited little interest. Months passed before Sinclair found a publisher. Doubleday agreed to print it in 1906, only after its officials were "convinced that *The Jungle* told the truth." Advertising the book as a "searching exposé of . . . the flagrant violations of all hygenic laws in the slaughter of diseased cattle, the farce of government inspection, and the whole machinery of feeding a world with tainted meat,"[8] the publisher fueled a controversy already swirling around the packers.

Between 1905 and 1906 hostility to the packers had mounted. The public was incensed by the Bureau of Corporation's sympathetic report on the industry. Few believed that the Sherman Act was effective against packer collusion. Even the courts seemed tainted by packer influence. A movement for a federal pure food and drug law, fitfully underway since the early 1890s, had gained momentum with the embalmed meat scandal of the Spanish-American War.[9] The dogged determination of Dr. Harvey Wiley, head of the Bureau of Chemistry, and civic-conscious women's groups, kept the issue of meat inspection before the public and meat on the government's diagnostic agenda.[10] A book that discussed both the packers and the dangers of adulterated foods and unhealthy meats was bound to create excitement. Doubleday's slick advertising strategy assured success. Within two and a half months after publication, over 25,000 copies had been sold.[11]

The book also struck a responsive cord in Washington. Having already placed the meat packers on his list of "bad" trusts, TR welcomed an opportunity to discipline them further. He moved cautiously, however, to determine first if the government inspection service deserved Sinclair's indictment. He ordered the Department of Agriculture to investigate "the condition of the meat-inspection service of the Bureau of Animal Industry at Chicago, the relations subsisting between the meat-inspection service of the Bureau and the meat inspection service of the city of Chicago, and the sanitary conditions of the abattoirs at Chicago."[12] The department's report, completed on April 15, 1906, revealed weaknesses in the existing inspection system but found Sinclair's charges of grossly unsanitary conditions, "greatly exaggerated," and his attempts to discredit federal inspectors, "willful and deliberate misrepresentations of the fact." The weaknesses of the system, concluded the department, resulted from the voluntary nature of the inspection, its application solely to the export trade, and from insufficient funding and staffing rather than from the employment of a cadre of corrupt officials. The authority of federal inspectors was extremely limited; they could not destroy condemned meat, supervise conditions under which finished products were prepared, or enforce sanitary regulations. The threat of withdrawal of inspection was the only form of coercion the department possessed. Furthermore, there was nothing in the law "to forbid any carrier from accepting for interstate transportation the carcasses and food products which had not had federal inspection."[13]

While the department was compiling its report, the packers grew restless. Sinclair's exposé made imperative a temporary change in the packers' public relations strategy. With "great reluctance," J. O. Armour departed from the "traditional corporation policy of secrecy under attack" to defend the family name and business. "Finding myself the responsible head of a business founded by a father who had put into its upbuilding the best energies of a long, active life and a very considerable genius for affairs," wrote J. O., "I found it increasingly difficult to keep silent."[14] In a series of articles in the *Saturday Evening Post* in March 1906, J. O. launched his own personal attack against the "professional agitators of the country," the "yellow magazines," the "sensation mongers," whose charges he denounced as "unfair, unjust, untrue and in most cases, maliciously bitter." As for government inspection, wrote Armour, "Attempt to evade it would be from the purely commercial viewpoint, suicidal. NO PACKER CAN DO AN INTERSTATE OR EXPORT BUSINESS WITHOUT GOVERNMENT INSPECTION. Self-interest forces him to make use of it.... This government inspection ... becomes an important adjunct of the packer's business from two viewpoints. It puts the stamp of legitimacy and honesty upon the packer's product and so is to him a necessity. To the public it is INSURANCE against the sale of diseased meats."[15]

J. O.'s declarations came too late to change public attitudes. They made almost no impact whatsoever upon TR. To avoid possible criticism that the departmental report was self-serving, he appointed a second committee, composed of a former labor commissioner, Charles P. Neill, and a lawyer turned social worker, James B. Reynolds, to probe further conditions in the industry.[16] Their report, first given verbally to TR in early May 1906, and formally finished on June 2, concentrated on describing the working and sanitary conditions in the industry. Whereas the report of the Department of Agriculture had detailed the activities of such functionaries as the microscopists who examined the hog for trichinae, Neill and Reynolds told of "girls and women... found in rooms registering a temperature of 38°F. without any ventilation whatever, depending entirely upon artificial light. The floors were wet and soggy, and in some cases covered with water, so that the girls had to stand in boxes of sawdust as a protection for their feet. In a few cases even drippings from the refrigerator rooms above trickled through the ceiling upon the heads of the workers and upon the food products being prepared."[17]

Along with their descriptions went a stinging criticism of the system of administration and of employers and managers who "completely ignored.... the ordinary decencies of life." "The various departments are under the direct control of superintendents who claim to use full authority in dealing with the employees and who seem to ignore all considerations except those of the account book. Under this system, proper care of the products and of the health and comfort of the employees is impossible, and the consumer suffers in consequence." They described "one notable instance," where "the privy for women working in several adjoining rooms was in a room in which men chiefly were employed, and every girl going to use this had to pass by the working places of dozens of male operatives and enter the privy the door of which was not 6 feet from the working place of one of the men operatives."[18]

Concerned with the effects of such conditions on the workers, they warned that "The whole situation ... in these huge establishments ... tends necessarily and inevitably to the moral degradation of thousands of workers, who are forced to spend their working hours under conditions that are entirely unnecessary and unpardonable, and which are a constant menace not only to their own health, but to the health of those who use the food products prepared by them."[19]

Revolted by conditions, TR decided "they should be radically changed."[20] However, he wanted to avoid hurting the "scores of thousands of stock growers, ranchers, hired men, cowboys, farmers and farm hands all over this country who have been guilty of no misconduct whatever."[21] He withheld publication of the report, preferring to use it as a club with which to secure a stringent meat inspection bill. So that his strategy would not be misinterpreted, he warned a congressional ally of the packers that he remained ready to publish the report "if it is necessary ultimately to hurt them in order that the reform shall be accomplished."[22]

He directed Neill and Reynolds to confer with the Secretary of Agriculture to write the administration's meat inspection bill. When Indiana Senator Albert Beveridge informed the President that he was working on his own bill, TR invited Beveridge to join forces. Beveridge was one of *The Jungle*'s most avid readers and a staunch believer in government activism. He set out to make meat inspection the cause célèbre of his political career.[23]

While the government trio was drafting its bill, the packers clumsily tried to play TR's game of feints and threats. As they soon discovered, the rules were as quick-changing and as unpredictable as TR's temperament. Louis Swift promised to clean up the plants and carry out any "reasonable, rational and just" recommendations within 30 days if TR would not publicize the report, but TR refused to deal, declaring that it was "absolutely necessary that we shall have legislation which will prevent the recurrence of these wrongs."[24]

The packers found the president's strategy exasperating. Not only was TR unwilling to arrange with them the kind of detentes that had characterized his dealings with United States Steel and other large corporations but,[25] by threatening to publish the Neill-Reynolds report before the administration produced its own bill, TR undermined the packers' attempts to devise their own strategy. Opposition to the Beveridge amendment became synonymous with opposition to meat inspection.

Reluctant players in a game beyond their control, the packers watched nervously as Senator Beveridge introduced what he humbly termed "the most perfect meat inspection bill in the world."[26] Clearly it was the most comprehensive and detailed measure to date. The bill made the inspection of export and interstate meat and meat products compulsory. Inspectors appointed by the Secretary of Agriculture were authorized to supervise all stages of production, lay down and enforce rules covering sanitation, and bar from shipment in interstate commerce all meats not inspected by the government. Labels on canned meats were to signify the date of canning and not merely the fact that meats had been inspected at the time of slaughter. The packers were to pay inspection fees. They were denied appeal from the rulings of the Secretary of Agriculture.[27]

The introduction of the Beveridge bill erased whatever doubts the packers had about the kind of bill the administration wanted, but in no way solved their dilemma. The packers had not pressed *for* meat inspection legislation in 1906. They were too busy building National and defending themselves in court. TR and the reformers had forced them on the defensive. Not only did the packers have to step softly in legislative hallways so as not to provoke TR into publishing the Neill-Reynolds report. They also were trying to figure out precisely where their interests lay with respect to the Beveridge bill.

They clearly saw the advantages of more stringent meat inspection. Testifying before the House Committee on Agriculture during hearings on the Beveridge bill, Thomas Wilson of Morris & Co. echoed J. O. Armour's earlier declaration that meat inspection was in the packers' self-interest. "We are and have always been in favor of the extension of the inspection, also to the adoption of sanitary regulations that will insure the very best possible conditions."[28] The packers had welcomed meat inspection in the 1890s. When Germany shut out American pork they had even offered to pay the costs of inspection.[29] However, in 1906, conditions in the industry had changed substantially, as had the packers' position in the industry and their perception of the industry's future. Far from dreaming of the profits that would rebound from a more stringent bill, the packers worriedly calculated the costs.

Already stung by publication of *The Jungle,* the packers calculated the possible effects of the Neill-Reynolds report on trade conditions in both domestic and foreign markets. About this time rates of growth of domestic production and consumption began to slow, and competition in the international market intensified as other countries began to imitate the methods of American packers in exporting fresh and preserved meats.[30] In the face of new problems, the packers considered the costs of possible publication of the Neill-Reynolds report not worth the risk. They opted for a face-saving strategy in the hopes that they could rebuild consumer confidence in their products and salvage their badly tattered image by convincing TR not to publish the report. Rather than risk provoking him, they counted on his favorite "stock-growers, ranchers, hired men, cowboys, farmers and farm hands" to do their work for them, while they concentrated on developing a strategy and position of their own. The packers sat in golden silence as the Beveridge bill breezed through the Senate without a dissenting vote on May 25.[31]

Meanwhile, they received assurances from their friends in the House that the Senate version would be challenged. Even before the Senate vote on the Beveridge amendment, Representative William Lorimer—the notorious "blond boss" of Chicago and a member of the House Agricultural Committee that handled the House meat inspection bill—had publicly declared that "this bill will never be reported by my Committee—not if little Willie can help it." Another packer ally was the chairman of the House Agricultural Committee and a wealthy stock raiser from New York's Gennessee Valley, James Wadsworth. Like other stockmen, Wadsworth blamed "the senseless agitation over meat inspection"[32] for the decline in the U.S. export trade. Although the real reason for the decline in the export meat trade lay in changing geographical sources of supply, stockmen focused on the immediate decline and feared that the new measure would further harm the export trade. They also worried that they would ultimately have to absorb the costs of inspection: "[When] all slaughterers must pay in the first instance to the government a fee per head, the man who owns the head will in the second instance have to pay that fee." Presently perceived common interests overcame past animosities between stockman and packer. Said Samuel H. Cowen, attorney for the National Livestock Association, "we have never been afraid to appear anywhere with anybody who represents a common interest with us. . . ."[33]

Despite stockmen support, the packers got nowhere with the President. When the National Livestock Association flooded the White House with letters and telegrams opposing the measure and pleading with him to withold publication of the Neill-Reynolds report on the grounds that it would damage the cattle raising interests, TR suspected packer influence. He rebuffed a personal visit from two spokesmen for the packers and livestock interests, who reiterated the packers' pledge to do whatever was necessary to clean up their plants if TR withheld the report.

Then, on May 28, two days after the unanimous Senate vote on the Beveridge bill, the *New York Times* exploded a bombshell when it printed portions of the Neill-Reynolds report leaked to it by an impatient Upton Sinclair, who had learned of the contents of the report from TR. With part of his trump card played for him, TR could do little except lecture the reformer: "You are not bound to me by any agreement or understanding not to make public anything you see fit," he admitted, but you have made and repeated "utterly reckless statements which you have failed to back up by proof." TR was particularly aggravated by Sinclair's public stand against the Beveridge bill. "You say in effect that the Beveridge Amendment, and, indeed, any legislative act of the kind, must be inoperative. [Yet] to 'give the people the facts,' as you put it, without pointing out how to better the conditions," TR scolded, "would chiefly be of service to the apostles of sensationalism and would work little or no permanent betterment in conditions."[34]

Compounding TR's troubles with Sinclair were new difficulties with Congress. When the Wadsworth-Lorimer substitute emerged from the House committee in late May, TR was enraged. There was no prohibition against interstate transportation of uninspected meats; inspection was confined to postmortem examination of carcasses, and the provision for inspection and dating of canned meats and meat products was struck out. An annual congressional appropriation of $800,000 replaced the packer fee requirement. A provision for judicial review was inserted to allow packers to appeal the "legality and constitutionality" of a departmental ruling.[35] Still seething over the packers' "immunity bath," TR charged that "the Committee substitute would make any judge whom the packers chose to designate, and not the experts of the Department of Agriculture, the man to decide on any question of any kind which the packers thought it worthwhile to dispute."[36] TR fired an angry letter to Wadsworth: "[It] seems to me that each change is for the worse and that in the aggregate they are ruinous, taking away every particle of good from the suggested Beveridge amendment." He finally decided to play the rest of his tattered trump card. "In view of the wide differences of opinion developed by these proposed changes, and the evident likelihood that there cannot be an agreement upon anything which would seem to me satisfactory," he told Wadsworth, "I do not feel warranted in any longer withholding my message to Congress transmitting the reports as to the conditions in the beef packing establishments, . . ."[37]

TR charged into Congress with the full Neill-Reynolds report and urged passage of the Senate amendment. J. O. Armour responded by publicly accusing TR of harboring "a strong personal animus against the packers of Chicago and [of] doing . . . everything in his power to discredit their business."[38]

The tip-toeing had stopped. The game of feints and threats was over. An all-out legislative struggle ensued to determine precisely what kind of meat inspection bill would result. Arrayed against the Beveridge amendment were the large packers, small packers, and the "scores of thousands of stock growers, ranchers, hired men, cowboys, farmers and farm hands" whom TR had wanted to protect. Congressmen fearful of a more active government also joined the packer bandwagon. Siding with TR and Beveridge were pure food and drug reformers, women's consumer groups, middle-class urban progressives, and congressmen anxious to carve out a stronger and more active role for government in the economy.

The struggle over meat inspection was bound to be a protracted one. For TR, meat inspection was above all a moral issue and had little to do with economics. For the packers meat inspection was less a moral issue than an economic and political one. Once the issue was thrown into the legislative hopper, it also invariably tested the relative power of various interest groups and of the President to control the outcome. Already, TR's strategy and the developments that it nourished had narrowed options for the President and widened those for the packers.

THE PACKERS TALLY COSTS AND BENEFITS

Of immediate concern to the big packers was the impact of the meat inspection controversy on exports. When the chairman of the House Agricultural Committee asked Wilson "how much trade had fallen off since the attack on packing house methods," Wilson declared,

> Our results now are very disastrous ... fresh meats and manufactured products [are] apparently cut in two. Every country in Europe has taken up this agitation and reprinted all these wild stories that have been circulated, and there are interests over there to whose advantage it is to crowd those things along, and they are doing it; and it is hurting us, and hurting us very, very materially. These other countries that are producing stuff in competition with us are taking advantage of it ... our competitors to-day are all getting the benefits of this agitation and we are standing the losses.[39]

Publicly, the packers doubted that they could find profitable markets for the surplus if exports declined and feared a renewed attack by angry livestock growers if livestock prices declined. "I do not like to think what the ultimate result will be," admitted Wilson. "[The] farmers when they send their stock in shall expect us to buy it and pay good prices. If we can not handle it I do not see how we can avoid a terrible calamity, in the western country at least."[40] Privately, the packers knew that unless they ran their plants "full and steady" and supply and demand were coordinated, unit costs would rise. Unlike their smaller competitors, the large interstate packers were saddled with huge overhead and fixed expenses that made it difficult to cut back on supply without risking excess capacity and increasing costs.

The packers had a clearer idea about what they did *not* want in a meat inspection bill than what they wanted. They did not want a bill that increased their costs or interfered with managerial decision making. Wilson admitted that the actual cost of inspection, estimated at between 5–8 cents per head of cattle, 1½–2½ cents per hog and sheep, was not unbearable.[41] Nevertheless, they balked at paying it. More important than the actual cost was the principle behind it. "There is no limit to the expense that might be put upon us," complained Wilson. "[Our] contention is that in all reasonableness and fairness *we are paying all we care to pay.*"[42] Publicly, the packers fretted that burdens would not be distributed equally. If interstate packers were saddled with the costs of inspection, smaller competitors in local markets might gain a competitive advantage. "Take one of the smaller packing houses in Chicago who do not have the inspection business," Wilson explained. "They have no losses for condemnation; they have no expense for this inspection. They have nearly every facility for doing business that we have and they have a tremendous advantage over us in the Chicago market in disposing of their meat products."[43] Privately, the packers were concerned that additional cost pressures, in the face of a slowdown in the rate of growth, might disrupt attempts to achieve stability in the industry and draw the oligopolists into ruinous price competition.

Ironically, the movement for regulation and the uncertainty surrounding TR's reform strategy convinced the packers that they could not rely on meat inspection to solve their problems. Instead, they began to reassess the relationship between domestic and export markets and to consider a new strategy to counter domestic difficulties. Sometime between 1906–1907, the packers moved abroad to secure new sources of supply. Swift moved first into Argentina, followed rapidly by his anxious rivals, who used the National Packing Co. to force a joint multinational strategy.[44]

It is uncertain whether the packers were contemplating this strategy during the debate over meat inspection. In June 1906 Wilson claimed that he did "not know of an American packer who has any interest whatever in any packing house in any foreign country . . . that is producing a large quantity of livestock."[45] The move abroad was a safer way to handle both the supply problem at home and to counter European attempts to limit American imports. It was also a way to escape federal regulations. Thus, while export markets remained important to the packers, they no longer played the same role as they had during the 1890s. Nor did meat inspection promise such direct economic benefits in 1906. Unlike the smaller packers and stockmen whose choices were more constrained by new economic conditions, the large packers exploited the advantages of size and circumvented foreign barriers to American imports to become beef importers as well as exporters. The new multinational strategy was an unintended consequence of the drive for more stringent meat inspection legislation.

Just as the possibility of more stringent meat inspection legislation prompted packers to think more carefully about changing conditions of supply and demand and of the impact of these developments upon the oligopoly, so too did it rekindle fears that government might use meat inspection to meddle in worker-management relations, a traditionally sacrosanct domain of private business. Whereas the moralistic TR joined the issue of meat inspection to worker welfare, the economically-minded packers separated the issues: to support meat inspection was one thing; to be told how to run their businesses and to conduct relations with their employees was another. "What we are opposed to," emphasized Wilson, ". . . is a bill that will put our business in the hands of theorists, chemists, sociologists, etc., and the management and control taken away from the men who have devoted their lives to the upbuilding and perfecting of

this great American industry."[46] The packers recognized that government could be of some help in certain areas of the business, but they
considered intervention in the workplace strictly beyond its prerogative and a challenge to their own power to make decisions affecting their
private businesses.

As businessmen, the packers saw workers as employees and factors in
the production process. They saw costs and profits in every job and
interpreted working and sanitary conditions in economic terms. The
packers were shocked that the public blamed them for conditions that
they considered to be a by-product of business and of human nature.
"The present criticism and the present destruction of our trade is not of
our doing and it is unjust and unfair," wailed Wilson. Conditions were
"not bad considering the nature of the work that is being done . . . We
cannot avoid handling the offal, or the entrails, and they carry some
odor with them," insisted Wilson, before adding rhetorically, "I do not
think that Doctor Neill would suggest their being perfumed, or anything
of that sort."[47] Agreeing with Wilson that the Neill-Reynolds report
exaggerated conditions, Illinois state representative Charles S. Charton
chimed, "I do not believe anybody ever expected to find a rose garden in
a slaughterhouse."[48]

When asked to comment on Neill-Reynolds' assertation that workers
"climb over . . . heaps of meat, select the pieces they wish, and frequently
throw them down upon the dirty floor beside their working bench,"
Wilson focused on work processes:

> If I understand the conditions right, that was in the cutting room in some one of the
> plants, and as the stuff came from the saw the rib was thrown to one side, and the
> chuck to the other for boning. Now, in our house they have little bins . . . for them to
> be thrown into . . . the men that bone these chucks, work on piecework, and it is their
> instruction to take always the first one they come to take to their table to bone. Now,
> unless you stand right over that man with a club—he is paid so much a piece for
> those that he bones, and he is not going to take the biggest one, but the littlest one
> that he can bone the quickest. It means just so much more money to him. Now, I
> think that if the foreman had his head turned, that man might reach pretty high and
> might, unless he was watched pretty carefully, step up there and pick out the one
> that he thought was easiest. We would not tolerate that in our house if we knew it.

The Chairman: "That is human nature, is it not?"
Mr. Wilson: "It is pretty hard to control the men in those matters
when it is a matter of dollars and cents to them."[49]

As for throwing meat down on the dirty floor, Wilson simply could:

> not understand what he would ever do that for. The workman does not cut out each
> bone separately; he just skins out the entire bone, and that he might throw on the

floor, and it would be all right to throw it on the floor. It goes to the tank, and all there is in it is grease and fertilizer. It is an unnecessary expense of labor to throw it on the floor however. It ought to be thrown in the truck and carted away. It would save the expense of handling twice.[50]

Asked if workers relieved themselves on the killing floor as Neill and Reynolds had reported, Wilson calmly pointed out that "Men are men, and it is pretty hard to control some of them."[51]

Packer attitudes about the workplace and their responsibilities to employees, like the public's attitudes toward classic price competition, lagged economic developments. Self-help, worker diligence, and *caveat emptor* may have sufficed to protect workers and consumers during an earlier era, when firms were small, competition was relatively free and independent, employees were few in number, and managers were also owners. These doctrines clearly were inadequate to safeguard workers or consumers in an era of big business, when the size and capital intensity of firms changed the nature of competition.

Oligopolistic competition during the period of empire-building in the late nineteenth century directed attention toward product development and cost-reducing strategies, and away from social consequences of those economic processes. Engaged in high volume operations that yielded a small margin of profit, and determined to win the race for market shares, the packers built fast and furiously, erecting plants and branches across the country.

Such hectic building created new problems of construction and engineering. When Neill and Reynolds criticized the packers for using brick and wood in their buildings when cement was preferable for sanitary reasons, Wilson acknowledged that cement was better, but complained:

We have not been able to get a cement floor that would stand the wear. We have tried it, but had to go back to brick. We put cement in our place in Kansas City in the hide cellar, and the place has been built just about a year and cost our folks about a million and a half of dollars, and to-day we have got to replace it.[52]

Improvements in existing plants were neglected in the race to build new plants in new locations, with the result that the older Chicago plants bore the brunt of the reformers' criticisms.

Too frequently it was the workers who suffered most from these cost-cutting strategies and the hectic pace of oligopoly building. Wage cuts and worker speed-ups were an integral part of competitive strategy. Packers supplied neither aprons, soap, toilet paper, nor shammy cloths for their workers.[53]

During the early phases of industry development, more attention was paid to product than to human development. Not long after the big packers began to compete in the same markets in the Northeast in the 1880s, they began to develop new forms of competition to replace risky price competition. They employed full-time chemists to extend and to improve by-product manufacture. To win customers they distinguished their products by advertising "quality." Swift chose the "Premium" label, Armour picked a "Star," and Morris, hoping to capitalize on the prestige of the Court, selected the "Supreme" label.[54]

The packers prided themselves on their accomplishments. Rather than public thanks, however, they were stung by public attacks. They simply could not understand why the public could not understand that "If [the packers] have bad meat, they have bad management, and they can not stay in competition and exist."[55]

Efforts alone, of course, did not guarantee quality any more than the local butcher's "word" guaranteed quality meats. However, such efforts did indicate how new patterns of competition had changed the economics of quality control. Whereas previously owners had relied on the market to send them signals regarding quality, as product competition came to supplement price competition, managers took a more active role in sending and interpreting market signals.

Consumers, on the other hand, found market signals more difficult to interpret and frequently less reliable, for there was now a brand as well as a price. From their standpoint, oligopoly had stripped away much of the "protection" of the marketplace. When consumers took the local butcher's word that his meat was quality, they did so knowing that if they complained to the owner of the shop and did not receive immediate satisfaction, they could take their business to any number of small competitors down the street. They also could observe first-hand, both the sanitary and working conditions in the shop. Oligopoly narrowed consumer alternatives at the same time it widened the distance between producers and consumers.

Urban consumers were most immediately and directly affected by new competitive patterns. In cities like Boston and New York, where population was large and concentrated, and local sources of supply were limited, packers controlled between 65 and 95 percent of the market.[56] Here, economies of scale in production and distribution had given large packers their greatest advantage. As a result, the giants had few effective rivals, and consumers had few real alternatives but to buy from the large packers. Consumers had little idea about working or sanitary conditions at the packers' central plants thousands of miles away and almost no influence whatever over packer decision making. Instead of getting immediate satisfaction when they complained to the butcher or retailer, they heard the familiar bureaucratic run-around, "Don't tell *me*, tell *them*."

The "public" who opposed the business methods and performance of the large packers was composed primarily of eastern, urban, white middle class reformers in revolt against economic changes that had dethroned consumers as kings and installed a small band of princely managers and corporate bureaucrats in their place.

Ironically, the public gave the packer princes more credit for "control" than they deserved. Mass production and mass distribution of a variety of goods by a large labor force, working at top speeds in plants and branch houses across the country, required expert administration by skilled managers. Managers, however, were not born; they were made, and the learning process took time—more time than the packers realized and more time than they allowed. The packers may have been good empire builders, but as owners of family firms they managed more on the basis of authority than skill. Their empires rapidly outgrew their ability to control every detail of the business, but the packer pioneers clung to their old roles as general entrepreneurs, delaying the trend toward managerial control inherent in big business.[57] Only with the slow-down in growth at the turn of the century and the passing away of the founders did the firms begin to address the problems of worker control as a problem of management rather than as a contest of authority and will.[58] In 1906 the industry was still in the midst of the transition from the old to a new era. Old attitudes died hard.

The legislative battle over meat inspection ultimately produced a policy that mirrored the intellectual and economic conflicts produced by the transition from a simple, personal, and knowable economy of the past, to one that was becoming increasingly complex, impersonal, and unknowable.

MEAT INSPECTION—A COMPROMISE OF SORTS

After weeks of intense lobbying and compromise on both sides, the Senate followed the House in approving a compromise measure worked out by a joint conference committee. The final measure eliminated the dating, labeling, and fee provisions, but retained the prohibition against interstate transportation of uninspected meats, and the provision for inspection before slaughtering and during processing. The government absorbed the cost of inspection and appropriations were increased from $800,000 to $3,000,000. The principle of judicial review was "resolved in ambiguity." No explicit provision was made for review, and the proposed stipulation that the decisions of the Secretary of Agriculture would be "final and conclusive," was simply eliminated.[59]

Who won the meat inspection battle? For supporters of the Beveridge bill, there was little doubt. "I feel as though I will go home like a licked dog," whined Senator Knute Nelson, "whipped by the packers and by the raisers of range cattle and nobody else." "We have met the enemy and we are theirs—indemnity $3,000,000." announced Senator McCumber of North Dakota. Massachusetts Senator Lodge credited the packers with doing "more to advance socialism and anarchism and unrest and agitation than all the socialist agitators who stand today between the oceans."[60]

Historians have drawn different scorecards without changing the good guy, bad guy plot. For Gabriel Kolko the fight for meat inspection was not a battle at all. It was a subtle game designed by rational-minded packers and played for profit. Government was merely the vehicle through which packers obtained their ends. Far from being staunch opponents of regulation, he argues, "the big packers were warm friends of regulation. . . ."[61] Other historians, more interested in the details of the legislative struggle than in the outcome, have portrayed the packers to be far less rational and more fearful of government intervention, with many more friends in the stock-growing and farming regions of the country and with more enemies in government. The spoils are more evenly divided. TR is applauded for his shrewd and tough-minded strategy while the packers are booed from the sidelines. "The legislation was not passed without a bitter fight," concludes historian John Braeman, "—and it was only T. R.'s masterful handling of the political situation that carried the day."[62]

This study has found some truth in each of these interpretations but has also shown the importance of going beyond *The Jungle* to examine the economic details absent from so many histories. In the final analysis, the packers did not support meat inspection as much as they fought to avoid paying inspection costs.

The significance of the legislative struggle for this study is what it reveals about changing patterns of competition and regulation. The battle over meat inspection in 1906 contrasted significantly with the quiet passage of the government's first meat inspection measure in the 1890s. In 1890 Congress passed a meat inspection bill that was limited in scope and voluntary in application in an effort to stimulate the export trade. The packers, who were then among the country's largest exporters, had little to lose and much to gain. Meat inspection legislation of 1906, on the other hand, was introduced not as an aid to business, but as a reform measure, to increase the power of the national government to deal with business wrong-doings. Beveridge himself had boasted that the bill was "THE MOST PRONOUNCED EXTENSION OF FEDERAL POWER IN EVERY DIRECTION EVER ENACTED."[63] It had, moreover, become costly and compulsory at a time when new conditions in domestic and foreign markets had already made the profit horizon more uncertain.

Far from enhancing packer power vis-à-vis the government, the emergence of oligopoly invited new attacks and created new problems of management and control that necessitated new strategies with regard to intra-industry competition, to government, and to the public. Packers influenced the policy outcome in 1906, just as they had during the 1890s, but their voices were diluted by the demands of many more interest groups with different economic concerns and by their own uncertainties about an optimizing strategy. As the rural-agrarian economy of the nineteenth century gradually gave way to the urban, industrial society of the twentieth, the packers encountered new social constraints on their behavior in the marketplace.

TR deserves credit for insisting that the big packers could not escape the moral responsibility that accompanied their increase in economic power. However, he also must accept part of the responsibility for the residue of bitterness that remained after the meat inspection controversy. In view of the changing economics of the meat industry and of the packers' desire to rebuild their blackened public image, TR may have secured just as stringent a meat inspection bill if he had not brandished such a big stick and brought others into the legislative process before it was too late for compromise. Instead, he frustrated the packers and Congress with a strategy that hardened old attitudes and slowed the coming of a new, more humane economic order.

"Public prejudice against the packer is inevitable," concluded J. O. Armour, "and will always continue without regard to the manner in which the packing business is conducted."[64] Considering their family firms to be their own private businesses and unaccustomed to dealing openly with the public, the packers interpreted the lessons of 1906 negatively. The battle bred a deep distrust of government officials and the press that soured the packers' relations with the public and the government in the future. Considering "prejudice inevitable," the packers did little to improve their relations with the public, except for occasional defensive thrusts. They continued to insist that the meat inspection debate involved unjustified attacks against the industry, one promoted by TR and a band of muckrakers for political and personal gain.

Meat inspection easily became a handy public relations tool, however. When consumers began to complain about rising meat prices in 1908 and 1909, the packers simply blamed TR and the new regulations: "The important result of his activities against the trade, aside from the discomfort, expense and general revolution created in the packinghouse business," complained the *National Provisioner*, "was a net increase in the cost of producing meat food products, and that cost will very probably be permanent. It may be conservatively figured at 3 to 5¢ per pound of meat when it leaves the butcher's counter, and unnecessary agitation caused by the _____ President is alone to blame for the existence of such a condition."[65] From 1906 to 1910 the packers continued to blame TR for their troubles. As he prepared to leave office, the *National Provisioner* eulogized: "It is now ex-President Roosevelt; perhaps the funny men will say he should go down in history as ax-President Roosevelt."[66] After a decade of trying to deal with the uncertainties of a policy of administrative and executive discretion, the packers sighed with relief when William Howard Taft became President.

NOTES

1. Upton Sinclair, *The Jungle* (1906: Signet Classic Edition, New York, 1960), p. 161.

2. *Ibid.*, p. 71.

3. *Ibid.*, pp. 133–134.

4. *Ibid.*, pp. 101–102.

5. *Ibid.*, p. 98.

6. Quoted in John Braeman, "The Square Deal in Action: A Case Study in the Growth of the 'National Police Power,' " in *Change and Continuity in Twentieth-Century America*, ed. by John Braeman, Robert H. Bremner, and Everett Walters (Columbus, O., 1964), p. 44.

7. Sinclair, *The Jungle*, p. 349, quoted by Robert B. Downs in "Afterword."

8. Braeman, "The Square Deal in Action," pp. 44–45.

9. The scandal prompted a congressional investigation known as the "Dodge Commission." See U.S. Congress, Senate, *Report of the Commission Appointed by the President to Investigate the Conduct of the War Department in the War with Spain*, 8 vols., S. Doc. No. 221, 56th Cong., 1st Sess., 1898. More generally, see Hunter Dupree, *Science in the Federal Government* (Cambridge, Mass., 1957), pp. 176–180.

10. Harvey W. Wiley Papers, Accessions No. 9810 and 10,134, General Correspondence No. 198-210, Library of Congress, Washington, D. C. Oscar E. Anderson, Jr., *The Health of a Nation: Harvey W. Wiley and the Fight for Pure Food* (Chicago, 1958), especially pp. 180–188, and "The Pure-Food Issue: A Republican Dilemma, 1906–1912," *American Historical Review*, 1 (April 1956):550–573; C. C. Regier, "The Struggle for Federal Food and Drug Legislation," *Law and Contemporary Problems*, 1 (December 1933):3–15; Thomas A. Bailey, "Congressional Opposition to Pure Food Legislation, 1879–1906," *American Journal of Sociology*, 36 (July 1930):52–64.

11. Braeman, "The Square Deal in Action," p. 45.

12. U.S. Congress, House, *Hearings Before the Committee on Agriculture of the so-called "Beveridge Amendment" to the Agricultural Bill* (H.R. 18537), 59th Cong., 1st Sess., 1906, p. 275.

13. The Department's report is reprinted in full, in *Hearings . . . "Beveridge Amendment,"* pp. 273–363. See also Melvin, "The Federal Meat Inspection Service," pp. 66–73; Braeman, "The Square Deal in Action," pp. 50–51.

14. J. O. Armour, *Packers, the Private Car Lines and the People* (Philadelphia, 1906), pp. v–viii.

15. Quoted in Kolko, *The Triumph of Conservatism*, p. 102. Kolko's interpretation differs substantially from that adopted here and from that of Braeman. See Braeman's comments, "Square Deal in Action," p. 74, n. 79a.

16. With a Ph.D. from Johns Hopkins, Neill had no experience in the packing business. He had been a professor of political economy at the Catholic University in Washington, D.C., for nearly ten years before accepting his first government job as commissioner of labor

in the Department of Commerce and Labor. A lawyer by training, James Reynolds headed the University Settlement of New York for eight years, after which he worked two years as secretary to Mayor Low of New York City. During that time he was also acting chief of the bureau of weights and measures, the bureau of city marshals, and the bureau of city licenses of New York City. A visit to the Berlin stockyards while in Germany was his only first-hand packing house experience. (*Hearings* . . . *"Beveridge Amendment,"* pp. 95, 141.)

17. *Hearings* . . . *"Beveridge Amendment,"* p. 269.

18. *Ibid.,* pp. 268–269.

19. *Ibid.,* pp. 269–270.

20. "Conditions in Chicago Stock Yards—Message from the President of the United States," in *Hearings* . . . *"Beveridge Amendment,"* p. 261.

21. Letter from TR, Washington, D.C., May 29, 1906, to Upton Sinclair, in Elting Morison, John Blum, and Alfred D. Chandler, Jr., eds., *The Letters of Theodore Roosevelt* (Cambridge, Mass., 1952), Vol. V, p. 288.

22. *Ibid.,* p. 283, letter from TR, Washington, D.C., May 26, 1906, to James Wolcott Wadsworth.

23. *Ibid.,* p. 282.

24. Braeman, "The Square Deal in Action," p. 54.

25. The detentes are discussed in Kolko, *The Triumph of Conservatism,* pp. 79–158.

26. Quoted in Braeman, "The Square Deal in Action," p. 57.

27. *Congressional Record,* 59th Cong., 1st Sess. (May 21, 1906), p. 7127; (May 25, 1906), pp. 7420–7421. See Braeman's discussion, "Square Deal in Action," pp. 55–56.

28. Testimony of Thomas E. Wilson, *Hearings* . . . *"Beveridge Amendment,"* p. 5.

29. *Ibid.,* pp. 71, 78. Wilson distinguished the German case by claiming that it was not "general inspection" but "microscopic inspection for trichinae." He claimed that the German tariff against American meats had created an "emergency" situation that made the packers glad to get the inspection "if it could not be gotten in any other way, to stand the expense" (p. 71).

30. In 1905 Argentina replaced the United States as the leading beef-exporting nation in the world. During the next four years exports remained large but continued to decline slowly. The decline accelerated after 1909 and by 1913 beef imports (including beef equivalent of trade in live animals) exceeded beef exports. Lynn Ramsay Edminster, *The Cattle Industry and the Tariff* (New York, 1926), pp. 41–42, attributes the declining exportable surplus not only to "the failure of production to keep pace with the growth of our population but to its failure to increase at all." Production declined so greatly that despite the great decrease in exports and even some increase in imports, the aggregate beef consumption also declined. The decline in production and consumption was absolute. Given the growth of population, the per capita production and consumption declined even more markedly. Edminster includes data on beef production and consumption, p. 43, and on foreign trade in live cattle and beef (p. 84).

31. Braeman, "The Square Deal in Action," p. 59, claims that the packers supported the amendment "in a momentary panic." This section interprets packer silence as part of a fitful legislative strategy. Not only would packer opposition at this point have been costly in terms of the packers' public image, since the President threatened publication of the Neill-Reynolds report, but given the antipacker feelings in the Senate it probably would have been futile. By not voicing opposition at this point, the packers demonstrated support for meat inspection without committing themselves to the Beveridge amendment.

33. S. H. Cowen, "Legislative Questions Affecting Our Industry," in *Proceedings of the Fifteenth Annual Convention of the American National Livestock Association, 1911,* pp. 95–96. Braeman, "The Square Deal in Action," overemphasizes the packers' abilities to manipulate stockmen. Stockmen were not likely to support a measure that they considered inimical

to their own interests. Moreover, stockmen did not go along with the packers when the latter devised their own meat inspection bill. Stockmen opposed the court review provision that the packers wanted and fought to have it eliminated.

34. Letter from TR, Washington, D.C., May 29, 1906, to Upton Sinclair, in Morison *et al.,* eds., *Letters of Theodore Roosevelt,* Vol. V, pp. 287–288.

35. The text of the Wadsworth-Lorimer substitute, with Wadsworth's explanation of the changes made, is given in U. S. Congress, House Report No. 4935, 59th Cong., 1st Sess. (June 14, 1906), p. 107. There were two minority reports filed the following day: House Report No. 4935, Pt. 2, 59th Cong., 1st Sess. (June 15, 1906), pp. 1–3; and House Report No. 3468, Pt. 2, 59th Cong., 1st Sess. (June 15, 1906), pp. 1–3. Nine Republicans and two Democrats voted for the Wadsworth-Lorimer substitute; three Democrats and four Republicans voted against it. Braeman, "The Square Deal in Action," p. 68, contends that the provision for the "right of appeal to the federal courts" was the focal point of contention in the meat inspection battle. The President clearly was outraged at this provision, but Thomas Wilson's testimony before the House committee, *Hearings . . . "Beveridge Amendment,"* p. 86, suggests that the packers were not as committed to the principle as Braeman implies. Wilson testified that he thought the packers "ought to be protected in that in some way, in whatever way you gentlemen, who are lawyers—I am not a lawyer, and I don't know. If the lawyers say that we have the appeal, and can satisfy you gentlemen that we have the appeal, we will be satisfied. All we want is to have that part in shape, so that we would be protected." The packers feared that a political appointee like the Secretary of Agriculture might not necessarily have the knowledge or expertise to make rules and regulations concerning inspection and sanitation. "That is a science," argued Wilson (p. 90). "It is an art; and there are men that are highly versed in it and are capable of passing upon it." They also feared that giving the Secretary of Agriculture such power might politicize the inspection service. "If we had a change to-morrow, or at the end of this Administration, or at any time, in the Secretary of Agriculture, and the new man comes in, and ideas of the new man may be entirely different. . . ."

Dating and labeling provisions, like many other aspects of the Beveridge Amendment, were opposed by different interests for different reasons. The large packers were concerned that dating inspection would create "complications" in inspection and marketing. Since some meat was packaged as fresh meat, and other as canned meat, with meat from animals inspected on different dates going into the same can, packers did not "see how they could follow and identify that particular meat. . . ." They also worried that dating would interfere with their efforts to coordinate the supply of animals with the demand for meats, especially the demand for canned goods. To assure a profitable and steady market for canned meats, the packers smoothed out meat flows by withholding some canned goods when there was not a market for them at acceptable price levels. These efforts, in turn, were related to the variable production and marketing schedule of animals. "Farmers seem to want to clean up . . . stock at certain periods of the year," explained Wilson, "and they come in large quantities, especially in the fall and late summer. We have got to buy those cattle and can them, and we can not find a market for the canned goods at the time we can the stuff; it is not possible to get rid of it immediately,"—at least not at the prices the packers hoped to secure. (Testimony of Thomas Wilson, *Hearings . . . "Beveridge Amendment,"* pp. 10–12).

Smaller packers who had carved out comfortable niches in local or regional markets by specializing in certain meat products were not as concerned with possible bottlenecks in the distribution system. They worried that labeling provisions that required the label to reflect accurately the contents of the package or can might force them to give up established trade names. Whereas the large packers advertised on the basis of quality, many smaller packers had chosen names like "Maple Leaf" or "Palm Leaf Lard," and had designed their labels accordingly. Pure Food and Drug Administration, Record File No. 88, National Archives, "Packer's Convention on Pure Food and Meat Inspection Law, August, 1906," p. 73, records the following exchange between Secretary of Agriculture James Wilson and several regional packers:

> Mr. Drier: "There is no objection to the leaves on the label, is there?"
>
> The Chairman: "I think there is."
>
> Mr. Steward: "How can we make a tree without leaves? It will be so ruled then, as I understand the Secretary. I would like to know how we can get our labels up."
>
> Secretary Wilson: "I think you are safe in making it."
>
> Mr. Stewart: "You think that would be the decision to strike off the leaf entirely and the picture and the leaves?"
>
> Secretary Wilson: "I think so."

Wholesale grocers wondered whether their position as middlemen between the manufacturer and the retailer would entitle them to exemptions from inspection, since the proposed law applied only to the packer or manufacturer, and since they "will receive only goods that are properly branded and stamped and passed" (p. 24). When they learned that all goods intended to be used for interstate or export trade required government inspection, regardless of the place in the distribution chain, they worried about possible losses from uninspected inventories. "But we have on hand now . . . a lot of goods that are not marked 'passed' and yet they are bought and delivered. We ought not to suffer the loss of those goods" (p. 24).

Meat importers faced a different set of concerns. "Suppose you buy that imported mincemeat and manufacture it in bond, and have done so for many years, and that branch of the business reaches millions of pounds?" asked one meat importer.

"Unless those goods bear the marks of inspection they could not be received by your establishment if you are operating your establishment under the regulations of this Department," replied a Department of Agriculture spokesman.

Unsatisfied, the importer blurted, "You are weeding out a business that exists—a lawful, legal business just for the benefit of a packing house monopoly" (p. 41).

Big packer opposition alone, then, did not defeat the Beveridge amendment. The President miscalculated the diversity of opinion on meat inspection. Far from being a clear-cut issue, it was multifaceted, and required far more delicate leadership than TR provided.

36. Letter from TR, Washington, D.C., May 31, 1906, to Wadsworth, in Morison *et al.* eds., *Letters of Theodore Roosevelt,* Vol. V, p. 291.

37. *Ibid.*

38. Quoted in Braeman, "The Square Deal in Action," p. 64.

39. *Hearings . . . "Beveridge Amendment,"* p. 75.

40. *Ibid.*

41. *Ibid.,* p. 76.

42. *Ibid.,* p. 79. Italics added. The question of fairness came up in regard to other commodities, like wheat, where the government absorbed the cost of inspection. Louis Filler discusses some of the ideological issues raised by meat inspection in "Progress and Progressivism," *American Journal of Economics and Sociology,* 20 (April 1961):297.

43. *Hearings . . . "Beveridge Amendment,"* p. 88. Under the old inspection system, packers absorbed the losses from condemnation.

44. See text, Chapter VI, pp. 158–160.

45. *Hearings . . ."Beveridge Amendment,"* p. 89. In Chapter VI above it was suggested that

Wilson may indeed not have known of Swift's move into Argentina, since Swift & Co. apparently moved first—and independently of other packing firms.

46. *Hearings...* *"Beveridge Amendment,"* p. 5.

47. *Ibid.,* pp. 72, 42-43.

48. *Ibid.,* p. 169.

49. *Ibid.,* pp. 50-51.

50. *Ibid.,* p. 51.

51. *Ibid.,* p. 51.

52. *Ibid.,* p. 49.

53. *Ibid.,* p. 46. Wilson claimed that workers furnished the soap "by choice," and that they "preferred" to carry their own towels since "there is no chance of conveying disease from one person to another." Charles Joseph Bushnell, *The Social Problem at the Chicago Stock Yards* (Chicago, 1902), provides information on geographical and racial conditions, art interests, health, including mortality statistics, crime, education, and community relations. Included in his study are several fascinating pictures of work conditions and of the layout of the yards.

54. The "Supreme" trade mark was first seen on refrigerator cars in 1909 (*National Provisioner,* March 12, 1909, p. 37).

55. Testimony of Wilson, *Hearings...* *"Beveridge Amendment,"* p. 23.

56. *Commissioner of Corporations Report on the Beef Industry, 1905,* p. xxi.

57. Thomas C. Cochran, *Railroad Leaders, 1845-1890* (Cambridge, Mass., 1953), discusses the delayed trend toward managerial control in the railroad industry.

58. The attitudes of Swift and Armour toward labor, particularly organized labor, are found in Leech and Carroll, *Armour and His Times,* pp. 217-234; Swift and Van Vlissingen, *The Yankee of the Yards,* p. 141. David Brody, *The Butcher Workman* (Cambridge, Mass. 1964), p. 6, claims that "labor policies of the packers did not extend beyond their cost sheets." Indicative of the authoritarian approach to labor relations is Armour's statement in a letter to two of his sons, Ogden and Phil, December 19, 1899:

> If the men about you think they can get back at any time they want to by a little missionary work through themselves or somebody else, or if they feel they can easily get at your soft side, you will never have any sort of respect or authority that is necessary to conduct a large business.... You of course want to be good and kind to your men. You don't want to be stuck on any of them, but simply just with them. You certainly must permeate the concern from one end to the other that you are not dependent on any one, two or three men to keep the business afloat (Leech and Carroll, *Armour and His Times,* pp. 222-223).

Gustavus Swift shared Armour's views of his workers, boasting proudly on numerous occasions, that "I can raise better men than I can hire" (Swift and Van Vlissingen, *The Yankee of the Yards,* p. 141).

59. The final bill was a compromise between the Wadsworth-Lorimer substitute and the original Beveridge amendment. Braeman, "Square Deal in Action," pp. 69-74, suggests that TR's concern for party unity made him more willing to accept a less effective meat inspection bill, since the vote on the Wadsworth-Lorimer substitute did not follow party lines. Facing a legislative impasse over the issue, TR called on a fellow Republican, Speaker "Uncle Joe" Cannon. Cannon shared TR's concern for party unity, but, as an Illinois Republican, also was well aware of packer demands and influence. To break the impasse, Cannon sent a ranking committee member, Republican Henry C. Adams of Wisconsin, to work out a compromise with TR. A former food commissioner in his own state of Wisconsin and an advocate of pure food and drug legislation, Adams was untainted by packer influence. He and TR quickly reached an understanding. Together with the solicitor of the Department of Agriculture and James Reynolds, they revised the Wadsworth-Lorimer

substitute. Then, while Lorimer and Wadsworth were away for the weekend, Adams called an informal meeting of remaining committee members and secured their approval. For details, see Braeman, "The Square Deal in Action," pp. 69–74; Regier, "The Struggle for Federal Food and Drug Legislation," pp. 13–15; Bailey, "Congressional Opposition to Pure Food Legislation," pp. 61–64.

59. Melvin, "The Federal Meat Inspection Service," p. 79; John Morton Blum, *The Republican Roosevelt* (New York, 1965), used the phrase "purposeful obscurity" to describe resolution of the provision for judicial review.

60. Quoted in Regier, "The Struggle for Federal Food and Drug Legislation," pp. 14–15.

61. Kolko, *The Triumph of Conservatism*, p. 107.

62. Braeman, "The Square Deal in Action," p. 74.

63. Quoted in Braeman, "The Square Deal in Action," p. 57.

64. J. O. Armour, *Packers, the Private Car Lines and the People*, p. 162. Robert E. Lane, *The Regulation of Businessmen* (New Haven, 1954), pp. 19–20, offers this general perspective on the effects of regulation on attitudes:

> The New Regulation, the events which prompted it, and the rationale which supported it . . . challenged the businessmen's belief system, profaned his idols, and deprecated his myths. . . . [It] denigrated the businessman himself, lowered his status in the community, and allocated him to a role subordinate to the one he had enjoyed. In this way it attacked what might be termed the business ego, psychologically a most traumatic experience . . . it frustrated men by depriving them of choices to which they had become accustomed . . . it aroused new anxieties and uncertainties in a time already tense with doubt and foreboding.

65. The *"Significant Sixty,"* p. 95. Compliance with regulations may have added to the packers' costs, but the slow-down in rates of domestic livestock production and in beef consumption is a more plausible explanation for rising meat prices. The *National Provisioner* suggested that there was simply not enough meat to feed the country's rapidly growing population: "With more consumers bidding against each other for a stationary or smaller supply, prices were bound to rise." An increase in demand could, of course, occur without an increase in per capita consumption of meat.

66. The *"Significant Sixty,"* p. 95.

Chapter IX

Packers Found Not Guilty:
United States v. *Louis Swift et al.*

The packers had reason to hope that they would fare better under TR's successor. A former justice on the Sixth Circuit Court of Appeals, William Howard Taft had a judge's rational, contemplative frame of mind. Preferring conciliation and compromise to combat and pressure tactics, he had faith in the Sherman Act and in the courts' abilities to enforce it. Moreover, he had made no arbitrary distinction between good and bad trusts. Rather, he distinguished between those combinations deliberately organized to restrict competition and those that had been organized for other reasons but which inadvertently, restricted competition.[1]

No longer forced to contend with arbitrary distinctions between good and bad trusts or a President who seemed determined to single out the beef industry for attack, packers felt confident that Taft's administration would treat them fairly. Ultimately, neither Taft nor the courts disappointed them. It was the National Packing Co. and its entanglement with an increasingly active Justice Department that caused the packers the most difficulty between 1908 and 1912.

During the uproar over meat inspection and the court battles of the Roosevelt administration, the operation of National had caused little concern or excitement. Since the company published no annual reports or any information on the volume of sales, not many people knew much about it. The Bureau of Corporation's report on the beef industry in 1905 had mentioned National, but did not give a clear picture of its functions. The Bureau stated very matter-of-factly that it "is distinguished from the other large packing concerns in that it is a merger of several independent companies, rather than a gradual development of a single organization."[2] Not until beef prices began to rise at the end of the decade did the government and public begin to reassess National's role in the industry.

219

In December 1908, the Justice Department undertook an investigation of the major packers, but no grand jury proceedings resulted. The government prosecutors' second investigation, undertaken a year later, initially appeared more promising. On March 21, 1909, the government brought criminal indictments against National and its ten subsidiaries for violations of the Sherman Act. At the same time, a bill in equity was filed, requesting the dissolution of National.[3]

Neither action went to trial, however. The government's case ran into a legal snag. The federal statute of limitations barred criminal prosecution more than three years after an alleged offense. Although the government had collected a great deal of information covering the period from 1890 to 1905, crucial evidence for the 1907–1910 period was lacking. Judge K. M. Landis of the Northern District Court of Illinois quashed the criminal indictments on the grounds that "the court is not clothed with authority to supply entirely by inference the complete ommission of so fundamental an element of the offense" as a charge showing that any statutory offense—fixing prices, dividing territory, restraint of trade—had been committed within the statutory period of the last three years.[4]

The government, fearing that the giving of testimony by indicted packers in a civil case might afford them immunity in its criminal case, then withdrew its civil petition against National and proceeded to try one of its criminal cases.[5] The packers' attorneys objected to dismissal of the civil suit. Confident that the civil case against National would be decided in their favor and undoubtedly hoping to strengthen the possibility of immunity pleas, they wanted a decision on the civil case before they took up the criminal trial against individual packers. Their requests, however, were denied.

On September 12, 1910, criminal indictments were returned, charging the directors with conspiracy and combination in restraint of trade. Specific charges were almost identical to those of the earlier 1903–1905 case against the packers, which resulted in the injunction. They included collusion in buying livestock, figuring list selling methods by a uniform system of accounting, keeping quotas for sales of each firm in different markets, and fixing the price of fresh meats. Packer attorneys filed demurrers arguing that the petition against the directors should be dismissed because it purported to be an original proceeding when in fact it was merely a proceeding in contempt for violation of the 1903 Grosscup injunction. District Judge George A. Carpenter of Illinois overruled their demurrers in May 1911, just a few days before the Supreme Court handed down its "rule of reason" doctrine in the Standard Oil case. The packers' trial was set for November 18.[6]

Attorneys for the packers could not ignore the implications of the

Standard Oil decision for their own case. In enunciating the "rule of reason," Chief Justice Edward Douglas White had reawakened the old controversy about antitrust revision that had been smouldering beneath the surface of progressivism since the early 1900s. Justice White argued, in apparent contradiction of the Trans-Missouri decision, that the Sherman Act would be read to prohibit only "unreasonable restraints" on interstate commerce. The way he established the "unreasonableness" of the Standard Oil combination, however, made the decision less a departure from precedent than was initially believed. He used the "illegal intent criterion" disavowed in Trans-Missouri but found proof of illegal means in the oil refiners' actions in joining in a combination. In so doing, Justice White linked Sections I and II of the Sherman Act; use of combination in restraint of trade that violated Section I, also directly violated Section II. Ironically, courts could now use the "rule of reason" to set aside the question of unlawful means, for any action to exclude competitors from the market forcibly was considered proof of illegal intent.[7]

White's doctrine invited numerous and conflicting interpretations. It could just as easily be read to stretch or to uphold legal precedent. Whereas some, like Attorney General George W. Wickersham, applauded the decision for narrowing the "uncertainty in the law" and defining more clearly its "scope and effect," others, like Judge Grosscup, complained that it increased the uncertainty of the Act and made enforcement even more difficult and dependent upon judicial discretion.[8]

The packers and their attorneys appeared uncertain about the general implications of the decision or its significance for their own pending criminal case. When the ruling was first handed down in May, after Judge Carpenter had overruled their demurrers, the *Chicago Daily Farmers and Drovers Journal* reported that the decision had given packers "new hope," and that their attorneys planned to file a motion to quash indictments on the grounds that they did not show "an unreasonable restraint" upon commerce.[9] Ultimately, however, no new motions were filed.

As the time for trial drew nearer, a new strategy emerged. Clearly, the packers hoped to capitalize on the uncertainties created by the Standard Oil decision to launch a new attack on the Sherman Act. The November 18 headlines of the *National Provisioner* read: "PACKERS TO TEST SHERMAN ANTI-TRUST LAW: WANT SUPREME COURT RULING WITHOUT JURY TRIAL DELAY." Filing a petition to take their case directly to the Supreme Court, defense attorneys asserted that the "reasonable doctrine" had, in effect, nullified the Sherman Act, for it had made impossible a determination in advance of a jury trial what was legal and illegal. "The indictment will depend entirely upon a particular jury's view of the reasonableness or unreasonableness of the particular case," charged the defense petition. "It will depend not on any standard erected by the law which may be known in advance, but on one that may be created by the whim, prejudice or arbitrary views of a jury. . . . There is not a set standard fixed, or attempted to be fixed, to guide the citizen to a knowledge of his guilt or innocence of an offense charged before it has been adjudicated. . . . The Act violates the sixth amendment to the Constitution of the United States, which required that the petitioners, severally, shall be informed of the nature and cause of the accusation."[10]

The Supreme Court did not agree. Having worked hard to develop the Sherman Act, it refused to grant the petition. The packer trial commenced formally on December 6, with U. S. District Attorney James H. Wilkerson charging "that the combination represented by the ten meat packers . . . is the most powerful engine or system for the suppression of competition and the fixing of prices ever known in the history of the industrial world."[11] The main contention of the government was that the packers used National as an instrument to carry out the functions of price fixing and regulation of output formerly accomplished by the old pools. As the government would argue in the Standard Oil and Du Pont powder cases,[12] the form of the "combination" made little difference. The creation of the National Packing Co. and the dissolution of the pools changed only the outward form of business. As far as the government was concerned, the packers still continued to restrain trade, fix prices, and suppress competition in defiance of the law. Prosecuting Attorney Pierce Butler asked:

> Can there be any difference, if your Honor please, between the present situation without fines? . . . Can there be any difference legally, your Honor, whether or not this understanding or agreement be cemented together by the brutal bonds of fines that only can control the conduct of untruthful and untrustworthy men? Or that this organization be bound together, if you please, by the silken cord of brotherly cooperation, as brother directors and as brother stockholders?[13]

A snag in the government's case, similar to that which had already prompted Judge K. M. Landis to toss out the indictments in 1908, was quickly spotted by packer lawyers. The indictment covered the years from 1907 to 1910, but depended upon facts that grew out of the operation of National, following the three-year limit covered by the indictment. Defense attorneys charged that "If there be eliminated all facts and circumstances of the National Packing Company for three years, beginning in 1907, there would be no shadow of a case to go to the jury. . . . All matters before that time are merely historical and cannot be the basis of a conviction."[14]

In pretrial response to government charges, packer lawyers insisted that National bore little resemblance to the pools and that the object of the pools was far different from National's operations. Whereas pools were designed to regulate shipments of fresh beef, National, they contended, was organized simply to hold different properties acquired in preparation for a merger that never materialized. "It is obvious," asserted Attorney John S. Miller for the defense, "that if these men wanted to continue the Veeder arrangement they didn't have to organize the National Packing Company to do it . . . they could have done it around a lunch table."[15] Although Miller's argument was neither obvious nor entirely correct (as the history of the National Packing Co. shows), it did sketch the broad outlines that the packers planned to adopt once it was their turn to answer formally the charges of the government.

The prosecution took a great deal of time to present its case and for weeks continued to produce piles and piles of data concerning prices, margins, and information on the operation of the packers' pools and the origins and operation of the National Packing Co.[16] Conspicuous by its absence, however, was any concrete information or evidence to prove that the packers, as individuals, had actually conspired to fix prices or eliminate competition. The prosecution attempted to compensate by arguing that conclusions were self-evident. "Any inference other than agreement runs counter to the hypothesis of competition, which is the equivalent here of the hypothesis of innocence. . . . [The] machinery runs well. It reaches the purpose for which it was organized—the division of supply between them. . . . [The] wonder is that it was possible to so perfect a system of dividing the supply to reach a result as close as that which has been reached."[17]

By January Judge Carpenter grew impatient. The packers had not yet formally presented their case, and the government appeared nowhere near the end of its arguments. "The government will have to show a combination of effort and concerted action on the part of each of these 10 defendants to commit conspiracy or there will have to be an end to this case," Carpenter warned on January 13. He continued: "The government is necessarily obliged to prove its theory in a case of this kind, piece by piece."[18]

Finally, nearly two months later, the government used the ideological underpinnings of the Sherman Act and the revered maxim of competition to tie the case together:

> The Sherman law is not the fog through which the ship of interstate commerce has been sailing; but the real fog has been contempt for and disobedience of the law . . . in this statute is crystallized the spirit of industrial freedom. It has not yet been necessary to wait until the entire country has been placed at the mercy of the gigantic combination before an assault could be made upon the combination.

The elimination of competition is public injury; the fixing, regulating and controlling of prices is a public injury, and it is no defense to say that it is impossible to measure in dollars and cents the exact amount of the injury which is inflicted upon the public.[19]

Confident of victory, the government rested its case.

Defense attorneys, however, were even more confident. Insisting that the government has presented "absolutely no evidence of guilt," they refused to put in any defense and rested the case with the jury on the evidence of the government's own witnesses and on the arguments of counsel.

Instructions to the jury followed. Then, one by one, attorneys for the prosecution and defense reiterated their main arguments.[20] Prosecuting Attorney James M. Sheean asked the jurors:

Is it conceivable that these packers who met Tuesday at the meetings in the National Packing Company and determined the course of business of the National Packing Company left the meetings and directed their business along different lines? The necessary and inevitable consequence was to bring about the actual operation of the concerns in harmony.... So gentlemen, let us bear in mind that the ultimate fact which the government charges and which it asks you to find to be a fact is that there is a combination in restraint of trade whereby competition is eliminated or restricted between the vast businesses of Armour, Swift and Morris. That, stripped of all cumbersome legal verbiage, is the ultimate controlling, central fact, the great high mountain peak of the whole case.

Defense Attorney John S. Miller responded:

The question is, are they in combination to restrain trade? Are innocent things which they did to be construed into violation of the law? The Supreme Court says evil done to the public is the test.

Defense Attorney John B. Payne continued:

Nobody claims anybody has been injured by these defendants. A verdict of guilty would characterize these men as criminals, brand their business as a fraud, and do great harm to this country and its people. Not a witness has testified that the price of fresh meat has been raised or the cattle price lowered.

Instructions from the defense then ended with a familiar ring:

Eliminate all except evidence of the Veeder meetings and what remains? For years these defendants have been the ball of the political, legislative, communistic, and socialist attacks. Cut out all the suspicion and probability and remove all the guesswork. Is there a case shown where these defendants purposely and consciously violated the anti-trust act?

The jury thought not. After being reminded by Judge Carpenter that the question of injury done to the public was not an element to be considered, and that "the law may be said to conserve political as well as industrial freedom,"[21] the jury acquitted the packers of all charges on March 26, 1912.

Interviews with jurors after the trial indicated that the government lost its case less because the theory on which it rested was unconvincing than because the evidence introduced did not substantiate the theory. "The reason on which the acquittal was based," explained juror J. H. Edwards, "was that we gave the defendants the benefit of the doubt. We did not believe the Government had made out a strong case." Adam Clow, another juror said: "There was certainly a whole lot said about a few facts, but none of us could find that the defendants should be convicted on such evidence."[22]

The 1912 case provided packers with a convenient defense of both future and past policies. Packers, then and since, have maintained that the verdict proved that National was "perfectly legal", that constant live-stock percentages were the result of "intelligent competition" rather than collusion.[23]

U.S. v. *Louis Swift et al.,* however, was clearly no landmark case. It established no new legal precedents. Nor did it have much of an impact upon the economics of the industry. Nevertheless, it was important. Not only did it demonstrate the difficulties of proving criminal collusion on the part of individual corporate officers, but it also, and more importantly, showed the difficulty of proving collusion in an industry where collusion had long ago been institutionalized.

The packers interpreted the verdict as a vindication not only of their own characters and integrity, but of their business policies and practices as well. "This verdict of 12 men under oath, chosen from all walks of life should forever silence the caluminator and muckraker," claimed M. W. Borders, general counsel for Morris & Co.[24] While the verdict did not in fact settle the question of the legality of National, the fate of that corporation had already been decided. Even before acquittal, packers were preparing to dissolve the company.

DISSOLUTION

Unlike the court-ordered breakups of the Standard Oil, American Tobacco, and Du Pont empires, the dissolution of National Packing Co. was suggested and carried out by the packers with the approval of the Attorney General of the United States. It was "absolutely a voluntary dissolution," insisted Henry Veeder, legal counsel for Swift & Co., when he testified before the House Committee on Agriculture in 1920.[25] Technically, Veeder was right, though it was obvious that the packers acted only under duress. Although the government had intended to bring a civil case against National and its ten subsidiaries in 1910, and had even filed a bill in equity requesting the dissolution of the company, it had abandoned this effort in 1911 in order to press a criminal case under the Sherman Act against the individual directors of National.[26] That case came to trial in November 1911. "The principal issue in that case and the principal issue upon which the court instructed the jury," Veeder maintained before the House committee, "was whether these men in the ownership of the National Packing Company, meeting in the director's room of that company, were at the same time undertaking to regulate the business of Armour & Company, Swift & Company, Morris & Company, so as make a combination in restraint of trade.... The question was not raised as to the legality of the organization of the National Packing Company. In my opinion that was a perfectly legal organization.... The charge in the bill was that we were engaged in an illegal combination, not in a legal merger.... There was no attack made on the National that its organization was illegal...."[27]

Prior to the resolution of the case, the packers went to the Attorney General and "informed him that they were just as anxious as he to dispose of the National Packing Company in some way, and if he would point out the method he wanted the packing company dissolved, they would be very glad to follow it."[28] Although the government eventually lost its case against the individuals, who were directors of the National Packing Co., evidence suggests that the Justice Department was intending to reintroduce the equity case against National following disposition of the criminal case.[29] Other facts were also important in the packers' willingness to dissolve the company.

By 1912 the need for and utility of a device like National had also diminished. Having interlocked the administrative networks of National with those of the Big Three, having routinized oligopolistic behavior and stabilized market shares, the packers may well have gained enough knowledge about each other's business to have come to consider National no longer necessary to the smooth functioning of the oligopoly. Such intimate acquaintance with the operations of the leading firms in the oligopoly facilitated such techniques as price leadership, as well as the full realization of the futility of traditional competition.

In addition, there was, of course, a positive and powerful inducement to dissolve the company once the federal government had taken action against it. As the behavior of other industrialists in similar predicaments had demonstrated, voluntary dissolution offered an opportunity to influence the outcome as well as a way to avoid prosecution.[30] If the National

Packing case came to trial, the packers risked an unfavorable verdict. Therefore, it was hardly surprising that dissolution was suggested by the packers and their attorneys in 1912 when no suits were pending against National as a corporation. National had worked moderately well, but the legal dangers it posed had come to outweigh its diminished utility as a vehicle for stability in the industry.

The government was receptive to the packers' offer. It promised the end of the National Packing Co. as an instrument for the suppression of competition in the industry. The "voluntary" dissolution of National seemed a good way to restore competitive conditions in the industry without investing additional time and money in the case against National. To bring about an effective dissolution, District Attorney James H. Wilkerson agreed with the packers that:

> there should be an actual distribution of the assets of the companies whose stock is now held by the National Packing Company among the three large packing interests which own the stock of the National Packing Company. A distribution of the stock of those subsidiary companies would be fruitless and the continuation of the corporate existence of the respective companies does not seem necessary to preserve any rights of private property, while the interests of the public would seem to be best subserved by the distribution of assets as above noted and the actual absorption of those assets by the respective packing interests to which they are turned over upon the distribution.... [If] they were to own the properties absolutely and be allowed to continue the names of the old subsidiary companies, they could maintain and dictate prices and still be within the law. In that way, the public would suffer more under the altered conditions than at present.[31]

In carrying out the dissolution, plants and branches were awarded as far as possible to the interests that had not previously had a plant or a branch at a particular place. For example, the Morris interests, which previously had no plant at Omaha, received the Omaha Packing Plant, along with 16 branch houses and 10 minor selling agencies, most of which were in the southern states. The other physical assets were parceled out to Armour, Swift, and Morris.[32]

By distributing the properties of National in such a manner, the Department of Justice tried to go "as far as possible in the attempt to restore competitive conditions as to the property acquired in 1902 and after the organization of the National *without actually parting with their ownership of the same.*" Competition was to be restored, but with the least possible violence to the protection of property rights. In Wilkerson's opinion:

> There is no way in which the property can be returned to those from whom it was purchased. To say that these corporations may not engage in interstate commerce so long as they are controlled by either Swift or Armour or Morris means either that they are to be driven out of interstate commerce or that if their property is sold through a receivership probably the only persons able to purchase it will be prohib-

ited from bidding at the sale. This would be to use the power of a court of equity not to prevent future violations but to punish past ones, and to overlook the fundamental purpose of the statute to protect and not to destroy property rights.[33]

Thus, although the distribution increased the volume of business of the Big Three (Armour & Co. by 21 percent, Swift & Co. by 25 percent, and Morris & Co. by 13 percent), the Justice Department remained convinced that:

> The condition created was not one where there will be a continued attempt to monopolize after the dissolution of the National Company. There is nothing suggestive of a monopoly by either Swift or Armour or Morris in adding to their equipment the plants obtained from the National. Nor do we have, as to the properties originally merged in the National, the situation of property acquired through unfair trade methods, so that the very control of the property by those who thus acquired it may constitute a continuing violation of the state. The situation here is clearly one in which an adequate measure of relief would have resulted from restraining the doing of the unlawful acts in the future; and the parties having voluntarily discontinued those acts, there is now no occasion for further resort to the courts for relief.[34]

The dissolution brought few arguments or complaints from the packers, but the Federal Trade Commission later complained in its own report on the industry in 1919 that "the decision left all the strong independents which had been absorbed into the National Packing Company in the hands of the packers."[35]

In effect, the dissolution simply reestablished the status quo that had existed before the formal incorporation of National and after the Big Three had acquired these previously independent competitors. It left the oligopolistic structure of the industry essentially unchanged and even strengthened somewhat by giving legal sanction to the 1903 purchases. The Big Three, together with Cudahy and S & S, continued to control a major share of the interstate dressed beef trade as they had done since the late 1880s.

If the dissolution of National made cooperation somewhat more difficult, it certainly did not restore the kind of competition the court had envisioned. Similarities in administrative networks, costing techniques, managerial philosophies, and years of cooperation and camaraderie enabled the packers to adjust relatively easily to the loss of the National Packing Co. By the end of January 1913, only five months after the dissolution of National, the packers had already agreed informally upon new percentages for livestock purchases.[36]

The government thus appears to have been more successful in preventing any possibility of monopoly in the industry than in restoring the traditional brand of competition that really had not existed since the old days before the refrigerator car. The packers had learned to live with the realities of oligopolistic competition, and, in fact, the industry changed very little in the wake of the destruction of the National Packing Co.

CONCLUSION

The National Packing Co. was a most unusual—perhaps even unique— institution in the corporate history of the late nineteenth and early twentieth centuries. When the packers, like so many other industrialists of the day, set out to effect a merger that would have created a single dominant firm, their efforts proved abortive. The collapse of the final merger try left Armour, Morris, and Swift with nearly fifteen new companies and no money to pay for them. They eventually resolved their difficulties by creating the National Packing Co., a strange sort of half-way house between pooling and combination.

Just as they had done to solve similar problems of coordination and control in their own companies, the Big Three created a complex administrative network at National. That network, however, did more than control product flows of companies held by National—it also served to coordinate information and product flows among the Swift, Armour, and Morris companies, though not so comprehensively as would probably have been the case under a real combination. Supplies were allotted; prices and market shares were stabilized. U.S. District Attorney James H. Wilkerson offered a good summary of National's stabilizing role in the industry in a letter to U.S. Attorney General Wickersham in 1912:

> [The] National Packing Company served a two-fold purpose. First, its very existence operated to check the competition among Swift & Company, Armour & Company, and Morris & Company, because the principal owners of the stock of those companies and those in the active management of their affairs were united in the ownership and management of a fourth corporation, whose business was large enough to make it an important factor in the industry in which they were jointly engaged. Competition on the part of Armour & Company as against Swift & Company, for instance, was necessarily competition against the National Packing Company, in which Mr. Armour had a large interest. The inevitable check upon competition growing out of this relation is perfectly obvious. Secondly, by acting as directors of the National Packing Company the representatives of Swift & Company, Armour & Company and Morris & Company were given a pretext for continuing the weekly meetings; and in view of their community of interest they could make arrangements as to output and prices for their own concerns in the guise of arrangements made with respect to the management of the affairs of the National Packing Company.[37]

When the National Packing Co. became more of a threat to industry stability than a vehicle for that stability, the packers saw the writing on the wall and offered to dismantle the firm. It is probably not accurate to say that its usefulness was over, but its utility had clearly been diminished by the fact that the partners in the oligopoly were much better disciplined in 1912 than they had been a decade earlier when National was created. That, coupled with the force of ominous government pressures, made the end of National, logical. And, despite the government's sanguine expectations, its disappearance made very little difference to the behavior or structure of the industry. As they probably knew very well, the big packers really gave up very little when they agreed to dissolve their half-way house. They received in return a respite from federal pressures.

NOTES

1. Alfred S. Eichner, *The Emergence of Oligopoly*, pp. 20–21, 299; Gabriel Kolko, *The Triumph of Conservatism*, pp. 159–188; Hans Thorelli, *Federal Anti-Trust Policy*, pp. 468, 482; William Letwin, *Law and Economic Policy*, pp. 250–253.

2. *Commissioner of Corporations Report on the Beef Industry, 1905*, p. 35.

3. For details and chronology, see Department of Justice (JD) File No. 60-50-0, National Archives. Letter from U.S. District Attorney James H. Wilkerson, Chicago, Ill., September 25, 1912, to U.S. Attorney General George W. Wickersham; U.S. Congress, House, *Hearings Before the Committee on the Judiciary, Investigations of Beef Industries*, 64th Cong., 1st Sess., 1916, p. 450.

4. Quoted in *The "Significant Sixty,"* p. 91.

5. *National Provisioner*, December 31, 1910, p. 15.

6. *U.S. v. Louis Swift et al.*, 188 Fed. Rep. 1002.

7. The decision and its implications are discussed in Letwin, *Law and Economic Policy*, pp. 253–265; Eichner, *The Emergence of Oligopoly*, pp. 18, 25, 203–306, 313; Chandler and Salsbury, *Pierre S. Du Pont and the Making of the Modern Corporation*, especially Chapter X.

8. *Chicago Daily Farmers and Drovers Journal*, June 14, 1911, p. 1.

9. *Ibid.*

10. *National Provisioner*, November 18, 1911, p. 15.

11. *Ibid.*, December 23, 1911, p. 15.

12. Chandler and Salsbury, *Pierre S. Du Pont*, pp. 259–300, provides an excellent analysis.

13. See text, Chapter V, p. 82, n. 11, regarding Swift & Co. holdings, *U.S. v. Louis Swift et al.*

14. Quoted in *National Provisioner*, December 23, 1911, p. 15.

15. *U.S. v. Louis Swift et al.*, p. 39.

16. Refer to text, Chapter VI.

17. *U.S. v. Louis Swift et al.*, p. 296.

18. Quoted in *National Provisioner*, January 13, 1912, p. 15.

19. *Ibid.*, March 30, 1912, p. 15.

20. *Ibid.*, March 23, 1912, p. 17.

21. *Ibid.*, March 30, 1912, p. 59.

22. *Ibid.*

23. U.S. Congress, House, *Hearings Before the Committee on Agriculture on Meat Packer Legislation*, 66th Cong., 2nd Sess., 1920, pp. 1021, 1018.

24. Quoted in *National Provisioner*, June 1, 1912, p. 17.

25. U.S. Congress, House, *Hearings Before the Committee on Agriculture on Meat Packer Legislation*, 66th Cong., 2nd Sess., 1920, p. 1295.

26. Department of Justice File No. 60-50-0. Letter from District Attorney Wilkerson, Chicago, September 25, 1912, to U.S. Attorney General Wickersham. In November 1911 U.S. attorneys were still optimistic about a successful prosecution. Referring to the packers' attempts to have the case dismissed, U.S. Attorney General Wickersham wrote District Attorney Wilkerson, November 14, 1911: "I take it that this is simply the last desperate wriggle before getting face to face with a jury of their peers. I don't believe it will be effective."

27. U.S. Congress, House, *Hearings . . . on Meat Packer Legislation,* 66th Cong., 2nd Sess., 1920, pp. 1301–1303.

28. *Ibid.*

29. Department of Justice File No. 60-50-0 details the legal developments. Letter from U.S. District Attorney Wilkerson, Chicago, September 25, 1912, to U.S. Attorney General Wickersham, explained that the government dismissed its civil petition and went to court with a criminal case in order to avoid the packers' objection that the civil case was not an original proceeding but "an information in contempt charging a violation" of the Grosscup injunction. However, the criminal case charging the packers with price fixing "presented the question of the direct criminal connection of the individual defendants with the alleged unlawful acts; and the Government was obliged to rely mainly upon circumstantial evidence to establish this personal participation within the period of the statute of limitations. There was convincing direct evidence of acts as late as 1906, the prosecution for which was not affected by the immunity claimed to have been obtained in 1906. . . ." Wilkerson admitted that "the situation of the government would have been stronger in a proceeding brought promptly after the failure in the immunity case than it was in the one which was ultimately tried" (p. 10).

As of February 13, 1912, before the National Packing Company was dissolved, there were still several cases pending against the packers in the District Court of Illinois (Nos. 4510, 4511, 4620, *U.S.* v. *Louis Swift et al.,* and 3626, *U.S.* v. *Armour*) but the government now seemed pessimistic about a successful prosecution. Letter from U.S. District Attorney Wilkerson, Chicago, February 13, 1912, to U.S. Attorney General Wickersham, indicated that packer attorney Sheean discussed the "advisability of dismissing the pending indictments against the Chicago packers," and suggested "that there would be considerable difficulty in making the proof conform to the averments . . . and that inasmuch as immunity was given to the individual defendants [in the 1905 case], attempted conviction of the corporate defendants was hardly worth the expenditure of time and effort which such an undertaking would impose." Sheean recommended dismissal of the cases.

30. For example, see the legal maneuverings of the Du Pont firm described in Chandler and Salsbury, *Pierre S. Du Pont and the Making of the Modern Corporation,* pp. 259–300.

31. Justice Department File No. 60-50-0. Letter from U.S. District Attorney Wilkerson, Chicago, September 25, 1912, to U.S. Attorney General Wickersham.

32. *Ibid.* Armour received the Anglo-American Provision Company of Chicago; the Fowler Packing Company of Kansas City, Kansas; the Hammond Packing Company of St. Joseph, Missouri; the Colorado Packing and Provision Company of Denver; Fowler's Canadian Company, Ltd., Hamilton, Ontario; and the New York Butchers' Dressed Meat Company of New York City. In addition, the company received the Stock Yards Warehouse Company and the North American Provision Company of Chicago; the Freidman Manufacturing Company, an oleomargarine concern of Chicago; the Fowler Brothers, Ltd., a selling agency in Liverpool, England; the Hamilton Beef Company, Ltd., of London, England; the Hamilton Stock Yards Co., Ltd. of Hamilton Ontario; and real estate at the Union Stock Yards, together with 51 branches and 19 minor selling agencies in the South. Swift was awarded the G. H. Hammond Company and the Omaha Packing Company of Chicago; the Plankinton Packing Company of Milwaukee;

the St. Louis Dressed Beef & Provision Company of St. Louis; Sturtevant & Haley Beef & Supply Company of Boston; the United Dressed Beef Company of New York City; and the Western Packing Company of Denver. Along with these plants came the Continental Packing Company, a warehouse in Chicago; real estate at the Union Stock Yards; 50 percent of the stock in the Denver Stock Yards; the Milwaukee Stock Yards; the Northwestern Glue Company of Chicago; the Northern Reduction Company of Bartell, Wisconsin; real estate in St. Joseph, Missouri; real estate in Chicago; 55 branch houses and 25 minor selling agencies. The 2600 refrigerator cars of the National Car Line Company were distributed as follows:

Swift	1214
Armour	1043
Morris	343
Total	2600

33. Justice Department File No. 60-50-0. Letter from U.S. District Attorney Wilkerson, Chicago, September 25, 1912, to U.S. Attorney General Wickersham.

34. *Ibid.*

35. FTC, *Report on the Meat-Packing Industry, 1919,* Pt. II, "Evidence of Combination Among Packers," pp. 22–23.

36. *Ibid.* includes information on the readjustment of livestock percentages following the dissolution of the National Packing Company. The livestock pool involved livestock purchasing agreements among the Big Five, whereby each packer was permitted to buy only a certain stipulated proportion of the animals offered for sale. Evidence from the so-called "Black Book" memoranda, written by German F. Sulzberger, vice-president of Sulzberger & Sons Co., January 1913 to January 1916, confirmed the pooling activities and provided fascinating insights into competitive relationships between the Big Five preceding the reorganization of Sulzberger & Sons into Wilson & Company.

37. Justice Department File No. 60-50-0. Letter from U.S. District Attorney Wilkerson, Chicago, September 25, 1912, to U.S. Attorney General Wickersham.

Chapter X

Competition and Regulation: Conclusion

The meat packing industry in 1912 remained oligopolistic, just as it had been for the previous quarter of a century. Its structure and behavior contrasted dramatically with the atomistic and unconcentrated industry that prevailed before the advent of the refrigerator car. Pre-oligopolistic competition involved price competition between numerous buyers and sellers, none of whom had large enough shares of the market to affect the price and output behavior of rivals. These competitive patterns prevailed because the undeveloped state of refrigeration and transportation technology restricted meat packing to a few months a year. Since meat was highly perishable in its fresh state, it had to be consumed immediately after slaughter or cured during the winter months before shipment to distant markets in the spring. The seasonal production of cured meats made entry easy and limited specialization in the industry. Curing required no heavy investment in plant or equipment, only a supply of livestock and a good curing recipe. Cured products were easily distributed through the traditional network of jobbers and middlemen. Since packing was a part-time, nonspecialized activity, almost anyone could enter the business. Roles were not clearly defined and relationships with others in the industry were fluid and unsystematic.

The refrigerator car revolutionized the industry. By enabling meat to be produced and slaughtered in the West near major sources of supply and distributed quickly throughout the year to major urban areas in the East, the refrigerator car created new opportunities to market a new product—western dressed beef. Western packers who utilized the new innovation and built the distribution networks it required were able to put western dressed beef on the market at a lower cost than meat obtained from livestock driven or transported on the hoof by railroad to eastern markets and then slaughtered. The competition spurred by the new innovation was a key element in the western packers' success. By capitalizing on the economies of large-scale production and distribution and exploiting the railroads' vulnerability on rate agreements, the innovators overcame resistance from the old orders in transportation and distribution and succeeded in launching a new industry. The new order in packing was based primarily on beef rather than pork and was oriented to the economic needs of concentrated urban cities rather than to the needs of diffuse and local markets. Packers were no longer primarily merchants but had become specialized meat manufacturers who produced, distributed, and transported their own meats and meat by-products.

Although packers were no longer at the mercy of the weather after the innovation of the refrigerator car, they faced a new set of problems. Since railroads were unwilling to build refrigerator cars and the old network of wholesalers either could not or would not provide the services and facilities necessary to handle the perishable product quickly and efficiently, the packers interested in utilizing the new innovation had to provide huge amounts of capital to build and operate an entire system—including plants, refrigerator cars, and branch houses—from the outset. To keep unit costs down and deliver meat quickly and safely, they searched for ways to increase both the volume of meat and speed at which it flowed through the enterprises. Coordination was essential, for only if the supply of meat on hand at the plants was carefully matched with demand at branch houses could the system operate effectively and efficiently. Not long after packers began to build their distribution outlets in the same markets, therefore, they began to rationalize their respective organizations. They created, independently of each other, centralized, departmentalized, administrative structures to define and clarify authority and responsibility for day-to-day routine activities and long-run planning decisions. Utilizing the telephone and telegraph, they built administrative networks to link the purchasing and selling departments with headquarters in Chicago. They devised new methods of cost accounting to relate costs more closely to price and achieve more effective coordination of supply and demand at profitable levels.

Oligopoly emerged quickly because the huge capital investments needed to build an entire system and the long lead time of the innovator limited entry to a few packers who had resources and determination to undertake a strategy of vertical integration quickly and effectively.

There was also an important geographic component to the emergence of oligopoly in meat packing. Because Swift and those who followed him directed their initial marketing efforts to the Northeast, where the demand for meat was concentrated and expanding rapidly, the battle for market shares centered there. By the mid-1880s Swift, Armour, Morris, and Hammond each had established sales outlets in many of the same cities in the Northeast. With a few giants pouring large shipments of beef into the same region, it did not take long for the market to fill up and price competition to set in. The market could hold only so much.

The first efforts to pool dressed beef shipments into the Northeast in the mid-1880s marked the emergence of oligopoly in the industry and indicated a shift in packer strategy from price competition to cautious cooperation. The scenario first played out in the Northeast was then replayed in the new market areas with continued expansion of the industry. In each market area, several stages of growth reappeared. There was an initial period of relatively rapid growth, when profits were high and expansion was relatively easy. Then, as the packers began to confront each other in the same markets and growth began to slow, the pools tried first in the Northeast were extended or revised to include the new market areas.

The development of oligopoly encompassed a lengthy learning period during which time packers attempted to cooperate and coordinate jointly the meat flows of the entire industry. Replicating the techniques first worked out at the level of the individual firm, packers standardized accounting methods so that they operated at roughly the same margins of profit. Utilizing their administrative networks, they channeled information on margins and sales to pool headquarters in Chicago. Cooperation was not easy, however. Only gradually, after the repeated break-up of their pools, did they finally learn the rules of the game, among the most important of which was that oligopolists had more to lose and less to gain by competing on prices. But by that time pools had become less necessary.

The packers arrived at oligopoly through a strategy of vertical integration designed to solve problems of marketing a perishable product. While firms in other industries, such as oil, sugar, and tobacco, first encountered production rather than marketing problems and solved them through a strategy of horizontal combination rather than vertical integration, eventually all firms ended up functioning similarly: that is, they came to compete oligopolistically, which meant that they competed through means other than prices—on the basis of brand names, advertising, or on considerations of quality and service. With a good knowledge of each other's costs, they practiced price leadership. Such an arrangement benefited all firms, placing a protective price umbrella over the least efficient firms and offering the most efficient firms higher profit margins and greater price stability. Having learned by experience the futility of trying to compete on prices for larger market shares, the oligopolists practiced the fine art of cooperation.

Just as oligopolistic competition came to characterize the competitive patterns of most giant firms, so too did oligopoly become the characteristic structure of most of the nation's center industries. Oligopoly came to dominate the nation's industrial structure largely because of the extreme difficulty of maintaining monopoly. As Alfred Eichner has expertly pointed out in his analysis of oligopoly in sugar refining,[1] despite the formation of the American Sugar Trust, its monopoly was continually eroded by new competition from the aggressive west coast refiner, Claus Spreckels, from new innovations, such as the sugar beet, or from court challenges, so that conditions in the industry more nearly approximated oligopoly than monopoly even before the government intervened to break up monopoly. In a few instances, like American Tobacco, government action against monopoly was directly responsible for the industry's oligopolistic structure, whereas in the cases of both oil and sugar, government policy simply hastened the emergence of oligopoly.

Monopoly was never achieved in the dressed beef industry, which was oligopolistic almost from the outset. Why the packers failed to create a monopoly in the 1880s and 1890s, as industrialists in oil, tobacco, and sugar had done, cannot be explained by government policy, which played an unimportant role in the industry until the turn of the century. The Sherman Anti-trust Act was passed nearly four years after the emergence of oligopoly. More than a decade passed before the government formulated an antitrust policy. Until then, enforcement was left to the courts, whose ambiguous opinions served more to confuse than to clarify the meaning of the Act. The explanation for the failure to create a monopoly lies, rather, in the history of oligopoly.

Like the pioneers of many of the first large corporations, the packers were reluctant to lose their identity in a merger. For them the corporation was still a personal institution, endowed with the family name and run for the sake of the family. Yet, other industrialists who shared the packers' familial loyalties eventually merged their family firms. Why, then, did the packers fail to follow the same route?

In the meat packing industry the pools formed during the 1890s worked far better than most other pools, such as those attempted in the oil industry. They worked better because the strategy undertaken to solve the problems of marketing perishable fresh meat produced an integrated, consolidated enterprise that purchased, produced, transported, and sold its own products. The building of an entire system raised barriers to entry. Then, with the creation of administrative networks that linked together various parts of the enterprise into an integrated whole, greater control and coordination were achieved, making joint control of the industry through pools easier. In many industries where firms had grown large through a strategy of horizontal combination, pooling preceded rather than followed attempts at administrative consolidation. In these industries entry was often easier and firms more numerous, so that joint control and cooperation were also more difficult.

More important in explaining why the packers did not build a monopoly rather than rely upon the pools, which after all, remained unstable throughout the 1890s, was the fact that dressed beef was a new industry that enjoyed a relatively fast and profitable growth period for a long time. Because geographical expansion occurred gradually, the packers' confrontation with the unhappy fact of saturated markets, which was the element that drove most other firms to merge, was staggered over time and place, occurring first in the New England region around 1886 and spreading to the Southeast in 1892, to Colorado, Illinois, Iowa, Missouri, Minnesota, and Nebraska in the mid-1890s. This made it easier for the packers to enjoy both the luxury of family firms and the growth, expansion, and good profits in less developed markets.

This phase of the industry's growth, however, applied roughly to the period 1886–1902. By the turn of the century the packers were at last coming to confront the problem of market saturation (at profitable prices) everywhere in the United States, each having built sales outlets in many of the same cities. The move to merge in 1902 not only signaled the packers' intent to monopolize the industry, it also marked the end of the industry's greatest and most extensive period of growth, when the foundations of the industry's basic oligopolistic structure were laid and individual fortunes were made.

By the time the decision to merge finally came, however, it was too late! After the turn of the century, government antitrust policy became a real force in the industry's development. With merger plans aborted by the abrupt withdrawal of financiers, the packers innovated a unique half-way house between the old pooling pattern and the newer, merged, consolidated firm, the National Packing Co. The new concern worked well for a short time. The government's continual harassment of National marred a performance record characterized by stable prices and profit margins. By the time National had become a definite legal liability, the oligopolists had reached the point where they no longer really needed a formal forum for collusion. By 1912 the packers had mastered the arts of cooperation and oligopolistic competition. They knew how to maintain price agreements without overt collusion.

While it must remain for the social historian to examine more fully the impact of oligopoly upon society, this study has suggested a promising strategy of inquiry. The forces of markets, technology, and competition, which provided the framework for this analysis of oligopoly, can also help to describe how individuals and groups in the industry acted and responded as they did to changing events. In the history of meat packing there was a close correlation among the emergence and maturation of oligopoly, the appearance and spread of protest, and changes in public policy. Those who spearheaded the first attacks against the "beef trust" were the meat wholesalers, butchers, and livestock shippers whose livelihoods were most immediately and directly threatened by the emergence of oligopoly. Fighting for their economic survival, they charged the packers with monopoly and conspiracy to monopolize the trade. The fact that the industry was oligopolistic rather than monopolistic made little difference to them. Viewing competition in traditional terms, they demanded that Congress outlaw monopoly and protect old patterns of free and independent competition among numerous small firms. The result was the antimonopoly Sherman Anti-trust Act.

As the courts developed a body of case law applicable to monopolistic industries, the meat packers continued to confront the realities of oligopolistic competition. They evolved patterns of cooperation and competition that were especially difficult to prosecute under the Sherman Anti-trust Act. While it is not accurate to say that the packers operated above the law, they worked around it without much difficulty, at least until the first decade of the twentieth century.

By that time protests had spread beyond special interest groups to the broad range of middle class consumers. Oligopolistic competition had encouraged a disregard for consumer welfare that invited federal regulation. Revolted by Sinclair's revelations in *The Jungle*, progressive reformers demanded that government regulate the conditions under which meat was processed. The Meat Inspection Act of 1906 marked the beginning of compulsory federal meat inspection.

The ebb and flow of competition and cooperation in the industry affected various groups differently at different times. Absorbed with the industry's competitive problems in the 1880s and 1890s, the packers made little time for or showed little interest in the well-being of their laborers. Their major concern was to reduce costs; wage cuts were one of many alternatives that the packers used to enhance their competitive position in the marketplace. It was during the 1880s and 1890s, while the packers were struggling to make their pools work, that labor received some of its severest setbacks. Cooperation on a common labor policy aimed at resisting wage increases or thwarting unionization efforts came quickly and easily during the depression of the 1890s when pressures to reduce costs intensified. Nevertheless, when the packers sought to stabilize the industry after the turn of the century and labor began to develop more effective organizations of its own, packers turned their attention to devising employee stock-sharing plans and wage-bonus schemes. While the antiunion sentiment remained, packers began to view unions less as a threat and more as a possible source of stability in the industry.[2]

Whether the social costs of oligopoly outweighed the benefits of aggregate employment to laborers or price reductions to consumers depends upon a comparison with a hypothetical alternative—either monopoly or free and atomistic competition, neither of which existed in fact. As this history has shown, oligopoly did initially offer consumers a great variety of lower priced meats than the existing system of small firm production and distribution through independent meat wholesalers. Nevertheless, the economies, size, and control that accompanied the development of oligopoly also augmented packer power, both potential and real. Just as the packers could and often did use this power to block the entry of newcomers or undercut smaller rivals, so too did they use their power to thwart labor's unionizing efforts.

In the half century after 1912, however, even so powerful an oligopoly as this one proved vulnerable to changes in the nature of markets and technology. The development of efficient, low-cost refrigeration facilities for the motor carrier, the building of a system of all weather hard-surfaced roadways, the advent of chain store distribution, and the establishment of a federal grading system whittled down barriers to entry in the industry and encouraged the movement of meat packing away from terminal markets to interior packing points near the sources of supply.[3] Whereas in 1923 the Big Four packers[4] purchased 90 percent of their cattle and calves, 86 percent of their sheep, and 76 percent of hogs at terminal yards, by 1961 only 65, 37, and 29 percent of each species, respectively, were purchased there.[5] Although pre-1920 figures are unavailable for comparison, the number of interstate meat packing firms entering the industry jumped from 1,106 in 1921 to approximately 2,646 by 1958. These new firms increased their share of the total commercial cattle slaughter at the expense of the oligopolists, whose share dropped from 49 percent in 1920 to 20 percent in 1956. The oligopolists' share of other species also declined, though not as significantly.[6]

The oligopolists were powerless to halt or reverse the decentralizing trend in the industry. The major problem was that the centralized system of rail transportation and distribution through branch houses was simply not as economical or as efficient as the newer system of motor-truck-highway transportation direct to large mass food retailers equipped with their own warehousing and meat departments. The motor truck not only offered lower freight charges than the railroads; it allowed smaller shipments and greater flexibility regarding route and time schedules as well. The result was to lower capital requirements for distribution and encourage the entry of smaller, more specialized, less costly plants that operated with much smaller capital outlays and fewer employees than the packers' enormous multi-species plants that fed their gigantic distribution networks.[7]

With the growth of a few large food chains and the resulting decrease in the number of smaller, more specialized retailers, the packers also faced a far different set of consumers with radically different purchasing methods and oligopolistic power of their own. Whereas previously packer salesmen had called on small retail merchants and solicited orders to be filled from the local branch houses or peddler routes, large retailers had their own central buyers who solicited orders in advance of delivery dates directly from packing concerns on a competitive bid basis by telegraph. In this changed world of retailing, where buyers had the power to choose their suppliers and enforce competitive bidding, the large packers had no special advantages over the smaller, more specialized packing concerns.[8]

Nor did the oligopolists' brands and advertising give them any particular advantages once the federal grading system appeared. By making meat products more homogeneous, the grading system reduced marketing costs and increased buyer information regarding standards and quality. Small firms could enter the market without plowing large sums of money into advertising.[9] Together, these changes in transportation and refrigeration technologies, in retailing, and in relations between manufacturers and wholesalers eroded the market shares and also the market power of the oligopolists, at least with respect to the interstate meat trade.

The packers did not sit idly by while competition gnawed away their market shares, but neither did they respond with the same quickness and innovativeness that characterized their strategies during the early, formative years of oligopoly. Much more slowly than other industrial giants they adopted the strategy of diversification that ultimately saved their economic lives. Only when profit margins fell in the 1950s did they begin to transfer part of their resources into lines not directly connected with their primary meat, food products and by-products.[10]

This relatively slow response to impending economic change reflected, in part, the limited range of alternatives available as well as their own reluctance, nurtured by years of oligopolistic competition and cooperation, to recognize the realities of what Joseph Schumpeter has described as "gales of creative destruction."[11] Heavy capital investments in plant, equipment, and personnel made reallocation of resources difficult and costly. As one historian of the industry explains, not until "the marginal cost of growth and expansion in new facilities and locations was as low (or lower than) the marginal cost of operating existing facilities was it economically feasible to write off their holdings."[12] Closer government regulation of some packer activities in the Packers and Stockyards Act of 1920, and a consent decree, voluntarily entered in 1920 after a particularly exhaustive Federal Trade Commission investigation, also may have narrowed packer options. Evidence indicates, however, that the most significant effect of the decree may have been psychological rather than economic.[13]

Operating in a changed economy, the packers saw few alternatives to the gradual dismantling of their transportation and distribution system. The number of packer-owned branch houses declined over 50 percent between 1924 and 1958. By 1948 fifty percent of the meat packing industry's sales of fresh and cured meats was being sold directly to food retailers, delivered by truck and train directly to customers' retail outlets or central warehouses. The oligopolists also rid themselves of refrigerator cars, reducing their share of the total number of cars from 90 percent in 1920 to 5 percent in 1956.[14]

The official closing of the Chicago Union Stockyards in the autumn of 1970 signified the end of the era of big packer dominance of the meat industry. Although the "Premium" and "Star" labels still identify the meat products of Swift and Armour, these firms have joined the ranks of the decentralized, diversified conglomerates that color today's industrial landscape. Armour absorbed Morris in the 1920s and was, in turn, swallowed up by Greyhound in the early 1970s. The conglomerate Esmark purchased Swift's fresh meat business and then, in 1980, unloaded it. Schwarzschild & Sulzberger, which became Wilson & Co. in 1915, is a major producer of sporting goods. While the oligopoly remains, it maintains a much weaker position within the meat industry, testimony again of the influential role of markets and technology in the development of oligopoly.[15]

This study, while concentrating primarily on the oligopoly's emergent and formative years, has shown that the causes of oligopoly lay much more in prosaic, interrelated forces of technology and markets than in the workings of entrepreneurial genius or in the implementation of some sinister master plan to dominate the industry. The coming of oligopoly was a process of economic change in which entrepreneurs were the agents rather than the instigators of change. Swift, Hammond, Armour, and Morris became the pioneers of the large, integrated packing corporation because they were the first to respond to changing markets and technology by using the refrigerator car and creating the distribution and administrative networks it required. The organizations they created enabled them to solve the problems of shipping a perishable product long distances and to meet the needs of an expanding urban market. As entrepreneurs, they affected the rate and pattern of change, but they themselves were not the fundamental cause of that change.

The study suggests that the changing patterns of competition and concentration in each industry depend primarily upon the technological, marketing, and organizational imperatives of business in that particular industry, and upon the strategies adopted to meet these requirements. Unlike the experience of industries such as oil refining and sugar refining, in the dressed beef industry vertical integration and oligopoly preceded horizontal combination and monopoly. Vertical integration and oligopoly came first in meat packing because the overriding initial problem in the industry was marketing, not overproduction, as had been the case in oil and sugar. Extensive vertical integration delayed (but did not eliminate) the pressure for horizontal combination in meat packing, for it helped these firms to secure a reliable flow of materials and to rationalize distribution and marketing. Such cross-industry comparisons of early oligopolies make it clear that the origins of oligopoly were different in different industries, and that two important causal patterns were (1) the need to overcome marketing problems and (2) the need to control overproduction. The second pattern has most often been emphasized, and this study helps to redress the imbalance.

In the history of meat packing, however, the firms in the oligopoly soon found themselves facing some of the same pressures that lay at the heart of the rise of oligopoly in the overproduction industries. Although its origins were different, the oligopoly in meat packing soon came to resemble the oligopolies in oil and sugar refining. The high capital investments required to build and operate large, integrated firms reduced profit margins and created severe pressures to keep resources fully employed. These pressures, in turn, intensified competition. Because a few firms dominated the industry and operated in the same markets, it soon became more important to cooperate than to compete in order to stabilize market shares and assure continuous high-volume flows. This suggests that there may have been underlying economic forces leading all oligopolists toward roughly similar behavior, despite the varying origins of concentration in different industries.

Once the meat packers set out to cooperate rather than to compete, public policy began to influence the industry. Its effect was more to prevent monopoly than to regulate oligopoly. Firmly-held attitudes about the sanctity of private property, the novelty and uncertainty of the nation's first antitrust law, and the lack of economic sophistication in the courts and in the Justice Department led the government to play a basically negative and passive role. It would not permit monopoly, but neither did it go very far in determining precisely how the oligopolists should behave. Unable or unwilling to confront the unique problem of oligopolistic competition, the government simply sought to characterize the industry as monopolistic and, therefore, to avoid seriously engaging the question of how best to regulate the new oligopolistic competition that emerged in numerous industries.

By analyzing one important example of oligopoly in terms of forces that are familiar to both economists and economic historians, this study has provided a foundation for interdisciplinary and comparative studies. Such studies should prove invaluable in understanding the process by which oligopoly developed in a technologically advanced economy, subject only to a basically passive set of public policies.

NOTES

1. *The Emergence of Oligopoly* (Baltimore, 1969).

2. There is still no comprehensive study of labor in the meat packing industry. The best is still David Brody, *The Butcher Workman* (Cambridge, Mass., 1964). See also Lewis Corey, *Meat and Man: A Study of Monopoly, Unionism and Food Policy* (New York, 1950); Mary Elizabeth Pidgeon, *The Employment of Women in Slaughtering and Meat Packing* (Washington, D.C., 1932).

3. The analysis of deconcentration, below, follows closely the work of Robert M. Aduddell, "The Meat Packing Industry and the Consent Decree, 1920–1956" (Ph.D. dissertation, Northwestern University, 1971): pp. 1–212; Robert Aduddell and Louis P. Cain, "The Consent Decree in the Meat Packing Industry" (mimeo.), pp. 1–39; Richard J. Arnould, "Changing Patterns of Concentration in American Meat Packing 1880–1963," *Business History Review,* 45 (Spring 1971):19–34.

4. Swift, Armour, Cudahy, and Wilson. In 1913 Sulzberger & Sons was reorganized as Wilson & Company. Morris & Company was acquired in 1923 by the North American Provision Company, a subsidiary of Armour & Company.

5. Arnould, "Changing Patterns of Concentration in American Meat Packing," p. 26.

6. Figures are those of Aduddell, "The Meat Packing Industry and the Consent Decree," pp. 130, 132. If the Big Four's slaughter of the various species is transformed into their share of total consumption of various types of meat, the Big Four suffered a reduction in market share from 46 percent of red meat production in 1920 to 34.5 percent of red meat production in 1956. The reduction in percentage terms over the entire period was 25 percent of their market share, or 11.8 percentage points in concentration of slaughter (p. 35).

7. Arnould, "Changing Patterns of Concentration in American Meat Packing," pp. 26–29; Aduddell, "The Meat Packing Industry and the Consent Decree," pp. 87–97.

8. The best discussion is Aduddell, pp. 100–127.

9. Arnould, "Changing Patterns of Concentration," pp. 28–29.

10. Alfred D. Chandler, Jr., *Strategy and Structure* (New York, 1966), p. 346.

11. Joseph A. Schumpeter, *Capitalism, Socialism and Democracy* (3rd ed., New York, 1950), especially pp. 81–86.

12. Arnould, "Changing Patterns of Concentration in American Meat Packing," p. 29.

13. Aduddell, "The Meat Packing Industry and the Consent Decree," especially pp. 170, 196, and the helpful condensation, Aduddell and Cain, "The Consent Decree in the Meat Packing Industry." The terms of the decree were extremely broad, enjoining the packers from entering the retail meat business, handling any other food items not directly a part of their meat operations, or owning any interest in concerns producing food operations. They also had to divest their ownership of stockyards and ancillary activities. Significantly, the consent decree did not attack the major packers' oligopolistic position in meat packing

itself. Its stated purpose was to reduce the major packers' total sales of nonmeat foods. Aduddell and Cain persuasively argue that the structural changes in the industry after 1920 were much more closely related to changing technology and markets than to the consent decree. They suggest, however, that part of the decline in the relative power of the major packers was related to the divestiture provision of the decree. (Aduddell and Cain, pp. 29, 24.)

14. Aduddell, "The Meat Packing Industry and the Consent Decree," pp. 173–174.

15. This is the conclusion of Aduddell and Cain, "The Consent Decree in the Meat Packing Industry," p. 27; Joe Bain, *Industrial Organization* (2nd ed., New York, 1968), p. 112; Carl Kaysen and Donald F. Turner, *Antitrust Policy: An Economic and Legal Analysis* (Cambridge, 1959), pp. 24f, used different classification systems for measuring concentration. See also, Ralph L. Nelson, *Concentration in the Manufacturing Industries of the United States* (New Haven, 1963), pp. 108–276.

Appendix A

Patent Drawings

Appendix A.1. Davis Refrigerator

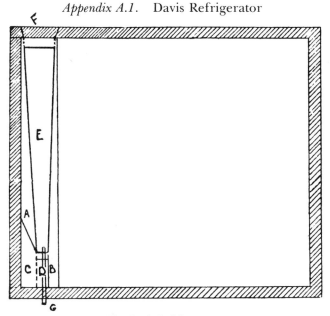

The Davis Refrigerator.
Patented June 10 and September 15, 1808.

A and B—Strips to Brace Ice Receptacle.   E—Ice Receptacle.
C—Space between Ice Receptacle and Wall.   F—Openings and Plug.
D—Stool under Ice Receptacle.   G—Waste Pipe.

Appendix A.2. Davis Refrigerator

Davis Refrigerator.
Patented June 10, 1808.

A and B—Supports to Ice Receptacle.   E—Ice Receptacle.
C—Space between Ice Receptacle and Wall.   G—Waste Pipe.   H—Hopper.

Source: Ice and Refrigeration, September 1894, pp. 166–167.

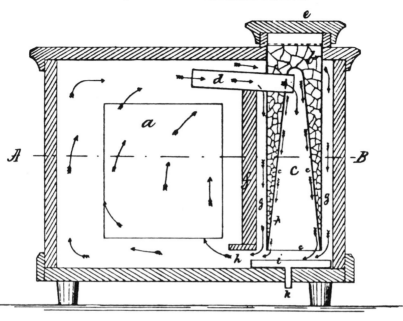

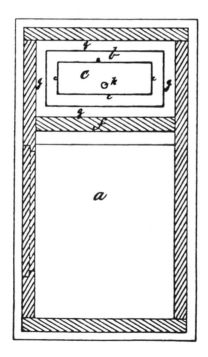

Witnesses.   Inventor:

Andrew J. Chase.

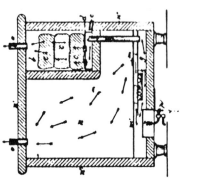

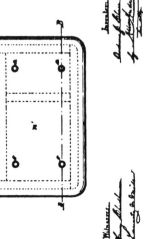

Appendix A.5.   A. J. Chase Refrigerator
No. 229,956.   *Patented July 13, 1880.*

Appendix A.4.   A. J. Chase
Purifying, Circulating, and Rarifying Air.
No. 215,572.   *Patented May 20, 1879.*

248

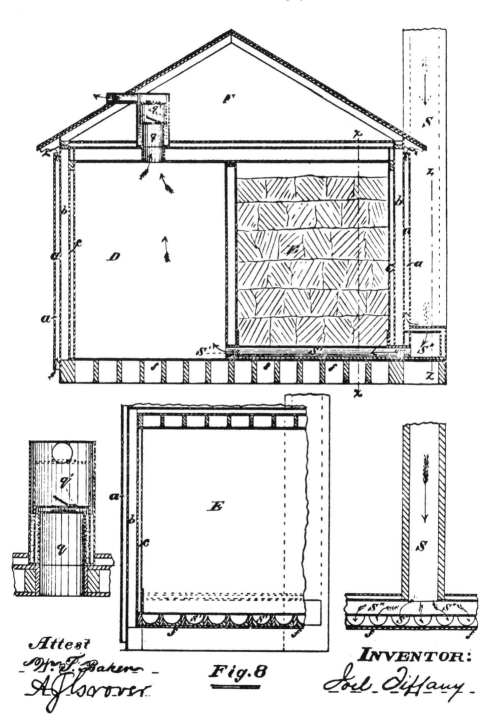

Fig.8

Attest

Wm T. Baker

A. J. Grover

INVENTOR:

Joel Tiffany

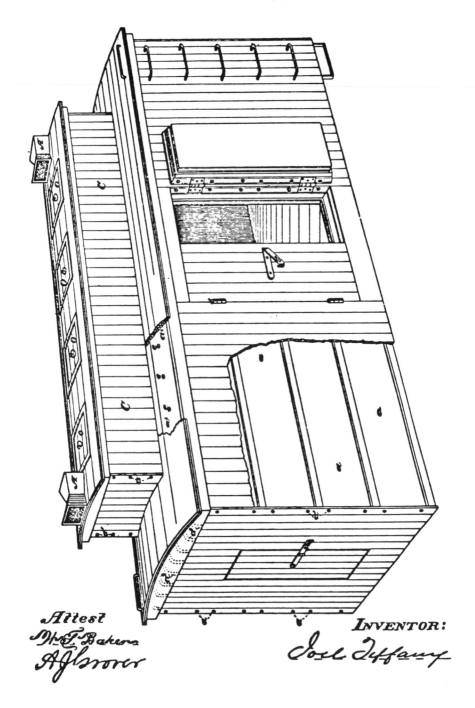

Attest

INVENTOR:

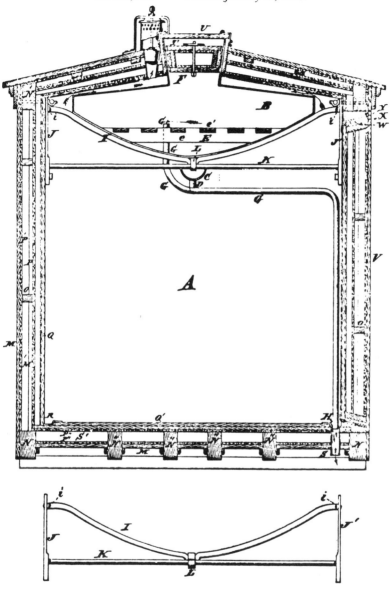

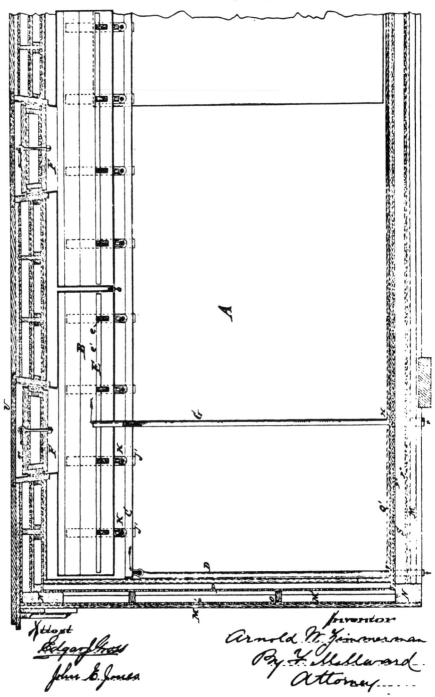

Appendix B

Cattle Slaughter, Market Shares, and Industry Growth

Appendix B.1. Cattle Slaughtered at Chicago by the Meat-Packing
Industry 1884–1890

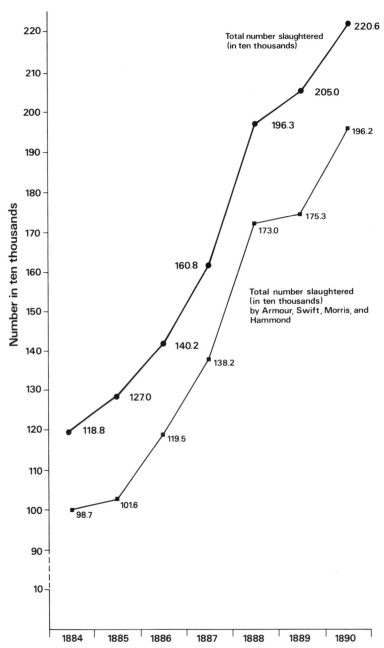

Source: Compiled from Chicago Board of Trade, *Annual Reports, 1884–1890,* and Cincinnati Price
Current, *Annual Report, 1888,* p. 18.

Appendix B.2. Growth Index of Total Cattle Slaughtered at Chicago for Dressed Beef, Packing, Canning, and Trade (Based on 1884 = 100%)

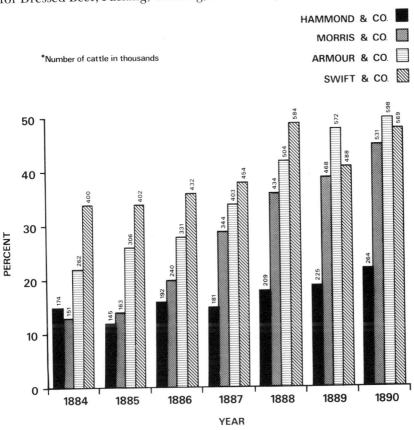

Source: Compiled from Chicago Board of Trade *Annual Reports, 1884–1890,* and Cincinnati Price Current, *annual Report, 1888,* p. 18.

Appendix B.3. Number of Cattle Slaughtered at Chicago for the Dressed Beef, Packing, Canning and City Trade 1870, 1871, and 1884–1890

Firm	1870	1871	1884	1885	1886	1887	1888	1889	1890
Armour & Co.	2,777	4,156	261,863	306,374	330,652	402,886	504,292	572,014	597,941
Cragin & Co.	788	—	—	—	—	—	—	—	—
Culbertson, Blair & Co.	3,860	7,709	—	—	—	—	—	—	—
Eastland & Duddleston	—	—	—	17,000	9,500	14,000	14,500	15,000	—
Fairbank Canning Co.	—	—	115,000	163,423	239,995	344,487	433,563	468,498	531,443
Hammond & Co.*	—	—	174,200	145,010	192,240	181,000	209,150	225,400	263,841
Hancock, J.L.	—	1,949	—	—	—	—	—	—	—
Hately, J.C.	—	—	—	—	—	—	—	11,700	34,449
Hess Bros.	—	—	—	—	20,000	20,000	20,700	23,100	—
Jones, Hough & Co.	996	—	—	—	—	—	—	—	—

Kent, A.E. & Co.	3,313	7,440	—	—	—	—	—	—	—
Lees, Hendricks & Co.	—	—	—	63,862	33,286	37,253	29,000	—	—
Libby, McNeil & Libby	—	—	120,928	112,215	106,284	109,645	125,922	180,549	141,699
Miller, Henricks & Co.	—	—	—	—	33,286	37,253	29,000	12,000	—
Morris, Nelson	—	—	36,000	—	—	—	—	—	—
Murphy, B.F. & Co.	229	—	—	—	—	—	—	—	—
Schoeneman & Co.	—	—	—	30,800	28,500	35,000	32,000	24,600	—
Swift & Co.	—	—	400,163	401,617	432,156	453,931	583,924	487,766	568,812
Smaller houses	—	—	80,000	30,000	30,000	30,000	10,000	30,000	25,000
Total	11,963	21,254	1,188,154	1,270,301	1,402,613	1,608,202	1,963,051	2,050,627	2,206,185

*Slaughtered at Hammond, Indiana and included in shipments of live.

Note: From 1885 to 1890 the figures are for the year ending March 1.

Source: Chicago Board of Trade, *Annual Reports, 1870, 1871, and 1884–1990*; Cincinnati Price Current, *Thirty-Ninth Annual Report*, 1888, p. 18.

Appendix C

Branch House Expansion of the Major Meat Packers in the U.S., 1884–1917

Appendix C.1.   Branch Houses of the Big Five—Number opened, by years, and cumulatively, 1884-1917.

Year	Armour	Swift	Morris	Wilson (Schwarzschild & Sulzberger)	Cudahy	Total for year	Total cumulative
1884	2		(1)			2	2
1885	(1)		1			1	3
1886	1		1			2	5
1887	3		1			4	9
1888	5		6		[2]1	12	21
1889	19		7		3	29	50
1890	12		13		2	27	77
1891	14		4	[2]2	2	22	99
1892	16		11	(1)	8	35	134
1893	17		8	12	2	39	173
1894	20		6	7	5	38	211
1895	16		3	10	5	34	245
1896	8		2	1	6	17	262
1897	16		7	4	7	34	296
1898	13		9	5	6	33	329
1899	12	[3]193	9	1	(1)	215	544
1900	26		9	2	10	47	591
1901	18	3	3	(1)	3	27	618
1902	18	30	6	9	4	67	685
1903	8	21	2	5	3	39	724

Year						Total	
1904	10	[1]	1	6	2	743	
1905	6	1	1	3	3	757	
1906	13	25	3	3	1	802	
1907	10	21	1	2	8	844	
1908	12	18	1	7	5	887	
1909	8	7	3	5	6	916	
1910	9	3	3	14	1	946	
1911	6	8	2	4	5	971	
1912	68	47[4]	19[5]	5	[1]	1,110	
1913	3	7	2	1	1	1,124	
1914	[1]	4	3	1	[1]	1,132	
1915	4	1	7	[1]	2	1,146	
1916	1	[1]	3	2	1	1,153	
1917	1	1	4	3	3	1,165	
Total[6]	395	390	161	114	105	1,165	
In operation, 1917	363	367	154	121	115	1,120	n.f.

[1] No branch houses opened.
[2] No figures prior to this year.
[3] Prior to 1900.
[4] 40 branch houses taken over from National Packing Co.
[5] 11 branch houses taken over from National Packing Co.
[6] Includes any that may have been closed since date of opening.

Source: Federal Trade Commission, *Report on the Meat-Packing Industry 1919*, Summary and Pt. I, p. 153.

Bibliography

MANUSCRIPT SOURCES

Baltimore, Maryland. Maryland Historical Society. Baltimore & Ohio Railroad Papers.
Boston, Massachusetts. Baker Library. Harvard University. R. G. Dun & Company, Mercantile Credit Reports.
Chicago, Illinois. Newberry Library. Chicago, Burlington & Quincy Railroad Papers. Record Group No. 33. File Nos. 2.1, 7.16, 7.2, 7.3, 7.31, 7.32.
_____. Illinois Central Railroad Papers.
_____. Swift & Company. Swift and Company Archives.
Montreal, Canada. Canadian National Railway Library. Grand Trunk Railroad Papers.
Washington, D.C. Archives of the Association of American Railroads.
_____. National Archives.
Bureau of Animal Industry. Record Group No. 17. File No. 16.
U.S. Bureau of Corporations. Record Group No. 122. File Nos. 623, 666, 705, 738, 833, 2295, 2680, 3943.
Department of Justice. Files #60-50-0, 25-0-116.
Food and Drug Administration. Record Group No. 88.
_____. Library of Congress. Manuscript Collection. Harvey W. Wiley Papers. Accessions 9810 & 10,134. General Correspondence, pp. 198–210.

GOVERNMENT SOURCES

United States—Federal Government:
U.S. Bureau of the Census. *Historical Statistics of the United States: From Colonial Times to 1957.* Washington, D.C.: Government Printing Office, 1965.
U.S. Bureau of Corporations. *Report of the Commissioner of Corporations on the Beef Industry, 1905.* Washington, D.C.: U.S. Government Printing Office, 1905.
U.S. Bureau of Labor. *Annual Report of the Commissioner of Labor for the Fiscal Year Ended 30 June 1904.* "Cost of Living and Retail Prices of Food." Washington, D.C.: U.S. Government Printing Office, 1904.
U.S. Bureau of Labor Statistics. "Wages and Hours of Labor in the Slaughtering and Meat-Packing Industry." Bulletin Nos. 472(1929) and 535(1931).

U.S. Census Office. *Fifth Census of the United States, 1840.* Washington, D.C.: D. Green, 1842.

———. *Eighth Census of the United States, 1860: Manufacturers of the United States in 1860.* Washington, D.C.: U.S. Government Printing Office, 1865.

———. *Ninth Census of the United States, 1870: Statistics of the Wealth and Industry of the United States.* Washington, D.C.: U.S. Government Printing Office, 1872.

U.S. Congress. House. *Annual Report and Statements of the Chief of the Bureau of Statistics on the Commerce and Navigation of the United States for the Fiscal Year Ending June 30, 1887.* 50th Cong., H.R. Executive Doc. 6. 1st Sess., 1887.

———. *Hearings Before the Committee on Agriculture on Meat Packer Legislation.* 66th Cong., 2nd Sess., 1920.

———. *Hearings Before the Committee on Agriculture on the So-called "Beveridge Amendment" to the Agriculture Appropriations Bill* (H.R. 18537). 59th Cong., 1st Sess., 1906.

———. *Hearings Before the Committee of Interstate and Foreign Commerce on Government Control of the Meat Packing Industry.* 65th Cong., H.R. 13324. 3rd Sess., 1918, 1919.

———. *Hearings Before the Committee on the Judiciary, Investigations of Beef Industries.* 64th Cong., 1st Sess., 1916.

———. *Hearings Before the Subcommittee of the Committee on Interstate and Foreign Commerce, Having Under Consideration House Bills Relating to Private Car Lines.* 58th Cong., H.R. 12767 & 16977, 3rd Sess., 1905.

———. *Proceedings of the Conference Relative to the Marketing of Live Stock, Distribution of Meats and Related Matters,* by D. H. Houston. 64th Cong., H. Doc. 855. 1st Sess., 1916.

———. *The Range and Ranch Cattle Traffic,* by Joseph Nimmo Jr. 48th Cong., Exec. Doc. 267. 2nd Sess., 1886.

U.S. Congress. Joint Commission of Agricultural Inquiry. *The Agricultural Crisis and Its Causes.* 67th Cong., H. Rept. 408, Pt. I. 1st Sess., 1921.

———. *Marketing and Distribution.* 67th Cong., H. Rept. 408, Part 4. 1st Sess., 1921.

U.S. Congress. Senate. Committee on Finance. *Wholesale Prices, Wages, and Transportation,* by M. Nelson Aldrich. Rept. No. 1394, Pt. I. March 3, 1893. Washington, D.C.: U.S. Government Printing Office, 1893.

U.S. Congress. Senate. Committee on Interstate Commerce. *Hearings Before the Committee on Interstate Commerce on S. 2793, Regulation of Motor Carrier Transportation.* 72nd Cong., 1st Sess., 1932.

———. *Exports and Imports—Exports to Foreign Countries 1789–1893.* 53rd Cong., S. Doc. 259, Pt. II. 2nd Sess., 1893–1894, Tables No. 2 and No. 7.

———. Committee on Interstate Commerce. *Regulation of Railway Rates. Hearings Before the Committee on Interstate Commerce.* 58th Cong., 1st Sess., 1905.

———. *Hearings Before the Committee on Interstate Commerce, Regulation of Railway Rates.* 59th Cong., S. Doc. 243. 1st Sess., 5 vols. Washington, D.C.: U.S. Govt. Printing Office, 1906.

———. Committee on the Judiciary. Sub-committee on Antitrust and Monopoly. *Administered Prices: A Compendium on Public Policy.* 88th Cong., 1st Sess., 1963.

———. *Decision in Beef Trust Case,* by Peter S. Grosscup. 57th Cong., S. Doc. 179. 2nd Sess., 1903.

———. *Hearings Before a Subcommittee of the Committee on Agriculture and Forestry on Amendment to Packers and Stockyards Act,* S. 3776 & S. 4387. 69th Cong., 1st Sess., May 28, June 3–4, 1926.

———. *Report of the Commission Appointed by the President to Investigate the Conduct of the War Department in the War with Spain.* 8 vols. 56th Cong., S. Doc. 221. 1st Sess., 1898.

_____. *Report of the Federal Trade Commission on the History and Present Status of the Packer Consent Decree.* 68th Cong., S. Misc. Doc. 15. 2nd Sess., 1926.

_____. *Report of the Select Committee on the Transportation and Sale of Meat Products, 1889-1890.* 51st Cong., S. Rept. 829. 1st Sess., 1890. (Known as *Vest Report.*)

_____. *Report of the Select Committee on Transportation Routes to the Seaboard.* 43rd Cong., S. Rept. 307. 1st Sess., 1874. (Known as *Windom Report.*)

_____. *Report of the Senate Select Committee on Interstate Commerce.* 2 vols. 49th Cong., S. Rept. 46. 1st Sess., 1886. (Known as the *Cullom Report.*)

_____. *Report on Transportation Interests of the U.S. and Canada, 1889,* by Shelby M. Cullom. 51st Cong., S. Rept. 847. 1st Sess., 1890.

U.S. Dept. of Agriculture. *Reports of the Commissioner, 1849-1884.*

_____. "Beef and Beef-Cattle of the West," by W. W. Corbett (1862):326-333.

_____. "Distribution and Movement of Neat Cattle in the United States," by Silas L. Loomis (1868):248-261.

_____. "The Hog and Its Products," by Charles Cist (1866): 383-393.

_____. "Hogs and Pork Packing," by H. D. Emery (1863):211-215.

_____. "Fresh-Meat Shipment to Europe" (1876):312-320.

_____. "The Market System of the Country: Their Usages and Abuses" (1870):250-253.

_____. "The Texas Cattle Trade" (1870):346-352.

_____. *Annual Reports of the Bureau of Animal Industry, 1884-1912.*

_____. "The Beef Supply of the United States and Conditions Governing the Price of Cattle" (1888):39-44.

_____. "Dressed-Meat Traffic" (1885):277-282.

_____. "Live Stock and Meat Traffic of Chicago," by Edward W. Perry (1884):245-269.

_____. "Meat Industries of the United States," by H. C. Clark (1887-1888):359-378.

_____. Bureau of Agricultural Economics. *Barriers to Internal Trade in Farm Products. A Special Report to the Secretary of Agriculture by the Bureau of Agricultural Economics,* by George Rogers Taylor, Edgar L. Burtis, and Frederick V. Waugh. Washington, D.C.: U.S. Government Printing Office, 1939.

_____. *The Patent Situation in the Food Industries,* by A. C. Hoffman. (mimeo.) Washington, D.C.: U.S. Government Printing Office, 1939.

_____. *Meat Situation in the United States.* U.S. Dept. of Agriculture Rept. Nos. 109-113. Washington, D.C.: U.S. Government Printing Office, 1916.

_____. Bureau of Statistics. Bulletin No. 55. *Meat Supply and Surplus, With Consideration of Consumption and Exports,* by George K. Holmes. Washington, D.C.: U.S. Government Printing Office, 1907.

_____. *Cooperative Livestock Marketing Came Early,* by C. G. Randell. Farm Cooperative Service Bull. No. 1. Washington D.C.: U.S. Government Printing Office, 1955.

_____. *Diets of Families of Employed Wage Earners and Clerical Workers in the City.* U.S. Dept. of Agriculture Circ. No. 507. Washington, D.C.: U.S. Government Printing Office, 1939.

_____. *The Direct Marketing of Hogs.* U.S. Dept. of Agriculture Misc. Publ. No. 222. Washington, D.C.: U.S. Government Printing Office, 1933.

_____. Division of Foreign Markets. Bull. No. 34. *Agricultural Exports of the United States, 1851-1902,* by Frank H. Hitchcock. Washington, D.C.: U.S. Government Printing Office, 1903.

_____. Division of Statistics. Bull. No. 15 (Misc. Ser.). *Changes in the Rates of Charges for Railway and Other Transportation Services,* by John Hyde, M. T. Newcomb, 1898.

_____. *A History of Livestock Raising in the United States, 1607-1860,* by James Westfall

Thompson. Agriculture History Ser. No. 5. Washington, D.C.: U.S. Government Printing Office, 1942.

———. *Studies of Family Living in the United States and Other Countries,* by F. M. Williams and C. C. Zimmerman. U.S. Dept. of Agriculture Misc. Publ. No. 223. Washington, D.C.: U.S. Government Printing Office, 1935.

———. *Trends in the Production and Foreign Trade for Meats and Livestock in the United States,* by P. Richards. U.S. Dept. of Agriculture Tech. Bull. No. 764. Washington, D.C.: U.S. Government Printing Office, 1941.

———. *Yearbook of Agriculture, 1929.* "Trends in the Dietary Habits in the United States," by H. K. Stiebeling. Washington, D.C.: U.S. Government Printing Office, 1929.

U.S. Dept. of Commerce. Bureau of Corporations. *Trust Laws and Unfair Competition,* by Joseph E. Davies. Washington, D.C.: U.S. Government Printing Office, 1916.

U.S. Dept. of Commerce and Labor. Bureau of Statistics. "The Provision Trade of the United States." In *Monthly Summary of Commerce and Finance of the United States for the Fiscal Year 1900.* Vol. III, pp. 2279–2306.

U.S. Federal Trade Commission. *Report on the Meat-Packing Industry, 1919.* Pts. 1–6. Washington, D.C.: U.S. Government Printing Office, 1919.

———. *Report on Private Car Lines,* 1920. Pts. 1–3, Washington, D.C.: U.S. Government Printing Office, 1920.

U.S. Industrial Commission Reports. Vol. 1, *Preliminary Report on Trusts and Industrial Combinations,* Pt. 1, Review of Evidence; Pt. 2, Testimony (1900). Vol. 2, *Report on Trust and Corporation Law* (1900). Vol. 6, *Report on the Distribution of Farm Products* (1901). Vol. 9, *Report on Transportation* (1902). Vol. 13, *Report on Trusts and Industrial Combinations* (1900). Vol. 19, *Final Report* (1902). Washington, D.C.: U.S. Government Printing Office, 1900–1902.

U.S. Interstate Commerce Commission, *Annual Reports, 1888–1904.*

U.S. National Commission on Food Marketing. *Organization and Competition in Food Retailing.* Tech. Rept. No. 7. Washington, D.C.: U.S. Government Printing Office, 1963.

U.S. Temporary National Economic Committee. *Competition and Monopoly in American Industry,* by Clair Wilcox. Committee Monograph No. 21. Washington, D.C.: U.S. Government Printing Office, 1940.

———. *Large-Scale Organization in the Food Industries,* by A. C. Hoffman. Committee Monograph No. 35. Washington, D.C.: U.S. Government Printing Office, 1940.

U.S. Patent 78,932, "Preserving Meat," William Davis. Detroit, June 16, 1868.

U.S. Patent 193,357, "Refrigerator Car," J. Tiffany. Chicago, July 24, 1877.

U.S. Patent 199,343, "Refrigerator Car," A. W. Zimmerman. New York, January 15, 1878.

U.S. Patent 210,995, "Improvement in Refrigerators," Andrew J. Chase. Boston, December 17, 1878.

U.S. Patent 215,572, "Purifying, Circulating, and Rarefying Air," Andrew J. Chase. Boston, May 20, 1879.

U.S. Patent 219,256, "Refrigerators," George Hammond. Detroit, September 2, 1879.

U.S. Patent 220,422, "Refrigerator Car," T. L. Rankin. Lyndon, Kansas, October 7, 1879.

U.S. Patent 229,956, "Refrigerator," Andrew J. Chase. Boston, July 13, 1880.

U.S. Patent 250,322, "Refrigerator," A. W. Zimmerman. Indianapolis, Ind., April 15, 1881.

United States—State Government:

Massachusetts. Bureau of Statistics of Labor. *Food Consumption: Quantities, Cost and Nutrients of Food Materials.* Annual Rept., No. 17, Pt. 3. 1886.

New York State Legislature. Assembly. *Proceedings of the Special Committee Appointed to Investi-*

gate *Alleged Abuses in the Management of Railroads Chartered by the State of New York,* Report and Testimony, 8 vols. Assembly Doc. No. 38 (1880). (This is the so-called *Hepburn Report.*)

_____. Senate. *Report of the Commission on General Laws on the Investigation Relative to Trusts,* March 6, 1888. New York: Troy Press, 1888.

Great Britain—Government Documents:
Great Britain. Ministry of Agriculture and Fisheries. "Report on the Trade in Refrigerated Beef, Mutton, and Lamb." Rept. No. 6 (1925).

_____. *Parliamentary Papers,* Vol. 15. "Minutes of Evidence Taken Before the Department Committee on Combinations in the Meat Trade." Cmd. 4661 (1909).

_____. *Parliamentary Papers,* Vol. 23. "Interim Report on Meat Prepared by a Subcommittee Appointed by the Standing Committee on Trusts." Cmd. 1057 (1920).

_____. *Parliamentary Papers,* Vol. 25. "Report of the Committee Appointed by the Board of Trade to Consider the 'Means of Securing Sufficient Meat Supplies for the United Kingdom.'" Cmd. 456 (1919).

NEWSPAPERS AND TRADE PERIODICALS

Boston Market Produce Report, 1877, 1880, 1886, 1888.
Boston Transcript, 1888.
Breeder's Gazette, 1883–1891.
Butcher's Advocate, 1881–1892.
Chicago Daily Drovers Journal and Farm News, 1905–1907.
Chicago Daily Drovers Journal and Farm News, Yearbook of Figures, 1911.
Chicago Daily Farmers and Drovers Journal, 1907–1912.
Cincinnati Price Current, 1882–1908.
Commercial and Financial Chronicle, 1902–1912.
Ice and Refrigeration, September 1894–1910.
National Provisioner, 1892–1912.
New York Daily Tribune, 1890.
New York Evening Post, March 4, 1905.
New York Evening Sun, September 19, 1912.
New York Times, 1875–1912.
Railway Age, 1873–1890.
Railroad Gazette, 1875–1905.
Railway Review, 1886.
Railway World, 1876–1895.

CORPORATION PUBLICATIONS AND ANNUAL REPORTS

American National Livestock Association. *Proceedings and Circulars of the Fifteenth Annual Convention of the American National Livestock Association, December 12–13, 1911.*
Annual Reports of American Corporations. Corporation Records Division, Baker Library, Harvard Business School, Boston, Massachusetts.
Armour & Co. Armour's Livestock Bureau. *Monthly Letter to Animal Husbandmen.* July 1924.

Trunk Line Association. Freight Department. *Agreement of the Trunk Lines and Terminal Roads at Chicago and Their Recommendations to Western Roads in Regard to Live Stock Traffic.* New York: Russell Brothers, 1879.

———. *Proceedings and Circulars of the Joint Executive Committee, 1879–1889.* New York: Russell Brothers, 1879–1889.

———. *Proceedings and Circulars of the Trunk Line Committees, 1879–1889.* New York: Russell Brothers, 1879–1889.

———. *Proceedings and Circulars of the Trunk Line Executive Committee, 1880–1889.* New York: Russell Brothers, 1880–1889.

———. "Report of the Commissioner Upon the Testimony Furnished at the Conference Held at New York, April 11 and 12, 1883, between the Trunk Line Executive Committee, the Chicago Committee and Dressed Beef and Livestock Shippers, regarding the Relative Cost of Shipping Dressed Beef and Livestock from the West to the Seaboard." *Proceedings and Circulars of the Joint Executive Committee, 1883.* New York: Russell Brothers, 1883, pp. 1–132.

———. "Final Report Upon the Relative Cost of Transporting Live Stock and Dressed Beef, containing Abstract of Proceedings of April 11 & 12, 1883, and Proceedings of the Trunk Line Executive Committee of May 31 and June 1, 1883." *Proceedings and Circulars of the Joint Executive Committee, 1883,* pp. 1–97. New York: Russell Brothers, 1883.

———. *Report of Messr. Thurman, Washburne and Cooley, Constituting an Advisory Commission on Differential Rates by Railroads between the West and the Seaboard.* New York: Russell Brothers, 1882.

Union Stock Yard and Transit Company of Chicago. *Forty-first Annual Livestock Report, 1906.*

LEGAL CASES AND RECORDS

U.S. Courts. *Decrees and Judgments in Federal Antitrust Cases, July 2, 1890-January 1, 1918,* compiled by Roger Shale.

State of Missouri v. Armour Packing Co., 265 Mo. 121 (1915).

St. of Mo. v. Hammond Packing Company and St Louis Dressed Beef and Provision Company. No. 16090, Joint Abstract of Record and Transcript of Evidence, 6 vols. (Swift & Company Archives). (Reported sub. nom. *State ex. rel. Barker v. Armour Packing Co.* 265 Mo. 121, 176 S.W. 382 [1915]).

U.S. v. Addyston Pipe & Steel Co., 1 F.A.D. 641 (1898); 175 U.S. 211 (1899).

U.S. v. Armour & Co., 142 Fed. 808 (1906).

U.S. v. Cudahy Packing Co., Cr. 520 (S.D. Ga., 1910).

U.S. v. E.C. Knight Co., 156 U.S. 1 (1895).

U.S. v. Hopkins, 82 Fed. 529 (D. Kan. 1897).

U.S. v. Swift & Co., 122 Fed. 529 (N.D. Ill., 1903), affirmed, 196 U.S. 375 (1905).

U.S. v. Louis F. Swift et al., 186 Fed. 1002 and 188 Fed. 92 (N.D. Ill., 1910).

U.S. v. National Packing Company, Cr. 4384 (N.D. Ill., 1910).

GAZETEERS, BUSINESS DIRECTORIES, AND COMMERCE AND TRADE REPORTS

Annual Review of the Commerce, Manufacturers and the Public and Private Improvements of Chicago, 1856–1857. Chicago: Daily Democratic Press, 1857.

Boston Board of Trade, 1880, 1882–1883.

Boston Chamber of Commerce Reports, 1888–1889.

Chicago Board of Trade. *Annual Reports, 1856–1912.*

——. *Annual Report of the Packing of the West, 1876–1877.* Chicago: Howard, White, Crowell & Co.

The Commercial & Financial Chronicle and Hunt's Merchant's Magazine, January–June 1883.

Connecticut Business Directory, 1888.

Child, Hamilton. *Gazetteer and Business Directory of Windsor County Vermont for 1883–1884.* Syracuse, N.Y.: Journal Office, 1884.

Fourth Annual Review of the Commerce, Manufactures, Railroads and General Progress of Chicago for the Year of 1885. Chicago: Iglehart & Co., 1886.

Fifth Annual Review of the Commerce, Manufactures and the Public and Private Improvements of Chicago, with a Full Statement of Her System of Railroads and General Synopsis of the Business of the City for the Year 1854. Chicago: Iglehart & Co., 1857.

Griffith's Annual Review of the Livestock Trade and Produce Trade of Chicago, Fifth and Eighth Annual Reports, 1869 and 1872.

Hunt's Commercial Chronicle and Review. Vol. XIX (July–December 1848).

Moody, John, ed. *Moody's Manual of Industrial and Miscellaneous Securities, 1900–1912.* New York: O. C. Lewis.

——. *Moody's Manual of Railroads and Corporation Securities.* New York: Moody Manual Co.

New England Business Directory and Gazetteer, 1871–1900.

New Hampshire Business Directory, 1883 and *1888.*

New York Produce Exchange. *Annual Reports, 1880–1905.*

Poor's Manual of Railroads. New York: H.. V. and H. W. Poor.

Poor's Register of Corporations, Directors and Executives, United States and Canada. New York: Standard & Poor's Corp., 1928.

DISSERTATIONS, THESES, AND UNPUBLISHED SOURCES

Aduddell, Robert. "The Meat Packing Industry and the Consent Decree." Ph.D. dissertation, Northwestern University, 1969.

Alspaugh, Harold P. "Marketing of Meat and Meat Products." Ph.D. dissertation, Ohio State University, Columbus, Ohio, 1936.

Atkinson, Eva Lash. "Kansas City Livestock Trade and Packing Industry." Ph.D. dissertation, University of Kansas, 1970.

Catton, William Bruce. "John W. Garrett of the Baltimore & Ohio: A Study in Seaport and Railroad Competition, 1820–1874." Ph.D. dissertation, Northwestern University, 1959.

Engle, Nathanial Howard. "Competitive Forces in the Wholesale Marketing of Prepared Food Products." Ph.D. dissertation, University of Michigan, 1929.

Erlenborn, James L. "The American Meat and Livestock Industry and American Foreign Policy, 1880–1896." Master's thesis, University of Wisconsin, 1966.

Roy, Bill, "Inter-Industry Vestings of Interests in National Policy Over Time: The United States, 1886–1905." Ph.D. dissertation, University of Michigan, 1977.

Unfer, Louis, "Swift and Company: The Development of the Packing Industry, 1875–1912." Ph.D. dissertation, University of Illinois, 1951.

Wyllie, Cleland B. "How the Grand Trunk Got to Chicago." Master's thesis, University of Michigan, 1953.

BOOKS

Adams, Walter, and Gray, Horace M. *Monopoly in America: The Government as Promoter.* New York: Macmillan, 1955.

Adelman, Morris A. *A & P: A Study in Price-Cost Behavior and Public Policy.* Cambridge, Mass.: Harvard University Press, 1959.

American Economic Association. *Readings in Price Theory.* Homewood, Ill.: R. D. Irwin, 1952.

American Meat Institute. *The Packing Industry.* Chicago: University of Chicago Press, 1924.

Anderson, Oscar E. *The Health of a Nation: Harvey W. Wiley and the Fight for Pure Food.* Chicago: University of Chicago Press, 1958.

_____. *Refrigeration in America.* Princeton, N.J.: Princeton University Press, 1953.

Appleton's Encyclopedia of American Biography. James Grant Wilson and John Fiske, eds. New York: D. Appleton and Co., 1894.

Areeda, Philip. *Antitrust Analysis: Problems, Text, Cases.* Boston: Little, Brown and Company, 1967.

Armour, Jonathan Ogden. *Packers, the Private Car Lines and the People.* Philadelphia: Henry Altemus Co., 1906.

Arthur, Robert Burns. *The Decline of Competition: A Study of the Evolution of American Industry.* New York: McGraw-Hill Book Company, Inc., 1936.

Asch, Peter. *Economic Theory and the Antitrust Dilemma.* New York: John Wiley and Sons, 1970.

Atherton, Lewis. *The Cattle Kings.* Bloomington: Indiana University Press, 1961.

Averitt, Robert L. *The Dual Economy: The Dynamics of American Industry Structure.* New York: Norton and Company, Inc., 1968.

Bain, Joe S. *Industrial Organization.* New York: John Wiley and Sons, 1959.

_____. *Price Theory.* New York: John Wiley and Sons, 1966.

Baumol, William J. *Business Behavior, Value and Growth.* Rev. ed. New York: Harcourt Brace Jovanovich, 1967.

Belcher, Wyatt. *The Economic Rivalry Between St. Louis and Chicago: 1850-1880.* New York: Columbia University Press, 1947.

Benson, Lee. *Merchants, Farmers, and Railroads.* Cambridge, Mass.: Harvard University Press, 1955.

Bergman, Arvid Mathias. *A Review of the Frozen and Chilled Trans-Oceanic Meat Industry.* Stockholm: Almqvist & Wiksell, 1916.

Berle, Adolph. *Power Without Property: A New Development in American Political Economy.* 1st ed. New York: Harcourt Brace Jovanovich, 1959.

_____. *The Twentieth Century Capitalist Revolution.* New York: Harcourt Brace & World, 1960.

Berle, A. D., and Means, Gardiner C. *The Modern Corporation and Private Property.* New York: Harcourt Brace Jovanovich, 1967.

Berry, Thomas S. *Western Prices Before 1861: A Study of the Cincinnati Market.* Cambridge, Mass.: Harvard University Press, 1943.

Blair, John M. *Economic Concentration: Structure, Behavior and Public Policy.* New York: Harcourt Brace Jovanovich, 1972.

Blum, John Morton. *The Republican Roosevelt.* New York: Atheneum, 1965.

Bock, Betty. *Dialogue on Concentration, Oligopoly and Profit: Concepts and Data.* New York: Conference Board, 1972.

Bonbright, James C., and Means, Gardiner C. *The Holding Company: Its Public Significance and Its Regulation.* New York: McGraw-Hill Company, Inc., 1932.

Brady, Robert A. *Business As a System of Power*. New York: Columbia University Press, 1943.

Brody, David. *The Butcher Workman: A Study of Unionization* Cambridge, Mass.: Harvard University Press, 1964.

Brown, P. W. *A History of the Grand Trunk Railway of Canada*. Quebec: Hunter, Rose, 1864.

Burns, Arthur Robert. *The Decline of Competition: A Study of the Evolution of American Industry*. New York: McGraw-Hill Book Company, Inc., 1936.

Bushnell, Charles Joseph. *The Social Problem at the Chicago Stockyards*. Chicago: Chicago University Press, 1902.

Butz, Dale E., and Baker, George L., Jr. *The Changing Structure of the Meat Economy*. Boston: Harvard University, Graduate School of Business Administration, 1960.

Cain, Louis P. and Paul J. Uselding, eds. *Business Enterprise and Economic Change: Essays in Honor of Harold E. Williamson*. Akron, O.: Kent State Univ. Press, 1973.

Campbell, E. G. *The Reorganization of the American Railroad System, 1893–1900*. New York: Columbia University Press, 1938.

Chamberlain, Edward H. *The Theory of Monopolistic Competition*. Cambridge, Mass.: Harvard University Press, 1933.

Chandler, Alfred D., Jr. *Strategy and Structure: Chapters in the History of the American Industrial Enterprise*. Paperback ed. New York: Doubleday & Company, Inc., 1966.

———, ed. *The Railroads: The Nation's First Big Business*. New York: Harcourt Brace Jovanovich, 1965.

———. *The Visible Hand: The Managerial Revolution in American Business*. Cambridge, Mass.: Harvard University Press, 1977.

Chandler, Alfred D., Jr., and Salsbury, Stephen. *Pierre S. Du Pont and the Making of the Modern Corporation*. New York: Harper & Row, 1971.

Cheever, Lawrence O. *The House of Morrell*. Cedar Rapids, Iowa: Torch Press, 1948.

Cist, Charles. *The Cincinnati Almanac for the Year 1846; Being a Complete Picture of Cincinnati and its Environs*. Cincinnati: Robinson & Jones, 1846.

———. *Cincinnati in 1841: Its Early Annals and Future Prospects*. Cincinnati. n.p. Publ. by the author, 1841.

———. *The Cincinnati Miscellany; Or Antiquities of the West and Pioneer History and General and Local Statistics*. Cincinnati: C. Clark, 1845–1846.

———. *Sketches and Statistics of Cincinnati in 1851*. Cincinnati: W. H. Moore, 1851.

City of Chicago: A Half Century of Progress, 1837–1887. n.a. Chicago: n.p., 1887.

Clark, John G. *The Grain Trade in the Old Northwest*. Urbana, Ill.: University of Illinois Press, 1966.

Clark, Victor S. *History of Manufacturers in the United States*. 3 vols. 1929; rpt. New York: Peter Smith, 1949.

Clarke, John. *Competition as a Dynamic Process*. Washington, D.C.: Brookings Institution, 1961.

———. *Studies in the Economics of Overhead Costs*. Chicago: University of Chicago Press, 1923.

Cleaver, Charles. *History of Chicago, 1833–1892*. Chicago, n. publ. 1892.

Clemen, Rudolf A. *The American Livestock and Meat Industry*. New York: Ronald Press, 1923.

———. *By-Products in the Packing Industry*. Chicago: University of Chicago Press, 1927.

———. *George Hammond, 1838–1886: Pioneer in Refrigerator Transportation*. New York: Newcomen Society, 1946.

Cochran, T. C. *Railroad Leaders, 1845–1890: The Business Mind in Action*. Cambridge: Harvard University Press, 1953.

Cook, P. Lesley. *Effects of Mergers*. London: George Allen and Unwin, Ltd., 1958.

Cowie, Frederick W. *Transportation Routes in Canada.* Montreal: The Engineering Institute of Canada, 1923.

Crawford, Sir William, and Broadley, H. *The People's Food.* London and Toronto: W. Heinemann, 1938.

Critchell, James Troubridge, and Raymond, Joseph. *A History of the Frozen Meat Trade: An Account of the Development and Present Day Methods of Preparation, Transport and Marketing of Frozen and Chilled Meats.* London: Constable and Company, 1912.

Cummings, Richard Osborn. *The American and His Food: A History of Food Habits in the United States.* Rev. ed. Chicago: University of Chicago Press, 1941.

——. *The American Ice Harvests.* Berkeley: University of California Press, 1949.

Currie, A. W. *The Grand Trunk Railway of Canada.* Toronto: University of Toronto Press, 1957.

——. *Economics of Canadian Transportation.* Toronto: University of Toronto Press, 1954.

Curry, Leonard P. *Rail Routes South: Louisville's Fight for the Southern Market, 1865–1872.* Lexington: University of Kentucky Press, 1969.

Cutler, Irving. *The Chicago-Milwaukee Corridor: A Geographic Study of Intermetropolitan Coalescence.* Northwestern University Studies in Geography, No. 9. Evanston, Ill.: Northwestern University Press, 1965.

Cyert, Richard M., and March, James G. *A Behavioral Theory of the Firm.* Englewood Cliffs, N.J.: Prentice-Hall, Inc., 1964.

Danhoff, Clarence H. *Change in Agriculture: The Northern U.S., 1820–1870.* Cambridge: Harvard University Press, 1969.

DeGraff, Herrell. *Beef Production and Distribution.* 1st ed. Norman, Oklahoma: University of Oklahoma Press, 1960.

Depew, Chauncey Mitchell. *One Hundred Years of American Commerce, 1795–1895.* 2 vols. New York: D. O. Haynes & Co., 1895.

Dewey, Donald. *Monopoly in Economics and Law.* Chicago: Rand McNally, 1959.

Dewing, Arthur S. *Corporate Promotions and Reorganizations.* Cambridge, Mass.: Harvard University Press, 1914.

Dictionary of American Biography. Dumas Malone, ed. New York: Scribner, 1933.

Dorsey, E. B. *English and American Railroads Compared.* New York: John Wiley and Sons, 1887.

Drummond, Jack Cecil, and Wilbraham, Anne. *The Englishman's Food: A History of Five Centuries of English Diet.* Rev. ed., London, Eng.: Jonathan Cape, 1958.

Drury, John. *Rare and Well Done: Some Historical Notes on Meats and Meatmen.* Chicago: Quadrangle Books, 1966.

Dupree, A. Hunter. *Science in the Federal Government: A History of Politics and Activities to 1940.* Cambridge, Mass.: Harvard University Press (Belknap Press), 1958.

Durand, Edward D. *The Trust Problem.* Cambridge, Mass.: Harvard University Press, 1915.

Dykstra, Robert R. *The Cattle Towns.* New York: Alfred A. Knopf, 1968.

Easson, Charles. *Statistics of American Railways.* London: Effingham, Wilson, 1886.

Easterbrook, Aiken. *Canadian Economic History.* Toronto: Macmillan, 1956.

Edminster, Lynn Ramsey. *The Cattle Industry and the Tariff.* New York: Macmillan, 1926.

Eddy, A. J. *The New Competition.* 4th ed. Chicago: A. C. McClurg, 1917.

Eichner, Alfred S. *The Emergence of Oligopoly: Sugar Refining as a Case Study.* Baltimore: Johns Hopkins Press, 1969.

——. *The Megacorp and Oligopoly: Micro Foundations of Macro Dynamics.* New York: Cambridge University Press, 1976.

Faulkner, Harold U. *The Decline of Laissez-Faire, 1897–1917.* New York: Harper Torchbook, 1968.

Fellner, William. *Competition Among the Few: Oligopoly and Similar Market Structures.* New York: Alfred A. Knopf, 1949.

Fine, Sidney. *Laissez Faire and the General-Welfare State: A Study of Conflict in American Thought, 1865–1901.* Ann Arbor: University of Michigan Press, 1956.

Fishlow, Albert. *American Railroads and the Transformation of the Ante-Bellum Economy.* Cambridge, Mass.: Harvard University Press, 1965.

Fogg, Charles J., Weller, W. W., and Struck, A. eds. *Freight Traffic Red Book.* New York: Traffic Publishing Co., 1955.

Fowler, S. H. *The Marketing of Livestock and Meat.* 2nd ed. Danville, Ill.: Interstate Publishers and Printers, 1961.

Galbraith, John Kenneth. *Economics and the Public Purpose.* Boston: Houghton Mifflin, 1973.

Gates, Paul W. *The Farmer's Age: Agriculture, 1815–1860.* New York: Holt, Rinehart and Winston, 1960.

Gerth, H. H., and Mills, C. Wright. *From Max Weber: Essays in Sociology.* New York: Oxford University Press, 1958.

Giedion, Siegfried. *Mechanization Takes Command: A Contribution to Anonymous History.* New York: Oxford University Press, 1948.

Glazebrook, G. P. de T. *A History of Transportation in Canada.* 2 vols. *Continental Strategy to 1867,* Vol. I; *National Economy, 1867–1936,* Vol. II. Rev. ed. Toronto: McLelland & Stewart, 1964.

Goodspeed, Thomas W. *Gustavus Franklin Swift.* Chicago: University of Chicago, Reprint from *Chicago Biographical Sketches,* Vol. I., 1922.

Gort, Michael. *Diversification and Integration in American Industry.* Princeton, N.J.: National Bureau of Economic Research, 1962.

Grand, W. Joseph. *Illustrated History of the Union Stockyards: Sketch Book of Familiar Faces and Places at the Yards.* Chicago: Thomas Knapp Printing & Binding, Co., 1896.

Gray, Lewis Cecil. *History of Agriculture in the Southern United States to 1860.* 2 vols. Washington, D.C.: Carnegie Institute, 1933.

Greer, Howard C., and Smith, Dudley. *Accounting for a Meat Packing Business.* Chicago: Univ. of Chicago Press, 1943.

Gressley, Gene. *Bankers and Cattlemen.* New York: Alfred A. Knopf, 1966.

Hampe, Edward C., and Wittenberg, Merle. *The Lifeline of America: Development of the Food Industry.* New York: McGraw-Hill Book Company, Inc., 1964.

Henlein, Paul C. *Cattle Kingdom in the Ohio Valley, 1783–1860.* Lexington: University of Kentucky Press, 1959.

Hewson, M. B. *The Grand Trunk Railroad of Canada.* Toronto: Bilford Bros., 1876.

Hidy, Ralph W., and Hidy, Muriel E. *Pioneering in Big Business, 1882–1911.* New York: Harper & Row, 1955.

Hilliard, Sam Bowers. *Hog Meat and Hoecake: Food Supply in the Old South, 1840–1860.* Carbondale: Southern Illinois University Press, 1972.

Hinman, Robert Byron, and Harris, Robert B. *The Story of Meat.* Chicago: Swift and Co., 1939.

Hirschauer, Herman. *The Dark Side of the Beef Trust: A Treatise Concerning the "Canner" Cow, The Cold Storage Fowl, The Diseased Meats, The Dopes and Preservatives.* Jamestown, N.Y.: Theodore Z. Root, 1905.

Hofstadter, Richard. *The Paranoid Style in American Politics.* New York: Alfred A. Knopf, 1965.

Hotchkiss, George B. *Milestones in Marketing.* New York: Macmillan, 1938.

Hubbard, Elbert. *Little Journeys to the Homes of Great Business Men.* 2 vols. East Aurora, N.Y.: The Roycrofters, 1909.

Hungerford, Edward. *The Modern Railroad.* Chicago: A. C. McClurg & Co., 1911.

———. *The Vermont Central–Central Vermont: A Study in Human Effort.* Boston: Railway and Locomotive Historical Society, 1942.

Innis, Harold A. *Essays in Canadian Economic History.* Toronto: University of Toronto Press, 1956.

Jackman, William T. *Economic Principles of Transportation.* Toronto: University of Toronto Press, 1935.

———. *Economics of Transportation.*, 1st ed. Toronto: University of Toronto Press, 1926.

Jenks, Jeremiah W., and Clark, Walter E. *The Trust Problem.* 5th ed. Garden City, New York: Doubleday, Doran & Co., 1929.

Jones, Eliot. *The Trust Problem in the United States.* New York: Macmillan Company, 1921.

Kaplan, A. D. H. *Big Enterprise in a Competitive System.* Washington, D.C.: Brookings Institution, 1954.

Kaplan, A. D. H., Dirlam, J. B., and Lanzillott, R. F. *Pricing in Big Business.* Washington, D.C.: Brookings Institution, 1958.

Kaysen, Carl, and Turner, Donald F. *Antitrust Policy: An Economic and Legal Analysis.* Cambridge, Mass.: Harvard University Press, 1959.

Kennan, George. *E. H. Harriman: A Biography.* 2 vols. Boston: Houghton-Mifflin, 1922.

Kirkland, Edward C. *Industry Comes of Age: Business, Labor, and Public Policy, 1860–1897.* New York: Holt, Rinehart, Winston, 1961.

———. *Men, Cities, and Transportation: A Study in New England History, 1820–1900.* 2 vols. Cambridge, Mass.: Harvard University Press, 1948.

Kolko, Gabriel. *Railroads and Regulation, 1877–1916.* Princeton: Princeton University Press, 1965.

———. *The Triumph of Conservatism: A Reinterpretation of American History, 1900–1916.* Chicago: Quadrangle, 1967.

Knauth, Oswald. *Business Practices, Trade, Position, and Competition.* New York: Columbia University Press, 1956.

Knickerbocker, Frederick T. *Oligopolistic Reaction and Multinational Enterprise.* Boston: Division of Research, Graduate School of Business, Harvard University, 1973.

Knorst, William J. *Interstate Commerce Law and Practice, 1953–1958.* 4 vols. Chicago: College of Advanced Traffic, 1958.

———. *Transportation and Traffic Management.* Chicago: College of Advanced Traffic, 1955–1957.

Lane, Robert E. *The Regulation of Businessmen: Social Conditions of Government Economic Control.* New Haven: Yale University Press, 1954.

Larmer, Forrest M. *Financing the Livestock Industry.* New York: Macmillan, 1926.

Larson, Henrietta M. *Guide to Business History.* Cambridge, Mass.: Harvard University Press, 1948.

Leech, Harper, and Carroll, John Charles. *Armour and His Times.* New York: Appleton-Century-Crofts, 1938.

Letwin, William. *Law and Economic Policy in America: The Evolution of the Sherman Antitrust Act.* New York: Random House, 1965.

Lippincott, Isaac. *A History of Manufacturing in the Ohio Valley to the Year 1860.* Chicago: University of Illinois Press, 1914.

Locklin, Philip D. *Economics of Transportation.* Homewood, Ill.: Richard D. Irwin, Inc., 1947.

Logan, Samuel H., and King, Gordon A. *Economies of Scale in the Slaughter Plants.* Research Rept. No. 260. Berkeley: University of California Press, 1962.

Longley, Ronald Stewart. *Sir Francis Kincks: A Study of Canadian Politics, Railways and Finance in the 19th Century.* Toronto: University of Toronto Press, 1943.

Lovett, H. A. *Canada and the Grand Trunk.* Montreal: n.p., 1924.

Low, Richard E. *The Economics of Antitrust: Competition and Monopoly.* Englewood Cliffs, N.J.: Prentice-Hall, Inc., 1968.

MacAvoy, Paul W. *The Economic Effects of Regulation: The Trunk Line Railroad Cartels and the Interstate Commerce Commission Before 1900.* Cambridge, Mass.: MIT Press, 1965.

McCoy, Joseph. *Historic Sketches of the Cattle Trade of the West and Southwest.* Kansas City, Mo., 1874; rpt. Columbus, O.: Long's College Books, 1951.

MacDonald, James. *Food From the Far West.* London: William P. Nimmo, 1878.

McFall, Robert James. *The World's Meat.* New York: Appleton-Century-Crofts, 1927.

MacGibbon, J. A. *Railway Rates and the Canadian Railway Commission.* Boston: Houghton Mifflin, 1917.

Mailer, Norman. *Miami and the Seige of Chicago.* New York: New America Library. Inc., 1968.

Malott, Deane W., and Martin, Boyce F. *The Agricultural Industries.* New York: McGraw-Hill Book Company, Inc., 1939.

Markham, Jesse W. *Competition in the Rayon Industry.* Cambridge, Mass.: Harvard University Press, 1952.

Mason, Edward S. *Economic Concentration and the Monopoly Problem.* Cambridge, Mass.: Harvard University Press, 1959.

Mazlish, Bruce. *The Railroad and the Space Program: An Exploration in Historical Analogy.* Cambridge, Mass.: MIT Press, 1965.

McCormick, S. D. *An Address Delivered Before the Annual Convention of the Butcher's National Protective Association, May 28, 1890, being a Review of the Cattle Industry and Showing the Spoilation of the Cattle Pool.* n.p.: Butcher's National Protective Association, 1890.

Means, Gardiner. *The Corporate Revolution in America.* New York: Crowell Collier & Macmillan, Inc., 1962.

Michaux, François André. *Travels To The Westward of the Allegany Mountains* (transl. by B. Lambert). London: J. Mawman, 1805.

Miller-Barstow, Donald H. *Beatty of the C. P. R. A Biography.* Toronto: McClelland & Stewart, 1951.

Moody, John. *The Truth About the Trusts.* New York: Moody Publishing Company, 1904.

Moore, John Hebron. *Agriculture in Ante-Bellum Mississippi.* New York: Bookman, 1953.

Morison, Elting; Blum, John; and Chandler, Alfred D., Jr.; eds. *The Letters of Theodore Roosevelt.* 5 Vols. Cambridge, Mass.: Harvard University Press, 1952.

Murray, K. A. H. *Factors Affecting the Prices of Livestock in Great Britain.* New York: Oxford University Press, 1931.

Nelson, Ralph L. *Concentration in the Manufacturing Industries of the United States.* New Haven, Conn.: Yale University Press, 1963.

————. *Merger Movements in American Industry, 1895-1956.* Princeton, N.J.: Princeton University Press, 1959.

Neyhart, Louise A. *Giant of the Yards.* Boston: Houghton Mifflin, 1952.

Nicholls, William H. *Imperfect Competition in the Agricultural Industries.* 1st ed. Ames: Iowa State University Press, 1941.

Nicholson, Michael. *Oligopoly and Conflict: A Dynamic Approach.* Toronto: University of Toronto Press, 1972.

North, Douglass C. *The Economic Growth of the United States, 1790-1860.* Englewood Cliffs, N.J.: Prentice-Hall, Inc., 1961.

Nutter, G. Warren, and Einhorn, Henry A. *The Extent of Enterprise Monopoly in the United States, 1899-1939.* New York: Columbia University Press, 1969.

Osgood, Ernest S. *The Day of the Cattleman.* Minneapolis: University of Minnesota, 1929.

Overton, Richard C. *Burlington Route: A History of the Burlington Lines.* New York: Alfred A. Knopf, 1965.

Parker, William N., ed. *The Structure of the Cotton Economy of the Antebellum South.* Washington, D.C.: Agricultural History Society, 1970.

Passer, Harold C. *The Electrical Manufacturers, 1875–1900: A Study in Competition, Entrepreneurship, Technical Change and Economic Growth.* Cambridge, Mass.: Harvard University Press, 1953.

Paul, Allen B. *Growth of the Food Processing Industries in Illinois from 1849 to 1947.* Chicago: University of Illinois, 1953.

Pelzer, Louis. *The Cattleman's Frontier: A Record of the Trans-Mississippi Cattle Industry from Oxen Trains to Pooling Companies, 1850–1890.* Glendale, Calif.: Arthur H. Clark Co., 1936.

Pennington, Myles. *Railways and Other Ways; Being Reminiscences of Canals and Railway Life During a Period of Sixty-seven Years with Characteristic Sketches of Canal and Railway Men, Early Tram Roads and Railways, etc.* Toronto: Williamson & Co., 1894.

Penrose, Edith. *The Theory of the Growth of the Firm.* Oxford, England: Blackwell, 1959.

Perren, Richard. *The Meat Trade in Britain, 1840–1914.* London, Eng.: Routledge and Kegan Paul, 1979.

Phillips, Almarin. *Market Structure, Organization and Performance.* Cambridge, Mass.: Harvard University Press, 1962.

Pidgeon, Mary Elizabeth. *The Employment of Women in Slaughtering and Meat Packing.* Washington, D.C.: U.S. Government Printing Office, 1932.

Pierce, Bessie Louis. *A History of Chicago.* 3 vols. New York: Alfred A. Knopf, 1957.

Porter, Glenn. *The Rise of Big Business, 1860–1910.* New York: Thomas Y. Crowell Company, 1973.

Porter, Glenn, and Livesay, Harold C. *Merchants and Manufacturers: Studies in the Changing Structure of Nineteenth Century Marketing.* Baltimore: Johns Hopkins Press, 1971.

Powell, Fred W. *The Bureau of Animal Industry: Its History, Activities and Organization.* Baltimore, Md.: Johns Hopkins Univer. Press, 1927.

Purcell, Theodore V. *The Worker Speaks His Mind on Company and Union.* Cambridge, Mass.: Harvard University Press, 1953.

Rhoades, E. L. *Merchandising Packinghouse Products.* Chicago: University of Chicago Press, 1929.

Riley, Elmer A. *The Development of Chicago and Vicinity as a Manufacturing Center Prior to 1880.* Chicago: University of Chicago Press, 1901.

Ripley, William Z. *Railroads, Finance, and Organization.* New York: Longmans, Green and Company, 1927.

———. *Railroads, Rates and Regulation.* New York: Longmans, Green and Company, 1924.

———. *Railway Problems.* Boston: Globe & Co., 1907.

———. *Trusts, Pools and Corporations.* Boston: Ginn & Co., 1905.

Robinson, Joan. *The Economics of Imperfect Competition.* 2nd ed. New York: St. Martin's Press, 1969.

Rosenberg, Nathan. *Technology and American Economic Growth.* New York: Harper & Row, 1972.

Rusling, J. F. *The Railroads, The Stock-Yards, the Eveners: Exposé of Great Railroad Ring that Robs the Laborer of the East and the Producer of the West of $5,000,000 a Year.* Washington, D.C.: Polkinhorn Printer, 1878.

Russel, Charles Edward. *The Greatest Trust in the World.* New York: Ridgway, Thayer Co., 1905.

Saloutos, Theodore. *Farmer Movements in the South: 1865–1933.* Berkeley: University of California Press, 1960.

Scherer, Frederick M. *Industrial Market Structure and Economic Performance.* Chicago: Rand McNally, 1970.

Schumpeter, Joseph. *Business Cycles: A Theoretical, Historical, and Statistical Analysis of the Capitalist Process.* 2 vols. New York: McGraw Hill, 1964.

_____. *Capitalism, Socialism and Democracy.* 3rd ed. New York: Harper & Row, 1950.

_____. *The Theory of Economic Development.* Cambridge, Mass.: Harvard University Press, 1934.

Seaman, Ezra C. *Essays on the Progress of Nations, in Civilization, Productive Industry, Wealth, and Population.* New York: Scribner, 1852.

Shannon, Fred A. *The Farmer's Last Frontier: Agriculture, 1860–1897.* New York: Harper Torchbook, 1968.

Shepherd, William G. *Market Power and Economic Welfare.* New York: Random House, 1971.

Sherman, Roger. *Oligopoly: An Empirical Approach.* Lexington, Mass.: Lexington Books, 1972.

The "Significant Sixty": A Historical Report of the Progress and Development of the Meat Packing Industry, 1891–1951. Chicago: National Provisioner, 1952.

Simons, A. J. *Holding Companies.* London: Isaac Pitman & Sons, Ltd., 1927.

Sinclair, Upton. *The Jungle.* New York: Doubleday & Co., 1906; Signet Classic Edition, 1960.

Smith, Peter H. *Politics and Beef in Argentina: Patterns of Conflict and Change.* New York: Columbia University Press, 1969.

Stevens, George Roy. *Canadian National Railways.* 2 vols. *Sixty Years of Trial and Error, 1836–1896.* Vol. I. Toronto: Clarke Irvin, 1960. *Towards the Inevitable, 1896–1922.* Vol. II. Toronto: Clarke Irvin, 1962.

Swift, Helen. *My Father and My Mother.* Chicago: n.p., 1937.

Swift, Louis F., and Van Vlissingen, Arthur. *The Yankee of the Yards: The Biography of Gustavus Franklin Swift.* New York: A. W. Shaw Company, 1927.

Sylos-Labini, Paolo. *Oligopoly and Technical Progress.* Cambridge, Mass.: Harvard University Press, 1969.

Taylor, George Rogers. *The Transportation Revolution, 1815–1960.* New York: Holt, Rinehart and Winston, 1951.

Thompson, N., and Edgar, J. H. *Canadian Railway Development from the Earliest Times.* Toronto: Macmillan, 1933.

Thomson, Dale C. *Alexander MacKenzie, Clear Grit.* Toronto: Macmillan, 1960.

Schubik, Martin. *Strategy and Market Structure: Competition, Oligopoly and the Theory of Games.* New York: John Wiley and Sons, 1959.

Thorelli, Hans B. *The Federal Antitrust Policy: Origination of an American Tradition.* Baltimore: Johns Hopkins Press, 1955.

Thorp, Williard. *The Integration of Industrial Operation: A Statistical and Descriptive Analysis of the Development and Growth of Industrial Accomplishments and of the Size, Scope and Structure of Combinations of Industrial Establishments Operated from Central Offices.* Washington, D.C.: U.S. Government Printing Office, 1920.

Towne, Charles Wayland, and Wentworth, Edward M. *Cattle and Men.* Norman: University of Oklahoma Press, 1955.

_____. *Pigs: From Cave to Corn Belt.* 1st ed. Norman: University of Oklahoma Press, 1950.

Trout, John M., and Trout, Edward. *The Railways of Canada for 1870–1871.* Toronto: Monetary Times, 1871.

Tucker, G. N. *The Canadian Commercial Revolution, 1845–51.* Toronto: Ryerson Press, 1936.

Walsh, Margaret. *The Manufacturing Frontier: Pioneer Industry in Antebellum Wisconsin, 1830–1860.* Madison, Wisc.: State Historical Society of Wisconsin, 1972.

Watkins, Myra W. *Industrial Combinations and Public Policy: A Study of Combination, Competition and the Common Welfare.* New York: Houghton Mifflin Co., 1927.

Wattenberg, Ben J. *This U.S.A.: An Unexpected Family Portrait of 197,926,341 Americans Drawn from the Census.* 1st ed. Garden City, N. Y.: Doubleday & Co., 1965.

Weld, L. D. H. *Private Freight Cars and American Railways.* Studies in History, Economics, and Public Law, edited by Faculty of Political Science of Columbia University. Vol. 31, no. 1. New York: Columbia University Press, 1908.

Weld, L. D. H., Kearney, A. T., and Sidney, F. H. *Economics of the Packing Industry.* 1st ed. Chicago: University of Chicago Press, 1925.

Weston, J. Fred. *The Role of Mergers in the Growth of Large Firms.* Berkeley: University of California Press, 1953.

Whitney, Simon. *Antitrust Policies: American Experience in Twenty Industries.* 2 vols. New York: Twentieth Century Fund, 1958.

Wilgus, W. J. *The Railway Interrelations of the U.S. and Canada.* New Haven, Conn.: Yale University Press, 1937.

Williams, Willard F., and Stout, Thomas T. *Economics of the Livestock-Meat Industry.* 1st ed. New York: Macmillan, 1964.

Williamson, Harold F., and Daum, Arnold R. *The American Petroleum Industry: The Age of Illumination, 1895–1899.* Evanston, Ill. Northwestern University Press, 1959.

Williamson, Harold F., ed. *The Growth of the American Economy.* 2 vols. 2nd ed.. Englewood Cliffs, N.J.: Prentice-Hall, Inc., 1951.

Wilson, Charles H. *History of Unilever: A Study in Economic Growth and Social Change.* 3 vols. New York: Frederick A. Praeger, Publishers, 1968.

Wing, Jack. *The Great Union Stockyards of Chicago.* Chicago: Religio-Philosophical Publishing Association, 1865.

Woolrich, Willis R. *The Men Who Created Cold: A History of Refrigeration.* New York: Exposition Press, 1967.

Young, James. *The Toadstool Millionaires: A Social History of Patent Medicines in America before Federal Regulation.* Princeton, N.J.: Princeton Univ. Press, 1961.

ARTICLES, STUDIES, AND PAMPHLETS

Abbott, Edith, and Breckinridge, S. P. "Women in Industry: The Chicago Stockyards." *Journal of Political Economy* 19 (October 1911):632–654.

Adelman, M. A. "Effective Competition and the Antitrust Laws." *Harvard Law Review* 61 (September 1948):1289–1300.

Aduddell, Robert M., and Cain, Louis P. "The Consent Decree in the Meat Packing Industry." (mimeo.)

Alsberg, C. L. "Some Economic Consequences of Commodity Control." *Law and Contemporary Problems* 1 (December 1933):144–149.

Anderson, Oscar E. "The Pure Food Issue: A Republican Dilemma, 1906-1912." *American Historical Review* 61 (April 1956):550–73.

Andrews, E. B. "Trusts According to Official Investigations." *Quarterly Journal of Economics* 3 (January 1889):117–152.

Arant, Willard D. "Wartime Meat Policies." *Journal of Farm Economics* 28 (November 1946):903–919.

Arnould, Richard J. "Changing Patterns of Concentration in American Meat Packing, 1880-1963." *Business History Review* 45 (Spring 1971):19–34.

"Attorney General Moody and the Beef Trust." *Harper's Weekly* (January 21, 1905):81.

Bailey, Thomas A. "Congressional Opposition to Pure Food Legislation, 1879–1906." *American Journal of Sociology* 36 (July 1930):52–64.

Bain, Joe S. "Pricing in Monopoly and Oligopoly." *American Economic Review* 39 (March 1949):448–464.

———. "Workable Competition in Oligopoly: Theoretical Assumptions and Some Empirical Evidence." *American Economic Review* 40 (May 1950):35–66.

Baldwin, William. "The Feedback Effect of Business Conduct on Industry Structure." *Journal of Law and Economics* 12 (April 1969):123–27.

Belcher, Wallace E. "Industrial Pooling Agreements." *Quarterly Journal of Economics* 19 (November 1905):111–123.

Berle, Adolf A. "The Impact of the Corporation on Classical Economic Theory." *Quarterly Journal of Economics* 79 (February 1965):25–40.

Berry, Thomas S. "The Effect of Business Conditions on Early Judicial Decisions Concerning Restraint on Trade." *Journal of Economic History* 10 (May 1950):30–44.

Bork, Robert. "Vertical Integration and the Sherman Act: The Legal History of an Educational Misconception." *University of Chicago Law Review* 22 (Autumn 1954):157–201.

———. "Legislative Intent and the Policy of the Sherman Act." *Journal of Law and Economics* 9 (October 1966):7–48.

Braeman, John. "The Square Deal in Action: A Case Study in the Growth of the National Police Power." In *Change and Continuity in Twentieth-Century America*. John Braeman, Robert Bremner, and Everett Walters, eds. Columbus, O.: Ohio University Press, 1964.

Brandeis, Louis. "Cut-Throat Prices: The Competition that Kills." *Harper's Weekly* (November 15, 1913):10–12.

Breithaupt, William H. "Outline of the History of the Grand Trunk Railway of Canada." *Railway and Locomotive Historical Society Bulletin* No. 23 (November 1930):37–74.

Bullock, Charles J. "Trust Literature: A Survey and Criticism." *Quarterly Journal of Economics* 15 (February 1901):167–217.

Burnett, Edmund Cody. "Hog-Raising and Hog-Driving in the Region of the French Broad River." *American History* 20 (April 1946):86–103.

Camp, William. "Reforms in the System of Food Distribution." *Journal of Political Economy* 29 (December 1921):824–825.

Chandler, Alfred D., Jr. "The Beginnings of 'Big Business' in American Industry." *Business History Review* 33 (Spring 1959):1–31.

———. "The Role of Business in the United States: A Historical Survey." *Daedalus* 98 (Winter 1969):23–40.

———. "The Structure of American Industry in the Twentieth Century: A Historical Overview." *Business History Review* 43 (Autumn 1969):255–281.

Charles, J. L. "Railways March Northward." *Canadian Geographical Journal* 63 (January 1961):2–21.

Comanor, William S. "Vertical Mergers, Market Power, and the Antitrust Laws." *American Economic Review* 57, Pt 1. (May 1967):254–265.

Commons, John R. "Labor Conditions in Slaughtering and Meat Packing." *Quarterly Journal of Economics* 19 (November 1904):1–32.

Conant, Luther, Jr. "Industrial Consolidations in the United States." *Publications of the American Statistical Association* 7 (March 1901):207–220.

Crawford, C. W. "Technical Problems in Food and Drug Law Enforcement." *Law and Contemporary Problems* 1 (December 1933):36–43.

Croxton, Fred. "Beef Prices." *Journal of Political Economy* 13 (March 1905):201–216.

Cyert, Richard M., and March, James G. "Organizational Structure & Pricing Behavior in an Oligopolistic Market." *American Economic Review* 45 (March 1955):129–139.

Davis, Lance E. "Capital Markets and Industrial Concentration: The United States and the United Kingdom, A Comparative Study." *Economic History Review* 19 (August 1966):255–272.

Duncan, C. S. "Legalizing Combinations for Export Trade." *Journal of Political Economy* 25 (April 1917):313–338.

Eichner, Alfred S. "Business Concentration and Its Significance." In *The Business of America*. Ivar Berg, ed., pp. 169–200. New York: Harcourt Brace Jovanovich, 1968.

Fife, George B. "The Great Business Combination of Today: The So-Called Beef Trust." *Century Magazine* 65 (November 1902):148–158.

Filler, Louis. "Progress and Progressivism." *American Journal of Economics and Sociology* 20 (April 1961):291–301.

Forbes, B. C. "'Right Organization Essential' says Thomas E. Wilson." *Forbes Magazine* (May 27, 1922):169–170.

Frank, Lawrence K. "The Significance of Industrial Integration." *Journal of Political Economy* 33 (April 1925):179–195.

Galbraith, J. K. "Market Structure and Stabilization Policy." *Review of Economics and Statistics* 39 (1957):124–133.

_____. "Monopoly and the Concentration of Economic Power." In *A Survey of Contemporary Economics*. Howard S. Ellis, ed. Homewood, Ill.: R. D. Irwin, 1948.

Galenson, David. "The Profitability of the Long Drive." *Agricultural History* 51 (October 1977):737–758.

Gallman, Robert E. "The Agricultural Sector and the Pace of Economic Growth: U.S. Experience in the Nineteenth Century." In *Essays in Nineteenth Century Economic History: The Old Northwest*. David Klingman and Richard K. Vedder, eds., pp. 35–76. Athens, Ohio: Ohio University Press, 1975.

_____. "Changes in Total U.S. Agricultural Factor Productivity in the Nineteenth Century." *Agricultural History* 46 (January 1972):191–210.

Gilchrist, D. T. "Albert Fink and the Pooling System." *Business History Review* 34 (Spring 1960):24–49.

"Government's Report on the Beef Trust." *Outlook* 79 (March 18, 1905):667–668.

Gunsaulus, Frank W. "Philip D. Armour." *American Review of Reviews* 23 (February 1901):167–176.

Gunton, George. "The Economics and Social Aspects of Trusts." *Political Science Quarterly* 3 (September 1888):385–408.

Hall, R. L. and Hitch, C. J. "Price Theory and Business Behavior." *Oxford Economic Papers* 2 (May 1939):12–45.

Hayes, Lauffer P., and Raff, Frank J. "The Administration of the Federal Food and Drug Act." *Law and Contemporary Problems* 1 (December 1933):16–35.

Hill, H. C. "The Development of Chicago as a Center of the Meat Packing Industry." *Mississippi Valley Historical Review* 10 (December 1923):253–273.

Hill, William. "Conditions in the Cattle Industry." *Journal of Political Economy* 13 (December 1904):1–12.

_____. "Relation of Packer's Credit to Panic and Prices." *Journal of Political Economy* 16 (February 1908):87–102.

Hough, E. "Swifts." *Cosmopolitan* (March 1909):399–407.

Howey, W. C. "Our Beef Supply as a Great Business." *Review of Reviews* 41 (March 1910):308–320.

Hutchinson, W. K., and Williamson, Samuel H. "The Self-Sufficiency of the Antebellum South." *Journal of Economic History* 31 (September 1971):591–612.

Irwin, E. P. "Facts About the Packing House." *Overland* 48 (August 1906):70–77.

Johnson, Arthur M. "Continuity and Change in Government Business Relations." In *Change and Continuity in Twentieth Century America*. John Bremner and Everett Walters, eds., pp. 191–219. Columbus, O.: Ohio University Press, 1964.

_____. "Theodore Roosevelt and the Bureau of Corporations." *Mississippi Valley Historical Review* 45 (March 1959):571–590.

_____. "Antitrust Policy in Transition, 1908: Ideal and Reality." *Mississippi Valley Historical Review* 48 (December 1961):415–444.

Jones, Robert Leslie. "The Beef Cattle Industry in Ohio Prior to the Civil War." *Ohio Historical Quarterly* 64 (April 1955):168–194 and (July 1955):287–319.

Kahn, Alfred. "Standards for Antitrust Policy." *Harvard Law Review* 67 (November 1953):28–54.

Kaysen, Carl. "Another View of Corporate Capitalism." *Quarterly Journal of Economics* 79 (February 1965):41–51.

Leavitt, Charles. "Some Economic Aspects of the Western Meat Packing Industry, 1830–1860." *Journal of Business of the University of Chicago* 4 (January 1931):68–90.

_____. "Transportation and the Livestock Industry of the Middle West to 1860." *Agricultural History* 8 (January 1934):20–33.

Livermore, Shaw. "The Success of Industrial Merger." *Quarterly Journal of Economics* 50 (November 1935):68–95.

Livesay, Harold C. and Porter, Patrick G. "Vertical Integration in American Manufacturing, 1899–1948." *Journal of Economic History* 29 (September 1968):494–500.

Mak, James, and Walton, Gary M. "The Persistence of Old Technologies: The Case of Flatboats." *Journal of Economic History* 33 (June 1973):444–452.

Mallman, Sharon M. "Milwaukee's John Cudahy." *Historical Messenger of the Milwaukee County Historical Society* 32 (Autumn 1976):70–87.

Markham, Jesse W. "Market Structure, Business Conduct and Innovation." *American Economic Review* 55 (May 1965):323–332.

_____. "Survey of Evidence and Findings on Mergers." In *Business Concentration and Public Policy*, pp. 141–212. Princeton, N.J.: National Bureau of Economic Research, 1955.

Mason, Edward S. "Monopoly in Law and Economics." *Yale Law Journal* 47 (November 1937):34–49.

_____. "The New Competition." *Yale Review* 43 (Autumn 1953):37–48.

"Meat Packing and Slaughtering." *Encyclopedia of the Social Sciences*. London, Eng.: Macmillan & Co., 1963.

Mercer, Lloyd J. "The Antebellum Interregional Trade Hypothesis: A Reexamination of Theory and Evidence." Unpublished paper presented at the Southern California Economic History Workshop, California Institute of Technology, May 1979.

Merwin, Samuel. "The Private-Car Abuses." *Success Magazine* VIII, No. 131 (April 1905), 249–254.

Modigliani, Franco. "New Developments on the Oligopoly Front." *Journal of Political Economy* 66 (June 1958):215–232.

Navin, T. R. and Sears, M. V. "The Rise of a Market for Industrial Securities, 1877–1902." *Business History Review* 29 (June 1955):255–272.

Nicholls, William H. "Market Sharing in the Meat Packing Industry." *Journal of Farm Economics* 22 (April 1940):225–240.

Nickerson, J. F. "The Development of Refrigeration in the United States." *Ice and Refrigeration* 49 (October 1915):170–175.

Oliphant, J. Orlin. "The Eastward Movement of Cattle from the Oregon Country." *Agricultural History* 20 (January 1946):19–43.

Osborne, Dale K. "The Role of Entry in Oligopoly Theory." *Journal of Political Economy* 72 (August 1964):396–402.

Patinkin, Don. "Multiple-Plant Firms, Cartels and Imperfect Competition." *Quarterly Journal of Economics* 61 (February 1947):173–205.

Penrose, Edith. "Biological Analogies in the Theory of the Firm." *American Economic Review* 42 (December 1952):804–819.

Perren, Richard. "The North American Beef and Cattle Trade of Great Britain," 1870–1914." *Economic History Review* 20 (August 1971):430–444.

Porter, Patrick G. "Origins of the American Tobacco Company." *Business History Review* 43 (Spring 1969):59–76.

Porter, Patrick G. and Livesay, Harold C. "Oligopolists in American Manufacturing and Their Products, 1909–1963." *Business History Review* 43 (Autumn 1969):282–298.

_____. "Oligopoly in Small Manufacturing Industries." *Explorations in Entrepreneurial History* 7 (Spring 1970):371–379.

Primeaux, Walter J., Jr., and Bomball, Mark R. "A Reexamination of the Kinky Oligopoly Demand Curve." *Journal of Political Economy* 82 (July–August 1974):851–862.

Putnam, George E. "Joint Cost in the Packing Industry." *Journal of Political Economy* 29 (April 1921):293–303.

_____. "Unit Costs as a Guiding Factor in Buying Operations." *Journal of Political Economy* 29 (October 1921):663–675.

Regier, C. C. "The Struggle for Federal Food and Drug Legislation." *Law and Contemporary Problems* 1 (December 1933):3–15.

Reynolds, Lloyd G. "Cutthroat Competition." *American Economic Review* 30 (December 1940):737–747.

Spengler, Joseph J. "Kinked Demand Curves: By Whom First Used." *Southern Economic Journal* 32 (July 1965):81–84.

_____. "Vertical Integration and Antitrust Policy." *Journal of Political Economy* 48 (August 1950):347–352.

Stevens, William S. "A Classification of Pools and Associations Based on American Experience." *American Economic Review* 32 (September 1913):545–575.

Stigler, George J. "The Division of Labor is Limited by the Extent of the Market." *Journal of Political Economy* 51 (June 1951):185–193.

_____. "The Dominant Firm and the Inverted Umbrella." *Journal of Law and Economics* 8 (October 1965):167–172.

_____. "The Kinky Oligopoly Demand Curve and Rigid Prices." *Journal of Political Economy* 55 (October 1947):432–449.

_____. "Monopoly and Oligopoly by Merger." *American Economic Review* 40 (May 1950):23–40.

_____. "Perfect Competition Historically Contemplated." *Journal of Political Economy* 65 (February 1957):1–17.

_____. "A Theory of Oligopoly." *Journal of Political Economy* 72 (February 1964):44–61.

Sweezy, Paul M. "Demand Under Conditions of Oligopoly." *Journal of Political Economy* 47 (August 1939):568–573.

Taylor, Alonzo E. *Corn and Hog Surplus of the Corn Belt.* Food Research Institute, Misc. Publ. No. 6. Stanford, Calif.: Stanford University, 1932.

Towne, Marvin W. and Rasmussen, Wayne D. "Farm Gross Product and Gross Investment in the Nineteenth Century." In *Trends in the American Economy in the 19th Century.* William M. Parker, ed., pp. 255–312. Studies in Income and Wealth, Vol. 24, by the Conference on Research in Income and Wealth. A Report of the National Bureau of Economic Research. Princeton, N.J.: Princeton University Press, 1960.

Veeder, Henry. "The Federal Trade Commission and the Packers." *Illinois Law Review* 15 (March 1921):485–503.

Virtue, G. O. "The Meat Packing Investigation." *Quarterly Journal of Economics* 31 (August 1920):636–650.

Walker, Francis. "The Beef Trust and the United States Government." *Economic Journal* 16 (December 1906):491–514.

Walsh, Margaret. "Pork Packing as a Leading Edge of Midwestern Industry, 1835–1875." *Agricultural History* 51 (October 1977):702–717.

———. "The Spatial Evolution of the Midwestern Pork Industry, 1835–1875." *Journal of Historical Geography* 1 (1978):1–22.

Wattersdorf, M. C. "Holding Companies." *Economic Journal* 36 (December 1936):586–597.

———. "The Meat Packing Investigation." *Quarterly Journal of Economics* 35 (May 1921): 412–420.

Wentworth, Edward N. "Livestock Products and the Tariff." *Journal of Farm Economics* 7 (July 1925):319–345.

White, Wilford. "The Refrigerator Car and the Effect Upon the Public of Packer Control of Refrigerator Lines." *Southwestern Political and Social Science Quarterly* 10 (March 1930):388–400.

Wilcox, Clair. "On the Alleged Ubiquity of Oligopoly." *American Economic Review* 40 (March 1950):67–73.

Williams, Faith M. "The Measurement of the Demand for Food." *Journal of the American Statistical Association* 24 (September 1929):288–295.

Wilson, James A. "Cattlemen, Packers, and Government: Retreating Individualism on the Texas Range, 1880–1920." *Southwestern Historical Quarterly* 74 (April 1971):525–534.

Wolfe, T. N. "The Problem of Oligopoly." *Review of Economic Studies* 21 (1954):181–192.

Wollman, Henry. "The Mortality of Trusts." *Albany Law Journal* 67 (August 1905):227–232.

Woodhouse, C. G. "The Standard of Living at the Professional Level, 1816–1817 and 1926–1927." *Journal of Political Economy* 37 (October 1929):552–572.

Worcester, Dean A. "Why 'Dominant Firms' Decline." *Journal of Political Economy* 65 (August 1957):338–347.

Index